NEGOTIATING MINEFIELDS

NEGOTIATING MINEFIELDS
The Landmines Ban in American Politics

Leon V. Sigal

Routledge
Taylor & Francis Group
New York   London

Routledge is an imprint of the
Taylor & Francis Group, an informa business

Published in 2006 by
Routledge
Taylor & Francis Group
270 Madison Avenue
New York, NY 10016

Published in Great Britain by
Routledge
Taylor & Francis Group
2 Park Square
Milton Park, Abingdon
Oxon OX14 4RN

© 2006 by Taylor & Francis Group, LLC
Routledge is an imprint of Taylor & Francis Group

Printed in the United States of America on acid-free paper
10 9 8 7 6 5 4 3 2 1

International Standard Book Number-10: 0-415-95414-2 (Hardcover) 0-415-95415-0 (Softcover)
International Standard Book Number-13: 978-0-415-95414-3 (Hardcover) 978-0-415-95415-0 (Softcover)

Library of Congress Cataloging-in-Publication Data

Catalog record is available from the Library of Congress

Taylor & Francis Group
is the Academic Division of Informa plc.

Visit the Taylor & Francis Web site at
http://www.taylorandfrancis.com

and the Routledge Web site at
http://www.routledge-ny.com

Table of Contents

Preface

The idea of studying the campaign to ban antipersonnel landmines was not my own. Tom Graham and Susan Sechler of the Rockefeller Foundation were interested in how a handful of nongovernmental organizations with almost no mass base got more than 100 countries to outlaw a weapon that their armies had long used. Their support and encouragement piqued my curiosity.

The deeper I dug into the subject, however, the more I was drawn to document decisions by the Clinton administration first to support a ban and then not to sign it, as well as the conflict and the cooperation between officials and ban campaigners. That story proved to be much more intriguing than I had been led to believe by accounts in the press and elsewhere.

Those accounts portrayed the story as a David-and-Goliath struggle pitting the International Campaign to Ban Landmines against the US military, but my interviews with campaigners and government officials revealed that the US Army and the other armed services were far from united about the need for antipersonnel mines—in Korea or anywhere else. The ban campaign, too, was deeply riven by fierce struggles over whether to allow loopholes in the treaty exempting some mines and whether to assist tens of thousands of landmine survivors.

This, then, is a story of intrigue and misperception, of clashing norms and interests, of contentious bureaucratic and domestic politics. It is also a story of effective leadership—of sustained commitment to a cause, of alliances between campaigners and government officials, of a US senator who championed the ban, and of adroit use of the news media.

I could not have told the story without the generous help of many people—some of them old friends—on all sides of the controversy who were willing to talk, usually on the record, and to share internal documents that cast many of the differences in a new light. I am grateful to those who chose to confide in me and hope I have not betrayed their trust even when I sometimes disagreed with their conclusions.

I am indebted to the Rockefeller Foundation and the Social Science Research Council for their generous support. I owe special thanks to my friend, Michael McLean; and my wife, Meg, who had the patience and persistence to plow through my earlier drafts and suggest improvements. Thanks, too, to my son, Jake, who understood the power of landmines to blow things up.

Leon V. Sigal
New York City

List of Acronyms

ACDA	Arms Control and Disarmament Agency
ADAM	area denial antipersonnel munition
AID	Agency for International Development
AP	antipersonnel
APL	antipersonnel landmines
AT	antitank
ATACM	Army tactical missile
ATWG	Arms Transfer Working Group
AV	antivehicle
CCW	Convention on Prohibitions or Restrictions on the Use of Certain Conventional Weapons Which May Be Deemed to Be Excessively Injurious or to Have Indiscriminate Effects
CD	Conference on Disarmament
CINC	commander-in-chief (of a regional or specified command)
CTBT	Comprehensive Test Ban Treaty
DFAIT	Department of Foreign Affairs and International Trade (Canada)
DMZ	Demilitarized Zone
DOD	US Department of Defense
DOS	(also, State) US Department of State
FASCAM	family of scatterable mines
HRW	Human Rights Watch
HI	Handicap International
ICBL	International Campaign to Ban Landmines
ICRC	International Committee of the Red Cross
IDA	Institute for Defense Analyses
IWG	Interagency Working Group
JCS	Joint Chiefs of Staff
LSN	Landmine Survivors Network

MAG	Mines Advisory Group
MI	Medico International
MND	Ministry of National Defense (Canada)
MOPMS	modular pack mine system
MTCR	Missile Technology Control Regime
NGO	nongovernmental organization
NPT	Non-Proliferation Treaty
NSC	National Security Council
OAU	Organization of African Unity
OSD	Office of Secretary of Defense
PDD	Presidential Decision Directive
PHR	Physicians for Human Rights
PM	Bureau of Politico-Military Affairs
ROK	Republic of Korea
SOLIC	Office of Special Operations and Low-Intensity Conflict
USCBL	US Campaign to Ban Landmines
USUN	US Mission to the United Nations
VVAF	Vietnam Veterans of America Foundation

1

An Irresistible Force Meets
an Immovable Object

The scope of a conflict determines its outcome.

E.E. Schattschneider[1]

The International Campaign to Ban Landmines was born on October 2, 1992, in modest circumstances: a cluttered warren overlooking the lion-flanked New York Public Library, where Human Rights Watch had its headquarters. The six nongovernmental organizations that spawned the campaign were drawn to a landmines ban from diverse directions. Vietnam Veterans of America Foundation was founded by Robert "Bobby" Muller, who had been grievously wounded in Vietnam. German-based Medico International and French-based Handicap International specialized in treating and rehabilitating landmine victims in many countries. An English NGO, Mines Advisory Group, engaged in the delicate, sometimes deadly task of demining swaths of earth—removing the many mines scattered, unmarked and unmapped, around the world. Physicians for Human Rights was dedicated to addressing the moral as well as medical consequences of human rights abuses. The host of the meeting, Human Rights Watch, a global advocate for rights, had co-produced a September 1991 report, "Landmines in Cambodia: The Coward's

War," with Physicians for Human Rights calling attention to landmines as an indiscriminate weapon whose use not only caused humanitarian distress but also raised legal objections. It had stopped just short of calling for a ban.

The ban was the brainchild of Bobby Muller, who was inspired by a trip to Cambodia in 1991 with fellow Vietnam veteran Ed Miles. "Ed and I had been wounded but had both put our lives back together," says Muller. "Ed was a special forces captain in Vietnam who had gotten blown up—a multiple amputee." Told about a place "where they were warehousing disabled people who became so pissed off that they threw grenades in the marketplace," the pair made their way in wheelchairs to the remote location. "People weren't supposed to go out there," Muller recounts. "It was truly one of the most depressing things that we'd ever seen. They had 79 guys who were either amputated or blinded or multiply amputated…sequestered with their families in three buildings that had no running water, no electricity, nothing—just waiting to die." The experience led Muller and Miles to set up a project to rehabilitate landmine victims and other war disabled. They returned to Cambodia later that year. "Everybody was talking about the landmines issue, saying that something should be done," Muller says. "It was a very small but critical step from saying that something should be done to just doing it." After returning to Washington, DC, "I was sitting in the office and the thought came to me: just get rid of them—ban them like poison gas after World War I. It's doable, and once the magnitude of what's going on in Cambodia gets appreciated, it ought to be a no-brainer."[2]

Muller conceived of a global campaign for a ban in the course of a November 1991 meeting with Thomas Gebauer of Medico International, who had been collaborating with VVAF on the treatment and rehabilitation of mine victims. "The idea was, if he'd raise his voice in Europe and we'd raise our voices here, that would make this an international campaign," says Muller. "We argued about who would hire some staff and I lost the argument."[3] At Gebauer's suggestion, Muller hired Jody Williams, an activist who had spent 11 years organizing opposition to US policy in Central America. For the next 11 months Williams canvassed NGOs trying to interest them in a ban. The culmination of this incubation period was the birth of the International Campaign to Ban Landmines in October 1992.

The founders had their differences. VVAF and Medico International wanted a global ban from the outset, says Stephen Goose of Human Rights Watch. Muller and others wanted the focus kept on antipersonnel landmines, but Medico had a more radical approach: "It called for the abolition of war, so it was always pushing harder to make the landmine ban movement part of a broader peace movement." Human Rights Watch and Physicians for Human Rights were initially lukewarm toward a ban. A report they did on landmines in Cambodia "doesn't call for a ban," says Goose. "It says we should think about it." Goose elaborates, "Everything here is seen through the prism of human rights law and humanitarian law. For Human Rights Watch to step out on this, it really had to feel that not only were we faced with something on a scale that had humanitarian interest, but also that there were legal issues involved." Human Rights Watch and Physicians for Human Rights soon came around to a ban. The NGOs dedicated to demining, Mines Advisory Group and Handicap International, "were a little slower, in part because they were field operations rather than political activist" in orientation.[4] Indeed, HALO Trust, another leading British NGO specializing in demining, viewed the ban campaign as a costly distraction from its main mission and refused to join.[5]

At the October meeting, the six NGOs agreed to draft a joint call for a global ban on antipersonnel landmines. Constituting themselves as the steering committee of the ban campaign, they appointed Jody Williams to be its coordinator. They also decided to convene the first-ever NGO-sponsored international conference on a landmines ban in London in spring 1993.

In just 5 years, the founding six would be joined by 1,200 NGOs in 60 countries and the ban campaign, launched inauspiciously, would exceed its founders' wildest dreams. On December 3–4, 1997, representatives from 122 sovereign nations gathered in Ottawa, Canada to sign a Convention on the Prohibition of the Use, Stockpiling, Production and Transfer of Antipersonnel Mines and on Their Destruction—the Ottawa Convention for short. That a small group of NGOs could succeed in securing entry into force of a global treaty to outlaw a class of weapons in the arsenals of most armed forces is a story that confounds the conventional wisdom of international politics.

In the 9 years since the signing, the ban is slowly but surely taking effect. Treaty compliance, with rare exceptions, has been faithful. The stigma attached to antipersonnel mines has constrained even nonsignatories, a sign that a new international norm is in the making. Mine use has been reduced. Manufacture of antipersonnel mines has dropped dramatically as 7 of the world's top 12 producers, the United States among them, have ceased all production. Sales are also down. US intelligence has detected no shipments of antipersonnel mines by signatory states, although some nonsignatories have reportedly shipped mines abroad and black market sales persist, albeit at a reduced volume.[6] Some states have begun to destroy mine stockpiles, although mines by the millions remain. El Salvador is mine-free and demining is regaining lost ground in Cambodia, Mozambique, and elsewhere. South Korea has even demined a strip through the Demilitarized Zone where a rail line and a road will connect it to North Korea. Yet vast tracts of the earth remain hazardous to inhabitants. Landmines still claim another victim every day somewhere around the globe. Survivors by the tens of thousands remain social outcasts with little government care or rehabilitation.

The United States did not sign the ban. President Clinton did pledge adherence to a legislative ban on the production and sale of antipersonnel landmines. He would later commit the United States to sign the treaty by 2006, but only if suitable military alternatives to such mines could be found. In the meantime, the United States reserved the right to use antipersonnel mines.

The United States has not used landmines since, not even in Iraq in 2003, but it is no closer to signing the Ottawa treaty than it was in December 1997. How the ban campaign affected the politics of US landmines policy is the subject of this book.

A GLOBAL POWER SHIFT?

The ICBL's success has been widely hailed as dramatic evidence of a revolution in world affairs: the rise of nonstate actors to supplant the nation state or challenge its centrality. In awarding the 1997 Peace Prize to the ICBL, the Nobel committee concluded that "as a model for similar processes in the future, it could prove of decisive importance to the international effort for disarmament and peace."[7]

NGOs are not new. Nor are networks of NGOs whose influence transcends international borders. Transnational relations, which Thomas Risse-Kappen defines as "regular interactions across national boundaries when at least one actor is a non-state agent or does not operate on behalf of a national government or an intergovernmental organization," have long been a feature of international politics.[8] Multinational corporations, for example, are nonstate entities that operate and exert political influence across borders. Perhaps a more pertinent example is the British and Foreign Anti-Slavery Society, founded in 1838, which aroused anti-slavery activism far beyond England's shores. The trade union movement also formed influential transnational networks by 1900, as did socialist parties.[9]

NGOs were no strangers to international diplomacy, either. NGOs were invited to participate in deliberations of the League of Nations, even to vote and sign League documents. NGOs were instrumental in incorporating the Universal Declaration of Human Rights into the United Nations charter. And perhaps the strongest challenge to state sovereignty has long come from the Catholic Church, an NGO that has been accorded diplomatic recognition.[10]

What is newer is the dispersion and density of NGOs, their ability to raise substantial financial support, private as well as public, and their use of the latest communication technologies to link and mobilize activists across more permeable borders.

Newest of all is the NGOs' influence over military matters. During the Cold War, national security policy in the United States was largely the preserve of the executive branch. Congress and a handful of NGOs did exert effective influence from time to time, but only in rare instances have mass movements mounted a successful challenge to state power. In the 1950s the antinuclear movement in the United States and abroad helped drive nuclear testing underground. Yet the pace of development and deployment of new nuclear arms did not slacken until decades later with the end of the Cold War. Similarly, the antiwar movement helped cap the commitment of American ground troops to Vietnam in 1968; but even as troops withdrew, US military involvement persisted for 7 more years with little discernible diminution in intensity and the war claimed more American and Vietnamese lives after 1968 than before withdrawal. In the early 1980s, antinuclear protestors across Western Europe and the freeze movement in the United States were unable to stop deployment of cruise and Pershing missiles or the Reagan nuclear buildup, although they did prepare the ground for radical nuclear arms reductions in the 1990s.

In contrast, the ICBL was global in scope. It also achieved its aim of an international treaty over the determined opposition of the United States and other world powers, among them, China, Russia, and India. For an NGO to accomplish such a feat does seem to call into question prevailing assumptions about the role of the state in making national security policy.

The antiwar movement of the 1960s rode a genuine groundswell of public opinion. Taking to heart Bob Dylan's injunction not to follow leaders, the movement had an acephalous, even amorphous, organization. Those who spoke for it were often self-promoted or anointed by the news media.[11] In contrast, the landmines ban campaign was much less spontaneous and had no mass following. It was a virtual mass movement with relatively few rank-and-file members and even fewer contributors.[12] Nor was it an ordinary pressure group organized to lobby within national borders or, like Human Rights Watch or Amnesty International, across borders. It was a transnational network of heterogeneous groups with quite different motives who coalesced temporarily around one specific aim: a global treaty to ban antipersonnel landmines.

For some, the campaign was a humanitarian crusade against an indiscriminate weapon; for others, it was a means to secure aid for mine victims or funds for demining; for still others, it was part of a broader struggle to reduce military spending or outlaw war. The campaign brought together activists whose usual strategy was to confront the state with groups accustomed to cooperation with, even cooptation by, government. In its ranks were antimilitarist and anti-American groups on the left, standing side-by-side with the International Committee of the Red Cross, which began as an NGO but has evolved into what the British call a quango, or quasi-nongovernmental organization, whose affiliates work closely with governments and draw much of their funding from public coffers. Also collaborating with the coalition were members of Congress and parliaments and their staffs, as well as officials in the executive branch and in allied governments. Getting such a diverse coalition with divergent aims to act in concert was no mean feat.

The campaign adopted the classic outsider strategy of mass movements, using transformative rhetoric—reframing an issue of national security or arms control as one of human security or human rights—in pursuit of a radical goal, the abolition of all antipersonnel landmines. At the same time it used insider tactics, exploiting access to the negotiating table and back-room bargaining with diplomats to word the treaty in accordance with its own draft. The campaign's ability to circumvent the diplomatic barriers to entry was an important feature of its success.

The campaign exploited new information technologies to link its far-flung members. It could quickly disseminate information to its affiliates and to the news media, sometimes putting it a step or two ahead of the US government in framing issues for negotiators, the news media, and the wider public. Staging visually compelling events and drawing on the star power of Diana, Princess of Wales, it was also able to attract media attention to its cause.

As a transnational network, the campaign amplified its effectiveness by concerted action with affiliates in many countries. Yet the campaign was not organized hierarchically. Its hub did not control its spokes. In organizing the campaign, the network was the solution.

The campaign used e-mail and Web sites to gather and transmit information that governments have traditionally managed to keep to themselves. Viewing information as a primary source of power, some observers see this new technology as a democratizing force, a countervailing trend to state domination of information in the polity and top-down communication within organizations.

Some observers worry that if power were to devolve from the public to the private sector, civil society would become even more fragmented, leaving individuals at the mercy of unregulated market forces, environmental decay, international migration, and other transnational forces. Other observers see NGOs as agents, instruments, or sub-contractors coping with those forces, or even as catalysts or linchpins of international cooperation.[13] Still others see NGOs not just supplementing, but supplanting the state, usurping government power without public accountability.[14] Some welcome NGOs as evidence of an emerging international civil society that will eventually transcend national identities and challenge the primacy of states as a source of world order. Did the ban campaign meet any of these expectations?

Where to negotiate the ban, in the Conference on Disarmament or a new stand-alone forum, was a hotly contested decision. Some scholars of international relations emphasize how international institutions facilitate cooperation among states. Others see such institutions as mere manifestations of state power, an arena for the inherent conflicts of interests among nations to play out without doing much to resolve them. Which of these views best fits the

Conference on Disarmament and the locus of international decision making that displaced it, the Ottawa process?

THE DOMESTIC AND BUREAUCRATIC POLITICS OF A BAN

Because of its prominence in the international community, the US government was the campaigners' ultimate target. They first sought to influence Washington directly, and when that failed, they tried to influence it indirectly, through other governments. In the end, the campaign succeeded in getting most states to sign the ban over US opposition, which had seldom happened during the Cold War. Canada played a pivotal part in winning acceptance for the treaty. Belgium, Germany, the United Kingdom, France, and Japan—all of them US allies—provided vital support. Still, the campaign failed to get the United States to sign.

President Clinton sensed the political appeal of the ban campaign, as did members of Congress. Clinton publicly endorsed the elimination of antipersonnel landmines. Congress repeatedly voted overwhelmingly for resolutions to impose a moratorium of exports and to extend it. In the end, however, the United States did not back the treaty to ban landmines. Why?

The usual explanation is military resistance to a ban. Yet careful examination calls that into question. The extent to which antipersonnel mines were regarded as a military requirement was a matter of heated dispute within the armed services. What accounts for inter- and intraservice differences over landmines?

Interests mattered. But what interests? It is a tenet of realism, the dominant way of thinking about the world in the government and the foreign policy establishment of the United States as well as an important school of thought in the study of international relations, that states pursue enduring national interests, narrowly defined in terms of security or power, and that other values do not count.[15] To realists, a landmines ban posed a conflict between morality and interest, or between humanitarian duty and military necessity. In such a conflict, they believed, morality must give way. This view was a strong undercurrent in the landmines controversy.

Yet, far from enduring and clear, as realists assume, the national security interest of the United States in landmines was politically contested. Indeed, few in the armed services deemed landmines to be a military requirement. The US need for landmines even in Korea was often misunderstood. A bureaucratic and domestic politics approach, by disaggregating the state, yields a more differentiated picture of competing government agencies with conflicting organizational interests.[16]

Not only realists, but also most students of political science interpret political activity as motivated primarily by interests. Yet normative appeals are also the stuff of politics, inspiring political action by citizens and politicians alike. By invoking moral norms to stigmatize landmines, the ban campaigners rallied groups of citizens and elected officials to their cause. Even some military officers and civilian officials proved amenable to the campaign's moral appeal.

This study examines the interplay of norms and interests in US bureaucratic and domestic politics. It begins by laying out in greater detail how the landmines ban was put on the political agenda in the United States and the part that was played by moral concerns.

2

Beyond the Limits of Arms Control

Pressure politics is essentially the politics of small groups.

E.E. Schattschneider[1]

To most Americans a landmine was a remote abstraction. Even in the US government, the armed forces, or the nongovernmental organizations involved in landmine policy, few had ever seen a mine explode or dug one into or out of the ground, let alone felt their shattering impact first hand. That was not the case for most people in Cambodia or Mozambique, where millions of mines lurk unseen beneath fields and footpaths, threatening to shatter limb and life at any moment. The radical difference in perspective cast a shadow over what to do about the antipersonnel landmine—whether to treat it as a cancer requiring radical surgery in the form of a ban, or a flu to be quarantined by regulating its spread through arms control.

The International Campaign to Ban Landmines, as its name signifies, did not want to regulate the use of landmines, but to ban them. That was a radical approach by the standard of arms control then prevalent in Washington. As if that were not enough of a challenge, the campaigners had to overcome public indifference as well.

Inside Washington, conventional arms control usually takes a back seat to nuclear arms control, and negotiations on landmines were no exception. The

9

nightmarish possibility that a single nuclear warhead could instantaneously vaporize an American city seemed more newsworthy than the unreported reality of two dozen landmine casualties a day in obscure places around the globe. Nuclear disarmament episodically inspired mass movements during the Cold War; conventional arms buildups since 1945 stirred no comparable passion. Negotiating limits on nuclear arms between two superpowers, however difficult, seemed a simpler task than convincing many states who manufacture and use conventional arms to agree on restraints and adhere to them. Superpower summitry was high drama; meetings of faceless diplomats to negotiate on landmines were rarely reported and almost never televised. Even the name of the treaty under negotiation in 1994 seemed inspired by obscurantists: the "Convention on Prohibitions or Restrictions on the Use of Certain Conventional Weapons Which May Be Deemed to Be Excessively Injurious or to Have Indiscriminate Effects," or CCW for short.

THE UNCHECKED SPREAD OF ANTIPERSONNEL MINES

A weapon of the weak, landmines were used by insurgents and governments alike, not only to restrict troop movements but also to terrorize and control the civilian populace. An armed force could briefly seize territory and before abandoning it, strew landmines to prevent it from being reoccupied, whether by foe or by innocent civilian trying to return home and earn a livelihood. Landmines were thus indiscriminate. They were also long-lasting. Once emplaced, they could lie in wait for years after the war was over, for any passerby to trip them. So long as landmines were readily available on arms markets at affordable prices, attempts to regulate their use seemed doomed to failure. Unless something were done to curb production and sales and to remove the millions of mines already emplaced, the human toll would only mount.

A landmine, like other explosive ordnance, has a firing train consisting of a fuze, which activates a detonator, a very small charge of sensitive explosive material. That in turn sets off the main charge, a larger mass of less sensitive explosive. Mines cause destruction by blast or by dispersing metal fragments across a target area. They lie dormant until someone or something comes in contact with the fuze, then explode instantaneously. The fuze can be mechanical, electrical, or chemical, either alone or in combination. A common fuze is a tripwire, which sets off the mine when someone or something touches it. A pressure-sensitive fuze activates the mine when it is stepped on or driven over. A magnetic influence fuze sets off the mine when it senses a vehicle's magnetic field. A seismic fuze uses a sensor to detect vibration and activate the mine. These fuzes typically cannot distinguish friend from foe, or noncombatant passerby. By contrast, command-detonated mines require a person to transmit a signal by radio or wire to activate them after detecting an enemy presence.

The use of explosive charges to breach or defend fortified positions dates back to the battle of Agincourt in 1415 and iron mines of sorts from the Ming dynasty have been unearthed in China, but antipersonnel landmines are a more recent development in the history of weaponry. In the Civil War, the mining of fortified positions was used to devastating effect at Vicksburg and Petersburg. At Yorktown in 1862, antecedents of antipersonnel mines were introduced by Confederate soldiers who buried artillery shells base down so they would explode as a Union soldier stepped on them. Prussia also used makeshift mines in the Franco-Prussian War of 1870. During World War I, in response to the introduction of the tank by the British, the Germans improvised mines from artillery shells and laid them out in rows to stop tank attacks. They later mass-produced antitank mines. The British countered by attaching rollers to the front of their tanks to set off mines in order to breach the German minefields.[2] Primitive versions of antipersonnel landmines were also introduced on a limited basis.

Modern pressure-detonated antitank mines were not fielded until the 1920s, after the invention of trinitro-toluene or TNT, a powerful, lightweight and relatively stable explosive. In World War II, all the major combatants used antitank landmines—more than 300 million by one estimate. Yet antitank mines had a significant shortcoming: enemy troops could remove them and relocate them to minefields of their own. That shortcoming was exposed during the German tank offensive in North Africa under Field Marshal Erwin Rommel, when the Germans dug up British mines and replanted them in "devil's gardens" of their own to offset Britain's advantage in tanks. The German advance was halted at El Alamein, where each side appropriated the other's minefields for its own defensive works. To inhibit enemy troops from clearing antitank minefields, both sides began scattering small metal or glass containers filled with a pound or less of explosive, which could be detonated by a tug on a tripwire or by direct pressure. They also booby-trapped antitank mines with hand grenades. In short, antipersonnel landmines designed to detonate when a person, not a heavy vehicle, tripped them, first saw extensive use as adjuncts to antitank mines.

It did not take long before these improvised explosives were deployed on their own. Japanese troops were the first to booby-trap flashlights, pipes, radios, and other harmless objects. Soon all sides were booby-trapping the bodies of the dead. Precursors of today's antipersonnel mines also came into vogue. An outmanned Finland made extensive use of fragmentation mines against Russia in 1939–1940 and Germany introduced the "bouncing Betty" or S-mine, which could be activated by command or set off by pressure or tripwire. It consisted of two charges, one that propelled the mine a meter or two into the air followed by a second that sent steel fragments up to 30 meters in all directions.[3]

The antipersonnel landmine came into its own in the Vietnam War when the North Vietnamese used simple booby traps to deadly advantage and the United States air-dropped "scatterable" mines to impede infiltration into the south through Laos and Cambodia. Not confined to marked minefields, the 20-gram devices detonated when stepped on and harmed friend and foe alike. As a result, mines and booby traps caused 65 to 70 percent of all Marine Corps casualties in 1965.

The experience led some in the military to favor acquisition of a new generation of so-called "smart" mines that were designed to deactivate or self-destruct after a preset time to replace dumb mines that could lie dormant for years until tripped by a passerby. It led others to question the utility of antipersonnel landmines. It led still others, mostly outside the military, to try to bring them under some form of international control.

The origins of the CCW can be traced back to 1974, when the International Committee of the Red Cross hosted a conference of governmental experts to devise ways of curbing the use of weapons that cause excessive or indiscriminate harm—so-called "weapons of ill repute," a normatively evocative name. With the extensive use of napalm by the United States in Vietnam still fresh in the memory of delegates, the incendiary bomb, not the antipersonnel mine, was the main bone of contention. A working paper submitted to the Conference on Disarmament in Geneva on February 7, 1975, by several nonaligned countries proposed that use of incendiaries, cluster bombs, small-caliber projectiles, and aerial delivery of antipersonnel mines be prohibited.[4] At the second session of the experts group in 1976, a working paper was introduced to regulate the use of landmines and booby traps.

Yet, so long as the antipersonnel mine, whether used on its own or in conjunction with antitank mines, was considered a military requirement by many states, no consensus was possible on which mines to regulate, let alone ban. Instead, on June 10, 1977, the Diplomatic Conference on the Reaffirmation and Development of International Humanitarian Law Applicable in Armed Conflicts adopted two protocols further codifying the law of war. Protocol I Additional to the Geneva Conventions of August 12, 1949, elaborated limits on the use of force in international armed conflicts and extended them to civil wars. Article 35 outlawed use of "weapons, projectiles and material and methods of warfare of a nature to cause superfluous injury or unnecessary suffering." Article 51 prohibited "indiscriminate attacks," those "not directed at a specific military object" and those "of a nature to strike military objectives and civilians or civilian objects without distinction." Protocol II extended humanitarian protection to combatants and noncombatants in civil wars.

The Reagan administration did not submit Protocol I to the Senate for its advice and consent, in part because of objection from the Joint Chiefs of Staff that complying with it would cause needless US casualties and leave US troops liable to criminal prosecution.[5] Fifteen years later the United States had yet to ratify Protocol I.

After the two protocols were signed, yet another conference was convened, this time under United Nations auspices, to address specific weapons. It yielded the CCW and three new protocols, which were adopted by the General Assembly on October 10, 1980. Landmines were covered by Protocol II on "Prohibitions or Restrictions on the Use of Mines, Booby-Traps and Other Devices." It regulated the use of landmines rather than banning them. It forbade the indiscriminate use of mines. It provided that their use be directed only at military objectives and that all feasible precautions be taken to avoid targeting civilians. It further stipulated that remotely delivered mines not be used unless their location was accurately recorded or they were equipped with an effective neutralizing mechanism. It urged that mines be cleared once the hostilities ceased. Yet it applied to international conflicts only, not civil wars, and its injunctions were largely hortatory: it had no provision for enforcement. The United States was one of 53 countries to sign the protocol, but a decade later had yet to ratify it. Only 32 countries had.

The protocol's defects proved fatal. Over the next decade, antipersonnel mines by the tens of millions were sown in civil wars around the world—in Afghanistan, Angola, Cambodia, El Salvador, Nicaragua, Somalia, Mozambique, Sudan, Eritrea, and Bosnia—deliberately targeting noncombatants and the arable land that sustained them.

It did not take long for this devastating trend to draw the attention of NGOs that had to deal first-hand with its effects. The most prominent of these was the International Committee of the Red Cross, which had been founded in the 19th century to care for the victims of war. The ICRC took the lead in April 1993 in calling for a CCW review conference to reexamine the protocol.

The review conference was an American idea, according to Michael Matheson of the Office of Legal Adviser in the Department of State. "As it became clear that something had to be done about this," Matheson says, "my shop, basically me, decided that a sensible thing to do would be to try and organize a review conference, which was provided for under the convention, to revise the landmines protocol radically. It turns out the French were of a similar mind, although their initial substantive impulses were rather conservative."[6] The two countries collaborated on a UN resolution introduced by France in December 1993 calling for a review conference on the Convention on Certain Conventional Weapons and asking the UN Secretary-General to convene a group of governmental experts to prepare for the conference.

The ICRC's recommendations for future action were also modest: extension of regulations on landmines to internal armed conflicts, "tighter restrictions" on the types of mines used, and a "study" of "arms control/disarmament measures" to reduce the number of civilian victims. It made no mention of a ban.[7]

Joining with other ICRC affiliates was the American Red Cross, whose president, Elizabeth Dole, had served in President Bush's cabinet and was married to Senate Minority Leader Robert Dole. The statement she issued was predicated on a ban, though she did not call for one: "The use of these weapons of terror is prohibited by international humanitarian law and immediate compliance must be demanded by all men and women of conscience."[8]

THE BAN GETS A CHAMPION

By then, the issue of landmines was no longer in no-man's land politically. It had what ban proponents needed to get it on the agenda in Washington: a champion in Congress. Senator Patrick Leahy chaired the Foreign Operations Subcommittee of the Senate Appropriations Committee. In that capacity, he held the purse strings for foreign aid, assuring attention for his concerns in the State Department and the Agency for International Development. A liberal Democrat from Vermont who knew how to move an issue on Capitol Hill, Leahy was adept at attracting news media attention and at reaching across the deepening partisan divide in Congress to line up Republican support.

The landmines issue was not much of a vote-getter back home in Vermont. Nor did it have the headline-grabbing appeal that attracts media-conscious politicians. If the issue had any constituency, it resided abroad and was ineligible to vote in US elections. Apart from a handful of NGOs, the people in Washington who cared most about landmines were Army and Marine officers who did not want to give them up. For Leahy, a landmines ban was more a matter of right and wrong than a political plus.

Leahy's concern about landmines was inspired by a 1985 visit to a contra base in Honduras run by the Central Intelligence Agency. At a field hospital to care for the contras and civilian victims of the war in neighboring Nicaragua, recalls Leahy, "There was a little boy there, probably 11 or 12, with one leg, hobbling around on a makeshift crutch. He had been there several years with no place to go."[9] Eric Newsom of his staff, who accompanied him, picks up the story: "Through an interpreter, Senator Leahy asked, how did this happen? I stepped on a landmine. It blew my leg off. Where did it happen? Up in the mountains along the border. Leahy said, whose landmine was it? The kid said, I don't know—what difference does it make?" Newsom recalls, "I thought it was terrible but this is war. I didn't think anything more of it."[10] It did trouble Leahy, however: "I realized, now I get on a helicopter, I leave, I fly back to Washington, a day later I'd be in Vermont with my wife and kids, living in comfort and safety. I couldn't get this little kid out of my mind."[11] En route home, says Newsom, "Leahy, who was clearly moved by what he had seen, said to me, I have to do something about this. I want you to think about what we can do to help and give me some ideas."[12]

On his return, Newsom talked it over with a fellow Leahy staffer, Tim Rieser: "Tim said there's a lot of concern out there about landmines and a lot of people think we ought to ban them." Newsom was skeptical, "I don't think that is conceivable in the near term, if ever, and we don't want to get off on some crusade that's not going to do anything." Within a few days Rieser had spoken to the manufacturer of a "simple low-cost, low-tech prosthesis that he called a Third World leg." It inspired the two aides to try to pay for prosthetic devices and physical therapy for landmine victims. When Senator Leahy showed enthusiasm for the idea, they contacted AID officials, who "reacted with horror at using foreign aid for this purpose," says Newsom. "Senator Leahy, being who he was, was able to persuade them to think that over."[13] The senator arranged to earmark money in the foreign aid bill for what became the "Leahy War Victims Fund."

Later the fund would lead Leahy to ally with NGOs working on landmines, both in the United States and abroad. One of the first was the Vietnam Veterans of America Foundation, which had opened a prosthetics clinic in Cambodia in 1991 and within a year would co-found the International Campaign to Ban Landmines. The driving force behind the alliance was Tim Rieser. "He was plugged into the activists in a way that I was not," says Newsom. "Because of this work, he was talking to me about them and about the idea of banning landmines."[14] Indeed, if the ICBL was a network, Leahy and Rieser would become its nexus.

A key node in that network was VVAF's executive director Robert "Bobby" Muller. "We felt we needed a champion and the only person we could think of was Leahy," says Muller. He ruled out one obvious place to look, the Senate Foreign Relations Committee, chaired by Claiborne Pell. "Because of the weakness of Pell as chairman, it had put out authorization legislation just once in 9 years. Leahy was chairman of the Foreign Operations Subcommittee on Appropriations, which put money into AID and State, and absent any policy considerations out of the Foreign Relations Committee, the budget tended to set the priorities."[15]

Muller leaves no doubt about Rieser's role in piloting the ban campaign. "From the very beginning through this very moment," he says, "we do not do anything without the absolute concurrence of, and usually at the direction of Tim. So we have been soldiers under the direction of Tim, who has been given the authority by Leahy to do what was necessary to get the job done."[16] Rieser is more self-effacing: "We consulted regularly. They did not act on anything significant without getting our views, and vice versa. By 'they,' I mean Bobby [Muller], Steve Goose, and a few others. I valued their technical expertise and they knew they needed Senator Leahy's support."[17]

Jody Williams of VVAF had just begun canvassing for ideas on what to do about landmines when Rieser first met with her on December 4, 1991.

He talked about the need for a ban campaign and offered to publicize it in the Congressional Record.[18] Leahy later arranged for a grant from the War Victims Fund for VVAF to provide prosthetics to war victims in Cambodia.[19] The funding, Rieser and Muller knew, would alleviate the impact of antipersonnel mines without getting at the root cause: the alarming rate at which the devices were proliferating.

AN EXPORT MORATORIUM

Bobby Muller wanted a global ban on antipersonnel landmines. Tim Rieser "was immediately sympathetic," says Muller, "but there was a little problem. He was not the staff director of Foreign Ops. The staff director was Eric Newsom, and Eric is a fairly cautious kind of guy. Rieser suggested that I go directly to Leahy."[20] Through a Democratic Party fundraiser he knew, Muller arranged to see the senator in July 1992. The meeting took place "just off the Senate floor. Tim was with him," recalls Muller. "I said I appreciate everything you're doing with the war victims fund, but we have to do something more than put artificial limbs on people. We have to go upstream and get rid of the weapon. I said we need somebody to lead that effort. Would you be willing to be that person? He hesitated just a second, thought about it and said, that's a good idea. I'll do it. Then he said, But you've got to understand a couple of things. This is going to take years. Nobody is talking about landmines in political terms and we're going to have to go a step at a time. Are you prepared to make that kind of commitment? I said, Senator, we are, and we'll stick with you for the duration. He said let me think about how I want to begin and I'll get back to you."[21]

A temporary moratorium on US exports seemed more feasible than a permanent global ban. Worldwide, the number of producers was dauntingly large: 41 firms and government agencies in 29 countries were known to have exported antipersonnel mines in recent years. Production and sales figures were slippery, but the Soviet Union, China, and Italy were the most prolific producers for export.[22] Conventional mines, like the Claymore, took little know-how to manufacture. Even more sophisticated scatterable mines, which could be dispersed from airplanes and helicopters or fired by mine launchers, artillery, or rocket launchers, were not beyond the capacity of low-cost producers in developing countries to manufacture. Plastic mines—lightweight, durable, and difficult to detect and deactivate—did not cost much to make. In the 1980s, as cheap mines flooded world markets, higher-priced US exports dried up. Exports that decade had totaled less than $2 million, a mere drop in the bucket of US arms sales. The State Department had issued just eight licenses for commercial export of antipersonnel mines valued at $980,000.[23] The Defense Department had approved sales of 13,156 mines worth $841,145.

The defense industry, often an obstacle to arms control, had little at stake in a US moratorium on exports, but it stood to benefit if, through pressure politics, it could ban so-called "dumb" mines without regulating "smart" mines, which were designed to self-destruct or self-deactivate. If the campaigners managed to mobilize support to ban all antipersonnel mines, however, US landmine manufacturers would lose.

Newsom had Rieser invite some of the campaigners to discuss what to do. "He brought in Bobby Muller, Jody Williams, and two or three others to talk about how we might work together," says Newsom. The NGOs favored banning all antipersonnel landmines, but Newsom was still skeptical: "I said I don't think banning use by US forces is achievable any time soon, but there is an approach that may be feasible." He and Rieser, he told them, had checked and found "only one company in the United States makes landmines for export and it sells only about 10,000 a year abroad. The US government does not export any landmines. That could be our entry point—a moratorium on exports of APLs [antipersonnel landmines] from the United States." Newsom proposed a 1-year moratorium: "The idea was, we could serve as an example to the rest of the world and push others to institute their own export moratoriums."[24] Newsom's impression is that he must have sounded like "such an accommodationist" to the NGOs. Perhaps so, but Muller recalls the NGOs readily accepting any idea that Leahy's staff was willing to back: "Let's get this straight. We do what we are told. Period."[25] Rieser's recollection is similar to Newsom's: "We thought about what was possible and we could see there were not significant exports of antipersonnel mines from the United States, so there was not strong industry interest in it. Exports did not prevent our own military's use of the weapon, so it seemed like a logical place to start to send a message to other countries to stop the trade in landmines. It was a way for the United States to set an example." His approach was a normative one, exploiting the power of example, not US economic or military power. Did Rieser see it as a stepping stone to a ban? "We knew that the export problem was only the tip of the iceberg so we always envisioned that as the first step. We did not have a clear strategy about what the next steps would be, however."[26]

Newsom talked it over with Leahy, who gave his assent. "A campaign to stop APL carnage among civilians appealed to Leahy a great deal," says Newsom, but "his real interest was the war victims. The thing he really wanted to do was help people who needed help, but couldn't get it. At first, he didn't seem too taken by this sort of incrementalist legislation."[27]

On July 29, 1992, Leahy introduced the Landmine Moratorium Act, calling on the Bush Administration to submit the CCW to the Senate for ratification and declaring it to be "the policy of the United States to seek verifiable international agreements prohibiting the sale, transfer or export, further limiting the use, and eventually, the termination of production, possession or deployment of antipersonnel landmines." As an example for other countries, it mandated a 1-year moratorium on the export or transfer of such mines from the United States.[28]

In an orchestrated gesture, the day Leahy introduced the bill, Muller faxed him a letter endorsing it.[29] Jody Williams, coordinator of VVAF's landmines campaign, faxed copies of the bill, Leahy's statement, and a press release to the news media and to other NGOs, who chimed in with praise.

Leahy began to warm to the campaigners, too. "When he met Bobby Muller, they hit it off," says Newsom. "They agreed to work together."[30] It was more than a mutual admiration society. Leahy and the NGOs began collaborating closely on tactics and strategy. The next day, Williams, who was in the process of organizing the international campaign to ban landmines, wrote Leahy asking him to serve on its committee of advisers.[31] Within days, senators were barraged by appeals from NGOs asking them to co-sponsor Leahy's bill.[32] The NGOs, says Tim Rieser, "helped educate the public. They helped interest the press. They encouraged people to support legislation. Their strategy and our strategy were similar."[33]

The export moratorium, in sum, was the handiwork of Senator Leahy's staff, not the campaigners. The NGOs, write Jody Williams and Stephen Goose of the ICBL, "wish they could claim 'strategic brilliance' in pressing for an export moratorium and that they immediately recognized the global impact such legislation would have. But that was not exactly the case. NGOs did support the congressional initiative, but its success was more the result of congressional strategy than NGO or grassroots pressure."[34]

Leahy used his personal touch, handwritten postscripts to "Dear Colleague" letters and face-to-face appeals, to line up 35 co-sponsors in the Senate, among them several Republicans, most prominently Minority Leader Robert Dole (R-KS), a wounded World War II veteran. Leahy got Representative Lane Evans (D-IL) to introduce similar legislation in the Democratic-controlled House. He then secured Senate approval in the form of an amendment to the pending military authorization bill. In conference committee, Leahy persuaded Sam Nunn (D-GA), chairman of the Senate Armed Services Committee, and John Warner (R-VA), ranking minority member, to attach his amendment to the authorization bill in return for deleting a reference to eventual "termination of...possession or deployment." Stripped of the ban language, the provision was signed into law by President Bush on October 23.

Leahy also earmarked military assistance funds in the fiscal year 1993 foreign aid bill for mine clearing and mandated a study by the Department of State on the extent of the problem. Released in August 1983, that study estimated that 85 to 90 million mines lay scattered in 62 countries. Mines killed or injured roughly 150 people a week, most of them civilians. Yet the armed services, which had mine detection and removal equipment, did not use it for the delicate task of humanitarian demining. They reserved its use for a purely military mission instead, to breach minefields, clearing a narrow avenue of attack by detonating mines or plowing them aside. As implied in its title, "Hidden Killers: The Global Problem with Uncleared Landmines," the report made a case for giving priority to humanitarian demining, but most of its arguments applied with as much urgency to a ban. The world's fighting forces were laying more mines each day, it noted, and "one of the characteristics of mines" is "that while they are extremely easy to lay, they are also extremely difficult to detect and destroy."[35] What sense did it make to remove mines without a prohibition on laying more?

LEAHY'S UNREQUITED COURTSHIP

After President Clinton moved into the White House in 1993, Senator Leahy came a-courting. In an article in the Arms Control Association's bimonthly, *Arms Control Today*, Leahy urged that he "immediately review *all* the laws of war agreements on which the Reagan and Bush administrations failed to act, with a view toward sending them to the Senate for prompt ratification." He expressed high hopes the new administration would build on the moratorium: "The next step is for President Clinton to use the influence that accrues from setting an example with this policy of unilateral restraint to negotiate a binding international ban on the sale, export, and transfer of antipersonnel mines."[36] Leahy enclosed a copy of his article in a letter to Secretary of State Warren Christopher calling for ratification of Protocol I on landmines, never submitted to the Senate by Reagan or Bush, as a first step and inquiring about administration support for mine-clearing in Angola. The courtship was unrequited. The reply, from an acting assistant secretary for legislative affairs, was noncommittal.

Elsewhere Leahy fared better. The International Campaign to Ban Landmines was formally founded in October 1992, just days before President Bush signed the Leahy moratorium into law. The ICBL was quick to laud Leahy's efforts and get NGOs at home and abroad to sing his praises. Even more important, a few European politicians took up his moratorium as their cause. Two years after Leahy first introduced his bill for a 1-year moratorium on exports, more than a dozen other countries would adopt similar measures. In ways unanticipated by Leahy and his NGO allies, the export moratorium put a landmines ban on the policy agenda.

On July 22, 1993, Leahy introduced a bill to extend the export moratorium for 3 years. This time, 15 Republicans were among its 60 co-sponsors, and again, Minority Leader Dole was one of them. "It became clear that Senator Leahy could get a lot of co-sponsors for his bill," says Eric Newsom, once word got around that "we exported so few landmines that the impact on jobs and US industry would be minuscule." The NGOs saw to it that word did get around. "They put out fact sheets. We had a lot of people working with us by this time, doing research and getting this material out. We became quite organized." Newsom's boss was also showing more enthusiasm for the legislative approach: "Leahy and his own political staff saw that, as one of them put it, this was an issue with legs."[37]

Enthusiasm was tempered in other parts of Washington. The Leahy bill convinced the military that an export moratorium could soon become permanent. It also aroused the leading US exporter of landmines, Alliant Techsystems. "The military came in and talked to us," says Newsom. "So did the manufacturer of modern self-destructing and self-deactivating mines for export, and asked, why are we being singled out?" They had a point, Newsom acknowledges. "Frankly, I was sympathetic to their argument that the self-destructing antipersonnel landmines were much less of a threat to civilians than the 'dumb' mines most countries used. But these high-tech APLs were expensive and complicated and there wasn't much of a foreign market for them. A simple export cutoff was clearly our best strategy at the time."[38]

On September 10, the Senate passed the bill on a roll-call vote of 100–0. Once again, however, unanimity came at a price: stopping short of a ban. The reference in Leahy's original bill to "eventually terminating the manufacture, possession and use of antipersonnel mines" was dropped. Blurring a distinction that would later become fighting words, the legislation urged that the administration "actively seek to negotiate, under United Nations auspices, a modification of the Landmines Protocol, or another international agreement, to prohibit the sale, transfer or export of antipersonnel landmines, and to further limit their manufacture, possession and use." It also earmarked $10 million for demining, with the proviso that no US troops would be used for that purpose.

Leahy was vigilant in overseeing implementation and guarding against policy initiatives that would make a ban less negotiable. In 1993 Robert Sherman, who was running the advanced projects office of the Arms Control and Disarmament Agency, attempted to distinguish "short-duration self-destruct" mines, which he felt "were not a humanitarian problem—at least no more than any other weapon," from "persistent mines, which cause the problem." He proposed that "all mines, including naval mines, had to be duration-limited." He called the policy "safemines" and floated it in inter-agency strategy meetings "as a holy grail," where the administration should try to go with landmines. It was classic arms control. "Within State it was very readily accepted," he recalls, but "DOD resisted." When Sherman briefed the NGOs on the idea, their response disappointed him: "I thought they would say, that's great, it solves the humanitarian problem. Instead they opposed it."[39] They told Senator Leahy, who complained to ACDA's acting director, Thomas Graham, Jr., in a letter co-signed by Representative Evans, "Recently, it came to our attention that some in ACDA are proposing an exemption from the moratorium for certain scatterable, self-destruct/self-neutralizing mines which are produced in this country." They objected, "It would nullify the effect of the moratorium since these are the only U.S.-manufactured antipersonnel landmines being produced for export." That would undercut negotiating efforts, they said. "It would set a double standard between the U.S. and other industrialized countries, and countries that produce low-technology mines, even before negotiation begins on stronger limits."[40] Leahy followed up by telephoning Frank G. Wisner, undersecretary of defense for policy, who upheld the blanket moratorium.[41]

Leahy lent his name to other NGO efforts as well. That month the Arms Project of Human Rights Watch and Physicians for Human Rights gave added impetus to a ban by issuing a compendium of information, *Landmines: A Deadly Legacy*, documenting the global trade in landmines and the status of international law governing mines and reporting on detailed field studies of the medical and social impact of landmine use in six countries. Leahy wrote the preface. "Altogether," it read, "this report makes a convincing case for an international agreement to prohibit the production, stockpiling, trade and use of antipersonnel landmines."[42]

Leahy soon found a kindred spirit in the administration, the ambassador to the United Nations, Madeleine Albright. Albright's formative experience on landmines, like Leahy's, was a visit to mine-afflicted countries, in her case, Somalia and Cambodia. A member of her staff, Ambassador Karl F. "Rick" Inderfurth, accompanied her. "We went to look at peacekeeping operations," he recalls. "As part of our briefing materials, the landmine issue was raised. It was not one that she or I had focused on prior to this." First-hand experience changed that. "The number still sticks in my mind that 1 out of every 236 Cambodians was a landmine victim," he says. "The briefing papers were one thing; seeing the amputees on the streets of Phnom Penh was another. On the way back she said, let's see what we can do in the United Nations about this."[43]

The US mission to the United Nations, USUN in State Department shorthand, is located in New York, marginalizing it in Washington. "We weren't the Department of State, we weren't the Department of Defense, we weren't the White House. We were this little engine that could up in New York," says Inderfurth. That meant "play the role of provocateur" within the US government on landmine policy. Albright sat on the Principals Committee and Inderfurth represented her on the Deputies Committee, the highest level interagency policy-making bodies, but their main point of leverage was responsibility for what the United States said and did at the United Nations, says Inderfurth. "The two best ways to address landmines was through what the president said in the UN General Assembly and through resolutions." At Albright's behest, he circulated a draft resolution in the General Assembly calling on all states "to agree to a moratorium on the export of antipersonnel mines." According to Inderfurth, "From the first resolution offered in 1993 until the last one offered before we left in 1997, we continued to raise the mark," nudging member states toward a ban.[44]

Leahy's staff, not the NGOs, inspired Albright's initial efforts at the United Nations. "At this point I was not fully aware of the parallel work being done on the NGO side by Bobby Muller and Jody Williams," says Inderfurth. "The connecting tissue was Patrick Leahy, because when I came back from that trip with Albright in 1993, I started looking into this and very quickly all roads were leading to Senator Leahy, with whom Albright was already good friends." Through Leahy, Inderfurth forged links with the NGOs. "Getting in touch with him and his staff assistant, Tim Rieser, immediately plugged us into what he was doing on the Senate side," he says, "and, of course, at that point he was already beginning to work with Bobby Muller."[45]

Albright and Leahy began to collaborate on landmines. On October 6, the very day Leahy was objecting to any exemption to the US moratorium, Albright wrote him to report that the 1980 CCW would be sent to the Senate for ratification "as early as this fall." She also sent him a copy of the draft resolution.[46] Two weeks later, Leahy was dismayed to discover that the wording "agree to a moratorium" in the draft was about to be watered down to "consider a moratorium." He had his legislative director, Eric Newsom, take up the issue with Inderfurth. The two, who had worked together on Capitol Hill, discussed having Leahy lobby for the moratorium at the United Nations. Leahy then wrote Albright opposing any weakening of the resolution. "In my opinion," he argued, "countries which are opposing the present U.S. draft should be isolated, forced to oppose or abstain, and exposed to what I antici- pate will be a major international campaign to persuade them to join us and others in a moratorium."[47]

Not content with stiffening the spines of US officials, Leahy wrote to ambassadors in Washington from key allied countries 2 days later lobbying for the stronger language.[48] As a result of discussions with Inderfurth, Leahy was invited to introduce the US moratorium resolution at the United Nations.

On November 17, the General Assembly adopted the resolution by consen- sus. It called on member states to halt the export of "antipersonnel landmines that pose grave dangers to civilian populations." That was not as all-inclusive as Leahy's bill imposing a moratorium on US export of "smart" as well as "dumb" antipersonnel mines. On December 7, the Clinton administration sent notes to 44 mine-producing countries asking them to halt antipersonnel mine exports for the next 3 to 5 years.

To Leahy an export moratorium was a way station to a ban. For many US allies, as well as for some US officials, it was an alternative to a ban, a way to placate pro-ban sentiment by doing something about landmines while dissipating pressure for a ban. Knowing this, Leahy began lobbying the administration to support a CCW review conference and involve NGOs in the process.

A meeting of governmental experts was due to lay the groundwork for the review conference. On October 26, Leahy wrote Inderfurth to urge that the United States "play a major role." He recommended bringing in outsiders. "The best way would be for the NGOs to participate in the group of experts," he wrote. "If this is not possible I urge that other ways be found for the NGOs to participate actively in the preparations for the conference."[49] For a conference it would host in Paris that November, Handicap International (HI) solicited a letter of endorsement from Leahy. They asked him to mention "very specifically (we know that this is one of the French government's wishes, too) that it is imperative that NGOs like MAG, HI, VVAF, HRW, PHR [the ICBL's co-founders] be closely involved and that they are also an important source of information, data, and field studies."[50] If it were left up to the diplomats, the review conference would turn into arms control as usual. Assuring NGO involvement would give a ban a chance.

On December 16, 1993, the General Assembly voted 162–0 to hold the review conference. The United States was one of just three members to abstain. It did so because it objected to the wording, added to the resolution by Mexico, that supported a ban on production, stockpiling, and proliferation of landmines as a goal for future talks.[51]

Feeling ill-used by the US abstention, Senator Leahy sent President Clinton a sharply worded letter expressing his dismay: "In adopting this shocking decision for the US to abstain on this key vote, I am concerned that perhaps some US officials are not aware of your personal interest in exercising US leadership in dealing with the landmines scourge."[52] He repeated his objections in a January 13 letter to the *New York Times*, prompting a telephone call from Secretary of State Christopher and a letter from Albright. In a handwritten postscript, she expressed regret that Leahy had aired the disagreement in public before "we had had a chance to talk," adding, "We really are comrades in arms on this and other issues."[53]

Leahy and his NGO comrades in disarming wanted more than a review conference. They wanted a ban. To get one, they would have to do more than engage in information politics, quietly lobbying negotiators in the executive branch. Leahy would have to bring the NGOs into the negotiations. The NGOs, in turn, would have to involve other outsiders.

3

A Campaign to Bring in Outsiders

The definition of the alternatives is the supreme instrument of power.

E.E. Schattschneider[1]

Making defense policy in Washington is an insiders' game, in which outsiders have not had much say over the past 50 years. The choice of weapons to develop, procure, and deploy was usually determined by the armed services in collaboration with defense contractors, occasionally by civilians in the Defense Department or members of Congress eager to bring home defense contracts. The same players dominated arms control. The United States did agree to negotiated limits on nuclear and conventional weapons, but seldom over the determined opposition of the armed services. Global bans were negotiated on chemical and biological weapons, but, according to the conventional wisdom in Washington, the armed services had found these weapons difficult to deploy advantageously and were willing to give them up. In contrast, the US Army, left to its own devices, still wanted landmines.

Believing this, and doubting the efficacy of regulating weapons that were as widely used and manufactured as landmines, the arms control community showed scant interest in limiting, never mind banning them. Were it left to the generals and the arms controllers, a ban on landmines would never happen.

When backers of a ban tried to muster the arms control community to lobby for Senator Patrick Leahy's legislation, the initial response was tepid. "I remember when I was at the Arms Control Association having Jody [Williams] come to my office and saying, we need to do something about landmines," says Lee Feinstein, who would later join the State Department's policy planning staff, "and I'm saying to myself, what's a landmine?"[2] In Spring 1992, Tom Cardamone of the Vietnam Veterans of America Foundation met with the Arms Transfer Working Group, a coalition of arms controllers, to interest them in landmines. "I remember during these ATWG meetings the question kept coming up, 'Why are we singling this issue out?'" recalls Scott Nathanson.[3] In the end Nathanson and Feinstein were both persuaded to back a ban on landmines.

Casting about for how best to achieve a ban, Cardamone asked those involved about their experiences with the chemical weapons ban in the Conference on Disarmament. "I was impressed with the way he was looking for a comparable model," recalls Lora Lumpe, director of the Arms Sales Monitoring Project at the Federation of American Scientists, "and chemical weapons were not comparable—it was a nightmarish model negotiated through the CD—but he wanted to find out how groups working for many years against an indiscriminate and inhumane weapons system had achieved what they did."[4] It was understandable why he might make that comparison. Chemical weapons had been used, indiscriminately at times, with horrific effects. So had nuclear arms. Yet norms against these weapons had developed over the course of the century and the taboos had been legally codified in the form of a comprehensive ban, the Chemical Weapons Convention, and, less definitively, in the nuclear Non-Proliferation Treaty.[5]

Lobbying, the arms controllers' usual strategy, was unlikely to prove effective, however. If the issue were left to pressure group politics, the US Army and the arms makers would get their way. Working the landmines issue behind closed doors in the executive branch would concede the high ground to those who favored the status quo. Going outside could conceivably change the outcome. With relatively little of their profits at stake—the global market in landmines was estimated at less than $100 million a year, a fraction of the $20 billion a year spent on arms[6]—US arms manufacturers were not inclined to counter the ban campaigners by mounting a well-financed public campaign of their own.

By the time they had established the International Campaign to Ban Landmines in October 1992, organizers saw the need for a mass movement of sorts. The ICBL's strategy was to expand the conflict over landmines to involve outsiders by allying with humanitarian and religious groups. Among the outsiders whom the campaign would draw in were people least likely to become active: survivors of landmines and inhabitants of mine-strewn lands. That was one way to involve still others, especially the news media.

To broaden the scope of the conflict, the campaign framed the land-mines issue as one of human rights, not arms control. Such a normative and legal frame was familiar to Human Rights Watch and Physicians for Human Rights, which had worked within it since their inception. It appealed to Mines Advisory Group, Handicap International, and Medico International, the NGOs that worked on demining and victim relief. It also made sense to the Vietnam Veterans of America Foundation, which was wise in the ways of taking on the Pentagon.

By framing the issue in human rights terms, the NGOs sought to cast a moral stigma on landmines and shame governments into banning them. It is all too common for scholars and practitioners to minimize the place of morality in international politics, but norms of acceptable behavior have long affected the behavior of states. Such norms, rooted in beliefs about right and wrong, underlie the protections accorded prisoners of war and diplomatic emissaries, for example. Some of those norms are codified in international humanitarian law limiting the use of force.

When a norm is embedded in a larger set of norms, argues Thomas Franck, it will exert greater influence on state behavior: "[A] rule is more likely to obligate if it is made within the framework of an organized normative hierarchy than if it is merely an ad hoc agreement between parties in a state of nature."[7] With that idea in mind, the NGOs consciously sought to graft a new norm against antipersonnel landmines onto an older norm against inhumane weapons, or "weapons of ill repute," and propagated it around the globe by deliberate political action.[8]

Most antipersonnel mines are designed to maim, not kill. The gratuitous suffering they inflict made them subject to banning as inhumane, just as mustard gas and dum dum (expanding) bullets had already been outlawed for causing excessive harm to combatants. Landmines, once emplaced, can harm friend or foe alike. They can also be set off by noncombatants, long after a war is over. The indiscriminateness and persistence of antipersonnel landmines made them better suited for banning than mustard gas and dum dum bullets that target combatants in battle or nuclear arms that deter foes without being used.

As dreadful a human toll as landmines exact, their economic impact may cause even more harm. They force fertile fields to lie fallow, restrict livestock from watering holes or feeding grounds, and impede goods from reaching markets, leading to the depopulation of large swaths of land. That said, the maiming of innocents is a more graphically compelling way to motivate people and mobilize them to outlaw a weapon on humanitarian grounds.

Stigmatizing antipersonnel landmines as cruel, barbaric, and inherently indiscriminate was justification not just for limiting their use, but for outlawing them.

Yet framing the issue as a normative one of human rights antagonized Army officers who never liked outside interference and resented having the ban campaign outlaw weapons that some of them wanted to use. Many campaigners, in turn, tended to treat the military as part of the problem, not part of the solution, which only reinforced a predisposition in some military quarters to treat the campaigners as the enemy.

HUMAN RIGHTS: LEGAL GROUNDS FOR A BAN

War is both a social act and a social construct. What would be the crime of murder if committed by an individual in peacetime is socially sanctioned in war. Yet war is governed by rules about who may be killed and what weapons may be used, how, and against whom. Some rules are formally codified in treaties. Other rules are unwritten, matters of social convention, shared expectations of behavior based on past practice or on reciprocal interaction in battle. Many of these rules are norms, widely shared beliefs about ethically appropriate conduct. Some norms are so deeply rooted in the past, so internalized in the belief systems of military officers, and so embedded in the operations of armies that they have become facts of social life whose ethical content has leached out in the sands of time. Other norms are still in the process of social formation and dissemination, a process usually characterized by scholars as reasoning, learning, and socialization. Such characterizations tend to depoliticize normative struggles.[9]

Military officers make moral judgments on how war should be waged. "War is hell," General William Tecumseh Sherman famously declared. His words had profoundly moral overtones. In Sherman's judgment, those responsible for starting a war are rightly damned for their sin. Those who were attacked are blameless for whatever they do to resist and repel aggression. Yet even an exemplar of the "anything goes" school of armed force like Sherman, whose troops burned and pillaged their way through Georgia, denounced the use of landmines by the Confederates as unethical—"not war, but murder."[10]

The law of war rests on the principle that war may be hell, but not unmitigated hell. That principle was formally enshrined in the St. Petersburg Declaration of 1868: "There are limits at which the necessities of war ought to yield to the requirements of humanity." That principle requires soldiers to avoid harm to noncombatants—even at some risk to their own life and limb. While the law of war is not a suicide pact, self-preservation is no excuse for violating it. The principle was restated in Article 22 of the Hague Convention of 1907: "The right of belligerents to adopt a means of injuring the enemy is not unlimited."[11]

This principle is codified in US military regulations as well. According to the Army's bible, the US Army field manual on land warfare, the law of war stipulates that noncombatants must be protected from "unnecessary suffering" and "requires that belligerents refrain from employing any kind or degree of violence that is not actually necessary for military purposes and that they conduct hostilities with regard for the principles of humanity."[12] Like the Bible, the field manual's strictures are not always followed, but going by the book in the US Army means governing military operations by the principle of "proportionality." The Army manual defines that principle: "Loss of life and property must not be out of proportion to the military advantage to be gained."[13]

Similar normative considerations prompted the International Committee of the Red Cross in 1969 to urge UN members to outlaw the use of antipersonnel landmines as "excessively injurious" and "indiscriminate." Stopping short of a ban, negotiators appended a protocol to the Geneva Convention regulating the use of landmines in war.

The mines protocol adopted by the United Nations in 1980 did little to restrain landmine use, which escalated in the ensuing decade, along with its toll on human lives. This humanitarian nightmare prompted NGOs to go beyond regulating use and call for a comprehensive ban not only on the use of antipersonnel mines but also on their production and sale on human rights grounds. As the Arms Project of Human Rights Watch and Physicians for Human Rights concluded in an October 1993 report, *Landmines: A Deadly Legacy*, "A total ban is supported by international humanitarian laws prohibiting the use of weapons which cause indiscriminate and excessive injury, and by disarmament principles forbidding the production, stockpiling, and transfer of weapons which exact unconscionable human harm."[14]

The report was part of a sustained effort by Human Rights Watch to lay the legal and factual groundwork for a ban. From the time of the ICBL's founding in October 1992, Human Rights Watch "wanted to commit to producing a basic resource on landmines for the global community," says Stephen Goose. "There was so little on landmines out there." The director of the Arms Project of Human Rights Watch, Kenneth Anderson, and a consultant who served as counsel to the project, Monica Schurtman, "spent an awful lot of time in 1992 and 1993 developing what are still the basic legal arguments against this weapon," according to Goose. The 1993 report was Anderson's idea. Executive director Aryeh Neier was "very report-oriented," he says, "so I don't know how much convincing of Aryeh he had to do." Goose recalls the impact of the report at a meeting of governmental experts to prepare for the CCW review conference, "It was a lot of fun watching the delegates fight over copies. They were supposed to be experts, but they didn't know that much about the subject."[15]

In a brief for the experts' meeting, the Arms Project made the case for a ban. Its title posed a pivotal question: "Why Is a Complete Ban Required?" The 1980 Geneva protocol regulating the use of landmines "has been completely ineffective in controlling harm to civilians," the Arms Project contended. Not only was the protocol a "practical" failure, but it was also a "theoretical" failure because it did not conform to "customary" international law.[16] The brief cited law prohibiting indiscriminate attack, law mandating a balancing test that weighed the military utility of a weapon against the expected human toll, and law proscribing means of warfare that "are intended or may be expected to cause widespread, long-term and severe damage to the natural environment" and "thereby to prejudice the health and survival of the population."[17] Invoking "customary" law, which usually refers to common law, the brief tried to graft a taboo against landmine use onto outlawed military practices. That was normatively appropriate, but it left the brief open to legal counterargument.

Senator Leahy sent a copy to Conrad Harper, legal adviser to the State Department.[18] In an unofficial response, the Office of Legal Adviser called the brief "an interesting and provocative paper"—lawyerly terms of disparagement. It cited the continued "widespread use of landmines" as grounds for drawing the opposite conclusion about customary law: "States have not refrained from the use of landmines on the basis that they are unlawful. Indeed, the use of these weapons is standard military operating procedure for most national military forces. Such practice belies the view that use *per se* is contrary to customary international law." The State Department lawyers contrasted US military "doctrine" with military practice elsewhere in dismissing the Arms Project's case for a ban: "In our view, the unfortunate misuse of these weapons by others does not make all uses of these weapons illegal." Nor did the mines protocol apply to civil wars, where landmine use had reached epidemic proportions. The legal adviser's reply, in sum, conceded only that "the indiscriminate or intentional use of landmines against civilians is a violation of customary international law."[19]

Senator Leahy asked the Congressional Research Service for a second opinion. Its response bore down heavily on the customary law issue, too. Prior to the mines protocol, it found "little concrete reference to use of landmines as being contrary to the customary laws of war." Any prior references would be superseded by the mines protocol. To argue that customary law prohibits the use of landmines "when many nations apparently do not adhere to that prohibition," it concluded, "seems inconsistent."[20] Although its reading of customary law might have made legal sense, its contention that widespread use of landmines was grounds for not banning them had an Alice-in-Wonderland logic to it.

THE POLITICAL APPEAL OF A NORMATIVE APPROACH

Invoking the norms of human rights had political as well as legal implications for a ban. Framing landmines as a moral issue turned the campaign into a cause. That made it easier to attract NGOs as affiliates and to recruit and motivate activists. "Issues that involve ideas about right and wrong," Margaret Keck and Kathryn Sikkink point out in their study of transnational NGOs, "are amenable to advocacy networking because they arouse strong feelings, allow networks to recruit volunteers and activists, and infuse meaning into these volunteer activities." Campaigns, they add, are more readily organized around "issues involving bodily harm to vulnerable individuals." To be effective, campaigns must translate an issue into a "causal story," one that "establishes who bears responsibility or guilt. But the causal chain needs to be sufficiently short and clear to make the case convincing."[21] The causal story of mines fit the bill. Antipersonnel landmines maim and kill innocent people. The surest way to spare lives was to ban the production, sale, and use of such mines and begin removing the ones already emplaced.

Moreover, by calling attention to the victims of landmines, past and future, the campaign turned the ban into a human interest story. That was one way to attract the attention of the news media and the wider public, something that technical, often arcane negotiations on CCW had had trouble doing. Drawing attention to the victims would have the unforeseen and, for some campaigners, unwelcome consequence of mobilizing victims whose aims extended beyond a ban to encompass aid and empowerment.

The human rights approach had a narrower purpose as well, to tilt the bureaucratic playing field by involving other players. "In the early days," says Stephen Goose of Human Rights Watch, the aim of the campaign was "to take it out of the hands of the arms control and military types and get it into the hands of the humanitarian types," officials who worked on economic development and foreign aid, "to get that kind of perspective brought to the table."[22]

Disarmament, not arms control, was the logical product of a human rights approach to landmines. The CCW was arms control, and arms control, unlike disarmament, had never caught the public's fancy. Nor was it intended to. Those who came up with the concept had sought to appeal to military strategists and realists, who were skeptical about, even hostile to disarmament, especially nuclear disarmament. Arms control, wrote Thomas Schelling and Morton Halperin in their path-breaking book on the subject, "rests essentially on the recognition that our military relation with potential enemies is not one of pure conflict and opposition, but involves strong elements of mutual interest in the avoidance of a war that neither side wants, in minimizing the costs and risks of the arms competition, and curtailing the scope and violence of war in the event that it occurs." To distinguish it from disarmament, they portrayed arms control as intrinsic to military strategy, complementary to deterrence, and essential for national survival in the nuclear age: "It is the responsibility of military force to deter aggression, while avoiding the kind of threat that may provoke desperate, preventive, or irrational military action on the part of other countries."[23]

The arms control approach to landmines was the one taken at a 3-day symposium of military experts, many of them combat engineers, arranged by the International Committee of the Red Cross in Geneva on January 10, 1994. These experts emphasized the military utility of landmines and the inadequacy of substitutes. Landmines are "an integral part" of war plans, they concluded. When used along with barriers, natural and man-made, landmines channel enemy attacks so that firepower can be concentrated on killing zones: "By combining the effects of artillery, direct fire weapons, and electromagnetic warfare with the shaping of the terrain through the use of mined obstacles, the maximum synergistic effect of the combined arms produces the most decisive effect."[24] Mines dispersed by air and artillery impede enemy maneuverability and disrupt sudden flanking attacks or block avenues of retreat. Antitank mines, protected by antipersonnel mines, counter the two keys to success in tank warfare, speed and mobility. They impede tank mobility and slow down tank attacks. They also hinder the flow of reinforcements and supplies from rear areas to the battlefield.

From the military experts' vantage point, the capacity of mines to maim contributed to their usefulness: "This inherent ability to inflict casualties also has a powerful demoralizing effect on the enemy soldier. Forces are likely to avoid areas where even there is merely a reasonable possibility of encountering mines."[25] The contrast between the military and the human rights perspectives could not have been starker: the very character of landmines that connoted combat effectiveness to military experts spelled humanitarian disaster to the NGOs.

In the military experts' view, landmines were indispensable. Every alternative had disadvantages. Ditches and barbed wire were more costly than mines to manufacture and deploy. Flooding was less reliable or flexible. Unlike mines, which needed relatively little maintenance or logistic support once laid and were less subject to the ravages of weather, artillery fire and aerial bombardment required repeated expenditure of shells and bombs whose accuracy could be marred by bad weather and visibility. Unexploded ordnance posed some of the same risks to civilians as did mines. The military experts, while noting research under way on novel substitutes for mines like glues, foam, and infrasound, harbored doubts that these innovations would meet military needs. Countermeasures could be devised to defeat them or else research would reveal that they had adverse side effects of their own.[26]

In contrast to the military experts, who wanted to regulate the use of mines, the campaigners wanted to ban them—to move beyond arms control to disarmament. "The original six groups were all human rights or humanitarian work-oriented," says Stephen Goose. "Both as a reality of our work and as a political strategy, everyone agreed that we had to focus on the humanitarian side of things and not get hung up on arms control."[27]

In the preamble of their 1992 call for a ban, the founders of the International Campaign to Ban Landmines cited the humanitarian need and failure of arms control to meet that need:

> Whereas antipersonnel mines that detonate on contact are indiscriminate weapons that remain hidden and lethal long after the end of a conflict;
>
> Whereas antipersonnel mines have killed or mutilated tens of thousands of civilians and rendered large tracts of agricultural and pastoral lands unusable, preventing the subsistence and economic development of rural populations; and
>
> Where the 1981 United Nations Protocol on Prohibitions or Restrictions on the Use of Mines, Booby Traps and Other Devices has failed to prevent the indiscriminate use of antipersonnel mines.[28]

The import of the campaigners' public call for a ban was clear. Arms control had proven inadequate; disarmament was necessary. On human rights grounds, antipersonnel landmines had to be banned.

A ban won endorsement from the International Committee of the Red Cross on similar grounds. For the governmental experts who met in Geneva from February 28 to March 4, 1994, to prepare for the CCW review conference, the ICRC prepared a report arguing that the 1980 mines protocol designed to limit use of landmines had failed. "International humanitarian law originally controlled the damage caused by weapons by altogether prohibiting the use of weapons that were perceived as excessively cruel or 'barbaric'," said the ICRC. "Since 1925, however, international humanitarian law has not made any significant progress in prohibiting the use of specific weapons but has instead concentrated on imposing limitations on their use in the hope of sparing the civilian population as far as possible." This approach, the ICRC argued, "has severe shortcomings in that it assumes that all actors in fact abide by the rules regulating the use of weapons and that this will indeed spare civilians" from their effects. "In reality, neither of these assumptions is correct, for not only are weapons in practice used indiscriminately by a very large proportion of the persons [who] have them, but also, even if used correctly, civilians frequently suffer the 'incidental' effects of these weapons. The result is that unless the use of certain weapons is altogether prohibited, civilians will inevitably become victims of them." Noncombatants were not the ICRC's only concern: "Further, the rule prohibiting the use of weapons of a nature to cause unnecessary suffering or superfluous injury to combatants" remains valid, but unless it is "applied to new weapons, it will in practice fall into desuetude."[29] That line of logic led to a ban.

The ICRC report examined a variety of less than total bans and found them wanting. One option was to ban the use of scatterable or remotely delivered mines that were not fitted with self-destruct mechanisms. A self-destruct mechanism was a timing device that could be preset to detonate the mine at a specified moment. To be effective, the self-destruct mechanism had to activate reliably after a short duration. It also had to be tamper-proof. Even if a self-destruct mechanism had a very low failure rate, however, the fact that thousands of mines were dispersed at a time would "continue to pose a serious threat to the civilian population."[30] To foreclose the temptation to use cheaper substitutes, scatterable mines not equipped with self-destruct mechanisms would have to be banned as well.

Since such a ban did not cover mines emplaced by hand or by other means, a more comprehensive alternative was to ban the use of antipersonnel mines not fitted with self-destruct mechanisms that caused them to explode at a preset time. That raised most of the same difficulties for the ICRC as the first option.

Antitank mines were too expensive and too lethal to equip with self-destruct devices. They often had another feature that was a source of indiscriminate harm: an antihandling device, often built into or emplaced alongside antitank mines to keep enemy troops from disabling them by detonating when disturbed. Antihandling devices, essentially antipersonnel mines designed to impede enemy mine clearing, could harm not only foes, but also humanitarian deminers who attempted to disarm the mine. Even after the war was over, they could be tripped by an innocent passerby, especially if the mine was not buried or had resurfaced as soil shifted or eroded. Banning antitank mines equipped with antihandling devices was another option.

Mines could also be equipped with a self-deactivation mechanism that would make them incapable of exploding after a while. Self-deactivation mechanism is a fancy name for a battery. Battery-powered mines are rendered inert once the battery runs down. Banning antipersonnel mines not equipped to self-deactivate was one possible solution. Yet, as anyone knows who has tried and failed to turn on a flashlight or start an automobile, batteries cannot always be relied on to run down at a precise time. The failure of mines to self-deactivate occurs at a high enough rate to pose risks to noncombatants or to humanitarian deminers.

The ICRC also considered banning the use of mines that eluded detection, such as the cheap plastic ones flooding the world arms market. One problem was that even if such mines were made detectable, the metal components that facilitated detection could be removed subsequent to manufacture.

Given the problems with the alternatives as it framed them, the ICRC opted to ban the use, manufacture, and stockpiling of all antipersonnel landmines. A total ban would codify the norm that such mines were taboo. It might also be simpler to verify: "There is no doubt that from the humanitarian point of view this would be the best option as a total ban would have the effect of *stigmatizing* the use of mines and a violation of the rule would be easily provable."[31]

A ban lay at the opposite end of the range of possibilities from regulation of mine use, which was favored by the military experts. Between these polar alternatives were various proposals to strengthen the 1980 mines protocol, short of a ban, by extending it to civil wars, tightening required precautions to protect civilians, imposing a stricter duty to keep records of minefields and to clear mines once hostilities end, and on-site monitoring to verify implementation of the protocol.

YOU CAN'T BEAT SOMETHING WITH NOTHING

The agenda of the preparatory meetings for the CCW review conference posed a dilemma for the International Coalition to Ban Landmines: strengthening the CCW's limitations on landmine use might divert pressure for a ban, but concentrating its efforts entirely on a ban and ignoring efforts to amend the CCW might condemn the coalition to irrelevance.

Anticipating that the conferees were inclined to reject a ban, ICBL organizers began drafting two texts of their own in March 1994, one by Kenneth Anderson, Stephen Goose, and Monica Schurtman to amend the CCW provisions to ban use of antipersonnel mines, and another by Françoise Hampson, who was on the law faculty of the University of Essex, to strengthen the mines protocol "if a ban is not, at this stage, achievable."[32] The authors of the text to ban mine use articulated their rationale this way: "Although we still think that the most effective solution to the landmine crisis requires a ban on production, stockpiling, and transfer, as well as use, we also believe that because the review conference is to amend the weapons convention—a convention that only addresses use—we realistically can only deal with use in our suggestions."[33] The ICBL circulated its draft ban, but not its amended CCW. "This was in-your-pocket stuff," says Goose. "It wasn't put out for delegates to look at."[34]

The first text proposed a number of amendments to the CCW. To distinguish antipersonnel from antivehicle mines, it defined an antipersonnel mine as "any munition placed under, on or near the ground or other surface area and designed to be detonated or exploded by the presence, proximity or contact of a person." It barred the use of such mines. By that definition the prohibition applied to antihandling devices on antitank mines as well, which was sure to raise strong military objections. It also applied to so-called mixed munitions, antipersonnel mines deployed with antitank mines to keep them from being disarmed.

The draft made any willful use a grave breach of the CCW—hence a war crime punishable by international tribunal—and held military commanders responsible for any grave breach committed by troops under their command. It extended the reach of the CCW to nonstate actors. It required signatories to enact laws imposing penal sanctions on persons committing such a breach and to arrest such persons and either try them or turn them over to other parties for trial. It made states legally responsible for clearing the mines they had laid and legally liable for the damage or harm caused by their mines.

Hampson's ban proposal, by contrast, was comprehensive. It would "ban all forms of use, laying, storage, production, transport, transfer or sale of antipersonnel landmines, their components, and technology." She defined antipersonnel landmines "to include antitank or antivehicle mines which are triggered by the passage of one or more persons."[35] That covered mines equipped with antihandling devices or those with fuzes sensitive enough to be set off by a passerby. The ICBL ended up adopting a narrower definition "to confine ban efforts to mines designed as antipersonnel devices and not antitank mines that may function on occasion in that way."[36] That made a ban more palatable to the military.

To strengthen the mines protocol, Hampson proposed a ban on nondetectable landmines and on antihandling devices. Her aim in both instances was "to reduce the risks of mine clearing."[37] A requirement that mines be detectable was widely accepted, but a ban on antihandling devices was certain to encounter objections from European armies that relied on such devices. Because of the ease of manufacture, a ban on mine production was not verifiable. Hampson pinned the ICBL's hopes on banning the transfer or sale of landmines to any state that was not a party to the revised protocol, having states enact laws to criminalize breaches of the ban by firms or citizens, requiring states to notify the United Nations arms registry of any landmines transfer, and making them legally liable for clearing mines not properly registered. Assigning the state legal responsibility for transfers or sales, however, assumed that landmines could be traced to their country of origin, an iffy assumption. To generate funds to aid mine victims and mine clearing, she levied a tax on all transfers.

Finally, Hampson proposed banning remotely deliverable or scatterable mines. That was bound to face determined resistance from a number of countries, especially the United States. As a fallback position, she required all landmines to self-destruct, but not self-deactivate. Self-destructing mines are equipped to explode after a preset period of time. Self-deactivation, as the battery runs out, renders a mine inert without detonating it. Hampson excluded self-deactivation from consideration because of the difficulty of determining whether a mine remained active or not, which required those clearing mines after a war to assume the worst. While ruling out requiring mines to self-deactivate, she expressed reservations whether self-destruct mechanisms were reliable enough to assure the safety of deminers. More reliable mechanisms would prove too costly, leading to illicit use of landmines that did not self-destruct. The period of time allowed for self-destruction would be "contentious" because countries that emplaced mines to defend their own frontiers "did not want to have to re-lay their mines at too frequent intervals." They preferred a longer duration than countries that wanted to use mines on a battlefield during hostilities without impeding their own forces from advancing later on.[38]

By this reasoning, even mines that self-destructed and self-deactivated posed an irreducible risk to noncombatants, including NGOs engaged in demining. "If I drop a thousand mines," says Tim Connolly, principal deputy assistant secretary of defense for special operations and low-intensity conflict and a leading ban proponent in the Pentagon from 1993 to 1996, "and you tell me, by virtue of the statistical quality control standard you say we can put in place, that one of them is still going to be alive, I have to demine that field as if every one of them were alive, and consequently the humanitarian impact is the same as if all of them are dumb mines." Even "smart" antipersonnel mines remain irremediably indiscriminate. Moreover, Connolly contends, the 99.9 percent quality control standard is too costly to meet by testing mines individually. Tomahawk missiles sell for about $1 million apiece, so manufacturers can run quality controls for each missile and still make a profit, he says, and Tomahawks still have a failure rate of 2 or 3 percent. Landmines are not as profitable to produce as Tomahawks, so manufacturers select a few at random from each lot to test, and based on that, conclude that landmines meet the 99.9 percent standard. "If I set FASCAMs to self-destruct in 2 days and throw a thousand of them on the south lawn of the White House," Connolly wonders how many members of Congress "who believe these things are needed would send their kids out there to play soccer 3 days later?"[39]

Had the ICBL drawn a line between "dumb" mines not designed to self-destruct and self-deactivate and "smart" mines that were so designed—between persistent and short-duration mines—it would have outlawed the mines responsible for most of the harm. That would not eliminate the risk, however. Negotiating a treaty based on that distinction would also "set a double standard," as Senator Leahy and Representative Evans put it, leaving countries that possessed and produced dumb mines at a decided disadvantage to the United States and other countries that can afford smart mines. Gaining the have-nots' adherence would be difficult unless the haves gave up something in return.

Following the lead of the International Committee of the Red Cross, the International Coalition to Ban Landmines expected that efforts to tighten CCW limits on use would prove impractical. By narrowly construing the ban to exclude antitank mines, even those which at times functioned like antipersonnel weapons, they tried to make the ban seem less of a radical alternative.

AN EXPORT MORATORIUM GAINS GROUND IN EUROPE

The ban campaign got a boost from an unexpected quarter. As the CCW process was grinding on, Leahy's export moratorium began to catch on in Europe, much to the surprise of ICBL organizers. To many new adherents, however, the moratorium was intended to be a roadblock, not a way station, to a ban. Some US officials were urging other countries to adopt moratoria for that very reason. Unlike an international treaty with binding commitments to other states, a moratorium could be done—and undone—by a state through legislative or executive action of its own.

In France, Handicap International had taken the lead. Venturing beyond its usual mission of treating and rehabilitating mine victims, it organized a conference at the Senate Palace in May 1992 attended by a hundred representatives of NGOs, along with prominent political figures, journalists, and students. Distributing a French-language edition of *Landmines in Cambodia: The Coward's War,* the report prepared by Human Rights Watch and Physicians for Human Rights, it used the conference as a springboard for a nationwide petition drive calling for a halt to the "coward's war." Among the first to sign were Simone Weil, president of the European Parliament; Bernard Kouchner, former minister of health and humanitarian affairs; Jean François Deniau, former minister of foreign affairs; Javier Pérez de Cuéllar, former UN secretary-general; and Elie Wiesel, a human rights activist. Within months the campaign had gathered tens of thousands of signatures. Handicap International also invited mine victims to seminars in government offices and lobbied the French foreign and defense ministries.[40] The human rights approach began to bear fruit when Weil and two colleagues introduced a resolution in the European Parliament for a 5-year moratorium on exports.

In February 1993, Handicap International convened a second conference on landmines and invited French officials to attend. In preparation for the gathering, it solicited a letter from Senator Leahy supporting a moratorium on antipersonnel landmine exports and calling on the French government to convene a review conference on the CCW.[41] "As agreed with Tim Rieser [of Senator Leahy's staff]," Handicap International's organizers wrote in a thank-you note to Leahy, "we used this letter to 'persuade' a rather reluctant foreign ministry to take a public stand on the issue, which they have now done."[42]

Rieser describes how the network extended Leahy's reach beyond the borders of the United States: "We were talking to people in the NGO community here; they were talking to people in the NGO community in France, Germany, Norway, and throughout Europe. The people they connected me with described what was happening over there, and we talked about how to get their governments to act. That was what we wanted to do because we knew we needed a global effort."[43]

Handicap International also wrote to President François Mitterrand and arranged to have his wife Danielle hand him the letter, along with petitions signed by 15,000 people. It did not take long for Mitterrand to respond. On February 11, while on a visit to Cambodia, he proclaimed an indefinite moratorium on exports of antipersonnel mines and invited other countries to join in the initiative. He also called for a review conference on the CCW.[44] In the assessment of ICBL strategists Jody Williams and Stephen Goose, "the demands of the NGOs" prompted Mitterrand to take the initiative to "get them off his back."[45] That was as far as he would go. "*NO* to antipersonnel mines," the demand that Handicap International had broadcast on television and radio and plastered on posters across France, did not gain Mitterrand's endorsement. Indeed, his embrace of the review conference and the moratorium were intended to forestall a ban.

The Italian government took a similar tack. Italy was a leading exporter, selling 200,000 landmines to Saudi Arabia and Egypt in 1992. Italian-made mines had turned up in Afghanistan, Angola, Cambodia, El Salvador, Mozambique, Nicaragua, Somalia, and Yugoslavia.[46] Iraq used them in the 1991 Gulf War and would do so again in 2003.[47] Italy had opposed the US resolution in the UN General Assembly calling for a moratorium on exports. The 1994 election seemed to change all that. It brought to power Silvio Berlusconi, a scandal-tainted media magnate, whose main claim to fame was ownership of Milan AC, winner of the Italian soccer championship in 1993 and 1994. He formed a party of his own, named it Forza Italia after the national soccer chant—what better way to rise above Italy's clannish politics—and used his control of Italy's three largest private television networks, American-style celebrity politics, and media savvy to vault into the premiership.

The new government was a beneficiary of the end of the Cold War and gradual secularization of Italian politics, which had weakened the sway of the Catholic Church and blurred the old left–right dividing line, producing a political realignment. The Christian Democratic and Socialist parties, long bulwarks against communist and fascist rule, were mired in scandal. Recipients of covert CIA funding, both parties were habituated to being on the take. The Communist Party was similarly tainted by money from Moscow, but *embourgeoisment* of its rank and file had spawned a reform wing, disenchanted with Marxist-Leninist orthodoxy, which took control of the party in the 1970s and distanced it from the Soviet Union. Communists now governed many of Italy's cities, gaining a reputation for effective municipal management relatively free of corruption. With its new respectability came invitations to join coalition governments by the 1990s. Revival of a moderate left and new competitiveness on the center-right seemed to mark an end to years of immobility in Italian politics.

Capitalizing on the opening, Berlusconi moved to preempt a few issues. Landmines was one. The moratorium had already made some headway before Berlusconi's election. On October 27, 1993, 3 weeks after receiving a copy of a resolution that the US delegation was circulating at the United Nations calling for a more inclusive moratorium on antipersonnel landmine exports, Senator Leahy had sent letters to several allied ambassadors in Washington lobbying on its behalf. One recipient was Italy's Boris Biancheri, who replied on November 8, "I have just today been advised—and you will be pleased to learn—that Italy is in agreement with the current draft of the UN resolution and I am confident that my country will also be involved in the follow up to the resolution," once it has been approved.[48]

In December, a meeting of NGO representatives was held in Rome to kick off an Italian campaign against landmines. It was the first of the national campaigns founded with the ICBL's help. "That was an important strategy we hit upon," says Goose. "Early on, there weren't any national campaigns." The ICBL had just been reaching out "to different NGOs in other countries" and assumed "they should know best what tactics would work." Still, more delegates came to the Rome meeting from abroad than from Italy. It was "an inauspicious start," recall ICBL strategists Williams and Goose.[49]

The Italian campaign would have made little headway without help in high places, including parliament, the Vatican, and the ministry of defense. Senator Edoardo Ronchi of the Green Party introduced a motion calling for a ban. Emma Bonino, secretary of the Radical Party and deputy speaker of the chamber of deputies, introduced similar legislation in the lower house of parliament. In June 1994, the Holy See condemned arms trafficking and called for a ban on landmines.[50] Just days later, on June 22, Defense Minister Cesare Previti, Berlusconi's personal lawyer and political ally, appeared on a widely watched television talk show with representatives of Italy's landmine campaign and said, much to their delight, "These weapons must be banned always and in any case." He called for "compulsory reconversion" of mine production plants to civilian purposes.[51] The defense ministry made it official the next day. On June 28, Previti informed Ronchi that he had issued instructions banning the production and export of antipersonnel mines and tightening export controls. The cabinet, he added, would take up a bill to ratify the landmines protocol the next day and Italy would raise the issue at an upcoming Group of Seven summit meeting in Naples.[52]

The Italian ban campaign did its part, too. On June 27, representatives of employees of a leading landmines manufacturer, Valsella Meccanotecnica, called on the Italian government to halt landmine production and exports and to support aid to landmine victims. The stigmatization of landmine makers prompted Fiat, which owned 50 percent of Valsella, to announce the sale of its shares in July. In September a coalition of 44 peace groups, religious and women's NGOs, and trade unions organized a concert and a 17-kilometer walk from Brescia, home to a number of military-industrial plants, to Castenedolo, the site of Valsella, which drew considerable media attention. The Castenedolo local council unanimously adopted a resolution supporting a ban on landmines, 1 of 160 councils to do so.[53]

On August 2, the Italian senate passed an export moratorium and ratified the CCW protocol by a lopsided vote of 162 to 7. The government pledged to "ready the necessary instruments for stopping production of such devices by Italian companies."[54]

Six weeks later the foreign minister issued a clarification of government policy. Distinguishing a moratorium from a ban, it said nothing about supporting a ban and left open the possibility of resuming exports. The moratorium, it read, "will have effect as of today and until the entry into force of a possible new international regime regulating the export and production of antipersonnel mines."[55] The ICBL's Jody Williams asked Senator Ronchi whether that meant exports could resume. "He was very unclear about long-term plans for Italy despite what seemed clear in the August 2 motion," she told fellow campaigners with her usual asperity. "Well, here is clarity. And it is predictable. And it sucks."[56]

By then, quite a few states had heeded the UN General Assembly's call for an export moratorium, evidence of the importance of international institutions in legitimating norms. On February 24, 1994, Spain announced a 1-year moratorium. Slovakia followed suit on April 12. On May 11, Switzerland announced a moratorium on sales of mines to states that refused to sign the landmines protocol. Later that month, Argentina announced a 5-year moratorium. The Czech Republic was next, proclaiming a 3-year moratorium to commence in October. On June 8, Germany instituted a 3-year moratorium. On July 27, Britain imposed an indefinite moratorium on mines that "cannot be made safe after they have been planted." A day later, Israel announced a 2-year moratorium.

Senator Leahy was not about to settle for a moratorium on exports or tighter regulation of use. During a September 11 conversation in Washington, Leahy told Ronchi and Bonino that the CCW review conference may "end up with a very weak document, filled with loopholes" and asked them to urge their government to "be a leader in getting rid of these weapons."[57] Heeding his plea, Bonino persuaded the chamber of deputies to adopt a motion on December 6 that went beyond the senate's. By a vote of 400 to 2, it called on the government "to support the Swedish position, and that of the other countries, in favor of the total ban on antipersonnel mines."[58] Bonino faxed Leahy the text 2 days later.

As is their wont in Italy, the bureaucrats ignored the legislature. In a note to Bonino 6 weeks later, Jody Williams reported from the meeting of governmental experts in Geneva that "the Italian delegation does not feel bound by parliamentary sentiment and is not supporting the Swedish position calling for an amendment to Protocol II to ban antipersonnel landmines."[59] Even worse, producers in France and Italy soon found an easy way around their nations' moratoria by relocating the final assembly of their mines in Singapore.

A POLICY REVIEW TO HEAD OFF LEAHY

The export moratorium was gaining ground. Could a ban be far behind? Or would the United States, France, and Italy use the moratorium to fend off pressure for a ban? That prospect worried Senator Leahy. Having secured a 3-year moratorium on exports in 1993, he moved to extend the moratorium to US production of antipersonnel landmines in 1994. Representative Lane Evans introduced identical legislation in the House. Leahy's personal touch was again in evidence in rounding up 53 Senate co-sponsors. Typical was his handwritten postscript on a "Dear Colleague" letter sent to Alan Simpson (R-WY), a maverick conservative, "Al—This is an issue we should all be able to agree on." Simpson signed on. Another letter went to another maverick conservative, John McCain (R-AZ), who had been a prisoner of war in Vietnam, "John—You are one of the few people here who really understands landmines." The personal touch did not work on McCain, who declined to co-sponsor the bill. A moratorium on production "raises some serious concerns that last year's ban did not," he replied. "Our servicemen and women need landmines for their protection."[60] McCain was an exception; most senators were inclined to go along.

The prospect of a moratorium on production kindled concern in the executive branch because it suggested that the moratorium on exports would soon become permanent, with serious implications for military strategy. "That's when we began to discuss the NATO and the Korea problems because an export ban meant no transfers," says Thomas "Ted" McNamara, acting assistant secretary of state for politico-military affairs. The United States had long had landmines in Europe, and plans called for some to be turned over to the allies in the event of war. The problem was even more acute elsewhere. "There were these huge stockpiles in Korea, which were largely the pre-1975 kind and therefore they had to be kept in controlled temperatures," says McNamara. "As soon as you put the stuff in the ground, it starts deteriorating. Every few years, they had to replace the old stuff because it had gone to pot." As a consequence, even in peacetime, the United States was transferring more modern mines from its own stocks in Korea and California to the South Korean army. "If the Leahy bill had gone through, then very suddenly we would have been unable to work with the allies on stuff that was really very sophisticated."[61] The armed services did not want to concede the right to transfer landmines to US allies.

Anticipating passage by solid majorities, the administration moved to head off the legislation. McNamara, along with H. Allen Holmes, assistant secretary of defense for special operations and low-intensity conflict, asked Leahy to defer action in order to allow time for a policy review. Leahy asked for and received assurances that the review would consider a ban on use as well. Meanwhile, Leahy was told, the administration would press for a global ban on exports of antipersonnel landmines.

The commitment came in a letter dated June 28, 1994, and signed by Secretary of State Warren Christopher and Secretary of Defense William Perry. Leahy's legislation was "counterproductive to the goal we all share of developing as quickly as possible an effective antipersonnel Landmines Control Regime," they wrote, because it "would prejudge the US negotiating position" and "impede our diplomatic efforts to build support both for the export moratorium and the eventual regime." They also noted

> We are committed to working toward an effective international anti-personnel landmine control regime. The administration is conducting an intensive policy review to determine the parameters of what the United States would propose for a regime, both in the near term and in the longer term. A broad spectrum of options is under discussion ranging from a total ban on APL to export controls on all types of APL, production and/or stockpiling restrictions, and transparency measures.[62]

In return for the policy review, Leahy deferred legislative action.[63]

WASHINGTON OPTS FOR MORE ARMS CONTROL

Although the secretaries' list of options included a ban, the study gave it scant consideration. "At this stage it was an effort to come up with a band-aid as opposed to trying to push the military to end the US use of landmines," says Nancy Soderberg, deputy assistant to the president for national security affairs and the third-ranking official on the NSC staff. "We were still trying to address it at the margins."[64]

Within the US government, the landmines issue was being handled routinely. Top policy makers played little part. "Part of it was there was just too much else going on," says Soderberg, but that was just part of it. "It wasn't our landmines blowing up little kids in Angola. There wasn't the urgency that others saw. There was just no way we were going to take the landmine issue on at the level that Leahy wanted us to. To his credit, he kept pushing and pushing." Leahy was not alone. "The veterans groups—Bobby Muller—were trying to get us to focus on this, but it was [worked] at the mid-level of the government," she says.[65]

In thinking about negotiations on landmines, the career bureaucrats who had the action drew on their own experience, which was arms control. McNamara chaired an Interagency Working Group conducting the policy review, but the main players were the joint staff and civilians in the Department of Defense. He put Eric Newsom in charge of formulating a new policy. Newsom, a recent recruit to the Bureau of Politico-Military Affairs, had worked with McNamara in PM in the late 1970s when both were junior foreign service officers, but had left to take a job as a member of the Foreign Relations Committee staff, then as staff director of the Foreign Operations Subcommittee, and later as Senator Leahy's legislative director. Capitol Hill was not his metier, however, and when Under Secretary of State Jacqueline "Lynn" Davis asked him to come work for her, he was only too eager to accept. "I'd always been proud to be an FSO," he says. His first day back at the State Department in March 1994, "I walked in, knelt down and kissed the floor, I was so glad to be back in the building." Newsom had deliberately not sought Leahy's help to land the job, but his past dogged him at Foggy Bottom. "Because of my identification with Senator Leahy's landmine efforts, I became Mr. Landmines from the day I walked into PM."[66]

The key people in State were Steve Solomon from the Office of Legal Adviser and Steve Costner from PM, says Newsom, but "if there was one guy who mapped out thinking in State on this, it was Dave Appleton," a foreign service officer who was a deputy office director in PM. "These men," Newsom says of the trio, "were brilliant in their understanding of what we were up against and what we needed to do to give ourselves the best chance of coming out where we wanted."[67]

What to do about landmines policy quickly became bogged down in bureaucratic in-fighting. "Obviously the implications of doing a review was that we would not continue the status quo," Newsom says. Yet any change in policy would have to pass muster by the armed services. In taking on the joint staff, PM would not have much help from top officials in the State Department, the Office of Secretary of Defense, or the National Security Council staff. "We started a laborious process, where State, mainly PM, did battle with the joint staff, with OSD basically supporting the joint staff." At the NSC, Robert Bell "delegated to Ann Witkowsky the job of coordinating this process."[68] By all accounts, she was too junior to exercise much clout.

There was no love lost between State and ACDA in the Clinton years, either. "ACDA could be counted on to oppose any arms control agreement that should be supported and support any arms control agreement that should be opposed," says Lee Feinstein, a State Department policy planner. "They opposed the landmines treaty, they opposed the Comprehensive Test Ban Treaty by backing the entry-into-force provision [that required ratification by all five permanent members of the UN Security Council before the treaty could enter into force], they opposed arms control in Bosnia, and they supported the African Nuclear-Free Zone Treaty, one of the stupidest things we ever signed, which required us to issue [a] nuclear threat against non-nuclear [states]."[69]

Open antagonism erupted between PM and ACDA after Under Secretary of State Davis secured Secretary of State Warren Christopher's backing to reorganize PM into two bureaus. ACDA, long a whipping boy of Senator Jesse Helms (R-NC) and the right wing, had seen its standing on Capitol Hill erode to the point that by the 1990s its very existence as an independent agency was in jeopardy. It saw the reorganization as a slippery slope to absorption by PM. Two liberal stalwarts, Claiborne Pell (D-RI), chair of the Foreign Relations Committee, and Paul Simon (D-IL), a ranking member, were determined to defend ACDA's quasi-independent status. "Hardly had I gotten there," says Newsom, "than ACDA went behind the scenes to tell Pell and Simon and they landed on Christopher."[70] The reorganization plan was quickly dropped, but Newsom, who had been slated to head one of the two bureaus as an assistant secretary of state, got caught in the crossfire. It took Davis 3 months to have a new slot created for him, principal deputy assistant secretary of state, and many months more for him to be confirmed.

One issue for PM in the policy review was a venue for the negotiations. ACDA, along with the Office of the Legal Adviser, had the lead in the Conference on Disarmament, where they were trying to address the issue by amending the 1980 landmines protocol. If PM were to take the lead on landmines, it would have to find another venue. One possibility was NATO, where PM had the action on arms control. Another was to set up a new stand-alone forum. ACDA was staunchly opposed to both.

Differences between ACDA and PM went well beyond turf. ACDA career officials had accumulated expertise on landmines in years of negotiating in the CD. That experience reinforced the agency's predisposition to treat landmines as the objects of regulation, a technical matter bound by the canons of traditional arms control. Moreover, hostility toward ACDA on Capitol Hill predisposed it to protect US landmine assets, lest it be accused by right-wing critics of giving away the store. The State Department, by contrast, was feeling pressure to be proactive about controlling landmines from Senator Leahy, who held the department's purse strings. "I got back to PM in the spring of 1993 and they were doing the research for the landmines publication, *Hidden Killers*," which Leahy had mandated, says Ted McNamara. "As a result of that and the pressure on the administration to do something about landmines, we convoked a group in Rome" in January 1995.[71]

The stand-alone forum carried the day when PM, with tacit support from OSD, overcame opposition from ACDA and JCS. What to do in that forum was another matter. At the start of the policy review, "when Leahy began talking about a permanent ban, the Army just crapped a brick," says Newsom. It began "looking for a way to contain this pressure." After a lot of in-fighting, "we came up with the idea of a Landmines Control Regime. The heart of it was over time to squeeze off worldwide exports of antipersonnel landmines except the self-destructing types, which would be much safer for civilians. We were going to have a program of technical and other assistance to countries to develop the self-destructing kind. We were going to move toward an international agreement, not under the United Nations, but a coalition of the willing." Some officials had reservations: "In State many of us weren't very enthusiastic about this idea. We were skeptical that it was going to attract much support. It was too complicated to compete with the simple slogan, 'Ban all APLs.' But we did our best to develop it into a real proposal."[72]

The first step was a moratorium on exports of antipersonnel landmines by European mine-producing states. "That's what Leahy and those up on the Hill were seeking," says Ted McNamara. "We also felt we could get a moratorium in place quicker because we were not telling anybody we want a permanent commitment." It was "a quick fix." The rationale of McNamara and others was "if you get a moratorium, you at least give yourself time to work out a more permanent solution."[73] Other countries already knew what the campaigners were learning to their dismay, that an export moratorium was a way to postpone a ban.

In conceiving of the Landmines Control Regime, McNamara drew on his own experience with the Missile Technology Control Regime. The MTCR functioned as a cartel of sorts, regulating the transfer and sale of missiles and missile technology in order to impede proliferation. "I negotiated the MTCR," says McNamara, "so there was a certain tendency on my part to use that, if not as a model, then [as a source of] useful elements and concepts that could be molded to what is obviously not high technology." Most mines, unlike missiles, were low-tech enough to be mass-produced and sold like hockey pucks: "You're talking about millions of landmines, as opposed to a couple of big contracts."[74] The more countries able to produce landmines, McNamara knew, the harder it would be to set up a long-lived cartel to control production.

At first the Landmines Control Regime encountered little bureaucratic opposition except from ACDA. "At that juncture," says McNamara, "there was not the kind of resistance over at the Pentagon that developed later when they went beyond the moratorium to outright bans." As the policy review proceeded, however, the joint staff's resistance intensified. "Those that didn't want to go beyond the hockey pucks, which were the real problem, were becoming more and more entrenched and they were saying, hey you guys, we've got to put a barrier up somewhere."[75] Senior officials took no interest at all. "Lynn Davis wasn't much engaged," says Eric Newsom. No meetings of the Principals Committee or Deputies Committee were convened on landmines and even the Interagency Working Group rarely took up the issue. "Usually they were just little informal groupings, some convened by Ann Witkowsky at NSC, some convened in PM," he says. "Occasionally, we'd have a formal IWG to make decisions."[76]

Without high-level attention, the Landmines Control Regime became mired in minutiae. "The more we worked it, the more Rube Goldberg it became," says Newsom. "It got so full of loopholes to suit our military that it was laughable. It was dying of its own complexity." Soon, he says, "The NGOs were absolutely shellacking the initiative. For them it was substituting one kind of landmine for another. All we were doing was legitimizing landmines."[77]

International discussion of a Landmines Control Regime joined a core issue for the first time, whether to do something "quickly and ad hoc," says Ted McNamara, "or to go more slowly and methodically." The countries opposed to stringent control of landmines preferred the CCW, which troubled McNamara. The group in favor of a Landmines Control Regime "was beginning to look like the choir saying it was not going to rob a bank—it had no bank robbers."[78] That problem would become more acute as the ban campaign caught fire in Europe and countries in favor of stricter control of landmines gravitated to an outright ban. Eric Newsom did not think it was prudent to wait that long. Soon domestic politics would outrace bureaucratic inertia. He tried to jump start the policy process before it was too late.

THE PRESIDENT SAYS HIS PIECE

On September 26, 1994, the ban campaigners won backing from yet another unexpected source. In an address to the UN General Assembly, President Clinton endorsed the "ultimate goal of the eventual elimination of antipersonnel landmines." As if "ultimate" and "eventual" did not make that goal provisional enough, he added yet another proviso, "as viable and humane alternatives are developed." Still, it was the first time that a major world leader had called for a ban.

The president meant what he said, according to those who worked closely with him. "The words at the UN reflected the president's genuine interest in doing something about landmines," says a White House official. "He cared about this."[79]

The president's interest did not propel the administration toward a ban, however. "We were working for the CCW and the Landmines Control Regime," says the White House official. "Eventual elimination was designed to set a long-term goal. It did not have a specific control regime behind it. It was like eventual elimination of nuclear weapons."[80] That is a reference to the words of the nuclear Non-Proliferation Treaty. Just how conditional the commitment of the United States and the other four nuclear powers was to the elimination of nuclear weapons is evident in the negotiating record of the NPT and their actions ever since. The US commitment to eliminate antipersonnel landmines was just about as tentative. Internal deliberations at the time reveal just how tentative.

President Clinton's interest in landmines was piqued the way presidential attention to an issue often is—by media coverage and Congressional action. On January 23, 1994, the *New York Times* had run a cover story in the Sunday magazine, entitled, "It's the Little Bombs That Kill You," which framed the issue in human rights terms. The story prompted Clinton to "ask about landmines policy," says a White House official. From then on, "Leahy drove the issue. It was a coming together" of those two influences.[81]

The story of just how Leahy came to drive the issue begins with Eric Newsom's frustration with the Landmines Control Regime and his appreciation of the ban campaign's normative appeal. "Early on," he says, "I seemed to be one of the few people in the government who actually had much experience with the NGOs on the APL issue, and I don't want to exaggerate how much I had. It was primarily through Tim [Rieser]. I'm a square professional, but at least I had dealt with them. A few of us in State began to sense the power of what they were trying to do. Many others didn't have much idea of who these people were and what this was all about. They insisted on treating this as a standard arms control issue." Another important exception, says Newsom, was "Larry Dodgen, an Army general in OSD, who got smart on them very fast once he moved into the issue."[82]

Newsom decided to take matters into his own hands, officials say. He found a pretext to travel to New York and call on Karl F. "Rick" Inderfurth at the US mission to the United Nations, whom he knew from their days on Capitol Hill. They discussed a new UN resolution on landmines that Inderfurth was drafting and what President Clinton might tell the General Assembly in a few weeks. Ambassador Madeleine Albright had asked Leahy to introduce the new resolution and lobby for it. "The only way that Senator Leahy could agree to go to the UN was if we felt comfortable standing up and introducing the resolution," says Tim Rieser. "We had many conversations with the UN mission about the language. We and the UN mission would fax drafts of language back and forth."[83]

Inderfurth's draft called for the "eventual elimination" of antipersonnel landmines. "We had to have a Deputies Committee meeting on being able to use that language," he says. Deputy National Security Adviser Samuel "Sandy" Berger chaired the meeting. "I was there, and we got it." How did they get the joint staff to clear the draft resolution? "Initially I think our military colleagues saw this in the same category as elimination of nuclear weapons—a good thing to say but it ain't going to happen within our lifetime."[84] Robert Sherman of ACDA, who disliked the language, elaborates, "JCS didn't like it at all," but OSD had "some political appointees who were ultra-dovish on this" and stories had run in the press about a civil-military rift in the Pentagon. The joint staff director, Admiral Richard Macke, "was concerned about that and didn't want to feed that speculation," says Sherman, "so he made the decision that, since OSD was signing off on it, JCS wouldn't object." That left Sherman odd man out. "This was a time when ACDA's existence was threatened and the State Department was trying to gobble us up. I made the judgment that ACDA just can't afford to be off by its lonesome on the right end of the bench—on the left end maybe, but not on the right end—so I reluctantly cleared on it. I spent many years regretting that."[85] Inderfurth concurs, "It was less a case of standing down than choosing not to fight." He remembers hearing some officials who were unhappy with the decision to call for "eventual elimination" console themselves as they left the meeting, "Well, we said the same thing about nuclear weapons."[86]

Some diplomats at the United Nations had a similar reaction. "When I first started talking to others about that resolution, my British colleague called it a gimmick," Inderfurth recalls. "I said it was not a gimmick."[87]

As the resolution began making the diplomatic rounds at the United Nations, preparations got under way for the president's address to the General Assembly. Inderfurth cabled the Bureau of International Organizations in State to recommend that "the president should include language tracking the resolution we were already circulating," specifically the reference to "eventual elimination." He is unsure how those words were included: "White House speeches were never circulated widely before being delivered, but we made it very clear to State."[88]

Proposed language from executive branch departments often makes its way into White House speechwriters' wastebaskets, but Eric Newsom found a way to prevent that from happening, say officials: he went back-door to Senator Leahy. Leahy, in turn, took the matter up directly with the White House. Having agreed to withdraw his legislation in July in return for a policy review, the senator was unhappy with the results. He took a tough stance on the UN speech in a heated conversation with Deputy National Security

Adviser Berger. "The study did not convince us that the issue was moving forward," says Tim Rieser. "Senator Leahy had an exchange with Berger over precisely what the president was going to say about eliminating landmines. Senator Leahy made it clear that if he could not get satisfaction, our only alternative was to go forward with legislation."[89] As a result, a commitment to "eventual elimination" was written into the president's address.

Usually the bureaucracy takes the president's words as a statement of policy, not empty rhetoric. The operating assumption of those who fought hard for the language was that his words would turn into deeds. "If we are voting in favor of resolutions with this language—solemn commitments—and if the president is speaking to these issues in opening the General Assembly each year," says Inderfurth, "that should have a policy impact in Washington."[90] It did not.

Even though elimination of antipersonnel landmines may have been the "ultimate goal" for President Clinton, it was not for working-level officials. "The president, because he is the kind of politician he is, understood before almost anyone else the international dynamic that would develop around this issue," says Lee Feinstein. "US bureaucrats absolutely did not. Having understood that, he was hoping somehow that the process inside the US government would develop to the point that the Pentagon would soften its opposition so that he could make the final nudge. That is not what happened."[91]

One reason was that the low-ranking military officers and lawyers working on the issue in the Pentagon were determined to hold onto landmines. "Unlike most esoteric nuclear theology, which dealt with the improbable and the unthinkable, this in their minds touched on a genuine force protection issue," says Eric Newsom.[92] They were immovable without pressure from above, pressure that never materialized.

High-level disinterest was endemic not only in the Pentagon, but also in the Department of State. "Neither Secretary of State Warren Christopher nor Deputy Secretary Strobe Talbott was engaged," says Newsom. "Under Secretary Lynn Davis paid little attention to it. So it was left to Ted McNamara, me, and a few others." Where did PM get the clout to do battle with other agencies? "It was bluff. It was just bluff."[93]

Bluff seldom worked in the lower reaches of the bureaucracy. Without a senior official to champion the ban, the president's expression of interest went unheeded. The national security adviser was one top official who could have driven the process, but both Anthony Lake and Sandy Berger saw themselves primarily as policy brokers, not policy entrepreneurs, and seldom pushed their own views on the bureaucracy. Anticipating strong military resistance to a ban, top civilians in the Pentagon were reluctant to break their lances on landmines when they were tilting with the armed services on other issues. Warren Christopher did not leave his mark on most issues. Perhaps the best candidate was Madeleine Albright, who did what she could as UN ambassador to back a ban. Once she took over as secretary of state, however, she was less exposed to ban sympathizers and more in the line of fire of ban opponents than she had been at the United Nations.

Two reasons for disinterest were common to all the top civilians. One is that they had many other pressing concerns. Another is that they could not be sure of President Clinton's commitment: they had watched officials venture out on a limb for him on other issues, only to have him saw it off.

The UN speech did not go unheeded outside the government. Ban campaigners began trying to hold the Clinton administration to account by exposing the gap between the president's words and the officials' deeds. The magnitude of that gap was soon apparent to them. On October 7, State Department and ACDA officials held a briefing for the US Campaign to Ban Landmines to outline the initiatives to be taken in pursuit of the president's goal. One was to toughen the CCW regulations on use. Another was the Landmines Control Regime. The officials, recalls Joe Volk of the Friends Committee on National Legislation, were "very keen on trying to see if they could convince [the campaigners] that we had a joint humanitarian concern and that our calculations on how to deal with it were naive and their Landmine Control Regime was the real humanitarian initiative."[94] The campaigners remained unconvinced. "We had not been consulted very much on the development of that initiative, which surprised me a little bit because many of us were talking to Bob Sherman on a regular basis," says Goose. "If they had talked to us more, they might not have been caught so off guard by the strong reaction against it they got from the NGOs."[95] A letter to President Clinton signed by 28 NGOs condemned the proposal as "a giant step backwards in what has until now been a promising US leadership initiative." Those pushing for a ban were not about to settle for arms control.

THE CONTROL REGIME FOUNDERS

Negotiations on a Landmines Control Regime proceeded as if the president's UN statement had no bearing on policy.

McNamara headed the US delegation at the Rome talks in January 1995. The prevalence of cheap landmines, he told the Europeans, was a recent phenomenon. "There's a hemorrhaging of this stuff in the third world, particularly the hockey puck landmines—the three- or four-dollar things." Their persistence was also new. "Nobody had ever focused on the reason the landmine problem was growing—technology," he says. "Previous landmines were metal and had unstable explosives. Now we had highly stable explosives and the plastic encasement meant they were weather-resistant." Until the advent of long-lasting mines, unexploded ordnance, not landmines, had been the most dangerous residue of past wars. A rare exception had occurred in World War II after the German tank campaign against the British in the North African desert, where it was so dry that landmines did not rust, exposing the explosive to moisture and causing it to decompose.

Now, he said, as a result of communal strife throughout the world, left-over landmines were endangering life and livelihood. The problem, as the United States defined it, was the change in mine technology. The solution was to regulate some mines. Consistent with realism, that would preserve US military superiority while constraining less technologically advanced rivals.

Even the first step in such a regime, an export moratorium, encountered resistance in Rome. "The Europeans were sitting there thinking, we've had war for a hundred years now with landmines," he says. They expressed "skepticism about whether or not this was the kind of problem we were saying it was." McNamara argued for a moratorium on exports: "Let's just stop the stuff from going." That was not what some Europeans wanted to hear: "On the continent, the French, the Germans, the Italians were all saying, you guys are heading off half-cocked on this thing, and I was telling them, you guys have no idea how serious this is." The ban movement in Europe was not yet the political force it would soon be. "What I was telling them in Rome was get on top of it now," he recalls. "There was reluctance on the part of many countries to move very fast."[96]

McNamara made the case for a stand-alone forum. "The people who didn't want to move fast on this wanted to do it in CCW." He tried to reassure them. "We don't have any preconceived notions as to what the control regime should be, how strict it ought to be," he said. "We can shape it." European diplomats were also "a lot more traditionally oriented about what they were doing in arms control. They said the Geneva Convention ought to suffice, but, of course, it didn't." Doubts about US motives also surfaced. "The Europeans said you just want to stop these little things because you guys don't make them. I said, yes, of course, we don't make them because we don't use them. They said, we're making an awful lot of money from them." Europeans cited Leahy's moratorium legislation as the reason for Washington's sudden interest, arguing that "the United States was trying to get other people out of the market because you have this problem in the Congress that is pulling you out of the market." McNamara tried to rebut the accusation, "How many have we exported other than to NATO and Korea? Almost zero." In the face of resistance, McNamara thought he made headway. "Nobody signed up to the moratorium," he recalls, but "at the end of Rome, we had individual countries saying, okay, we can go along with the moratorium but we've got to know where it's heading."[97]

The United States began consulting with Britain on where to go beyond the moratorium. The two agreed on a Landmines Control Regime. "It defined what we were going to control, whether in a moratorium or a more permanent ban," says McNamara. "We weren't headed toward a ban on manufacture, although we wanted people to declare what they were manufacturing."[98]

Some 30 countries attended a second meeting in Budapest early in July 1995 to discuss the proposed regime. At a press conference the following week, McNamara characterized the US position, "We are in favor of...strictly controlling the use of landmines. We also wish to see controls placed on the export, on the stockpiling, and on the production of landmines. It is our considered opinion, after many months of working on the issue, that an outright ban on landmines is not possible at this time."[99]

A reporter posed a telling question, "It seems to me you are in a rather peculiar situation here, really. On the one hand, you have American companies making mines. On the other hand, you have American taxpayers dishing out money to dig them up. Isn't there rather an internal contradiction in this?" A way out of this Catch-22, replied McNamara, was to ban the production of cheap mines, "Part of what we are doing, in the convention and in the control programs that we are suggesting countries sign up for, would make mines more expensive. If they are to be self-destructing landmines, they are going to be more expensive than the cheap $3 landmines that are now on the market," McNamara noted. "And the productive capacity of the developed world which has created the landmine crisis cannot be reproduced by the underdeveloped world."[100] Why that was a good deal for less developed countries was not self-evident.

Yet the US military's insistence that they needed mines rather than the desires of US mine producers was the impetus behind the US stance. "It is the position of the Department of Defense and the position of the US government that there is still, even in a post-Cold War environment, a military utility or need for antipersonnel landmines," Tim Connolly told reporters. "It is a hotly contested policy issue within the US government." Connolly, who favored a ban, left little doubt where he stood, "There is, at this point, a conclusion that we need to move toward the eventual ban of antipersonnel landmines. And we are aggressively pursuing an alternative to antipersonnel landmines to provide the same capability as they provide on the battlefield, but we are not prepared at this point to abandon them."[101]

If the armed services' unwillingness to give up landmines was the main reason for the US stance, it was not the only one. "The skepticism in Europe was enormous," says McNamara, especially among countries still manufacturing landmines. "The Brits were also out of the business, which didn't help." McNamara discerned a pattern in the Europeans' views: "who wanted to do what depended upon the geopolitics of each country." The pattern was evident in the contrasting positions of Sweden and Finland. "The Swedes were all for a moratorium," he says. "The Finns were not sure it was a great idea." Finland, which borders on Russia, acts as a buffer state for Sweden. "The Finns put it very bluntly at one point," McNamara recalls. "Sweden doesn't need landmines because Finland is the Swedish landmine, but how do we stop a massive neighbor [from invading]. We do it by mining the border. You're telling us that we can't import and export these things, that we've got to make them all ourselves. Eventually, you're telling us under the control regime that we may not manufacture certain kinds of landmines. This has fundamental implications for our whole defense strategy." McNamara sensed a similar contrast between Austria, which favored controls, and the Czech Republic, which did not. "The Russians are worried about a populous China and use them in the Far East where they don't have much population. The Belgians and Canadians don't have such problems," he notes. After Soviet disunion, "Russia became more and more obdurate," fearing instability on its borders.[102]

McNamara's assessment was rooted in realism, the dominant way of thinking about the world in the government and the foreign policy establishment of the United States and an important school of thought in the study of international relations. Realism asserts that states are motivated by national interests, not the play of internal politics. Realists define national interests narrowly in terms of security or power and assume other values do not count. Armed force, they believe, exerts a strong pull on the behavior of states. Ethical norms do not.

Realists deem international law to be ineffective either because it is toothless or because, unlike domestic law, it is rooted in beliefs about right and wrong that are not shared by the international community, but differ from culture to culture and society to society. "Law is regarded as binding because it represents the sense of right of the community," E.H. Carr puts it. "International law is a function of the political community of nations. Its defects are due, not to any technical shortcomings, but to the embryonic character of the community in which it functions."[103] The international system is governed by anarchy and states have to look after their own security. That makes them unwilling to pay the price of enforcing the law, whether that price entails alienating an ally or confronting a lawbreaker with armed force. Realists regard law and morality as manifestations of interests and power. As interests change or power shifts, the rules of the international order are rewritten. In that sense, might makes right.

Among the realists' most formidable opponents in politics are liberals, who define interests in terms of values other than just power and who regard cooperation, not just conflict, as intrinsic to international politics. Liberals do not marginalize international norms and institutions, but see them as essential tools for facilitating cooperation. In their view, norms, rules, and procedures help the dominant states advance their own interests and preserve the existing international order.[104]

Even more fundamentally, in the view of liberals, community standards constrain how far the behavior of any state, even a great power, can deviate from the norm. States legitimate their actions by espousing community values and adhering to them. Their words and deeds are tempered by normative obligation and ethical constraint. Repeated deviance can stain states' reputations, causing their loss of legitimacy and influence with others and ultimately their repudiation and isolation as pariahs. States comply with norms not only because of calculations of costs and benefits, but also because norms define who they are and what they want. In short, norms are more than instrumental, a means to other ends. They are ends in themselves, intrinsic to states' identities and interests.[105]

The ban campaigners would soon overwhelm the realists. Appealing to a sense of right and wrong, they would stigmatize antipersonnel landmines. The power of their normative challenge would become evident in the CCW review conference, a development that Ted McNamara and Eric Newsom were quicker than most US officials to anticipate. Between January 1995, when McNamara and Newsom first broached the idea of a Landmines Control Regime in Rome as a way to head off a ban, and the Brussels Conference in June 1997, the ban campaign caught on in Europe, prompting governments to change stances. "At first they were all against it," recalls McNamara. "Now they'd flanked us on the other side."[106] After Brussels, "Ted came back saying, we're not going to make it," says Newsom. "By this time, the Europeans and others we had been talking to were getting a blowtorch put to their rear ends by the landmine ban activists and they were backing away from us like mad."[107]

4

Beyond Regulation to a Ban

Competitiveness is the mechanism for the expansion of the scope of conflict. It is the *loser* who calls in outside help.

E.E. Schattschneider[1]

As the CCW review got under way, the International Campaign to Ban Landmines adopted a two-track strategy, lobbying delegates to strengthen regulations governing the use of landmines and at the same time waging a public campaign to underscore the need for a ban by exposing the inadequacies of the regulatory approach.

Those inadequacies were readily apparent to the campaigners in the run-up to the CCW review conference. The four preparatory meetings of the group of governmental experts in 1994 and 1995 resisted most proposals for tighter regulation of use, let alone curbs on landmine production and exports. The review conference seemed likely to follow suit.

While ICBL strategists worried that too much emphasis on strengthening regulation would sidetrack a ban, the trouble with the two-track approach was more basic: if many governments were unwilling to accept more stringent arms control, how could the campaign get them to support disarmament? The ICBL's answer was to change strategy and try to broaden the coalition behind a ban. The campaigners moved beyond lobbying behind closed doors to mobilize more visible activism intended to dramatize the tragic legacy of landmines, publicize the limits of arms control, and shame governments into seeking a ban.

Not in the United States, however, where the ban campaign remained focused on lobbying. "Out of the blue, with Leahy's leadership, we managed to get an export moratorium in 1992," says ICBL strategist Stephen Goose. "That woke everybody up. It was an issue that governments had to take seriously." The moratorium was largely Senator Patrick Leahy's doing, not the ICBL's, he says. "The campaign was hardly under way." The legislative triumph reinforced the US campaigners' commitment to their strategy. "We were lulled by our success," says Goose. Even though "the Europeans from the very beginning seemed more intent on grassroots organizing," the US campaign "had more of a focus on Washington policy-makers—much more of an insider's game. Ultimately, I think, that did not suit us well."[2]

Outside the United States, the ICBL enlisted religious, humanitarian, and other NGOs in its cause and aggregated these new affiliates into national campaigns.[3] "We were trying to get groups whose focus was not naturally the ban," says Goose, "to become part of the coalition, to contribute as much as they could to the coalition, to view coalition work as part of their activity, even if it was not their focus."[4]

In expanding its coalition, however, the ICBL drew in groups with very different priorities. Even though the NGOs could agree on the overarching goal of a ban, NGOs that did demining wanted the ban to cover not only so-called dumb mines but also smart mines, designed to self-deactivate or self-destruct; NGOs that trucked in humanitarian relief were as eager to ban antivehicle mines as antipersonnel mines; disarmament groups were intent on banning all landmines, antitank and antipersonnel, dumb and smart, and cluster bombs, too; NGOs trying to curb arms exports wanted to bar the sale or transfer of landmines; still other NGOs were preoccupied with relieving the plight of landmine survivors. Although the ICBL tried to define a common interest that kept the disparate NGOs on board, campaigners faced tough tradeoffs among competing priorities in negotiating landmines.

Holding the coalition together was easier to do because the ICBL was not an organization or a mass movement, but a network, in which affiliates interacted by fax and e-mail, yet acted with considerable autonomy, if not entirely on their own.

Networking also helped mobilize activism. Campaigns have trouble attracting grassroots activists and even more trouble keeping them active. As campaigns struggle against long odds in pursuit of a distant goal, even dedicated activists drift away. It is easier to enlist existing groups and hold them together than to recruit individual activists and sustain their commitment to a cause.

Studies of NGOs suggest that narrow self-interest does not motivate much activism.[5] That was the case with the ban campaign, where few participants stood to benefit directly from a ban, even from empowerment of survivors or from funds for demining. Except for a handful of leaders, few could achieve power or fame. What then motivates people to contribute time, money, and energy to a movement? A mix of normative and personal incentives, studies show.[6] Altruism is enough for some activists to become involved and stay engaged, but for others, social motives like working with friends and sharing intense experiences matter more. Group membership sustains activism for those who care about association and involvement. Even if the unselfish pursuit of values does motivate some activists, the possibility of realizing those values helps keep them active. That is easier to do in a group. Members tend to go along with the group when it joins with other groups in a common cause. Groups hang together better than unattached individuals; group solidarity helps sustain hope for success.

Frequent communication between leaders and followers and involvement in decision making also boost collective effort. The ICBL aided coordination among campaigns in various countries by regularly sharing strategies with affiliated groups and, through contact with the news media, giving the groups name recognition. "One of the conscious decisions made by campaign leadership early on was that it had to be a loose coalition responsive to national or local conditions, so to become a part of the campaign you simply had to agree with the objectives," says the ICBL's Stephen Goose. The ICBL counted on the affiliates "to know best what tactics would work" in their own countries and wanted "to invest them with responsibility," Goose adds. "That's why we didn't have a secretariat. That's why we didn't have an ICBL staff. That's why there was only one person with a title [coordinator Jody Williams] and that person was seconded from another organization, just as everyone else working in the campaign was. We called ourselves a steering committee, but we didn't steer very much."[7]

Communications from the ICBL were not directives. Their main effect was to maintain affiliates' morale. "Sharing stories of their successes and failures," wrote Williams, "empowered all organizations and lessened the possibility of isolating any one group."[8] The message to small groups toiling in the trenches from Cambodia to Canada was: you are not alone.

The ICBL also became the public face of the disparate and dispersed pro-ban forces. Reporters need authoritative sources to represent various points of view in public discourse. The ICBL was the answer to the question, who speaks for the ban?[9] It provided timely statements and pungent quotes to reporters covering the review conference and telegenic visuals, not just talking heads, for television cameras. By serving as a convenient source for the news media, the ICBL put itself on the map.

In so doing, the ICBL defined the landmines issue for the news media. So long as US policy was caught in contradiction between the president's desire and the bureaucrats' inertia, no top official articulated US policy. With a clean slate to write on, the ICBL and Leahy cast landmines as a humanitarian disaster that only a global ban could forestall. First impressions proved longlasting with public opinion.

THE US DELEGATION PROTECTS ITS OWN

The ban campaign had yet to attract much public attention in the United States. Until it did, working-level officials in the US government were left unusually free to set landmines policy. The preparatory meetings leading up to the CCW review conference were not on the radar screens of top civilians. In the Pentagon, says Jan Lodal, principal deputy undersecretary of defense for policy, "Nobody really pays attention until Ottawa is going to happen and we're forced to pay attention to it."[10] It was the same story across the Potomac at the Department of State. "In the first Clinton administration, there was a lot of discomfort in dealing with arms control issues, which was a subset of dealing with foreign policy in general," says Lee Feinstein of the policy planning staff. It was as if the president had sent "a tacit marching order to the secretary of state to keep problems off my plate." As a result, high-level attention to landmines was cursory at best. "There was almost no adult supervision in the White House or the State Department on this issue," he says. "It was not an issue on which there were Principals Committee meetings or Deputies Committee meetings."[11]

What disturbed Feinstein about the policy process was a source of satisfaction for the US deputy chief CCW negotiator, Robert Sherman, who attributes the delegation's ability to shape the US negotiating position to its success at remaining "below the NSC's radar screen. We were not important enough for them to involve themselves. We didn't even have a separate backstopping group. So we could be both efficient and effective."[12] Without overseers in Washington, negotiating team members were also freer to logroll among themselves. That strengthened the hand of landmine enthusiasts within the US Army.

Within the Pentagon, a small group of low-ranking military officers worked on CCW, but the key player by all accounts was a civilian, W. Hays Parks, special assistant to the judge advocate general who had specialized in the law of war since 1979. "He had a great deal of weight because he was an Army staff counsel. He didn't embrace the notion of the United Nations in general and he clearly didn't embrace the notion of any kind of civilian or international organization trying to regulate weapons systems," says Tim Connolly, principal deputy assistant secretary of defense in the Office of

Special Operations and Low-Intensity Conflict. Landmines were not an issue that the armed services cared passionately about, according to Connolly. "It wasn't gays in the military. It wasn't the readiness of the armored divisions." The issue mattered more to a handful of officers in the Pentagon than most others out in the field: "It wasn't something that the line commander woke up in the morning and worried about. It was an insider's game." Within the Office of the Secretary of Defense responsibility for CCW fell to SOLIC, run by H. Allen Holmes, a career Foreign Service officer. Holmes "was agnostic on the issue," says Connolly, but "he was clearly not disposed to doing anything to disturb the force."[13]

Still, how could a lawyer in the Judge Advocate General's Office and a few low-ranking officers drive landmine policy? "They saw quite correctly that there was no leadership on this issue," replies Connolly, "that the secretary wasn't interested, that the undersecretary for policy wasn't interested, that the assistant secretary of defense for special operations, who was my boss, wasn't engaged. At the table was Joni Charme, occasionally Patricia Irvin [deputy assistant secretary of defense for humanitarian and refugee affairs], and me," he says. "That was the extent of the civilian side of the house." Charme, the OSD representative on the CCW delegation, operated at a distinct disadvantage, he adds. "She is a woman, which put her behind the power curve in policy formulation in the Pentagon, she's young, and she has no military background. Every day she is doing battle with people who have medals on their chest and stars on their collars and trying to make an argument against what they believe their client desires the outcome to be," says Connolly. "In an adversarial process you are inclined to plea bargain if you believe that you are going to get a worse outcome by failing to plea bargain. Hays Parks and his crowd did not have to have the political skills of a James Carville to figure out that there was no leadership on the civilian side, and consequently there was nothing to prevent them from getting 100 percent of what they wanted if they simply refused to cooperate at any level."[14]

The CCW delegation was headed by Michael Matheson, a lawyer who had served in the State Department since 1972, mostly in the Office of Legal Adviser. He began work on landmines as assistant legal adviser in the Bureau of Politico-Military Affairs in 1974, when the subject came up in Geneva, and he had been acting head of the US delegation in Geneva in 1980, negotiating the landmine protocol. Matheson was now principal deputy legal adviser, too lowly a position to exercise much bureaucratic clout even if he had wanted to. He saw no need to. "The law of war activity," he says, "was almost always done directly between the State and Defense Departments and basically between the legal adviser's office and the military lawyers. We almost never went to the NSC for decisions," a step Matheson was loathe to take. "Whenever humanly possible, don't ask the NSC to decide an issue. Then it gets into politics in a big way," he says. "All those people at the top are wonderful but sometimes the results are kind of quixotic." His approach to NSC coordination was low-key and low-level: "We just got a pro forma blessing. Basically, I would keep Ann Witkowsky fully informed and from time to time I would talk to her boss, Bob Bell. Since there were no interagency disagreements there was nothing for the NSC to do."[15]

These arrangements guaranteed that military representatives on the delegation would get what they wanted. "The proposals of May 1992, which for their time were reasonably radical, happened to coincide exactly with military interests," says Matheson. "By that point, and perhaps earlier, the military had already adopted unilaterally what became most of the substance of what became the revised protocol," he explains. During the 1980s Army adoption of a new doctrine that put increased emphasis on the use of mobility to seize the initiative in military operations had led to revived concern about friendly casualties, a legacy of Vietnam. As a result, the Army "had already developed and put into the inventory self-destruct antipersonnel mines" and was punctilious about the demarking and monitoring of minefields. CCW posed no problem for defense firms, either. "We were not telling them they couldn't manufacture landmines. We were telling them they had to manufacture landmines with some new features," says Matheson. "So all we really had to do was to figure out how to conceptualize these practices which the military had already adopted," he says, "and then convince other countries—obviously the hardest part—that they were militarily feasible and made sense in humanitarian terms."[16]

The result was classic arms control, where the aim is to protect weapons used by the US armed forces from regulation while trying to regulate weapons used by other countries. Asked if military requirements had special sway during the CCW review conference, Robert Sherman of ACDA replies, "The military representatives on our delegation were very firm on this. I mean, intense. But so was ACDA."[17]

The services wanted seven landmines left free of constraint, all of them self-destructing and self-deactivating. Of the seven, six were remotely delivered, commonly called FASCAMs, which stands for family of scatterable mines.

One was delivered by artillery, the area denial antipersonnel munition. Packaged in a 155-millimeter artillery round, 36 per round, the ADAM is a pop-up mine that deploys seven 20-foot triplines. When disturbed, the tripline triggers the mine to pop up 2 to 8 feet into the air and spray shrapnel up to 40 feet in all directions. ADAMs could be preset to self-destruct in 4 or 48 hours and to self-deactivate in about 14 days. An ADAM variant used by special operations forces, the pursuit deterrent mine, was emplaced by hand and activated by a device resembling a hand grenade. It self-destructed after 4 hours. Another was a remotely delivered antitank munition, the remote anti-armor mine system. It self-deactivated and self-destructed and like the ADAM was triggered by magnetic sensing. If detonated between the tracks of an armored vehicle, a RAAM could bring it to a halt. Nine RAAMs were delivered in a single 155-millimeter artillery shell. About one in five was equipped with an internal antihandling device.

The others were all mixed munitions that combined antitank with antipersonnel mines intended to impede foes from disarming the antitank mine. One was the RADAM, still under development, which was designed to combine ADAM and RAAM for delivery in a 155-millimeter artillery shell. A second was the Volcano, fired up to 50 meters from racks of mortar-like tubes. Each tube held one antipersonnel mine and five antitank mines. Configured in arrays of 160 tubes (160 antipersonnel and 800 antimines), the Volcano could be dispensed from moving tracked vehicles, 5-ton trucks, or helicopters. A third, the Gator, was a cluster bomb delivered by fixed-wing aircraft. The Air Force version dispensed 44 antipersonnel mines along with 72 antitank mines; the Navy version, 15 antipersonnel mines along with 45 antitank mines. The antipersonnel mines deployed 40-foot triplines while the antitank mines were triggered by magnetic sensing. Prior to takeoff, the mines could be preset to self-destruct at 4 hours, 48 hours, or 15 days. Self-deactivation took about 60 days. A fifth munition, the modular pack mine system, took four men to carry. The MOPMS could be deployed by a hand-held remote control radio transmitter, dispensing four antipersonnel mines and 17 antitank mines from seven launch tubes in a 35-meter semicircle. It had a timer that could be turned on and off to allow friendly forces to pass through. It could also be command-detonated. The MOPMS had a maximum self-destruct time of 16 hours and self-deactivated after about 14 days.[18]

The Army also wanted mines in Korea exempted. It succeeded. The CCW would permit antipersonnel mines co-located with antitank mines so long as they lay in marked minefields. "None of this is dealing with removal of emplaced mines," says Robert Sherman of ACDA, "so they can keep the stuff that's in the ground."[19]

The US aim in CCW was to curb the export and stockpiling of scatterable dumb mines while protecting antipersonnel mines of use to it. "For CCW," says Sherman, "I created the requirement that unmarked or remotely delivered APL had to self-destruct and self-deactivate. Mike Matheson thought we'd never get agreement on this, but he was willing to let me take the ball and see how far I could run with it."[20]

Disagreement arose when the military representatives tried to protect a long-lived mine that was not yet under development. Such a mine could be remotely delivered in advance, timed to deploy and to self-destruct at a preset interval. "The longest thing they had was 15 days," but the armed services had an idea for a new long-lived mine, "a notional plan for a turn-on/turn-off system," says Sherman. "They had no budget request, no cost projections." The mine's lifespan was a problem. "There was a general consensus that you needed a 4-to-1 ratio between self-destruct and self-deactivate time," he says, "so that you could be confident that the batteries are going to be live when you need them to be live. ACDA—that's me—wanted to have a 2-day self-destruct. JCS wanted 6 months." By the 4-to-1 rule of thumb, a 6-month self-destruct mine would have a 2-year self-deactivation period, a very long time for mines to remain a risk to passersby or deminers. "Because the CCW clock begins when the mine is emplaced, it doesn't matter when the mine is turned on." The dispute, says Sherman, was "between ACDA and JCS. State and OSD basically sat on the sidelines." Eventually the negotiating team settled on 30 days. That became the standard adopted in the CCW. "Once the United States had its fixed position, those were the numbers that CCW used."[21]

THE EXPERTS TRY ARMS CONTROL

The governmental experts proceeded incrementally, as arms controllers do, to regulate landmines and stop far short of disarmament.

The experts held four meetings in Geneva in 1994 and 1995. Three issues dominated the proceedings: strengthening regulation of use of landmines, extending coverage of the CCW to internal conflicts, and devising a procedure for verification.

"The details of the technical regulation of mines," says Michael Matheson, chief US negotiator, "was a problem for the Europeans." As the United States framed the issue, remotely delivered mines posed a greater risk of indiscriminate use and had to be equipped to self-destruct or self-deactivate, or else be banned. "The whole idea of self-destruct and self-deactivating was basically not very familiar to everybody else," Matheson says. "Putting this in treaty text and convincing them that this made sense and was feasible took a bit of time and education. We had to have our military work an awful lot with their militaries because at first it sounded like a bunch of gobbledygook which probably represented to them Americans trying to sell American weapons." The ban campaign was also a help: "We would not have succeeded without the painstaking working out of the details with the other militaries, but we used the public arousal to move the militaries along."[22] Still, US success was limited. When the Europeans refused to apply the requirement to antitank mines, the United States gave in. Only antipersonnel landmines would have to self-destruct or self-deactivate.

Getting the allies on board was key to Matheson's strategy: "The first thing we had to do was get solid Western support, and after that we had to get the Russians on board." That left "the harder cases" for last.[23] Once the

Europeans had accepted US standards on self-deactivation, the US delegation tried to win the others over.

"Nobody really challenged the numbers; they challenged the whole concept," says deputy US negotiator Sherman. China was the most determined challenger. Unsure how reliable its mines were, China preferred to set the reliability standard at 90 percent or lower. Under the US proposal, the 99.9 percent standard required, in effect, that if 1,000 mines were programmed to self-destruct in 30 days, all but one would do so. "The Chinese wanted to say, we'll accept the 99.9 percent specification for reliability or we'll accept the 120-day specification for duration, but we won't accept both," says Sherman, "which would be meaningless."[24]

A turning point on the duration standard came in bilateral talks with the Russians in Moscow on December 10, 1995. "One of the most difficult issues," says Sherman, "regarded the Russian VP-13, which has about a 1-year active life. It used six size-D flashlight batteries." Expecting to get nowhere, the Americans were surprised at the Russians' willingness to accept the 30-day standard—and more: "The Russians said we can modify it so that big batteries can't be installed." What accounts for the change of heart by Moscow? "We still don't understand why it happened," says Sherman. "We conjecture that the army saw this as a chance to modernize their mines." Moscow's shift put pressure on Beijing to go along. "The Chinese did not want to be the last holdout, blocking consensus on a humanitarian measure."[25]

A number of developing countries also objected to expanding the scope of the CCW to cover internal conflicts. Matheson chose to concentrate on China, India, and Pakistan. "If we could get these three, the others were not going to object," he says. "Both the Indians and the Pakistanis look at these issues through the prism of Kashmir. The Indians didn't want outsiders looking over their shoulder at what they were doing in Kashmir" and neither did the Pakistanis. "The Chinese attitude was more generalized anti-international intrusion."[26]

Yet, as Matheson told Senator Leahy in a private briefing, the review conference was unlikely to reach consensus on further limits unless a number of states withdrew their objections to key provisions. Some states, Russia and China among them, said they would need a "grace period" of 10 to 20 years, not 5 years, to replace their dumb mines with smart ones. Other states, notably China, were reluctant to specify 8 grams of metallic content as the minimum needed to make mines detectable, reducing the risk to deminers. A number of states, among them, France and Sweden, wanted to allow anti-tank mines equipped with antihandling devices. China, Mexico, and others opposed strong verification or enforcement provisions as infringements on their sovereignty, a raw nerve for nations with a colonial past.[27]

OUTSIDE, BUT NOT IN THE DARK

To the ICBL, the run-up to the CCW review conference was an occasion to expose the shortcomings of regulation. The experts' meetings also gave campaigners an opportunity to lobby the diplomats. With these goals in mind, the ICBL appealed to the UN secretary-general to permit NGO participation—without success.

It followed up that request with a letter to the secretary of the review conference proposing its own agenda for the conferees. Instead of amending the existing landmines protocol, it wanted a new one. It asked that conferees regulate production, stockpiling, and export of antipersonnel mines, not just their use. It wanted the regulations on use extended to internal, not just international conflicts. It sought a more precise definition of antipersonnel landmine. It wanted to ban mines that could not be safely removed by prohibiting antihandling devices hazardous to deminers and requiring all mines to be detectable. It sought a ban on remotely-delivered mines and mandatory demarcation of all minefields. It insisted all mines be equipped to self-destruct and self-deactivate. It wanted minelaying states held legally responsibility for clearing mines and mine offenses stipulated to be "grave breaches" of the CCW. It sought verification and enforcement that provided for fact finding and inspections.[28]

Barred from direct participation, the ICBL monitored the proceedings with the help of UN agency representatives and sympathetic delegates. Stuart Maslen of UNICEF, for example, passed along his notes on the second experts' session, with his trenchant critique of proposals and his insights into proponents' equities. A proposal by France and Germany to ban nondetectable mines and remotely delivered mines without self-destruct or self-deactivation mechanisms Maslen called "unacceptable" because it did not require the mines to contain a specific quantity of metal that could not be removed—one gram would suffice especially if it was shaped and positioned in the mine to facilitate detection—and because all mines, not just remotely deliverable ones, had to be self-deactivating *and* self-destructing. A US–Danish alternative requiring that all antipersonnel landmines be either self-destructing or self-deactivating was "preferable in some respects" but still unacceptable because it did not cover antivehicle mines. States were reluctant to extend coverage, Maslen noted, because of the cost of converting the mines they had. With an estimated 100 million mines, perhaps more, stockpiled around the world, "even at the price for conversion (parts, labor, etc.) of a couple of dollars, states are already bemoaning the financial considerations." Maslin saw two ways to mitigate their concern: allow a grace period of, say, 10 years for states to convert or use up stockpiles and replace the mines already sown, or else ban all antipersonnel mines, sparing states the cost of converting them. Ireland was the only country to call for a ban at this point.[29]

A critical issue was how to define "antipersonnel mine." The landmines protocol had defined "mine" as "any munition placed under, on or near the ground or other surface area and designed to be detonated or exploded by the presence, proximity or contact of a person or vehicle." Austria, with US backing, proposed the definition of antipersonnel landmine recommended by the technical subcommittee of the review conference: "a mine primarily designed to be exploded by the presence, proximity or contact of a person and that will incapacitate, injure or kill one or more persons." The definition was intended to exclude antitank mines equipped with antihandling devices or pressure fuzes as well as so-called mixed munitions in which antipersonnel mines were not integral to the antitank mine but were deployed nearby. The humanitarian problem was that as long as these mines remained active, they could be tripped by an innocent passerby who had no intent to tamper with or disable the antitank mine. The ensuing explosion could also detonate the antitank mine.

An April 28 memo from Leahy aide Tim Rieser urged the ICBL to press for a restrictive definition: "The insertion of the word 'primarily' in the definition of antipersonnel mines really worries me." He had the prescience to recognize broader implications of the definition: "I am obviously afraid that this will become the definition of antipersonnel mine used by governments not only with respect to this protocol, but in whatever unilateral actions they take."[30]

Rieser's memo reveals how closely he collaborated with the campaigners. It also shows how artfully he exploited his quasi-insider role. "I have discussed this with Steve Solomon of the US delegation," he notes, "and urged him to construe the definition narrowly in speeches or an annex to the protocol, which he says they are inclined to do." He also informed the campaign of Senator Leahy's intent to send a letter to Matheson and Thomas "Ted" McNamara. Rieser then recommended a direct appeal on the word "primarily" to the chair of the conference, Johan Molander of Sweden, who was preparing a rolling text: "I gather the ICRC has opposed this to no avail, and that we may very well not succeed, but I would still encourage you to consider making this a priority in your press strategy. Perhaps Molander could be persuaded to delete it, if he has that authority." Rieser also enclosed a statement by Leahy for use by the campaign in its press releases and lobbying: "It is a sad irony that governments that are ostensibly meeting to strengthen the Landmine Protocol would instead narrow the definition of 'antipersonnel mine' to exclude antihandling devices on antitank mines. This is a terrible mistake. It is common knowledge that the effect of these devices is to transform an antitank mine into a far more powerful antipersonnel mine. A child or deminer who disturbs one is instantly pulverized. Rather than further weaken the protocol by creating a whole new way to circumvent its rules, I would hope that the delegates would restore the original definition before it is too late."[31]

In contrast to its close collaboration with Leahy, there was less of a meeting of minds between the ICBL and US negotiators. The flavor of their interaction is captured in a memorandum of conversation by Stephen Goose after meeting with US delegation head Michael Matheson: "Mike took notes on several things we asked him to follow up on, told us to feel free to call him in Geneva for updates…and offered to debrief us on his return. If only his policies were as good as his manners."[32]

The misgivings were mutual. "In the rest of the delegation," recalls deputy US negotiator Robert Sherman, "the general attitude was these people are shameless self-promoters and they don't deserve any respect, but we've got to deal with them so let's just give them this briefing. I came from a background of 25 years on the Hill where I'd worked with NGOs and I had the feeling, these are my kind of people and they should be helpful, they should be rational, and when they weren't, I got very resentful and some harsh words were exchanged between me and the NGOs." He recalls no harsh exchanges between the NGOs and others on the delegation: "They didn't expect anything from the NGOs, and I did."[33]

Just after the second experts' meeting, Stephen Goose met with him, at Sherman's request. The State Department, Sherman said, wanted to focus exclusively on an export control regime while ACDA sought to ban all antipersonnel mines not equipped both to self-deactivate and self-destruct. The Joint Chiefs of Staff, Sherman thought, "would—reluctantly—go along with a production ban on nondouble-deactivating mines," but wanted to exempt barrier minefields, like those in the Korean demilitarized zone and did not consider Claymores to be mines because they were command-detonated and could not be set off by a passerby. "JCS," he adds, was "very resistant to the notion of destroying existing stocks of mines" but planned to replace them within 10 years with self-destructing self-deactivating mines.[34]

China showed the limits to what the campaigners could do for the negotiators. "I remember talking with Steve Goose when he was about to meet a holdout country, just drop a hint that the campaign might start a boycott of its goods if it didn't come to agreement," says Robert Sherman. "Afterward I asked him what had happened and he said he didn't get around to it."[35] Accommodating Sherman on China would have been awkward for Goose, who was still trying to convince the Chinese to allow NGO participation at the review conference. In Matheson's view, such an approach would not have been fruitful anyway: "The Chinese did not give a shit about American NGOs."[36] Goose agrees, "The head of the delegation would spit when she'd be around us."[37]

Matheson briefed Goose and Robert Muller on August 2, 1994, a week before the third experts' meeting. He described how the requirement for all remotely delivered mines to self-destruct and self-deactivate was encountering opposition from British, French, German, and Italian representatives, who wanted self-deactivation only. The Europeans, he acknowledged, were not alone in opposing the requirement. So did the United States, which wanted to exempt minefields in Korea and at its Guantanamo base in Cuba. Matheson said the United States favored treating antitank mines with anti-handling devices as antipersonnel mines. When Muller and Goose "stressed the need for an anti-handling prohibition," he agreed to pursue it. He was less accommodating on other issues. He parried their desire to do more than regulate use. The chances of getting stringent limits on production, stockpiling, and exports were better, he argued, if these issues were discussed outside the review conference, where the rule of consensus would not govern and the "lowest common denominator" might not prevail. That was an allusion to the stand-alone forum where the Landmine Control Regime was under discussion. Separate protocols, however, could undercut a comprehensive ban by allowing countries to choose which aspects they would adhere to.[38]

On this occasion, US negotiators and the ICBL worked in concert. They discussed opposition by China to NGO involvement: "He said the US would strongly back NGO participation in the review conference and would be willing to go through the whole rigmarole all over again with the Chinese, but he did not seem optimistic." If officials helped the campaign, that help was occasionally reciprocated. When Matheson noted that Mexico was objecting to having the CCW cover internal conflicts, not just wars between states, "I wondered aloud if NGOs couldn't help with Mexico," reports Goose, "and he said, please do."[39]

Long sensitive to outside interference in its internal affairs, Mexico remained unalterably opposed to expanding the scope of the mines protocol. Joining Mexico, noted Stuart Maslen of UNICEF in a report on the third government experts' meeting in August 1994 which was circulated to the ICBL, were China, Cuba, Iran, India, and Pakistan. No consensus was emerging on how to strengthen the prohibitions in the CCW, either. Sweden proposed a total ban on the production and stockpiling as well as use of antipersonnel mines. That won the support of Austria, Cambodia, Estonia, Ireland, and Mexico. Switzerland offered an interim solution, prohibiting all mines except those equipped with an effective self-destruct or self-deactivation mechanism. This was backed by Ireland and the Netherlands, Maslen reported, and could attract more support if it provided a sufficient "grace period" for countries to convert existing stockpiles and if it assured that the necessary technology would be shared. Denmark and the United States offered "an even weaker compromise" requiring that remotely delivered mines and all other mines self-destruct or self-deactivate but making an exception for minefields that were fenced in or otherwise demarcated to keep out civilians. France and Germany wanted to permit the use of nonself-destruct mines and unmarked minefields in the event of war or imminent threat of war. "This defeats the object of the clause, which is to protect civilians from the effects of mine laying in time of combat," Maslen wrote. "Pressure must be brought to bear to ensure that this proposal is not adopted."[40]

The fourth session of governmental experts, in January 1995, was the last before the review conference, which was scheduled to open that September. The International Committee of the Red Cross urged the experts gathering in Geneva to move toward a ban. "We are deeply concerned," the ICRC said, "that none of the proposals currently under consideration in this body, other than a total ban, are likely to significantly reduce civilian casualties from landmines." It criticized "the most widely supported initiative currently under consideration" requiring that all mines used outside marked fields be equipped with effective self-destruct mechanisms: "Because this same proposal explicitly permits the continued production, sale, and use of nonself-destruct mines for classical use in minefields, these 'dumb mines' will continue to be available and to be used indiscriminately." A reduction in casualties is likely, it said, only if the production, transfer, and use of dumb mines are prohibited and that prohibition is backed by strict verification and strong sanctions. Short of a ban, the ICRC would combine "a stringent interim requirement that antipersonnel mines be used only within marked, fenced, and guarded minefields; an impartial and nonpolitical verification regime to identify violators; and the appropriate use of sanctions." If states could not agree on a ban, the Red Cross deemed two other measures "indispensable": a prohibition on mines that are not readily detectable and adoption of the "principle" that the party laying mines is responsible for their removal.[41]

The work of the experts was arms control in action and that suited the US delegation just fine. "This was really a model negotiation," says deputy negotiator Robert Sherman. "We started out with just three countries agreeing on self-destruct and self-deactivation, the United States, Australia, and Denmark, and over 2 years we got an agreement. The way we did it was first to work on the Western group. In the beginning we even had the Brits against us." At every turn, when the United States would float a proposal, "we would encounter a French–Russian–German proposal to neutralize ours. By the time we got to the homestretch, the Brits and Germans were not only supporting us, but being very effective and active advocates."[42] A White House official shares Sherman's assessment: "We drove those negotiations." The United States tried "to bring the rest of the world up to our practices," the official says, although in the course of the negotiations some of its proposals "were watered down."[43]

If the US delegation was proud of its handiwork, the NGOs took it as testament to the shortcomings of arms control and the need for a ban. The fourth meeting of the group of governmental experts in Geneva on January 9–21, 1995, had "mixed results," reported the International Committee of the Red Cross. While welcoming the experts' recommendation that CCW restrictions on the use of landmines be extended to internal armed conflicts, the ICRC remained "concerned that the proposed new restrictions on landmines which have achieved the most support to date are both too complex and too weak" and "will fail to have a significant impact on civilian casualties." New restrictions required that all antipersonnel landmines be detectable, that all hand- and vehicle-emplaced mines outside of marked, guarded and fenced minefield, and that all remotely delivered mines self-destruct and self-deactivate. Yet the sale of dumb mines was permitted, making it difficult to enforce the prohibition on use. An exception adopted by consensus suspended the obligation to fence in minefields "in situations where direct enemy military action makes it impossible to comply." In keeping with the NGOs' two-track approach, the report concluded, "The ICRC remains convinced that a total ban on mines is the only effective means of containing the current global disaster."[44]

On January 26, Bobby Muller and Stephen Goose, along with Caleb Rossiter of the Project on Demilitarization and Democracy and Tom Cardamone of the Council for a Livable World, were debriefed on the results of the final experts' meeting by three members of the US delegation, Robert Sherman, Steve Solomon, and Joni Charme. The officials expressed optimism that the CCW would be extended to internal conflicts. While the experts were in agreement that all antipersonnel landmines should be detectable, they disagreed whether to specify how many grams of metal they had to contain or merely to stipulate that they be detectable by common means. Some states also objected to making antitank mines detectable, prompting concern by the ICBL that they might try to reclassify antipersonnel mines as antitank mines. The officials reported "a pretty good consensus" that use of nonself-destruct mines would be confined to minefields marked by fencing or other means that effectively excluded noncombatants. It appeared unlikely that the review conference would require all mines to self-destruct and self-deactivate. Instead, states would be allowed a choice of either self-destructing or self-deactivating mines with a phase-in period of 15 years to comply. There was disagreement on the time limit for self-destruction with the debate likely to range from 7 to 90 days. Proposals for the duration that mines could remain live before self-deactivation ranged from 30 to 365 days. They were not optimistic about gaining acceptance for a verification commission with a two-thirds majority needed to block a fact-finding investigation. A ban was not on the agenda. No one had even proposed language in the preamble calling for "eventual elimination of antipersonnel mines." Although the United States is telling other nations that it supports eventual elimination, "Sherman thinks this gets us in trouble and is counterproductive," the report notes. With others far from accepting the idea, "pressing for elimination can impair our ability to get near-term restrictions."[45]

The next day, NGOs learned from Michael Matheson they would be allowed to attend the review conference: "He said the Chinese finally softened after much pressure. According to Matheson, the rules will allow for NGOs to participate and speak in the plenary sessions and to participate in the committee sessions, unless a vote is taken to exclude them from individual sessions."[46]

Matheson's report proved premature. The review conference opened with the campaigners still on the outside looking in. "The Chinese," says Matheson, "were absolutely dead set against the NGOs having any part of anything. They didn't want the NGOs to be able to come to plenary sessions, let alone negotiating sessions. We did work out some kind of access for the NGOs, but not much—certainly not what they wanted." To compensate for their lack of access, Matheson says, "Every couple of days or after a major meeting, I would come out and assemble the major American NGOs and tell them what happened."[47] By then, the campaigners had found sympathetic government insiders willing to disclose what was happening in the conference, and much more. They were also preparing to take their opposition public.

GRAZING IN THE GRASSROOTS

In lobbying behind closed doors in Washington or Geneva, the campaigners concluded, they could exert greater leverage if they attracted more public attention and mobilized broader public support, especially in the United States. In June 1993, the ICBL's founders convened a diverse gathering of American NGOs in Boston for that purpose.[48] Reaching beyond arms control and disarmament groups, they drew in religious, humanitarian, peace, women's, veteran's, and other NGOs, including the American Friends Service Committee, the Church World Service, Lutheran World Relief, World Vision, CARE, the American Refugee Committee, Oxfam America, Bread for the World, the US Committee for Refugees, and the International Medical Corps. By March 1996 some 70 NGOs had affiliated with the US coalition; 2 years later, its ranks had swelled to 300.

Like the charter members of the ICBL, however, all but a handful were letterhead organizations with no mass base. The US Campaign to Ban Landmines was sparse at the grassroots—a mass movement in appearance only.

Nor was it much of an organization. It was not until March 1996, over 3 years after the founding of the ICBL, that the US campaign took on a semblance of structure, when American NGOs would form a steering committee to map overall strategy. The nine NGOs that volunteered for the job included three founding members of the ICBL, Human Rights Watch, Physicians for Human Rights, and Vietnam Veterans of America Foundation. A VVAF staff member, Mary Wareham, served as coordinator.[49]

Meanwhile, the ICBL was reaching out to NGOs abroad. When the ICBL convened its first international conference in London in May 1993, 70 people attended representing 40 NGOs. Attendance doubled at the second conference a year later, co-sponsored by UNICEF in Geneva. "The early and ongoing support from UNICEF was very important in increasing the credibility of the campaign," say Jody Williams and Stephen Goose of the ICBL.[50] By the 1994 conference the ICBL was not just aggregating NGOs into a global coalition. It was helping to organize national campaigns.

To extend the ICBL's reach into the mine-afflicted countries of the third world, the ICBL held its third conference in Phnom Penh, Cambodia in June 1995. It drew 450 participants from more than 40 countries. Six new national campaigns in third world countries were established at the conclave.

The conference host, the Cambodia Campaign to Ban Landmines, was typical of these national campaigns. A coalition of NGOs, few of them indigenous, founded in August 1994 with the help of the ICBL, it did not penetrate deep into the grassroots. That was understandable in Cambodia, where little else resembled the rest of the third world or other nations. Cambodians by the millions had perished in bombing by the United States in the early 1970s, a genocidal war on their own people waged by the Khmer Rouge from 1975 to 1979, an invasion by Vietnam to oust the Khmer Rouge in 1979, and an ensuing civil war that pitted Vietnam-backed forces of the government led by Hun Sen, himself a former officer in the Khmer Rouge, against an alliance of three resistance forces—the Khmer Rouge; Prince Sihanouk's United Front for a Independent, Neutral, Peaceful, and Cooperative Cambodia (FUNCINPEC); and the Khmer People's National Liberation Front under onetime prime minister Son Sann—which raged until a peace accord was signed in 1991, only to flare up again in 1993 and die down after 1996. Civil war was followed by a power struggle among Hun Sen and two rivals in the royal family, in which Hun Sen emerged victorious. Mines were a weapon of choice for all the warring parties, as one side, then another, would mount an offensive, seize territory and sow mines, then pull back. Torn apart by the conflict, the state collapsed. So did agricultural production in the mine-strewn countryside, leaving much of the populace dependent on handouts from abroad. From 1992 on, Cambodia was in UN receivership.

Like much else in Cambodian politics, its landmines campaign was the work of outsiders. In July 1994, an internationally funded local demining organization, Cambodia Mine Action Center, and the UN Special Rapporteur on Human Rights issued a statement to the press in Phnom Penh calling on the Hun Sen government to "declare a total and permanent ban on the import, stockpiling, and use of antipersonnel mines," including "the destruction of all existing stockpiles of mines." It also urged the UN secretary-general to "take a new and imaginative initiative" and "completely redraft the 1980 Convention." Within a month, the NGO Forum on Cambodia, together with indigenous and international NGOs, established the Cambodia Campaign to Ban Landmines and launched a nationwide petition drive at temples, schools, and marketplaces. By the time of the 1995 ICBL convention in Phnom Penh, it had collected 340,000 signatures, including King Sihanouk's.[51]

The ICBL encouraged petition drives in other countries as part of its strategy to drum up public activism in preparation for the opening of the review conference in Vienna on September 25, 1995. The activism was intended to complement its lobbying.

The ICBL was also evolving from a coalition into a network. Coalitions consist of groups that cooperate for a common purpose. A coalition typically has a hub-and-spokes structure, with a council or coordinating committee at the hub and high-level representatives from the affiliates conferring face-to-face or by telephone to coordinate activities. A network is more reciprocal and less hierarchical, with dense linkages, formal and informal, at all levels, not just at the top. It is a web, not a wheel.

At the review conference, the ICBL would establish itself as an authoritative source of information both for the delegates and for the news media. The ICBL had several advantages in lobbying, especially with the understaffed delegations from smaller states. It could draw on technical expertise from the International Committee of the Red Cross and other NGOs. It had up-to-date information from NGOs in countries around the world with whom it kept in touch by telephone, fax, and, in a few cases, e-mail. It had informants in sympathetic delegations willing to reveal what was going on inside the conference. The campaign could gather information in Vienna and circulate it more quickly to governments back home than could most diplomats.

Cooperation was not confined to sympathetic delegations. In France, a ban supporter, Xavier Emmanuelli, was named secretary of state for humanitarian affairs in 1995 and became a conduit for the campaigners. "Through this very privileged contact inside the government, the mass of information collected via the international campaign network was transmitted to the highest officials," wrote Philippe Chabasse of Handicap International. "NGOs were often the first to be informed of the evolution of the position of certain countries and obtained detailed information on personalities, locations, and meetings important to the decision-making process. This privilege allowed us to send timely letters and organize public events for maximum effect."[52]

Within the US government, campaigners found allies in unexpected places like the Pentagon. One was Tim Connolly, principal deputy assistant secretary of defense for special operations and low-intensity conflict. After serving in the special forces starting in 1979, including a 1-year tour of duty in Iraq and Kuwait, Connolly had worked on the 1992 Clinton campaign, scheduling Hillary Clinton's appearances. "The Pentagon thought Hillary had sent me," he chuckles. He attended the ICBL convention in Geneva in 1994. "I had heard about it," he says, "and at this point the building did not know enough about me to know they shouldn't have let me go, so I went over." He made his presence felt. "I agree with you, antipersonnel landmines suck, and here's what I think you need to do to reverse the policy," he told startled NGO representatives at a strategy session organized by the ICBL's Stephen Goose. "You need to buy a couple of shares of stock in every company that makes landmines, go to every stockholders' meeting, and hold up pictures...of maimed children and say, do we really want to continue this?" He also told the NGOs they were "correct in not getting sucked into the debate on whether you could, in fact, produce a self-destructing, self-neutralizing landmine—whether it was a technological standard that could be achieved."[53] Connolly impressed Goose. "He was freely dispensing his campaign advice and he was probably the most professional campaigner at the meeting." The "enthusiasm for a ban" from a Pentagon official, says Goose, "sure surprised a lot of the internationals."[54]

It was the start of open collaboration between a dissident defense official and the campaigners. "In fact, every time I saw Jody Williams from that moment on, within the first 5 minutes she would always say she didn't understand how I hadn't been fired yet," says Connolly. Not that he saw Williams often: "I primarily dealt with Goose," telling him "where we were on the CCW process." By 1996, he was also talking to "Bobby Muller and Tim Rieser on what we should be doing about public information and where the pressure points were."[55] Goose says, "It certainly opened up a clear channel of communication that we kept up over the years. He was an ally and we caught up with each other every so often, and when important things would happen, he would touch base." Connolly was not Goose's sole source inside the Pentagon. In the 1994–1996 period, he recalls, "I had three people from three different offices who were willing to talk to me in open fashion—besides people on the US delegation."[56] Goose would not identify them but did note that one was a military officer.

After Ambassador Madeleine Albright had invited Senator Leahy to introduce a resolution at the United Nations in the fall of 1994 calling for "eventual elimination," campaigners reached out to her. "It was very clear that once we started making these noises in New York, there was a place within the US government where they would have a sympathetic hearing," says Karl F. "Rick" Inderfurth. "So at that point I began getting calls from Bobby Muller, Jerry White, Jody Williams, Steve Goose, and others wanting to see me in New York and informing me of what they were doing."[57]

US delegates also passed information to the campaigners in the expectation that the ICBL would make use of it to lobby other delegations. A notable instance occurred just before the final session of the review conference when a US official, in the course of a briefing, shared a portion of a letter that ACDA Director John Holum had sent to China's deputy foreign minister, a US nonpaper turned over to China, and talking points for use with Chinese delegates, along with the identity of the Chinese delegate to lobby. Holum's letter cited a number of differences with China "of great importance to the United States." Stressing that "all landmines must be detectable," he insisted that they contain the equivalent of 8 or more grams of iron. He wanted that standard phased in quickly, within 5 years of the adoption of the revised convention, not 12 years as China wanted, but he offered a compromise: "all [China] needs to do by the end of the transition period is to convert those mines being made ready for use," not its entire stock of nonmetallic mines. Holum sought a "99.9 percent overall reliability requirement," not the 90 percent that Beijing favored on self-deactivation, but noted that China had the technology to meet that standard, "possibly by using smaller batteries."[58] "We tried that," says Stephen Goose, with no discernible results.[59] The official also provided the campaigners with the US talking points and a nonpaper for use with Russia and the name of a Russian official to contact.

When to cooperate with the US delegation was a contentious question within the ICBL. "The United States thought that if the NGOs with a ban agenda would have pushed some of these somewhat positive steps that were being proposed in CCW and worked on China and worked on Russia and worked on some of the other troublesome countries, that might have helped them along," says Goose, and "we would have ended up with a better amended protocol—not the ban that NGOs wanted, but a better amended protocol." Over the course of the experts' meetings, the ICBL cooperated on a selective basis. "Most of the things they wanted us to work on we rejected, that is, the smart mines versus dumb mines approach and buying into many of the technical fixes," says Goose. "The NGOs did have a small cluster of issues on which we did push. We did push for expansion of the convention, which did got through. We did push for verification provisions, which failed." Cooperation had its limits, however. "It wasn't our focus," he says. "We wanted to seize and maintain the high ground, and we didn't really think that we would have much influence on India and Pakistan."[60]

The ICBL drew the line at cooptation: "Mike Matheson and Hays Parks invited Jody and me to become part of the delegation. We had any number of NGOs that did that. NGOs from about a dozen countries were on the official delegations," says Goose, assuring the ICBL of plenty of informants inside. "Everybody was a little concerned about it but we relied on the judgments of individual NGOs whether this was a legitimate attempt to build bridges or whether someone was trying to coopt you and silence you." Whether or not to accept the US invitation was not a difficult call to make. "In the first or second experts' meeting," recalls Goose, "Mike and Hays said, we talked it over and if you guys want to join the delegation, you can and come in the room, but if you do it, you have to take US government positions, not just if you speak publicly, but if you have private discussions with other delegates."[61] That was a bridge the ICBL would not cross.

Cooperating with the US delegation eventually proved too trying for the ICBL. Before the start of the review conference, says Goose, "we made a long discussed decision to avoid the daily back-and-forth of what was happening inside the negotiations and instead to educate governments and to help win over international opinion for the necessity of a ban, concluding there was just no chance that what was going to emerge from here was going to make a significant difference." Adoption of an outsider strategy, with an emphasis on attention-getting ploys and grassroots protest, had been years in the making, much debated at meetings of ICBL leaders and at ICBL conclaves in Geneva in 1994 and in Cambodia in 1995. The Cambodia conference, says Goose, "had quite a few workshops about CCW strategy and brainstorming about the creative ways that we took over [the review conference] and had an impact on delegates through campaigning tools."[62]

At the same time that the ICBL adopted an outsider strategy, campaigners were seeking out allies at the CCW review conference. "The ICBL consciously tried to develop a group of like-minded governments with whom they could build some kind of trust," says Goose. "That grew out of campaign meetings during the September 1995 negotiations." The campaigners made little headway at first. "There were not many governments that we worked closely with until the third round of CCW negotiations in April and May. The now-famed partnership really wasn't forged until 1996"—and then largely at Canada's initiative.[63]

By engaging in *information politics*, using its network not only to exchange information but also to coordinate political action, the campaign was able to put more muscle into its advocacy. Its political activity took various forms: *symbolic politics*, staging events to dramatize the landmines issue and attract media attention; *leverage politics*, holding up states to moral scrutiny and shaming them into action; *accountability politics*, monitoring the behavior of governments to see that they live up to their own pretensions of principle or policy; *pressure politics*, mobilizing NGOs to activate legislators or party leaders and motivate them to influence their country's delegations at the negotiations; and *linkage politics*, using allies in one government to influence other governments.[64] Some of the campaign's political actions were local initiatives by affiliated NGOs; others were coordinated by the ICBL.

The information campaign was aimed as much at the news media and its own affiliates as at the conference delegates. The ICBL held regular press briefings in Vienna and circulated a biweekly newsletter, the *CCW News*. Intent on holding states accountable, the *CCW News* ran a column entitled "The Good, the Bad, and the Ugly" that drew attention to discrepancies between the public statements of governments and their not so public negotiating positions. The ICBL also invited delegates to explain their positions to the campaigners. Perhaps most important of all, it spread success stories, like big-name endorsements or countries that had moved from imposing export moratoria to backing a ban, which maintained morale and fueled activism among campaigners struggling around the globe.

Pro-ban campaigners used eye-catching displays to dramatize the landmine peril for the mass media covering Vienna. UNICEF, Pax Christi, and Save the Children Austria collected 6 tons of shoes, symbolizing the footwear that past and future landmine victims no longer needed, and piled them in front of the Austrian parliament. A photography exhibit displayed portraits of mine victims. Petition drives by affiliated groups gathered 1.7 million signatures in 53 nations calling for a ban. Landmine victims from Afghanistan, Cambodia, Mozambique, and the United States presented the petitions to Johan Molander, chair of the review conference, at a well-covered ceremony. When the conferees reconvened in Geneva in 1996, they had to file through a simulated minefield in the outer hall of the conference center. There was no avoiding the campaign outside the center either, where delegates found another massive pile of shoes, ban posters plastered on city buses, demonstrators demanding demining, and "ban mines" stickers wherever they turned.[65]

The media campaign reached well beyond the elite press to generate unprecedented coverage for an arms control negotiation. For the first time in its history, the International Committee of the Red Cross ran a large-scale advertising campaign with unpaid television spots and print ads to raise public consciousness of the landmines plague and the need for a ban.[66]

Even comic books were drawn into the media blitz. DC Comics produced *Death of Innocents: The Horror of Landmines*, in which Batman was enlisted in the ban campaign, and *Deadly Legacy*, a collaboration with UNICEF in which Superman soared beyond "truth, justice, and the American way" to spread mine awareness in Bosnia and other mine-afflicted countries. "We originally did that in New York at the suggestion of Tim Connolly. I sat down with Madeleine [Albright] and we called our friend, singer Judy Collins, who said she knew the president of DC Comics, Jenette Kahn," says Rick Inderfurth. It became a "joint enterprise" with Department of Defense funding. "Bobby Muller came up to advise. That got us connected with this broader community."[67] If Batman and Superman were not identifiable characters to children in remote war-torn regions where American television has yet to penetrate, the comic books still made a media splash.

The star of the show, Princess Diana, had yet to put in an appearance. When she did, not only would she draw media coverage around the world, but her presence would also put the landmines story in front of audiences that arms control had never before reached—from readers of supermarket tabloids to viewers of afternoon talk shows.

The US Campaign to Ban Landmines remained less visible than the ICBL. It was also sparser at the grassroots than in Washington. To succeed, it would have to depend on effectiveness at lobbying and the links it could forge in Congress and abroad.

EXPOSING THE SHORTCOMINGS OF REGULATION

The meeting of governmental experts had come out in favor of extending the landmines protocol to internal armed conflicts and to ban remotely delivered mines that were not self-deactivating. It took note of, but did not endorse, a moratorium on exports.[68] This was classic arms control.

These and other amendments to the 1980 mines protocol formed the core of a "chairman's rolling text" of the draft protocol circulated by John Molander, a Swedish diplomat who had chaired the group of governmental experts and was chosen to chair the CCW Review Conference when it opened on September 25, 1995. Intended to expedite negotiations, it contained language that had achieved consensus at the expert-level meetings, along with alternative formulations of wording that had not yet been agreed in brackets. Molander's rolling text was pockmarked with brackets.

The rolling text played into the two-track strategy of the campaigners and their allies by strengthening the limits on the use of landmines while underscoring the need for a global ban.

The spearheads of the landmines ban in Congress, Senator Leahy and Representative Evans, also took a two-track approach. In a letter to Secretary of State Warren Christopher, Secretary of Defense William Perry, and Arms Control and Disarmament Agency Director John Holum on April 11, 1995, they "strongly" urged the administration to support Sweden's proposal for a ban. "Failing that," they continued, it should agree to language in the protocol committing it to "the ultimate goal of a complete ban." They urged it "to seek the strongest possible limits on antipersonnel mines" at the review conference and to insist on having those limits apply in "all circumstances"—in internal armed conflicts. They listed five ways to strengthen those limits. First, they sought to preclude remote delivery of antipersonnel landmines by requiring that "all mines, including self-destruct mines which are as indiscriminate as other mines," be located "in marked and guarded minefields." That would have prohibited a number of landmines that the US Army wanted to protect. Second, they wanted no exception for "situations where direct enemy action makes it impossible to comply." Third, they wanted to require mines to self-destruct within 4 to 48 hours and, since "large numbers" of such mines "failed to self-destruct in the Persian Gulf War," to self-deactivate within 60 days. Fourth, they sought the "shortest possible phase-in time," not the 5 to 15 years under discussion, for self-destruct mines. Fifth, instead of the transparency measures then under consideration, which they deemed "grossly inadequate," they asked for "effective verification procedures and sanctions for non-ratification and non-compliance."[69] They forwarded a copy of their letter to Ambassador Molander, who thanked them for backing Sweden's ban proposal and, speaking personally, expressed pessimism about convincing China and the nonaligned states to accept verification.[70]

It took the administration over a month to reply to the Leahy–Evans letter. The reply came not from the addressees, but from Wendy Sherman, assistant secretary of state for legislative affairs, in effect, the department's lobbyist on Capitol Hill, who offered to have Michael Matheson brief them.

On June 15, Leahy and Evans, after recruiting 49 co-sponsors, introduced legislation to place a 1-year moratorium on the use of antipersonnel mines "except along internationally recognized borders or in demilitarized zones." The bill passed the Senate on August 4 by 67–27 as an amendment to the defense authorization bill for fiscal year 1996.

Passage came despite Republican capture of both houses of Congress in the 1994 elections, which had stripped Leahy of his committee chairmanship. It was made possible by bipartisan support, most significantly from the Senate majority leader and frontrunner for the Republican nomination for president in 1996, Robert Dole, an internationalist who stood up to rising pressures from the unilateralist wing of his party. Leahy then attached the identical amendment to the foreign operations bill, which was approved by both houses of Congress as part of a continuing resolution. President Clinton signed it into law on February 12, 1996.[71] It was the high point of Leahy's legislative efforts.

In the run-up to the review conference, Ambassador Albright also tried to give added impetus to a ban. "The CD process, while possibly helpful, was seen as certainly not a solution," says Rick Inderfurth, who accepted the main premise of the ban campaign: "To regulate the use of landmines was missing the point. The point was that until they were banned by all countries, large and small, users and nonusers, you were not going to make it clear that—smart and dumb—this was a weapon of war that the international community is not going to tolerate any longer. The normative point is essential."[72]

Inderfurth drafted a letter from Albright to National Security Adviser Anthony Lake, urging introduction of a resolution in the UN General Assembly, "Rather than merely reaffirming commitments, we should replace last year's call for the eventual elimination with a new goal, namely, the elimination as soon as possible." The resolution would have undercut the US negotiating position in CCW and aided campaigners' effort to shame governments into banning landmines. It did not secure approval. "Rick Inderfurth, when he was at the UN, did propose some kind of an APL ban," says Robert Sherman, "but when he came down to Washington, we had an interagency meeting and everyone else was against it."[73] By this time, says Inderfurth, "the military began clearly to dig in its heels, saying we can't go down that road."[74]

Others were moving to settle for less than a ban. In preparation for the review conference, the International Committee of the Red Cross circulated a nonpaper commenting on the rolling text. "While firmly believing that a total ban is the only effective solution," the ICRC noted, "it is recognized that agreement on this may not yet be possible at the forthcoming review conference. Therefore, we are submitting this document in order to give an indication of which alternative proposals within the present rolling text are considered preferable."[75]

The ICRC commended the government experts for applying the landmines protocol to internal armed conflicts, but objected to weakening the obligation by exempting "situations of internal disturbances and tensions, such as riots, isolated and sporadic acts of violence and other acts of a similar nature" and by reaffirming that "nothing in this protocol shall be invoked for the purpose of affecting the sovereignty of a State or the responsibility of the government, by all legitimate means, to maintain or reestablish law and order in the state or to defend the national unity and territorial integrity of the state." It also objected to having antivehicle mines exempted from the requirement that landmines be detectable.[76]

The ICRC argued in favor of prohibiting not only the use, but also the manufacture, stockpiling, and transfer of dumb mines. "As long as dumb mines continue to be available," it said, "they will inevitably be used by armed groups that do not conform to the rules" prohibiting their use. Although it was willing to allow self-destruct mines, it expressed concern about "their reliability" unless they were "checked by a central body" and equipped so that they "inevitably self-deactivate in a short period of time." It insisted on "compulsory control" of their reliability and "as short as possible" a "grace period" for replacing dumb mines with self-destructing ones.[77]

The provision on mine clearing "may well be the most important achievement of the review conference," the ICRC contended, but it wanted demining to commence "without delay after the cessation of active hostilities," not after "the meaningful withdrawal of forces from the combat zone," lest the removal of mines be delayed by disagreements over withdrawal. To ensure that landmines would be detectable, the ICRC wanted them to contain enough metal to distinguish them from the spent cartridges and other fragments that littered most battlefields. It also wanted to prohibit mines designed to be detonated by standard mine-detecting devices used in mine clearing.[78]

Finally, the ICRC backed several proposed provisions to verify the protocol and to redress and sanction violations. These would require states to enact national legislation implementing the protocol and to report on compliance, make states responsible for all acts committed by their armed forces personnel and liable for compensation, establish a permanent commission to investigate complaints of noncompliance and conduct fact-finding missions, and have cases of noncompliance referred to the Security Council for further action.

Taken together, the ICRC recommendations highlighted just how far toward a ban the review conference would need to go to make up for the shortcomings of the experts' deliberations. Getting states to go the distance would require the NGOs to go public.

CIRCUMVENTING THE ARMS CONTROL IMPASSE

The CCW review conference, as expected, made little progress toward a ban. It was confirmation to the ICBL that arms control was going nowhere. In keeping with their two-track strategy, campaigners condemned the result as a retreat. Instead of playing an inside game of lobbying delegates to improve the CCW protocol, the campaigners adopted an outside strategy emphasizing the use of symbolic politics and leverage politics to press for a ban.

The campaign to shame states into seeking a ban and hold them accountable went into high gear in Vienna. The aim was not to convert delegates who opposed a ban, but to stop sympathetic states from throwing in the towel. "The ICBL," say strategists Jody Williams and Stephen Goose, "worked to convince the media and friendly governments that not only were the negotiations *not* moving towards a ban, but they were, in fact, weakening the already horribly weak CCW landmine protocol." The ICBL "put tremendous pressure on governments extremely wary of 'bad press' on the issue."[79]

With predictable results: it made states do more, but still stop short of a ban. On September 26, for instance, France had announced a moratorium on production of antipersonnel landmines and plans to reduce its stocks of mines. That garnered favorable publicity but fell well short of a comprehensive ban.

With even "friendly" governments reluctant to appear to yield for the sake of consensus, negotiations deadlocked, and the conferees agreed to hold another round of talks in Geneva in January 1996. That round, too, was abruptly suspended after only a week. "It wasn't intended to happen that way," says Michael Matheson. "I just could not get the Russians anywhere close to agreeing, so basically I pulled the plug on the conference." He convinced Molander to suspend the proceedings and reschedule a 2-week session in late April, allowing time for "a lot of work in capitals."[80]

"The Russians took an awful lot of work," says Matheson. The political winds were mercurial in Moscow as conflicts intensified between the communists in the Duma and pro-Western circles around Yeltsin, making coordination of entrenched bureaucracies all but impossible. Washington, with its impassioned partisanship and bureaucratic in-fighting, was a model of coherence by comparison. "We went to Moscow twice and it was really a circus scene," he recalls. "We would be across the table from this huge variety of people," each representing their own views as their government's. Matheson's ploy caught the attention of those close to Yeltsin. "The Russians were a bit shocked by the fact that we stopped the conference and quietly blamed it on them. I think it was a very useful reality check because politically they didn't wish to be the reason for failure. To their credit, they did take an entirely new look at the problem and came around to the view that we were right, these were militarily acceptable provisions."[81]

In the end, Russia's larger interest of working together with the United States prevailed over its narrower military interests. "For the Russians," says Matheson, "this was no small potatoes because they had so many nonconforming mines and they used them so extensively—not only their fixed minefields on the Chinese border, but also in Chechnya—so they were in a position of having to give up very large amounts of their inventory and acquire new devices." In a cash-strapped government it would not be easy for the armed forces to acquire new self-destructing self-deactivating mines. He recalls a moment during the first session when he was summoned to an anteroom outside the main conference room and "some colonel-general came in to tell us where to get off." The Russian officer was beefy, "300 pounds and no neck," says Matheson, who recalls telling him, "Look, general, we wouldn't do this if we thought it was inconsistent with our military interests. Why don't you talk to my colonel who can tell you how wonderful these things are and how they are consistent with advanced Western military doctrine." Reasoning with the Russians "may have had some educational effect," he says, but what brought them around was being placed "in a politically undesirable position." They wanted "to be seen as a responsible co-power with the United States."[82]

That approach did not work with the Chinese, says Matheson, who "did not have any desire to be partners of the United States." Efforts to get China to acquiesce to the US-proposed provisions were buffeted by "the ups and downs of the US–China relationship, and we never were able to get ourselves invited to Beijing." The Chinese were eventually persuaded to go along with strengthened regulation on technical grounds. "Their inventory of landmines met the requirements but they didn't believe this up to the very end," Matheson recounts. "We made special arrangements to have their devices tested by the Austrians and it turned out, thank god, that their devices passed the test."[83]

Extension of the CCW to internal conflicts and verification were concerns for India and Pakistan, not the regulation of use, because "they realized it was consistent with what they were doing," notes Matheson. "The saving grace for all of these powers was the possibility of having fixed long-term minefields as long as you mark them." The regulation of use was consistent with the military requirements of most nations. That was classic arms control.

On April 13, 1996, just before the start of the final round, seven campaigners were invited to a briefing with Matheson, who told them that China and Russia had made additional concessions, citing China's acceptance of the requirement that all mines be detectable. That development did not impress Stephen Goose, who e-mailed his ICBL colleagues, "It seemed clear to me that the priority now is getting agreement on a protocol, almost any protocol, and that states are ready to cut deals to get it done. I found it very telling that Matheson mentioned, sort of off-handedly, that China's insistence on a 90 percent reliability rate on self-destruct, instead of 95 percent, 'was likely to prevail.'" Confirming earlier suspicions in the ICBL, the United States had settled a moratorium in lieu of a ban. Matheson, in Goose's view, was "putting a somewhat new spin on the importance of a revised protocol, saying that the key thing would be an immediate prohibition on the transfer of non-detectable mines." Goose found "the emphasis on the transfer provision ironic" given earlier US opposition to it and the fact that most nations had since adopted more comprehensive moratoria of their own unilaterally than the limited regulation to be incorporated into the CCW.[84]

Despite differences with US diplomats over a ban, the campaigners did aid and abet Matheson's attempts to line up allied support for the US proposals. "Fortunately, at the same time, there was political momentum developing behind concern about antipersonnel weapons," says Matheson, "and their militaries came to the perception that our military had, which was you can't fight something with nothing. It's much better to have something that has humanitarian value and can be seen to have humanitarian value as an antidote to a total prohibition." It helped with Russia "both to have some influence politically in Moscow and to be able to say credibly to the Russian military, look, which game do you want to play?" The campaign was of less consequence in the other countries central to his CCW strategy. "The Chinese didn't care. I don't think the NGOs had very much influence on the Indians and Paks, but some Indians were politically sensitive. The Indian ambassador didn't want to be criticized for having obstructed the conference. She was very worked up about that."[85]

While US negotiators were trying to convince countries to accept more restraints on landmines, the US armed forces began chafing at the bit. They wanted to relax the restrictions on the transfer or sale of antipersonnel landmines imposed by Leahy's moratorium legislation. On January 26, 1996, the NSC staff informed the president that "the interagency agreed option goes too far in loosening transfer restrictions." Aware of Clinton's concern that US landmine policy was "too weak," NSC favored revising the 1994 policy to

allow limited transfer of long-lived antipersonnel landmines to other countries on two conditions, that they are parties to the CCW and they join in
the Landmine Control Regime. JCS opposed NSC. It wanted the president to
allow transfers without attaching those conditions.[86]

On March 20, JCS won presidential approval for an exception to the ban
on transfers, but on NSC's conditions. The president also approved the distinction between dumb and smart mines to be proposed in CCW negotiations.
Dumb mines would be permitted but only in marked minefields, not in well-
traveled areas, with the exception of Korea. He also accepted a transition from
dumb to smart mines "if JCS can't develop substitutes in 3 years," according
to an NSC official. Again, Korea was an exception. The official recalls "some
discussion" about "whether to make all the Korean ones smart, but we ended
up never getting them [JCS] on board because of the cost."[87]

When the review conference resumed on April 22, 1996, the outsiders
were let in, albeit briefly. Jody Williams, coordinator of the ICBL, was invited
to address the delegates. The campaign, she told them, "is a voice for those who
all too frequently are not considered when negotiations deal with weapons—
and those are the victims, present and future, of antipersonnel landmines."
She again took a two-track approach. Noting that 29 states had now joined
the ICBL in calling for a ban, she acknowledged that, "had it not been for the
focus of attention on landmines provided by the [review] process, perhaps we
would not have had the dramatic movement that we have seen in such a short
time. And yet, while we recognize the tremendous value of the process, we are
discouraged that the likely changes to the CCW are not more far-reaching and
immediate. And we must ask: how many more people will fall victim before
the international community bans antipersonnel mines?"[88]

What especially exercised the ICBL was the change in the definition of
antipersonnel landmine to "a mine *primarily* designed to be exploded by the
presence, proximity or contact of a person." The word "primarily" was ostensibly intended to exempt antivehicle mines, including those equipped with antihandling devices, and a variety of munitions—some 35 in all, according to a
Pentagon study, including cluster bombs and bomblets for destroying airfields.
The ICBL opposed that exemption because it would cover "hybrid mines,"
antitank mines that were equipped with antihandling devices designed to keep
people from defusing them, as well as directional fragmentation (Claymore)
mines detonated by tripwire and "mixed munition systems," antipersonnel
mines deployed together with antivehicle mines. Antitank mines, argued
Stephen Goose of ICBL, "pose a very similar danger to the population as do
antipersonnel mines. They are the functional equivalent of APLs."[89] It was
"the mother of all loopholes," said Celina Tuttle of Mines Action Canada in an
April 26 e-mail to other NGOs calling for "urgent action" to seek its removal.

To no avail. The revisions of the CCW adopted by the review conference defined landmine to exempt dual-use mines. It required all mines to be detectable, but allowed countries 9 years, not 5, to replace their undetectable mines. It allowed a similar phase-in period for the replacement of dumb antipersonnel mines by smart ones that self-destructed and self-deactivated. It did not prohibit antihandling devices on mines. It did not limit the placement of remotely-delivered mines to allow their location to be recorded. It did not impose any new regulations on antitank mines. Above all, the revisions did not preclude mines from being produced, transferred, or used.[90]

Yet the review conference did make progress on arms control. It extended the landmines protocol to internal armed conflicts; it required that antipersonnel mines be emplaced within marked and protected minefields or else be equipped with self-destruct and self-deactivation devices reliable enough to ensure that no more than 1 in 1,000 could still function 120 days after emplacement; it prohibited the transfer of mines that did not meet these specifications; it required minelaying parties to record the location of all mines, not just those in preplanned minefields, and held them responsible for mineclearing; it added a provision for enforcement in the event of serious violations; and it accorded protection to Red Cross and other humanitarian workers. All these provisions had the backing of the United States.[91]

In a statement at the conclusion of the review conference, Matheson accentuated the positive, citing these accomplishments and calling the revised version "a very significant improvement over the current protocol" and "an important first step toward the goal of the eventual elimination of antipersonnel mines altogether." The revision, he said, "will, if widely observed, result in a substantial decrease in civilian casualties." Yet, he acknowledged, it "did not include all the improvements sought by the United States." He cited the absence of any mechanism to investigate noncompliance, inadequate restrictions on antitank mines that pose special risks to noncombatants and mine-clearing personnel, and an excessive 9-year grace period for countries to comply with some provisions.[92] Deputy US negotiator Sherman remains proud of the result: "CCW was a huge humanitarian benefit and the United States could take full credit for it." His main disappointment was that "Clinton never gave a speech on it."[93]

Consistent with their two-track approach, the campaigners highlighted the shortcomings of the regulatory approach. In its closing statement, the International Committee of the Red Cross condemned the results as "woefully inadequate." It concluded, "The ICRC is convinced that the 'public conscience' of people throughout the world is revolted both by the indiscriminate nature of antipersonnel mines and by the horrific suffering they have caused. The question now before us is whether there is sufficient political will to establish an absolute prohibition on these weapons and to ensure respect for such a norm."[94]

"The review process," the ICBL declared, "has been degraded to such a level that it actually encourages the production and use of a new generation of landmine"—in "cynical disregard of the humanitarian principles which are central to international laws for the conduct of war." The ICBL's bill of particulars included the loophole created by the definition of landmine that allowed mines "made, or claimed to be made, with a dual purpose to fall outside control provisions" and the failure to regulate antitank landmines fitted with antihandling devices or "booby-trapped in such a way as to make them de facto antipersonnel mines." The revised protocol "further legitimizes the use of remotely delivered (scatterable) landmines and encourages the use, design, and production of so-called smart mines." It called for such mines to be banned. The ICBL also objected to the lack of effective arrangements for verification and enforcement. Key provisions, it concluded, may not take effect for a decade or more. In the meantime, "another 260,000 people will fall victim to landmines. How many more will it take before a universal ban is reached?"[95]

Echoing the ICBL, Senator Leahy was similarly downbeat, calling the revised protocol "a deplorable failure to deal effectively with this humanitarian crisis. Rather than move us towards ridding the world of antipersonnel mines, it encourages the production and use of a new generation of this indiscriminate weapon." Seeing the need for "forceful US leadership," he called on President Clinton to "renounce these inhumane weapons."

A study by the Institute for Defense Analyses also suggested the limits of arms control. Because landmines were so inexpensive to produce and use, it reasoned, arms control agreements would have to impose "significant" costs for evasion and concealment of production and transfer and punitive sanctions for violators "to effect a large reduction of landmine use." The CCW protocol did neither. "What the present analysis *does* show is that *only* by assuming that stigmatization will work can one conclude that landmine arms control is likely to have a decisive effect on landmine use." The study gave little comfort to ban proponents in this regard, however. Because of limited experience with treaties stigmatizing a weapon system—the Chemical Weapons Convention was just entering into force and compliance provisions of the Biological Weapons Convention were not comparable—the IDA concluded that "no analysis has yet been provided to show that confidence in stigmatization is warranted as more than an unproven assumption."[96]

The arms control approach supported by the United States and all the other major powers had carried the day, but the two-track strategy of the campaigners gained ground: by the close of the review conference, 34 states were in favor of a landmines ban, up from 14 at its start, 7 months earlier.[97] Behind the scenes, other states were reassessing their positions as well. One was Germany. In March 1996, says Robert Sherman, the German diplomat covering the issue in Washington mistakenly "reported to Bonn" that the United States would soon change policy and accept "a total APL ban," and the German government decided, "if this is where the train is going, let's get out in front of it. So it did, and that gave the APL ban mainstream support and put pressure on France and the UK to do the same. If there was a point at which the Ottawa Convention reached critical mass, it was probably the German decision."[98]

The NGOs had a similar impression. "Quite a few people were convinced that the movement by certain countries in late 1995 and early 1996 all happened in anticipation that the United States was going to do it," says campaigner Stephen Goose. "Germany, Canada, and France had all seen the same signals that we had seen and were trying to beat the United States to the punch."[99] Even more dramatically, some states were openly allying with the ICBL.

To shore up support in Vienna, the ICBL had begun caucusing with "friendly" governments and international agencies. By the last day of the third session, the collaboration was flourishing. One sign was a press conference held by the ICBL, Canada, UNICEF, and the UN Department of Humanitarian Affairs to call for a ban. A more far-reaching form of collaboration emerged from the caucus, recall Jody Williams and Stephen Goose. Ban campaigners began considering how to get "avowedly pro-ban governments" to "work together as a bloc to move beyond the CCW impasse." One idea borrowed from nuclear arms control was to establish regional "mine-free zones" as "building blocks to a global ban."[100]

Canada had a better idea: Why not turn the caucus into an international conference and invite the NGOs to participate? It was the origin of the Ottawa process, which would move beyond arms control to disarmament.

5

Canada Takes Charge

The end product of party politics is inevitably different from that of pressure politics.

E.E. Schattschneider[1]

The landmines file is a loser at home and abroad, or so Mark Gwozdecky was warned in August 1995 when he took over as deputy director of non-proliferation, arms control, and disarmament in Canada's Department of Foreign Affairs and International Trade. "Nobody here is interested in this file, and nobody else in the world will let it go anywhere," his predecessor told Gwozdecky in bequeathing the portfolio.[2] It may have sounded like the voice of experience, but it was not good advice.

Instead of going nowhere, Canada went from deploying and exporting landmines in 1995 to spearheading negotiations for a global ban by 1997. What catapulted Canada into the lead on landmines, in direct opposition to the United States, long its NATO ally?

Part of the answer is to be found in Canadian politics, where taking a moral stance can help a politician stand out in a crowd. So does a display of independence from the United States, especially in the Liberal Party, which came to power with a solid majority on October 25, 1993. "It never hurts at election time," affirmed an aide to Prime Minister Jean Chretien in 1997, "for us to be at odds with Washington over something."[3]

Another part of the answer lies in the transformation of Canada's military role from staunch ally manning the front lines in the Cold War to international peacekeeper. In the 1950s the DEW line of defense early warning radars transected Canada, ready to alert the United States if Soviet bombers were approaching American air space, and Canadians fought alongside GIs in Korea. It was there that they had last used landmines in war. Yet peacekeeping had been Canada's main military mission ever since 1957, when Foreign Minister Lester Pearson was awarded the Nobel Prize for his part in promoting the idea. Peacekeeping had become the sole reason for deploying troops overseas after the demise of the Soviet Union. Canadians served on almost every peacekeeping mission authorized by the UN Security Council—over 30 in all—often honorably, like General Romeo Dallaire's mission in Rwanda, sometimes not, like General Lewis McKenzie's in Bosnia.

By 1995 Canada's armed forces were a fraction of their cold war size: active duty personnel totaled 70,000, down from 87,000 in 1990.[4] Just 2.5 citizens out of every 1,000 were serving in the armed forces, compared to 6.2 in the United States, 5.8 in Sweden, and 4.0 in the United Kingdom.[5] Some 2,800 Canadians were engaged in peacekeeping, a far greater proportion than the United States, if the disparity in population is taken into account. One of the peacekeepers' duties was humanitarian demining. "Close to 8,000 Canadian soldiers have risked their lives clearing mines in such countries as Kuwait, Afghanistan, and Nicaragua," Canada's ambassador for disarmament noted in October 1994. "Five Canadians have been killed or injured."[6]

With NATO no longer on guard against a Soviet threat to invade Western Europe and no borders to secure against attack, Canada's armed forces planned for the use of landmines primarily to protect its peacekeepers. Deployed in small units from the Balkans to Kuwait, peacekeepers might use landmines to secure the perimeter of their base camps. Not that landmines were much of a requirement for Canada's troops—far from it—mine clearing took priority over mine laying. Nor did Canada's defense industry have any equity in landmines. Arms exports totaled US$625 million in 1995, none of it landmines. Mine production had ended in 1992.

A third part of the answer lies in Canada's approach to the world. In contrast to the United States, which had both the inclination and the power to act unilaterally, Canada was wedded to multilateralism. Moreover, Canada had long been less adversarial and more cooperative than the United States in its approach to other countries, deemphasizing the threat of armed force in favor of other, arguably more effective instruments of foreign policy. By 1995 Canada's defense budget was down to US$7.2 billion; its foreign aid budget was US$2.4 billion. The figures for the United States were $279 billion and $12.3 billion. Only Spain and Luxembourg among NATO allies spent a smaller percentage of GDP on defense than did Canada at 1.6 percent but foreign aid was 0.41 percent of Canada's GDP (comparable percentages for the United States were 3.6 and 0.12).[7] During the 1993 campaign, the victorious Liberal Party had pledged to cut the defense budget and redirect more spending to sustainable development.

Development assistance was the responsibility of Canada's foreign minister, and the incumbent, André Ouellet, took that responsibility seriously. Some of Canada's aid went to demining. To Ouellet that seemed a waste of money when ever more mines were being sowed. Canada's landmines campaign had yet to move public opinion much, but Ouellet, aware that rank-and-file Liberals preferred to spend less on defense and more on development and anticipating that a landmines ban could become as popular as motherhood, knew a good issue when he saw one. In Summer 1995, at the urging of his senior policy adviser, Michael Pearson, Ouellet began pressing Defense Minister David Collenette to get rid of Canada's stock of landmines and change its landmines policy.

To career defense officials, that policy was carved in stone, and Collenette was not one to challenge civil servants. Collenette countered with his department's standard contention that it could not destroy its landmines until it had "effective and humane alternatives."[8] The Defense Department's stance was driven by the close relationship that Canada's armed forces had long had with their US counterparts. Their budget and their political prestige rested on remaining a loyal NATO ally. Even though Canada had parted company with the United States on occasion, most recently over the Reagan administration's enthusiasm for missile defense and disdain for arms control, Canada's role in NATO was often to act as a check on US unilateralism and a broker of compromises rather than an open dissenter, like France.

Foreign Minister Ouellet saw his opening in September 1995, when, at Senator Patrick Leahy's urging, the United States asked Canada to co-sponsor a resolution it was about to introduce in the UN General Assembly calling for a moratorium of landmines exports. By coincidence, UN officials had inadvertently included Canada on a list of states observing an export moratorium, and Ouellet argued that instead of drawing attention to the mistake, Ottawa should rectify it by adopting a moratorium. Warned by defense officials that this was just a ploy by arms controllers in the Department of Foreign Affairs and International Trade to wrest control of landmines policy from him, Defense Minister Collenette refused to play along.[9] A frustrated Ouellet determined to act on his own.

Canada's diplomats, unaware of their minister's attitude and accustomed to deferring to the military's aversion to challenging the Pentagon, were not spoiling for a fight. So when Mark Gwozdecky was promoted and turned over the landmines file to his successor Robert Lawson in October 1995, it was understandable that he passed along his predecessor's advice: a ban, however desirable, was not in the cards. Gwozdecky underestimated his minister.

On November 9, announcing the start of a review of landmines policy, Ouellet told an interviewer from Canadian Broadcasting Corporation that landmines "should be banned not only in Canada but everywhere in the world." A surprised Lawson soon got a call from a CBC reporter asking for his comment on the minister's remarks. Ducking the question, Lawson asked for a transcript and took it to Gwozdecky and Jill Sinclair, director of the division of nonproliferation, arms control, and disarmament. "You won't believe what just happened," he told them.[10] The news "secretly delighted" his colleagues. "Okay," Sinclair said, "we've got some direction from our minister on this one so let's go for it."[11]

Lawson promptly faxed the transcript to Mines Action Canada, of the fledgling coalition of ban campaigners in the country. He followed up the fax by telephone. Coordinator Celina Tuttle lost no time making common cause with officials, e-mailing fellow campaigners to stimulate a burst of congratulatory letters to Foreign Minister Ouellet. "That was the beauty of e-mail," says Tuttle. "Within hours people were patting him on the back."[12]

CANADA'S CAMPAIGNERS

At first, few of Canada's NGOs heeded the ICBL call for a landmines ban. Celina Tuttle of Physicians for Global Survival, the only Canadian to attend the second international conference of the ICBL, took the lead in 1993 with a letter-writing campaign. She was subsequently joined by other NGOs and churches working on development, social justice, health, peace, disarmament, and the disabled. By fall of 1994, some 20 NGOs came together to form a loose coalition, Mines Action Canada, and set objectives. Its formal founding came in March 1995, when the NGOs established a steering committee of six, chose Warmington to chair it, and appointed Tuttle coordinator.[13]

Mines Action Canada, like its US counterpart, was a coalition of mostly letterhead organizations without much of a mass base. Many had been working on third world development. Under Conservative rule, when development assistance had fallen into disfavor and the government had reduced spending for development education to zero, the NGOs had to scratch for funding. Even so, founding Mines Action Canada was a roll of the dice. Waging a campaign for a landmines ban meant a change of mission from development to disarmament, which had still less resonance with the Canadian public—even in 1983 at the peak of fervor over deployment of missiles in Europe and Ronald Reagan's Star Wars speech. For the NGOs to press for a ban was a high-risk strategy, recall the organizers of Mines Action Canada, Valerie Warmington and Celina Tuttle, which "could lead them to exceed the proportion of funds legally allowed to be devoted to lobbying government," and in turn "jeopardize an organization's charitable status" under Canada's tax laws. "In the past this constraint had steered some NGOs away from direct involvement in disarmament issues, despite the obvious links between disarmament and development and humanitarian issues."[14] Yet advocacy on landmines had two things in its favor compared to third world development, according to a campaign organizer, "It was black and white and something could be done about it."[15]

NGOs were already pressing the new Liberal government to live up to its campaign pledge and make sustainable development and social justice, not armed force, the touchstones of Canada's foreign policy. They also wanted to democratize foreign policy making by giving NGOs a meaningful role in the process. The new government conceded the need for a "more consultative foreign policy process" and began meeting regularly with NGOs to update them on landmines policy.[16] The campaigners took advantage of the encounters to impress upon officials the humanitarian toll of widespread mine use.

Jill Sinclair, director of the nonproliferation, arms control, and disarmament division, convened one such meeting on February 22, 1995. Jon Allen, deputy director of the legal operations division, briefed the NGOs on the results of the fourth session of governmental experts and Canada's preparations for the Review Conference. Allen emphasized Canada's desire for intrusive verification, but noted that nonaligned states remained opposed, "There may be some kind of verification, but not the kind we like." Parting company with the United States, which wanted a ban on exports negotiated outside CCW, Canada would press the review conference to ban the transfer of mines to nonsignatories of the CCW, violators of the CCW, and nonstate actors.

Not all that the officials said at the session was as sure to please the NGOs, however. When NGOs questioned whether smart mines were an improvement over dumb mines in humanitarian terms, the officials defended the difference. The requirement for self-destruct, self-neutralizing mechanisms, Lieutenant Colonel Ernie Fafard of the military engineering directorate in the Department of National Defense acknowledged, "did not come about for humanitarian reasons but for military reasons and has nice spinoffs" for CCW. Allen addressed the "balance of military gain and humanitarian impact, as much as one wants to buy that argument," by saying that "given military and government budgets, the best thing is to tighten restrictions" and "broaden the scope" of the landmines convention. Based on these comments, Celina Tuttle faxed a copy of her notes to Jody Williams of the ICBL, along with her conclusion, "It is clear the impact of mines on the basic rights of civilians has not been the basis of discussions for amending the convention and that the military are directing these discussions."[17]

Mines Action Canada was determined to right this imbalance. Its thrust was partly bureaucratic: within the Department of Foreign Affairs and International Trade, the nonproliferation, arms control, and disarmament division had the lead in landmines negotiations while the human security division was responsible for demining and other humanitarian matters. Objecting to the fact that the Department of National Defense was represented on Canada's delegation to CCW negotiations while the human security division was not, Mines Action Canada insisted that an official experienced in humanitarian affairs be added to the delegation. The NGOs also argued that if Canada was unwilling to back a ban, it would bear responsibility for the consequences. Their advocacy was underscored by news reports that Iraq had used landmines in its repression of the Kurds and that Canadian-made antipersonnel mines had been found in Iraqi stockpiles after the Gulf War.[18]

Mines Action Canada did more than make private appeals to officials. Starting in the summer of 1995, it launched a media campaign to publicize the plight of mine victims and a petition drive to endorse a ban. Following the lead of the International Committee of the Red Cross, it made a public case for outlawing antipersonnel mines on grounds that their use was inconsistent with international humanitarian law and that proposed revisions of the CCW were inadequate. "Images of seriously injured children, women, and men were used to underline the reality of the risk to civilians and the merits of NGO arguments for a ban," say Warmington and Tuttle. "Stories accompanying these images described what the person was doing at the time of his or her accident," featuring "innocent day-to-day activities like playing, planting food, collecting water, and walking to work or school."[19] Canadian musician Bruce Cockburn toured the country with Mozambican singer Chude Mondlane in support of the petition drive. Editorials favoring a ban began cropping up in the press. The campaign soon registered with the public. By the spring of 1996 the petition drive would gather some 50,000 signatures and a Gallup poll would find 73 percent of Canadians in favor of an international agreement to ban the use of landmines with only 8 percent opposed.[20]

The NGOs also tried to sway politicians directly. They sent information packets to the constituency offices of every member of parliament and later arranged for a Liberal MP, Jane Stewart, to visit Cambodia for a firsthand look at that mine-afflicted country. Keith Martin and other opposition MPs raised questions about the government's landmine policy in the House of Commons.

No MP could do what Senator Leahy had done for landmines, however. Unlike Congress, where members try to make a name for themselves by becoming identified with an issue, party lines are firmly drawn in Canada's parliament and members transgress them at their peril. "If you play by the parliamentary rules of the game, you don't get anywhere," says one MP. "In parliament, your objective is not to solve problems, but to destroy the other side." MPs can play a constructive role only if "public pressure is persistent, consistent, in-your-face, and in the media."[21] In time, the popularity of a land-mines ban, especially if the United States opposed it, and sustained activism by pro-ban campaigners would exert that effect, but not before one canny politician in the government had grabbed the issue and run with it.

The campaigners' initial encounters with officials, recall Warmington and Tuttle, were "often mutually frustrating" as "entrenched positions were repeated to no discernible positive effect." The government's response to their call for a ban was "highly defensive."[22] The November 1995 fax and phone call from Robert Lawson was just one sign that at least some officials were now ready to go on offense.

MOVING THE GOALPOSTS

Events soon confirmed the premonition of defense officials that their turf could become a slippery slope. Ouellet's outburst had an immediate effect. On November 12 he received a letter from Defense Minister Collenette accepting an export moratorium. In return, foreign affairs officials agreed not to seek any further change in policy. Behind the scenes, however, a ban sympathizer in the Department of Foreign Affairs and International Trade apprised Mines Action Canada of differences it had with the Department of National Defense. Campaigners, in turn, inspired reporters to look into the interagency dispute, which put the DND on the defensive.[23]

No sooner had the DND agreed to a moratorium on exports than the dis-armament division advised Foreign Minister Ouellet to press his advantage and extend the moratorium to production and use of antipersonnel landmines. The DND had to "acquiesce," sourly accusing the diplomats of "movement of the goalposts."[24] On January 17, 1996, just before the second session of the review conference was due to open in Geneva, Foreign Minister Ouellet and Defense Minister Collenette announced a unilateral halt to the export, pro-duction, and use of antipersonnel landmines by Canada and backing for a ban. "With these moratoriums in place," said Ouellet, "Canada moves to the forefront of countries seeking a global ban on these weapons." Not to be out-done, Collenette declared, "Antipersonnel landmines sown at random with no regard for the laws of war have become a scourge of humanity. Canada has not been part of the problem, but we will certainly be part of the solution."[25]

Ouellet retired a few days later. In contrast to Ouellet, a political pro who was astute enough to get on the popular side of an emerging issue, his succes-sor, Lloyd Axworthy, was looking for a good cause. Axworthy, wrote Canadian political scientist Brian Tomlin, "saw politics as a way to advance policy goals."[26] One of Axworthy's first official acts was to solicit recommendations on foreign policy priorities. Disarmament officials identified two such priorities: small arms and antipersonnel mines. On the advice of Michael Pearson, senior policy adviser to the foreign minister and a holdover from Ouellet, Axworthy chose landmines. He backed efforts by the nonproliferation, arms control, and disarmament division to turn the moratorium into a permanent ban and destroy Canada's stocks of mines. That met with determined resistance from defense officials who were feeling "nickeled and dimed."[27]

THE ORIGINS OF THE OTTAWA PROCESS

With Axworthy's encouragement, the division undertook two initiatives in March 1996 that prefigured the Ottawa process. It drafted a "Canadian Action Plan to Reduce the Global Use of Landmines" which followed a two-track approach. Canada would continue participating in the CCW review conference in April even though officials believed the conferees would deadlock. It would also host "a small international meeting of officials and NGOs to develop an action plan on landmines" that June.[28]

The division sought to ally officials with campaigners by inviting Valerie Warmington of Mines Action Canada to join the Canadian delegation to the CCW negotiations. Even though it had invited NGO representatives to attend international conferences and had included Warmington on a delegation to a July 1995 UN meeting to establish a trust fund for demining, the government had opposed inclusion of an official with humanitarian experience on the CCW delegation for the past year. Now it was willing to include an NGO leader. The government was having difficulty shielding its negotiating position from public scrutiny, now that landmines were getting media and parliamentary attention. If the review conference was destined for deadlock or disappointment, officials could at least claim they had done their best. "Let's throw open the books," one put it. "If Valerie can agree there is nothing to be done, then we're at an impasse."[29]

Far from leaping at the invitation, campaigners were leery of cooptation. "This was a huge issue," said one. "We did not support the CCW because they were negotiating something we felt had been outlawed in the Geneva Convention. How could we support the CCW when it was negotiating something that would be less than what was already in place. We did not want to legitimize the CCW."[30] Their first impulse was given added impetus by a March 17 briefing paper from the International Committee of the Red Cross objecting "that the proposed new restrictions on landmines which have achieved the most support to date are both too complex and too weak" and "will fail to have a significant impact on civilian casualties."[31] Other campaigners worried about alienating ICBL allies already suspicious of Mines Action Canada's close ties to government. "We were concerned about being coopted," says a campaign leader who was amenable to participating. Yet the NGO representative could always resign in protest. "Partnership with government means you share objectives. My view was, 'I'll support the government as long as I can, but if it goes off track I will be the first to criticize'."[32] After heated debate, Mines Action Canada agreed to join the delegation.

At the same time, it kept up its outside agitation, with a renewed emphasis on the politics of accountability. "Warmington's involvement," says one organizer, "meant access to a new level of information, but off-the-record discussions mean nothing in the big picture. They don't mean anything unless politicians make their views public so you can hold them to it. We kept hammering away for public declarations and statements, because they had been saying one thing and doing another."[33]

Meanwhile, foreign affairs officials were elaborating track two diplomacy, involving nonofficials and former officials. Starting in January 1996, when the second session of the Review Conference opened in Geneva, Robert Lawson met discreetly with eight pro-ban states and the NGOs to "explore a new track of diplomatic action on the AP mine issue."[34] Campaigners harbored suspicions at first. "When the Canadian government began floating the idea of hosting a meeting to strategize about a ban, some in the ICBL were skeptical, to say the least," recall Jody Williams and Stephen Goose. "One campaigner remembers wondering if the move was really designed to ensure that momentum for a ban would be sidetracked by more government discussions leading nowhere."[35] Williams, in particular, had her doubts. "I was on the side of wanting to embrace the Canadians pretty wholeheartedly," says Goose. "Jody was on the side of those who treated it with some skepticism." So did "many people in the Canadian coalition—Celinda Tuttle was one. But [there was] a realization that if you want to make progress, you have to have government champions. We had occasion to remind some of our NGO colleagues that no matter how many draft treaties we in the ICBL produced, eventually a government would have to write one, governments would have to negotiate it, and only governments would sign it. If we wanted a good one, we would have to work with the core group."[36] That view prevailed and "the ICBL invited pro-ban states to a meeting to discuss a cooperative way forward."[37]

All eight of the states that showed up at the first session in January—Austria, Belgium, Canada, Denmark, Ireland, Mexico, Norway, and Switzerland—had participated regularly in UN peacekeeping that exposed their troops to landmines left over from communal strife. A second meeting, over dinner hosted by the Quakers at the start of the review conference final session on April 22, drew 14 states. "We were shocked that so many showed up at the dinner," recalls the ICBL's Jody Williams.[38] Eleven came to a third meeting at the close of the review conference in May.

The US delegation was vaguely aware of the meetings. Mark Moher, the chief Canadian delegate, made an announcement at one point, recalls deputy US negotiator Robert Sherman. "He said we are doing this, and anyone who wants to can come, so we knew they were talking about some kind of total ban on APL, but beyond that we didn't know."[39]

The diplomacy that emerged from these sessions had four key political premises. First, what would become the Ottawa process was a gathering of the like-minded in a stand-alone forum. That meant countries had to opt in or opt out. By implication, a ban could emerge with or without Washington's participation, indeed, over its objections. Even at that point, however, they considered it "absolute heresy" to talk about a total ban, observes Jill Sinclair of the disarmament division.[40] Second, the NGOs were inside at last. Third, not just present and participating, NGOs were also influential in shaping policy and instrumental in attracting media attention to the ban and shaming governments into action. Fourth, the diplomats adopted the campaigners' way of framing the issue in moral terms, as a matter of basic human rights. This moral framing presupposed going beyond regulating the use of landmines on utilitarian grounds to outlaw them. The campaigners' aim, as they said on April 22 in Geneva, was to "contribute to the development of new global norms with respect to landmines."[41]

The Ottawa process was, at heart, public diplomacy. It was also normative: believers in the new global norms would try to proselytize others and put political heat on those who remained cool to a ban.

After the January meeting, Werner Ehrlich, an Austrian diplomat "stepped outside his foreign ministry [role] and took it upon himself to produce an early draft" of a ban, recalls Goose. Ehrlich was soon replaced by Thomas Hajnoczi, much to the campaigners' initial consternation, but Hajnoczi "turned out to be just as strongly supportive."[42] Drafting was expedited by the active involvement of the senior legal adviser in the defense ministry, Thomas Desch, whose pro-ban sympathies made it possible to circumvent resistance in the Austrian army.[43] Their aim, according to Hajnoczi, "was to keep it as short and clear as possible," grafting language from existing treaties to "demonstrate that a convention could be negotiated quickly."[44] Hajnoczi circulated the draft to the core group in advance of its April 22 meeting.

By then the small international meeting of officials and NGOs had grown into an "International Landmines Strategy Session" to be held in Ottawa. As more and more states expressed interest in participating, the June meeting was rescheduled for fall to allow further time to make arrangements. Lawson and his colleagues also framed a proposal to turn Canada's moratorium into a permanent ban on production, use, and transfer of antipersonnel landmines and to sponsor a UN resolution calling for a ban.

In so doing, the Canadians were moving to transcend arms control with a deliberately normative approach intended to establish a new taboo. "What we are seeking is not a traditional arms control treaty but the establishment of a new humanitarian norm against these weapons," Foreign Minister Axworthy would say in March 1997. "It will do what the world has already done to dum-dum bullets, poison gas, and blinding laser weapons."[45] Grafting a new norm onto existing ones would be Canada's aim at Ottawa. To accomplish that, it would move the negotiations into a new venue and ally with the campaigners.

A CHANGE OF VENUE FROM GENEVA

In May, as the review conference was wrapping up without a consensus on anything like a ban, diplomats were deliberating what to do next. Dropping the issue was out of the question: the ban campaign had become too prominent to ignore. Doing something about it was another matter. The United States, France, and the United Kingdom, Canada's allies, were inclined to refer the issue to the Conference on Disarmament. Like the review conference, the CD operated by consensus, which would perpetuate the stalemate.

For proponents of a ban, the choice of venue mattered. Taking the issue to the CD would sidetrack negotiations and derail a ban. Their critique of the CD was summed up by Peter Herby in an internal memorandum for the International Committee of the Red Cross. "As with the CCW Review Conference," Herby wrote, "the rule of consensus will probably make agreement on far-reaching measures impossible." Rule 18, adopted at the behest of the United States and other nuclear powers to forestall nuclear disarmament, provides, "The Conference shall conduct its work and adopt its decisions by consensus." Although the chemical weapons ban and nuclear test ban were negotiated in the CD, Herby noted, these treaties "affect the relatively few countries which possess these technologies" and "are backed up by nearly universally accepted norms." In contrast, most states possess antipersonnel mines. The CD has not negotiated any treaty on conventional weapons and progress "is likely to be held hostage to progress on nuclear disarmament." That was the intent of Mexico, Indonesia, and other third world countries. Of the 37 states represented in the CD, Herby said, only nine supported a ban and Algeria, China, Cuba, Egypt, India, Iran, Myanmar, Nigeria, Pakistan, and Russia were opposed. Moreover, the CD "is likely to accentuate the security aspects of the landmine issue and to deemphasize humanitarian concerns. Neither the ICRC nor UN humanitarian agencies nor NGOs have access to CD negotiations." In a standing forum like the CD, "negotiations usually face no deadlines for completion of work, which is often conducted on a less-than-intensive basis spread over months and years." Anticipating what would become the Ottawa process, Herby concluded, "If conducted in good faith in a forum dedicated to [antipersonnel landmines], negotiations could be concluded in several sessions of a few weeks each. Such a process would highlight the urgency of the landmines crisis and could more effectively integrate humanitarian interests."[46]

Canada's diplomats agreed with Herby. "Traditionally, international norms have been established using a top-down approach. State representatives sat in the chambers of international organizations and negotiated until consensus was reached," write Gwozdecky and Sinclair. "This often meant inordinate delay and inaction. The landmine campaign started from the premise that civil society can play a decisive role in establishing norms, and states can be brought along gradually to adopt them."[47]

With top officials in the department preoccupied by the war in Yugoslavia and NATO enlargement, the landmines issue was left to Sinclair and her staff in the division of nonproliferation, arms control, and disarmament. The division's original draft resolution to be submitted to the fall session of the UN General Assembly called for negotiating in the CD, but that reference was dropped. Instead, at the conclusion of the review conference in May, Sinclair authorized Robert Lawson to announce that Canada would host a meeting of states and NGOs committed to a ban, in order to plan further action, global and regional, to eliminate antipersonnel landmines.[48]

Reaction from all five permanent members was hostile, recalls Lawson. China and Russia rejected the very idea of a ban. "The United States, Britain, and France supported the ban in principle, but were all openly critical of the Ottawa process," he says. "All five states shared suspicions of the process and its strategic alliance with the NGO community and each continued to reserve the right to use antipersonnel mines."[49]

Their opposition put the Canadians in a quandary about whom to invite to the strategy session in Ottawa that fall. They could hardly leave the United States, France, and other allies off the invitation list, but as one official put it, "We couldn't invite everyone, or we'd get the lowest common denominator—all the rats trying to hijack our agenda."[50] Mark Gwozdecky came up with a way out: open the meeting to all, but let each country decide for itself whether to come. In May the ICBL had drawn up a "Good List" of 41 states supporting a ban. "The challenge," diplomats in the disarmament division recognized, "would be to find out which states were really supportive."[51] The division had already begun drafting a political declaration for endorsement by the conferees that committed them to take unilateral steps toward a ban. Why not circulate the declaration in advance? States willing to endorse it would be invited to participate; others could come as observers or not attend at all. Some states might even embrace the new norm by changing their own landmines policy in advance of the Ottawa session. Signatories who failed to live up to their commitment would be subject to shaming by ban campaigners.

Over the summer, as Canada firmed up arrangements for the Ottawa strategy session, more and more countries decided to participate. What to do for an encore became the issue for the Department of Foreign Affairs and International Trade. Jill Sinclair, director of the nonproliferation, arms control, and disarmament division, presented two options to Axworthy. One was a resolution to introduce in the UN General Assembly calling for an export moratorium and an end to landmine deployments. That idea would be dropped out of deference to the United States. The other was an alternative to the CD, a new "stand-alone" landmines negotiating forum for "like-minded states" modeled on the Ottawa strategy session. Gwozdecky suggested that Canada host the forum, but that was initially ruled out on grounds of cost.[52]

The diplomats also wanted to set a good example by turning Canada's moratorium into a permanent ban and destroying its stockpile of antipersonnel landmines, but defense officials were still opposed. On the eve of the Ottawa strategy session in September, Sinclair and Ralph Lysyshyn, director-general of the international security bureau, asked the Privy Council Office to intervene and break the deadlock. It brokered a deal to destroy one-third of the stockpile immediately and dispose of the rest "in the context of successful negotiations."[53]

In other respects, the Canadians were taking steps to lower the profile of the session and allay foreign concerns. Plans for a special logo were dropped. So was the idea of getting conferee agreement on a common plan of action. A week before the scheduled start of the session, Sinclair proposed to Lysyshyn that Canada issue a call for countries to begin negotiating a ban within a specified period of time, say, 2 years. Lysyshyn thought that would only antagonize some countries without grabbing public attention. Only bureaucrats, he said, could get excited about a commitment to begin talks in 2 years.[54]

Yet the Canadians were unwilling to relegate the issue to the CD, believing that negotiations there would be hamstrung by the need for consensus. When the French, in bilateral talks on the eve of the strategy session, insisted that any statement to emerge regarding the future of landmines negotiations should refer to the CD, the Canadians were noncommittal.[55]

The Ottawa session was originally supposed to serve as the spawning ground for a coalition of the like-minded. Instead of "a small international meeting of officials and NGOs" to map strategy, it was turning into a venue for states to commit themselves to a new norm and negotiate a global ban.

6

Civilian Deference to Service Interests

> The opposing tendencies toward the privatization and socialization
> of conflict underlie all strategy.
>
> **E.E. Schattschneider**[1]

While the ban campaign was gaining traction, US policy was stuck in the mud. The prevailing view of why the United States remained opposed to a ban is that the US military was firmly wedded to landmines. By most accounts, landmines were a military requirement and the ban was anathema to the armed services. Military opposition, they conclude, was decisive in defeating a ban in Washington.

Yet the military requirement for antipersonnel landmines was a matter of some dispute within the armed services. Evaluations of their utility varied from service to service. Even inside the Army, enthusiasm for landmines was decidedly lukewarm.

The differences in military views were not well understood by civilians in the Clinton administration, the news media, or the ban campaign itself. Nor was their source—interservice and intraservice differences in *organizational interests*, mainly capabilities, roles and missions, autonomy, and budget shares. Antipersonnel mines did make some military officers morally uncomfortable and their discomfort was evidence of norms at work. Yet the evidence suggests that the varying degrees of enthusiasm for landmines in the military were largely interest motivated.

Unaware how weak the support for landmines was in the armed services, the Clinton administration assumed that they were unalterably opposed to a ban and were loath to challenge them.

LANDMINES—A MILITARY REQUIREMENT?

Much of the public debate turned on how essential landmines were and what effect they had on US casualties. Evidence was mostly anecdotal. Typical was a *New York Times* op-ed by Bernard Trainor, a Marine general who later became the *Times'* military correspondent and directed the national security program at Harvard's Kennedy School of Government. Trainor described how his platoon had seized Hill 59 near Panmunjom during the Korean War in a firefight with Chinese troops. Making his way down the hill, he tripped a mine. "I heard a 'thip' as it activated a mine," he recalled, "and I steeled myself for the explosion that would rip off my legs. Nothing happened. The mine had malfunctioned." Expecting the Chinese to try to recapture the lost ground, his platoon mined the approaches to its position. The counterattack came 2 nights later. "The mines saved us from being overrun," wrote Trainor. "Yet I feel ambivalent about mines. I know they have both threatened and saved my life." He had no ambivalence about a ban, however: "Trying to outlaw mines is much like trying to outlaw war itself, an exercise in futility. An international agreement restricting their sale might help protect civilians, but not letting our troops use them could cost American lives."[2] Military opposition to a ban was sometimes more visceral than well reasoned.

The armed services' own conclusions were not as clearcut as Trainor's. As General Joseph Ralston, vice-chairman of the Joint Chiefs of Staff, summed them up on May 16, 1996, "The historical record is mixed concerning antipersonnel landmines. We know that they cause casualties, some enemy and some friendly. We know that they inhibit movement—enemy and friendly—and the significance in battle is variable. You will talk to combat-seasoned veterans who will tell you that antipersonnel landmines saved their life. You will also talk to veterans who will tell you that their best friend was killed by an antipersonnel landmine, one of ours. So you have conflicting stories."[3]

Tactical use of mines could conceivably prove decisive in some hypothetical situations—like air-dropping scatterable mines to fix in place two Iraqi divisions on the right flank of the VII Corps as it stormed into Iraq during the 1991 Gulf war, a much debated hypothetical that, a US study concludes, never happened—but the utility of mine use was scenario dependent, a synonym for anecdotal in the lexicon of Pentagon planners. Army doctrine stressed mobility, downplaying static defenses that relied on landmines. "It takes imagination to integrate them into fast-paced maneuver warfare, given the traditional association of mines with static situations," wrote Colonel Richard H. Johnson, an Army landmines expert.[4] Whether landmines did more to protect forces or to impede maneuver varied with the circumstances and it was difficult to demonstrate how landmines were a requirement for victory in any theater, even Korea. Antipersonnel landmines were not indispensable; other capabilities, combined with different tactics, could perform the same function.

Even the claim that landmines could spare the lives and limbs of US troops was open to dispute. The Army had generated a paper contending that landmine use could cut combat losses in half, but that conclusion was sensitive to a number of conditions and not at all generalizable.[5] Had it been done, a net assessment might have cast doubt on whether US-deployed mines had saved more US troops than they killed or maimed in recent wars.

The dearth of compelling analysis to support the military requirement for antipersonnel landmines was evident to the International Committee of the Red Cross in 1966: "[T]he military value of AP mines has almost always been accepted without question. It appears that no systematic studies of whether their actual military effects have lived up to expectations under past combat conditions have been undertaken by professional military organizations or military analysts. Historical records in the public domain give little or any attention to [the] role that AP mines have played."[6] The ICRC commissioned Brigadier Patrick Blagden, a retired British combat engineer with experience in weapons research as well as demining, to survey public records of landmine use in 26 countries. The conclusion was unanimously endorsed by a group of military experts convened by the ICRC: "The material which is available on the use of AP landmines does not substantiate claims that AP mines are indispensable weapons of high military value."[7] The experts also questioned the utility of antipersonnel mines as an impediment to mine clearing in war: "Their use to protect antitank mines is generally claimed to be an important purpose of AP mines, but there are few historical examples to substantiate the effectiveness of such use. Where minefields are cleared by roller, plow, flail, explosive-filled hose, fuel-air explosive or bombardment, the value of AP mines has not been demonstrated."[8]

The US Army had no studies demonstrating the military utility of landmines as of 1994, when Tim Connolly of the Office of Special Operations and Low-Intensity Conflict asked for one. "What they gave us was the PowerPoint slides of their standard dog-and-pony brief on mine doctrine. That was it," he says. "They would not do a position paper. Nobody would force them to." So Connolly commissioned a study of his own: starting with "the Army's doctrine as they currently articulate it, take the Army's simulation software [Janus, Army version 3.17] they use to analyze this sort of thing, and run enough iterations so that we have some statistically supportable cells that we can base some judgments on." The $250,000 contract to the Institute for Defense Analyses was small, but politically sensitive. "They recognized what I was going to do with it, which is go out on the street and say we've taken the Army's own doctrine, we've put it through the Army's own simulation system, and it turns out that landmines are unnecessary under current doctrine," says Connolly. "So IDA went off and did their thing, and as expected, APLs were of little or no value in the scenarios in which they were most defended by the military, for instance, the defense of the Korean peninsula, unless you believed that the major attack was going to be a million ground troops running screaming across the border toward Seoul." Moreover, most mines in Korea are not emplaced in the ground. "They're in depot stock because the contraction and expansion of the earth in winter causes them to go off," he found out. "So if, in fact, the North Koreans were able to turn on a dime and start heading south within hours, we would have to put them in and we wouldn't be putting them in." Use of antipersonnel landmines to protect antitank mines was also called into question. "The Army's own doctrine said that you don't put a minefield in and then leave it. It's always covered by indirect fire in some way, so if tanks started coming through, you bring steel down through artillery." These conclusions were Connolly's own, however: "IDA," he says, "was unwilling to make declarative statements in its final report because it realized the political implications of doing so."[9]

IDA simulated four scenarios in which heavy US brigades under attack by a Soviet-style tank division adopted either a pure tactical defense or defense in combination with a tactical counteroffensive—and with or without a very extensive mix of antitank and antipersonnel landmines. US vehicle losses were, on average, 40.0 percent with mines and 67.2 percent without mines in the pure defense scenario, and 74.8 percent when mines were used in counterattack simulations and 92.5 percent when they were not. The results were mostly attributable to antitank mines. They were also highly scenario dependent. Antipersonnel mines were ineffective in open terrain against armored attack but were more useful in rough terrain against assaults by dismounted infantry. IDA also studied two Korea-like scenarios in which a US mechanized battalion conducted a purely tactical defense against a Soviet-style tank regiment that attacked it along two converging axes. Two dismounted motorized battalions conducted a flanking attack along one axis, a forested slope. Two other tank battalions attacked the heart of the US position simultaneously along a second axis with more trafficable terrain. In the first scenario, US defenders deployed extensive minefields with antitank and antipersonnel mines in about equal proportion. In the second scenario, they used no antipersonnel mines, only antitank mines. Without antipersonnel landmines, US losses increased by 10 percent in close terrain, or less than the standard error. IDA couched its conclusions in tempered terms. "Antipersonnel mines are of substantially more restricted utility than antitank mines," the study reads. "For the utility of antipersonnel mines to be so high as to preclude further consideration [of arms control] requires an especially demanding set of assumptions about the nature of future warfare. It is far from obvious that the required assumptions can be sustained."[10]

Connolly was in the audience when IDA briefed the study to the joint staff and other Pentagon officials: "The bottom line was that the absence of antipersonnel landmines in a couple of isolated cases—[like] a special operations 'A team' in retreat—caused a 1 or 2 percent increase in casualties. It did not factor in US casualties from friendly fire. The military spin was, so you're asking us to accept two percent casualties that we otherwise could avoid." As a result, he says, "The IDA report basically went nowhere. No one cared that this was the only legitimate piece of analysis about whether landmines were useful or not," says Connolly. "It had nothing to do with whether or not the landmine was effective, was necessary, was doctrinally supportable. It had to do with, we're not going to be forced by Jody Williams and Bobby Muller and all of these tree-huggers and pacifists to take a weapon systems out of the US inventory. We don't care if we never use the weapon system."[11]

Eric Newsom, principal deputy assistant secretary of state for political-military affairs, also remembers being briefed on the study. "It showed that in the event of a major North Korean attack, with the ability to use landmines our casualties would be X, but without landmines our casualties would be 2X or 3X," he says. "Well, when you're faced with that, what can you do? You can't say, I don't care, so it's only three times as many American dead." Military briefers knew how to disarm civilians: "It was whether you were for saving the lives of American soldiers or not."[12]

Jan Lodal, principal deputy under secretary of defense for policy, drew a different conclusion from the briefings he attended, that assessments of the military utility of landmines in Korea were sensitive to assumptions about advanced warning. "I saw simulations that the joint staff had done," he says. In the worst-case scenario of an attack without warning, landmines could help slow the North Koreans' advance and stop them from overrunning Seoul. "If they start from a no-warning situation, they get to Seoul fast. You have a chance to hold them back by picking up a few hours. If you have a lot of warning, the landmines still help, but they help less because you have a big buildup. You have a lot of artillery and airpower there."[13]

SERVICE STAKES AND STANDS

Conclusions about the need for landmines varied from service to service and from regional command to regional command, or CINC in Pentagon parlance. That was due to differences in organizational interests, mainly capabilities, role and missions, autonomy, and budget shares. Norms did matter, not because most military officers believed that antipersonnel landmines were morally suspect, but because a taboo codified in a treaty would deprive them of capabilities that they preferred to keep.

All the armed services are loath to give up capabilities without a fight and the US Army was no exception. "The Army obviously had a great vested interest in landmines," says an Army officer with high-level experience in landmines policy making. That interest did not end with antitank mines. "The big issue was always antitank," he says, but when he hears someone argue, "you haven't got a lot of antipersonnel landmines—it's all antitank," he has a quick rejoinder: "That's baloney. You've got to have both together; otherwise it's not an effective barrier. It's just not."[14] The Army's position was "very basic," concurs Lee Feinstein, deputy director of policy planning in the State Department, "We've got tools. We want to be able to use as many as we can."[15]

Norms matter to the military. So does international law. A new norm codified by treaty could impede the Army from using its capabilities—capabilities it thought it needed to protect the lives of US soldiers on the battlefield. US landmines were not the ones "blowing off the legs of little kids in Africa," says a senior official who favored a ban, "so landmines are not viewed by anybody in the US government, particularly in the Pentagon, as an immoral weapon."[16] Military officers "were very concerned about a weapon they use being labeled indiscriminate," says Feinstein. "They're very serious about the chain of command and the circumstances under which they can break the chain of command. One of these is when they've been given an illegal order. They don't want any of their people to be put in circumstances in which they would have to disregard international law or disobey their superior officer, so they pay a tremendous amount of attention to the evolution of humanitarian law."[17]

Just how seriously the military takes normative obligations was evident in the air war against Yugoslavia in 1999 and against Iraq in 2003 when collateral damage assessments and legal reviews were incorporated into the target selection process. In the case of Yugoslavia, targets where civilian casualties were likely, like those in downtown Belgrade, were also reviewed by the 19 NATO governments, often at senior levels.[18] In the case of Iraq, no target projected to have more than 30 civilian casualties could be struck without the personal authorization of the Secretary of Defense. According to a study by Human Rights Watch directed by a former Air Force targeter, the process worked very well for fixed targets, less well for strikes with cluster bombs or attacks on the Iraqi leadership when time was of the essence and "haste contributed to excessive civilian casualties because it prevented adequate collateral damage estimates."[19]

While the US military takes international norms and law to heart, many officials act as if US adherence to norms and laws has no bearing on the behavior of other countries. They believe that miscreants will violate international norms and law even if the United States complies and that a law-abiding state will turn miscreant if its security is endangered. These beliefs are shared by senior civilians and military officers alike and are as prevalent among ban supporters as ban opponents. "Norway is one of the core Ottawa Convention countries and the ban on APL use on one's own territory is one of the core provisions of that convention," says ACDA's Robert Sherman. "We had a meeting with the Norwegians, in which one of their diplomats said quite openly, 'The only time we'd ever consider using antipersonnel landmines or letting anybody else use them in our own country is when we're invaded, and if that happens, you don't think we're going to care about this treaty.' This does give one a certain perspective."[20] Officials who backed a ban expressed similar views. "We sign these treaties and we obey them," says Lee Feinstein. "A lot of other governments, like the French, will cite Article 51 of the UN Charter on self-defense as a reason not to do anything that's in the treaty."[21] These views were imbued with realism. Military officers were typically realists, which reinforced their doubts about the efficacy of a ban.

Yet, if landmines were not morally suspect to the military, they were doctrinally doubtful. Within the Army, the roles and missions for landmines were a matter of doctrine, and doctrine had changed radically since the early 1980s. Current US Army doctrine placed a much heavier emphasis on rapid maneuver—move, shoot, communicate. "Maneuver-oriented commanders have a natural bias against the use of tactics (such as mine warfare) traditionally associated with attrition warfare," wrote Colonel Richard Johnson, who spent much of his career developing mines for the Army at Picatinny Arsenal. "It is inherently difficult and unglamorous to train troops in emplacement and removal of mines (including countermine operations). The large logistical requirement of conventional mines is a deterrent to training because it is time-consuming and requires static positioning of maneuver forces while troops construct minefields." In 1995, Johnson pointed out, "Training simulations for scatterable mines and unexploded ordnance are just now being introduced, and the effect on mine usage is hard to judge."[22] It is axiomatic in the military that armies fight the way they are trained to fight.

The Army's emphasis on rapid maneuver marginalized mines even in Korea. Yet the legacy of static defense was still strong in that theater and the Army continued to insist that abandoning antipersonnel mines would require it to change tactics and strategy in Korea. As a high-ranking officer put it in a May 1996 Pentagon briefing, "We have built our plans in Korea really from the fifties on and we've trained all of our troops on the assumption that we have [landmines] in the inventory and one of the major aspects of the policy review here was to look at the transition aspects of this and how complex it is. It's very much of a serious issue if you just go in, in a very short period of time, a few months, maybe a year, try to change all this and retrain everybody, redo all the plans and so forth. And so, given that, we have not had an opportunity yet to even understand all the implications of this because this has been this way for such a long time and it's so ingrained in everything we do—that's another important reason for this exception."[23] This was the gist of the case for a transition period to allow doctrine to evolve.

Yet other officials talked as if strategy and doctrine in Korea were immutable, a natural consequence of Seoul's proximity to the North Korean border. "One of the reasons we currently have the Korea exemption," a senior Pentagon civilian told reporters in January 1997, "is because one of the few places in the world we are forced to fight in a static defensive position against an enemy who is very close with large forces is, in fact, Korea."[24] The implication was that US forces could not defend Seoul without landmines.

Yet the force posture in Korea was due more to the Army's choice of strategy than to geographic necessity. That strategy had evolved over time—as had the Army's need for landmines.

For two decades after the 1953 armistice, US war plans had called for allied forces to fall back to the Han River in the event of a North Korean attack and assume a defensive posture until reinforcements arrived from the United States. Those plans were revised in 1974, a time of tense relations with South Korea. At the heart of the disaffection in Seoul was the Nixon Doctrine, stating that the United States would "look to the nation directly threatened to assume primary responsibility of providing the manpower for its defense." That doctrine, along with withdrawal of 20,000 US troops from Korea and detente with China, seemed to portend US disengagement from the peninsula. That alarmed South Korea's military dictatorship under Park Chung Hee and prompted him to enter into talks with North Korea. It also led him to order covert development of nuclear arms.

In this uneasy climate, General James Hollingsworth took command of I Corps, responsible for the defense of Seoul, and drew up a new plan to take the war to the North in the event of aggression. Under Op Plan 5027, Hollingsworth had the US 3rd Marine Division and the ROK 1st Marine Division land at Wonsan and attack Pyongyang from the east. Redeploying most of his artillery far forward near the DMZ, he assigned two brigades of the US 2nd Infantry Division to march north and seize Kaesong, North Korea's southernmost city. That left a static line of allied forces to defend Seoul. To fortify that line, Hollingworth relied heavily on air power, artillery, and landmines. To impede North Korean forces from massing for an offensive, he planned to have B-52s bomb potential axes of attack and lines of supply. To beef up Seoul's defenses he deployed more barriers and landmines. The Hollingsworth line was a defensive wall to facilitate an offensive strategy.

That strategy, with some modifications, still guides allied forces today. As the North's military inferiority vis-a-vis the South worsened, Op Plan 5027 was revised to bolster the offensive and provide for preemptive strikes against North Korea's bombers and artillery in the event of unambiguous warning of preparations for attack. In 1992 the role of the 2nd Division was changed. It became a mobile mechanized reserve whose mission was to pinch off breakthroughs and counterattack locally—"expand the battle space"—until reinforcements arrived from the United States, then to join the mechanized 3rd Corps and amphibious and air mobile forces in a counteroffensive into North Korea.

In its new role the 2nd Division relied on rapid maneuver instead of static defense, so it no longer planned to emplace landmines. Its redeployment, however, stretched the defensive front line manned by two ROK corps, prompting them to rely more on barrier defenses and landmines. These changes led the US command to turn over responsibility for the barrier plan, including landmines, to South Korea and gradually to transfer US stocks of landmines to ROK forces.

As a result, *the United States has no mines of its own deployed in Korea as part of the barrier plan of the combined forces command.* All the million or so landmines emplaced in the ground in defense of Seoul belong to South Korea. "All the mines in the ground were Korean. We had given them away years earlier," says Jan Lodal. "We didn't actually have any mines in the ground out there."[25] A White House fact sheet entitled "U.S. Requirements for Landmines in Korea" delicately skirted that fact: "Because North Korean forces are so close to Seoul and so outnumber allied forces in place, *the United Nations command* relies on preplanned and emplaced minefields to counter and slow a possible North Korean advance."[26] "United Nations command" is a diplomatic way of referring to the US CINC in Korea who takes command of ROK as well as US forces in the event of war.

The ROK Army has 2 million mines in its own stockpiles. It also has some 685,000 mines in US stocks earmarked for its use. The United States has gradually turned over its stocks of dumb mines to South Korea and replaced them with self-destructing self-deactivating mines. "They couldn't immediately afford the newer types of explosive mines," says Thomas "Ted" McNamara, assistant secretary of state for politico-military affairs. "This was not a high priority item in the Pentagon. It was part of a logistical upgrading process that was going to take years."[27] Were a ban to enter into force, it would preclude transfer of antipersonnel mines in US stocks to ROK forces. That was a problem for the US commander in Korea in his role as combined forces commander.

The smart mines in the US inventory were not well-suited for use in barrier defenses. "The need for the barrier there is in effect because of the heightened alert at all times," says Lodal. "The problem with the self-destruct stuff is that the clocks run pretty fast." They can be preset to self-destruct, "but it's basically hard to keep a self-destruct minefield alive for more than 2 weeks." Why? Self-destruct mines are not designed for use in a barrier defense of Seoul but were intended for an altogether different purpose: "They're deployed tactically after the battle starts." Lodal explains, "The trouble in Korea is you have a no-warning situation. You don't have time to use them in that mode." Preparations for attack must be detected in advance, and "all of them have to be emplaced on strategic warning." The problem is, if "the war is not going to start in 2 weeks, and in any event, you don't want to give the North Koreans the simple option of waiting 2 weeks [for the mines to self-destruct] and then attack. You can't really use the existing stockpiles of self-destruct mines for the Korea barrier."[28]

More than half the US inventory of antipersonnel mines in Korea intended for use by US forces are self-destructing, self-deactivating mixed munitions, which are not ideal for tactical use there, either.[29] FASCAMs, or family of scatterable mines, are delivered by air or artillery rather than buried in the ground or emplaced in prechambered holes once war seems imminent. FASCAMs, like the Volcano, are not designed for pinpoint deployment in Korea's mountainous and wooded terrain. Launched from a distance, they can land on a hillside with enough momentum to bound and roll rather than come to rest where they are dropped. Landslides caused by heavy snow or monsoon rain dislodge them. "They didn't work quite right and maybe we needed a new generation of them with some better technology," says Jan Lodal. Yet OSD's efforts to come up with replacements encountered resistance in the Army, which "doesn't want to spend money on something like that."[30]

US war plans are closely held. Some civilian policy makers who worked on the landmines issue did not know the details. Nor did most officers who served in Korea before 1990, when strategy changed along with US use of landmines. When Ted McNamara first took over the landmines portfolio, for instance, he was unaware that most landmines in Korea did not belong to the United States. "I was tabula rasa. I just walked into this," he says. "I learned more about Korea over time."[31] Lee Feinstein's experience at the policy planning staff at State was similar. "Did I know they were Korean weapons and not American weapons? No. Not early on."[32] Asked whether it was widely known in the US government, Robert Sherman of ACDA replied, "Some people understand it; some people don't."[33] Indeed, Jan Lodal, the senior civilian in the Pentagon working on landmines policy, was unaware that the United States no longer had mines emplaced in Korea when he was developing a new policy in 1996. It was only afterward, Lodal says, that "it turns out that none of our mines were actually deployed."[34]

Ban proponents were also unaware of the reality on the ground in Korea. It was not until December 2000, 3 years after the ban treaty was signed, that campaigners found out. The US command in Korea, at Senator Patrick

Leahy's urging, gave a high-level briefing to two retired Army officers who were consultants for the Vietnam Veterans of America Foundation, General Robert Gard and Major Edwin "Ed" Deagle, Jr. During the briefing the two were handed a table itemizing landmines in the US stockpile. "The table was dumbfounding," says Deagle, amazement still evident in his voice months later. "I thought, my God, we've been listening to all kinds of generals who believe that South Korea is going to die if we don't have the landmines and we don't even plan to use them."[35]

US forces do maintain a stockpile of 225,000 landmines in Korea which are held in reserve for US reinforcements, but they are intended for use in a counteroffensive against the North, not for defense of the South. "Is the 2nd Division going to use those for a staged delaying action?" Deagle recalls asking the briefer. "He said, no, no, these are going to be for the reinforcements. I said, you mean the people who come in at Pusan?" Pusan lay across the peninsula from the landmine stockpile sites in Korea.

Deagle's question points up other problems with landmines. Guarding and dispensing stockpiled mines depletes scarce manpower needed for other urgent tasks when war is impending. Without advanced warning, stocks may be overrun or destroyed by advancing enemy forces before they can be deployed. "When the balloon goes up," says Deagle, "they'd have to send an engineer company to the ROK warehouses and an engineer company to the US warehouses to try to blow them up before the North Koreans get there."[36] Worse yet, if landmine stocks that are not prepositioned have to be shipped overseas from depots in California, they would likely arrive too late to be of use in a sudden attack and would levy an onerous logistical burden on US capacity for rapid deployment. That burden would be borne—reluctantly, if at all—by the Air Force and the Navy.

Air-delivered mines have even less military utility. Why use air power to drop landmines when it could be attacking targets with smart bombs or other ordnance? Air power was a particularly acute problem for the Army. The Marine Corps has fighter-bombers of its own to conduct air strikes, but the Army, barred by interservice agreement from acquiring fixed-wing aircraft, only has helicopters. The Army is uneasy about relying on the Air Force for close air support—and for good reason. From its inception as a separate armed service, the Air Force had regarded strategic bombing as its essential mission. It resisted providing close air support of ground forces on or near the battlefield, which meant sacrificing its organizational essence to perform a subservient role for the Army. It balked at acquiring aircraft like A-10s for close air support and was reluctant to divert aircraft to perform that mission in every war from Vietnam to Kosovo. That reluctance extends to air delivery of landmines. No wonder the Army feels a need to rely on its own devices. Yet air-dropping landmines would require the Army to divert attack helicopters for that purpose, which it prefers not to do.

Except for the Korea command, none of the CINCs had much of an interest in retaining landmines. Pacific Command (PACOM), by tradition, was a Navy command, and littoral mines were not at issue in the ban negotiations. Atlantic Command (USACOM) had used landmines to protect the perimeter of the US base in Guantanamo, Cuba, but by 1996 General John Sheehan, a Marine, had issued orders to begin removing them.[37] Even two traditional Army CINCs, European Command (EUCOM) and Central Command (CENTCOM), no longer regarded landmines as essential.

During the Cold War, when the Red Army kept its readiest tank divisions in East Germany, EUCOM had constructed extensive barriers to retard their advance. How much it relied on landmines even then is a matter of some dispute. Deagle reminisced with one major-general, a classmate of his from West Point, about serving in armored cavalry regiments along the East German border in the 1960s. "Remember when we used to get alerted," Deagle asked him. "Did you have landmines? Yes, he replied, I had 5-ton truckloads full of stuff." Deagle asked whether he planned to use them. "I wouldn't have thought we could have gotten them down before we had to withdraw. Nobody in my squadron ever did, he replied. I said we didn't, either. We moved much too quickly, whether it was counterattacking or withdrawing. But I don't remember them ever being issued to the troop commander—and they weren't."[38] With the Army's adoption of a doctrine of maneuver warfare, AirLand Battle, EUCOM put less emphasis on barriers, including landmines. After the disintegration of the Warsaw Pact, the Soviet Union, and the Red Army, EUCOM's focus shifted from the Fulda Gap to the Balkans, where mines were less a military necessity than a deadly danger to US peacekeepers.

CENTCOM has responsibility for the Middle East and Southwest Asia, theaters well suited to wars of maneuver. Because they impede mobility, landmines proved more of a hindrance than a help during the 1991 Persian Gulf war. An Army officer opposed to the ban who later played a role in landmine policy making recounts his own experience with landmines during the war. "I commanded a battalion in the Gulf. I carried them all the way out and even planned to use them," he says. "I was assigned to the 2nd Armored Cavalry Regiment, which was the lead attack force in the 7th US corps." His mission was to "make contact with the enemy and cause him to commit his heavy forces," a diversion designed to let US tanks pass through. From his vantage point as an artilleryman, "cavalry units have a nasty habit of bypassing pockets of resistance, which, if you're riding around in an Abrams is one thing, but riding around with howitzers is a totally different question." On "a couple of occasions" he encountered problems with dismounted Iraqi infantry armed with antitank rockets, he says. "I proposed to the regiment, and the regiment agreed with me, if we know a particular area has dismounts, I just fill it full of these FASCAMs." FASCAMs can be preset to deactivate in hours or days. "Firing the short-term stuff in there basically freezes those guys in place." The regiment was denied authority to use them, however. "The follow-on heavy divisions didn't want us to deploy those things because they were fearful that the short-term mechanism wouldn't work and they would run over them." He has some sympathy for their view: "They'd already begun to experience problems, not with mines, but with unexploded ordnance," in particular, cluster bombs. "You only need to run over one and you don't want to go near them. I know an officer—one went off under his vehicle and he came within a millimeter of losing his manhood."[39] Doubtful that self-destruct mines would perform as advertised, commanders refused to deploy them.

Despite this experience, he sees military utility in mines. "If I had been with the 2nd Division and arrived in August 1990, knowing there's nothing between me in Dharan and the Kuwaiti border but a lot of dust, this stuff would have been very useful." The problem lay elsewhere, he says. "We didn't want different types of ammunition hauled around." According to this officer, units came equipped with their standard load and had no time to reconfigure it, even if some of it, like smoke ammunition, was useless and they needed more FASCAMs. "So it's more a question of logistical requirements as opposed to operational requirements."[40]

The experience of General Paul McCurran, a brigade commander in the 2nd Division, suggests otherwise. Deagle recounts how McCurran's brigade arrived on August 24, 3 weeks after the Iraqi invasion of Kuwait, and was ordered to man an outpost in the desert. The brigade was equipped with landmines but did not deploy them. Why not, Deagle asked McCurran. "He said we had a mobile defense plan in the event that the Iraqis crossed into Saudi Arabia that involved multiple options for maneuver-based attack. If we used landmines, even FASCAMs, they would have restricted our maneuver."[41]

A 2002 study by the General Accounting Office confirms these personal recollections. US forces transported over 2.2 million landmines, antipersonnel and antitank, self-destructing and not, to the Persian Gulf, but used just under 118,000, all of them smart mines.[42] The Air Force dropped some 103,870, mostly to inhibit movement by SCUD missile transporters. Navy and Marine Corps aircraft dropped another 13,564 for the same purpose. The Marine Corps used 48 RAAM and 12 ADAM artillery rounds "to supplement a defensive position." The Army never used any mines at all.[43] In a joint service report on lessons learned, officials concluded, "Commanders were afraid to use conventional and scatterable mines because of their potential for fratricide."[44]

No Iraqi armored vehicles were confirmed to have been destroyed as a result. Indeed, no enemy losses at all were attributed to US use of landmines in armed service reports. "Similarly, neither DOD, the Joint Chiefs of Staff, nor the US

Central Command provided us with any reports or other evidence clearly indicating that US landmines used during the Gulf War had been the direct or indirect cause of enemy casualties, equipment losses, or maneuver limitations."[45]

Mines did impede US mobility. In areas seeded with Gator mines dropped by air, US units were under orders to maneuver "with extreme caution." A contractor hired to clear mines in Kuwait reported 1,977 mines equipped to self-destruct failed to do so in the specified time.[46]

Of the 1,364 US casualties in the war, landmines caused 81, or 6 percent, and unexploded ordnance, including cluster bombs, caused 96. At least 142 other casualties resulted from unidentified explosions. According to the GAO report, "Some portion of the 142 casualties caused by an unknown type of landmine or unknown or misidentified type of unexploded ordnance might have been caused by US or other landmines, but there is no way of knowing."[47] "Friendly" casualties suffered in the war and a higher-than-predicted malfunction rate sapped what scant enthusiasm CENTCOM ever had for mines. CENTCOM was not alone. The CINCs had little use for landmines.

The budgetary consequences of replacing landmines did matter to the Army. If ordered to find substitutes, the Army would delegate that task to the combat engineers, who would come up with more expensive versions of landmines to replace them. Unless money were added to the Army budget to pay for them, buying new mines would mean sacrificing other Army programs. If, instead, the Air Force were ordered to buy new reconnaissance and attack aircraft for the mission once performed by landmines, its budget share could increase at the Army's expense. "Mines are not mission-essential," one general summed it up, "but they are budget-essential."[48]

If the Army as a whole had less than a compelling interest, that was not so for the combat engineers. They were the keepers of the flame within the Army, preserving pride of place for landmines. "The reason the flame is still lit is because they belong to engineers, who write up M20/32," says Major Deagle. M20/32, the field manual setting out Army landmine doctrine, contemplates a rich menu of uses for antipersonnel mines: force protection, impeding infiltration and early warning of attack; inflicting frightful injuries that shake enemy morale; delaying hostile forces to increase their vulnerability to attack by air and armor, shaping the battlefield along with obstacles to channel enemy forces and allow firepower to be concentrated with greater effectiveness; and protecting antitank mines.

Why do combat engineers have such an abiding interest in keeping landmines? In a word, morale. "The issue for the corps," says Deagle, "was the loss of slots in combat engineering units who lay the mines."[49] Thanks to landmines, the engineers retain officer billets around the globe, which are essential to morale.

For the Army engineers, the Korea requirement was a wedge to destroy the ban. An article by Colonel John Troxell, director of national security studies at the Army War College and former chief of the engineer plans division in the combined forces command in Korea, made that aim clear in the authoritative Army journal, *Parameters*. "The Korea exception argues that because of the nature of the threat and geography on the Korean peninsula, antipersonnel landmine requirements in Korea must be excluded from any ban until such time as suitable alternatives are developed and fielded," Troxell put it. "The logic behind the need for antipersonnel landmines in Korea should be viewed not as an exception, but as the rule."[50] In other words, Army engineers wanted to be able to use antipersonnel landmines everywhere. The engineers' enthusiasm was not shared by others in the Army.

Last but not least, the ban campaign infringed on the Army's autonomy, one organizational interest that all military officers could appreciate. It was unthinkable for outsiders to deprive an armed service of any weapon that some officers believed they might need. Playing on the Army's interest in autonomy and greatly exaggerating the influence of the campaigners, some officers were determined to draw a line in the sand. The NGOs inspired paranoia in military ranks that a landmines ban was the opening salvo in a campaign to disarm them. "The media-oriented Ottawa process, which allows no room for compromise or the legitimate review of military requirements, is a dangerous model to apply to national security policy formulation," Troxell wrote. "NGO involvement in this issue and their success may change forever the way that security policy agendas are established and the direction that policy takes." Troxell saw a need to "guard against losing control of the national security policy agendas to NGOs and their associated special interests."[51] Others expressed this fear in even more intemperate terms. "We need to think about the Ottawa process before we are moved to total disarmament," said one highly placed general. "The pace, the participants, and the process were new. Military advice was not sought. Standard arms control methodology was not used—verification, none of that. It was just a race to get Ottawa," he declaimed. "Our capabilities sheet will look like Swiss cheese if we keep this up."[52] Although few campaigners had any interest in disarming the military, his paranoia is more understandable given the inherent expansiveness of the norm against inhumane weapons.

The other armed services were much more relaxed. The Marine Corps, whose strategy of amphibious assault and rapid breach of defenses puts a premium on mobility, was divided on the need for landmines. The Air Force's only stake in the issue was dropping mines on behalf of the Army, a role it preferred to avoid. The Navy had only the most marginal of interests at stake, that of its special operations Sea-Air-Land force. "With the exception of the SEALs' use of denial mines," says Tim Connolly, "the Navy had zero equities in this because we weren't talking about littoral mines."[53] Yet the Navy and Air Force would defer to the Army on an issue it cared about. As one retired officer characterized their view, "We don't have a dog in that fight."

OUT OF CIVILIAN CONTROL

The armed services' interests in landmines put General John Shalikashvili in a bind. His role as chairman of the Joint Chiefs of Staff was to represent the views of the armed services to the president, and vice versa. That was not an easy job in the best of times, and the Clinton years were hardly the best of times.

Civil-military friction was especially abrasive in Clinton's first term in office. Assailed in the 1992 presidential campaign for avoiding the draft during the Vietnam War, he began his first term with a self-inflicted defeat over gays in the military, then waged bruising battles over intervention from Haiti to Bosnia. The alienation was mutual. Feeling beleaguered by a White House that showed little understanding and even less sympathy, the military reacted by adopting what one retired officer calls a "bunker mentality." That, in turn, made civilians in the White House and the Pentagon skittish about dealing with the military. "The policy gap was quite troubling," says a senior Defense Department official. To narrow it was "critical for this administration, which got off on the wrong foot with the military." This official, who had worked more closely with the senior military than most other Clinton appointees, says, "They take it for granted that this administration is not doing a good job."[54]

The reason why President Clinton did not order a ban even though he "really wanted to," says an Army officer with high-level involvement in landmines policy after 1996, was "this administration's concern early on that in going against the military, it hadn't had the experience of a lot of others."[55] That inexperience, especially prevalent in the White House, also led the president's political advisers to exaggerate the armed services' antipathy to a ban in 1996 instead of probing military sentiment. "The great political skills that they possessed to gauge the will of the American people and to respond to that will in the domestic policy arena does not exist in the defense policy arena." says Tim Connolly. "They weren't able to read the signals correctly. All they saw was, if we do something, we'd get beat up by the military and we can't afford to do that in an election year."[56]

Until early 1996, many top civilians in the Pentagon and elsewhere in the administration who did have experience in political-military affairs preferred to duck the landmine issue in the belief that a ban would require yet another skirmish with the armed services. "Consequently," says Connolly, "the chairman was not prodded by anyone in the building."[57]

Yet General John Shalikashvili, or Shali, as he was called in the Pentagon, did not need much prodding. He was favorably disposed to reexamine the military's need for landmines. He anticipated that President Clinton would opt for a ban on landmines and order him to make the best of it.

Many officers who reach the highest ranks are firm believers in civilian control and recognize that the president has broader responsibilities and concerns, domestic as well as foreign. So long as he gives them a fair hearing and does not call their professional judgment into question, even if he overrules them on political grounds, they are usually willing to acquiesce.[58] Shalikashvili was one such officer. A Polish-born immigrant of Georgian and Russian descent, Shalikashvili also had strong bonds of personal loyalty and affection to a commander-in-chief who had promoted him to the highest military position in his adopted land.

Yet a chairman cannot command the service chiefs, only cajole them. His hand was strengthened by the Goldwater-Nichols Act of 1986. Shalikashvili's predecessor, Colin Powell, had strengthened it further by giving the joint staff a preeminent role in policy making and relegating the services to the sidelines. "The service staffs' input into policy, which had been much more direct, became much more indirect either through the joint staff or in the tank when the chiefs of service met," says an officer with extensive policy-making experience.[59] Despite repeated mandates from Congress empowering the chairman and encouraging jointness, each service's control of promotion within its ranks assures that officers seldom forget the color of their uniforms while on the joint staff. As a consequence, the service chiefs retain some influence over military policy making and functional bureaus in the armed services, like the combat engineers and the Office of Judge Advocate General, occasionally stand up to the CINCs.

The chairman customarily defers to regional commanders as well, especially in time of war. A rare exception came in 1999, when opposition to waging the war in Kosovo motivated the armed services to withhold Apache helicopters and other capabilities from the CINC responsible for operations there, General Wesley Clark. When the chiefs insisted on holding the Apaches in reserve for two major regional contingencies, a remote possibility, an exasperated Clark confronted the vice chairman, General Joseph Ralston: "Joe, surely you're not saying that we're going to give up and lose in the only fight we have going, in order to be ready for two other wars that are not threatening in any way now?"[60] Even in this exceptional case the CINC got his way in the end.

Goldwater-Nichols was also supposed to strengthen civilian control of the military. Whether it succeeded is an open question. Civilian control may be part of the American political canon, but the armed services still jealously guard their autonomy against encroachment by outsiders. Symbolizing that autonomy is "the tank," by custom off-limits to civilians except by invitation, where the service chiefs gather to logroll and make deals in an effort to avoid open splits. When the chiefs present a united front to the outside, they have the clout to get what they want, especially when it comes to military doctrine and capabilities.

Accusing officers of playing politics with defense may sound like slander in military circles, but political warring inside the Pentagon is never-ending. "Military officers are relentless infighters, although they portray themselves as above politics," says a deeply involved Defense Department civilian. As a result, says the official, "The civilians pretend to give orders; the military pretends to take them."[61]

Yet what seems like military assertiveness to some looks like undue civilian deference to others. "In the culture of the Pentagon, if you have any sort of rank on your shoulders, for some reason your view was regarded as significantly more valued than someone else's," says Tim Connolly. "Successive defense secretaries—and I put the blame on them—do not view these two as equivalent." Civilian deference may also be due in part to fear of looking uninformed in front of battle-tested veterans with presumed expertise. "The military essentially relies on the ignorance of civilians to razzle-dazzle them," says Connolly, whose years of service in the special forces before he became a policy-maker gave him an advantage: "I could throw the bullshit flag when these guys would come in and try some razzle-dazzle." By contrast, he says, a civilian policy maker at a briefing on landmines was "like a hog looking at a wrist watch."[62]

Civilian deference also permeated "the dual-tracked policy process in the Pentagon," says Connolly. One action channel is the joint staff; another runs through the under secretary of defense for policy. In contrast to civilians, he says, the joint staff, "by virtue of being in the military, is significantly more disciplined and better at moving paper and getting reactions to what is going on over here [on the civilian side]. They can make decisions within our decision cycle. We cannot make decisions within their decision cycle." That is not all. "As I move paper upstream to get to the secretary," he says, "I have to coordinate with the joint staff. I can't even move a paper to the next level, out of my office to Walt Slocombe, unless the joint staff concurs. The joint staff, of course, has no corresponding requirement. They can move paper all the way up to the chairman without anybody else knowing what is going on." One consequence is that "the joint staff gets a vote on what's presented to the secretary," Connolly says, "and the joint staff gets a second vote in the meeting with the secretary when the proposal gets presented."[63] Whether out of military assertiveness or civilian deference, civilian control of the military is honored more in the breach than the observance.

The norm of civilian control is also supposed to inhibit overt partisanship among military officers, but that inhibition has attenuated in recent years. The officer corps has long been politically more conservative than the American public. With the waning of Democratic Party dominance, the once-solid South, where a disproportionate number of officers hale from, had increasingly become avowedly Republican as well.[64] Military nonpartisanship was sorely tested by the November 1994 election, which not only produced Republican Party control of both houses of Congress for the first time in 40 years but also bolstered a right wing within the GOP that favored higher military spending as a matter of principle, not just pork, whatever the fiscal consequences. In the House the right wing controlled the Republican caucus and the Republican leadership—Newt Gingrich, Tom DeLay, and Tom Armey—reflected that control. Moderates still retained a slim majority in the Senate caucus, and felt pressure to toe the party line, a line set by Majority Leader Robert Dole, staunch backer of a ban. That line would change once Dole resigned his Senate seat to run for president in 1996 and Trent Lott, a right-winger, was elected majority leader. By then a Republican Congress flaying a Democratic president for being soft on defense was not about to give him the leeway to ban landmines. By 1997 prevailing winds on Capitol Hill blew at the backs of those in the Army who wanted to stand up against a ban.

The struggle over the Comprehensive Test Ban Treaty also affected the landmines ban. Shalikashvili had just gone to the mat to win military acceptance for a zero-yield standard on nuclear testing. True, the armed services no longer had much interest in new nuclear arms—the Army had abandoned them altogether, the Navy had taken all warheads off aircraft carriers and other surface ships, and even the Air Force had downgraded its nuclear roles and missions. Yet some top Pentagon civilians had scant enthusiasm for zero yield, weapons designers in the national laboratories adamantly opposed it, and so did the Republican majority in Congress. "The Pentagon had to swallow zero yield and did not have a lot of appetite for [a landmines ban]," says Lee Feinstein of the State Department policy planning staff. "On a range of issues—on peacekeeping, on the test ban, and on landmines—Shali was much more open-minded than some other people, but he also picked his battles." Given the bad blood between the White House and the military, he could not fight on too many fronts at once. "Shali made the same calculations everybody else did...CTBT is more important than landmines," says Feinstein, who supported both bans.[65]

In short, the political terrain on which Shalikashvili tried to negotiate the landmines issue could hardly have been more treacherous. He "made his views known but he wasn't going to insist on them," says Feinstein.[66] "Shali was very much trying to be helpful," concurs Nancy Soderberg, the third-ranking member of the NSC staff. "He would never say no. He'd say, here are your options."[67] He did more than that, according to Ted McNamara, who had gotten to know Shalikashvili working on counter-terrorism and discussed the landmines issue with him from time to time: "He was convinced that his guys were not being flexible enough and he was very helpful in breaking the logjam."[68] Eric Newsom agrees, "We were told that General Shalikashvili was trying to work the issue for the president, but that he was having enormous problems internally with the Army."[69]

It was a battle he could not win without civilian help. Yet civilians in a better position than Newsom were reluctant to give him that help. Shalikashvili needed an order to bargain with the Army. No top official advised President Clinton to issue such an order. "The president wouldn't do what Shali needed," says Connolly. "Shali, therefore, wouldn't do what he wanted to do because he figured if the White House wasn't going to give him cover, he was not going to be the only one out there."[70]

Deference to the military was at fault, says Connolly. "This was a case where even a modicum of civilian interest and a slight exercise of commander-in-chief power would have moved us from the lose column to the win column because Shali was prepared to be big-footed on this and only asked to protect his ability to function in his environment."[71] Instead, the chairman was left to muster the military without authorization or support from civilians. There was only so much he could do under those circumstances.

7

The President Fails to Push the Military

If you go out to any commander, in any theater anywhere, at any time in history and say, Do you need more troops? I don't know how that guy can ever say no.

Nicholas Katzenbach[1]

The armed services took President Clinton's September 1994 endorsement of the "ultimate goal of the eventual elimination of antipersonnel landmines" at the UN General Assembly as a sign of his pro-ban sympathies. It was just one of several such signs. The next one came on February 12, 1996, when the president signed into law a 1-year moratorium on use of antipersonnel landmines introduced by Senator Patrick Leahy. By that time, says a White House official, "JCS knows the president is interested and wants a serious review." JCS also had to contend with legislation that "did not actually exempt Korea though it looked like it did."[2]

Some military officers made no secret of their displeasure. "The president signed it into law," one unidentified general told reporters, but "we have not been happy with it." Treading close to insubordination without stepping over the edge, he added, "The president did accept it, and we believe we can live with it, but we don't think it's an adequate—I didn't say we didn't support it—I mean, we don't think it's an adequate answer to the problem."[3] Less obtrusively, other military officers began lobbying on Capitol Hill to repeal the moratorium on use.

The chairman of the joint chiefs had a more tempered response. Anticipating that his commander-in-chief would opt for a ban and order the armed services to comply with it, General John Shalikashvili began studying the military requirements for antipersonnel landmines. He found them less than compelling.

The reaction in some quarters of the Army was visceral. It infuriated those who believed they were being set up for a ban. It also led the Army chief of staff, General Dennis Reimer, to hand off the hot potato. "Reimer wasn't very helpful, didn't play much, and turned it over to [General Ronald] Griffiths," his vice chief, says a top Pentagon official. He feels Reimer's abdication was ill-advised, "Griffiths went on a talk show and said a bunch of really dumb nuts things."

The internal struggle in the Pentagon soon surfaced in the news. On February 4, the *Washington Post* ran a story by John Mintz quoting a Pentagon source that an "acrimonious and table-pounding debate" was raging in the Department of Defense over whether or not to renounce the use of landmines. Asserting that the Joint Chiefs of Staff viewed mines as "a valuable military tool," the story paraphrased Shalikashvili that the United States should not unilaterally give up a weapon that irresponsible foes would continue to use.[4] On March 17, Raymond Bonner of the *New York Times* contradicted the *Post* story. He quoted a senior Pentagon official, who said that Shalikashvili had told the joint chiefs he was "inclined to eliminate all antipersonnel landmines."[5]

Neither story quite captured what was going on behind the scenes. Most CINCs saw no great need for antipersonnel mines. Nor did Shalikashvili. The Navy and the Air Force had no interest in landmines. The Army and the Marine Corps were internally divided: some officers firmly believed antipersonnel mines were a military requirement, one that should not be sacrificed on the altar of humanitarianism. Others disagreed. Most did not care. Aware of the sentiment, Shalikashvili began preparing for a possible ban. At the same time, top civilians in the Pentagon and the White House, fearing restiveness in the armed services, were shying away from a ban.

As a result, the administration never gave Shalikashvili the authority or support he needed to turn the president's words into action. Instead of ordering the Pentagon to abandon antipersonnel landmines and rely on other weapons and tactics, the president deferred US participation in a global ban until after he left office. He made US accession to the ban contingent on devising an alternative to antipersonnel landmines, something the Army had little interest in doing. That gave the landmine enthusiasts in military ranks leeway to ignore the commander-in-chief's desire to move toward a ban and they took full advantage of it.

The campaigners' impression, which they conveyed to the news media, was that entrenched opposition in the armed services had forced President Clinton to back away from a ban in April 1996. That impression is incorrect. Instead of a tribute to military intransigence, the new landmine policy, formally inscribed in Presidential Decision Directive 48 on June 26, 1996, reflected a lack of civilian leadership.

THE CINCS' NEED FOR ANTIPERSONNEL MINES

Enactment into law of Leahy's moratorium on landmine use started "a clock running," recalls Jan Lodal, principal deputy undersecretary of defense for policy, but did not concentrate the minds of top Pentagon civilians. It prompted "lawyerly arguments" that "if we don't do something by this date, the Leahy bill requires us to pull this out of Korea," he says. That did "force some kind of low-level agonizing, but the basic attitude around the Pentagon was, look, we're just not going to do that." The ban campaign was gaining traction in Europe and the core group was meeting on the margins of the CCW review conference, but, says Lodal, "no one thought it was really going to go very far and we didn't pay much attention to it." Prodded by Shalikashvili, the military was beginning to pay more attention, however. So were a few administration officials. "As the ban picked up steam," says Lodal, "Nancy Soderberg at the NSC, in particular, got interested in it, pushed heavily from State. Inderfurth was involved. Albright was involved."[6] Soderberg concurs, "In the 1995–96 period, the issue started heating up and the president started getting hit on it on all sides, and that's when I started getting involved."[7] High-level involvement led to another interagency review of landmines policy.

The trigger for the review was a letter dated February 13, 1996, from UN Ambassador Albright to National Security Adviser Lake, Secretary of Defense Perry, and General Shalikashvili, arguing that decisive action on landmines was "urgently needed." Albright had just returned from Angola, where she saw mothers tether children to keep them from wandering into mine-strewn fields. Ambassador Karl F. "Rick" Inderfurth of her staff, who accompanied her, drafted the letter. Citing her impressions of Angola and the peacekeeping mission in Bosnia, where mines posed the principal danger to US peacekeeping troops deployed and had already caused 28 casualties and seven fatalities in the implementation force (IFOR), Albright argued that unless the administration moved beyond current policy, the president's goal of eventual elimination would not be met "within our lifetimes." Taking note of the administration's advocacy of the Landmines Control Regime and strong action in the United Nations in response to pressure from Congress, she said that failure to formulate an operational policy was preventing more meaningful action. It was also forfeiting US leadership on the issue to France, Germany, and Canada. She called for a policy review by the Deputies Committee or a senior review group to be completed in 2 months' time that addressed the military utility and the humanitarian implications, distinguish "good" versus "bad" landmines, and examined the economic and military viability of alternatives.[8] Where she had written, "We must get rid of these," Clinton had scrawled in the margin, "I agree with you."[9]

Not everyone did. The letter contained "all kinds of factual errors and trashed CCW," says Robert Sherman. "My judgment at the time was that was a letter written to be leaked."[10] Maybe so, but it took 2 months for Albright's letter and President Clinton's reaction to it to wend their way to the news media. Over lunch Albright herself shared a copy of the letter with VVAF's Robert Muller, who disclosed Clinton's marginal notation to Washington Post columnist Mary McGrory.[11] "I had a meeting with Madeleine a couple of days before I spoke to Mary," admits Muller. "Madeleine was mad at me for that."[12] A VVAF staff member who attended college with Albright had helped arrange the lunch. "Albright called her and said, you tell Bobby Muller that's the last lunch he's ever having with me," recalls Mark Perry of VVAF. "She was ripped."[13]

Shalikashvili sent Albright a brief noncommittal reply, according to an official familiar with its contents, saying that he and the chiefs agreed the issue needed to be resolved and that he planned to discuss it with them at an upcoming meeting.

Albright's letter and the president's reaction to it prompted National Security Adviser Anthony Lake to take up the issue. A December 1994 visit of his own to Angola had given Lake a first-hand impression of the devastation that moved Albright. "We went to a hospital where a lot of children had been hit by landmines," says Nancy Soderberg, Lake's deputy, who accompanied him on the trip. "This one woman died in front of our eyes in the hospital." Lake was particularly moved by starvation that was the result of landmine-strewn fields lying fallow. "Tony, I remember, focused on a mango tree on the other side of a field that they couldn't get to because of the landmines. The children and the devastation of Angola shocked Tony." They also went to Mozambique where they spoke to deminers from Halo Trust.[14]

A year after their trip, with the issue heating up, Lake was prompted to act. "Tony took it over and tried to come up with a proposal," says Soderberg. By now, "a ban had become the test of US leadership. It didn't matter that our landmines weren't the ones blowing up kids." Yet Lake was not prepared to ban the use of antipersonnel mines: "He was trying to work up something that would enable us to ban the production of landmines."[15]

Lake convened an ad hoc meeting of top officials to address the issue. "Tony actually established somewhat of a precedent in handling this issue by not taking it through a formal process," says Rick Inderfurth, "but trying to work this out among a small group of principals—Albright, Perry, Shali."[16]

The meeting set off alarms. "That triggered a frantic call to Shali from his mole over at the NSC," says Tim Connolly, deputy assistant secretary of defense, to report that "Albright had given this impassioned speech and everyone was nodding and tears were in their eyes." Warning that "they're buckling and they're going to ban landmines," the caller urged the chairman to telephone the president to head off a ban. Shalikashvili refused, according to Connolly, who was the most outspoken ban proponent in the Pentagon. "That should have told everyone in the system he wants this to go the way we want it to go."[17]

Less than a month later, in the second week of March, Lake formally directed a interagency policy review. Terms of reference for the review were drafted by Kurt Campbell, deputy assistant secretary of defense, with help from the NSC staff. It went well beyond the perfunctory review done to head off Leahy in 1994: "There was an effort to get a 'reasonable Department of Defense policy' out," says Lodal. "I ended up being the senior person short of the secretary willing to pay attention to this."[18]

Even before Albright's letter or Lake's directive, however, General Shalikashvili had quietly instituted his own far-reaching reexamination of landmine policy. In early February the chairman took up the issue with the joint chiefs. "He brought it up in the tank and went around the room," says Tim Connolly. "Essentially, the Air Force chief said, I just deliver them. I don't care. The Navy guy said, you're not touching my mines. I don't care. Wayne Downing from SOCOM [Special Operations Command] said, the only guys we have who use them is an 'A team' that needs to retreat. We can just throw Claymores if that's necessary. The Marine Corps commandant was the most vocal in defending the need for them. So I think that was the proximate cause for Shali to say, we're going to solve this one."[19]

Connolly did not sit on his inside information. He told John Mintz of the Washington Post, which ran a story on February 4 about the Pentagon's "acrimonious and table-pounding debate" over landmine policy. "I don't think the debate is over," Mintz quoted Connolly as saying, "I hope passionately landmines become part of the [historical] folklore of war."[20]

On March 8, Jan Lodal informed the NSC staff that Shali had told Perry he was setting up "a 'tiger team' to spend 1 week developing strategy for eventual elimination of APL and in particular for a date certain for elimination of nonself-destructing landmines." A "tiger team" is the joint staff's way of expediting policy formulation by bringing together interested parties in the armed services to thrash out differences. "Shali was trying to be helpful here," says a senior member of the NSC staff. "He understood the politics for Clinton and he said, let me try to work this."[21]

The tiger team's assessment of the utility of landmines was inconclusive. General Joseph Ralston, vice-chairman of the joint chiefs of staff, succinctly summed up the findings in a May 16 White House press briefing: "The historical record is mixed concerning antipersonnel landmines. We know that they cause casualties, some enemy and some friendly. We know that they inhibit movement—enemy and friendly—and the significance in battle is variable."[22] Later that day he was asked specifically whether landmines were needed to stop a North Korean invasion. He replied, "We ran excursions using every technique and war game and modeling that we could do in simulation and we ran it both with landmines and without and there are thousands of casualties—additional casualties—that take place if we do not have antipersonnel landmines in place and available in Korea." The reporter pressed him, "Did it change the outcome?" Answer: "Well, the outcome by thousands of casualties."[23] In sum, the military's conclusion was that antipersonnel landmines were not needed to repel a North Korean invasion, but they could hold down US casualties. No one questioned what assumptions lay under that conclusion or whether a net assessment of enemy and friendly casualties was ever done.

On hearing from the tiger team, the chairman called a meeting of CINC representatives on short notice. "Shali sends a message to all the combatant CINCs," says Tim Connolly. "He tells them that I, Shali, am rethinking this landmine issue. I am interested in getting your input. On the basis of that, I am going to decide whether we are going to support the elimination of landmines or not." The CINCs' response, in Connolly's view, was yet another sign of the tepid enthusiasm for landmines in the military. "Now, if I'm a combatant CINC and I believe that I need antipersonnel landmines in order to prosecute my war and defend my area of responsibility, I'm going to send the biggest dog I can find, besides myself, because I want to make sure my voice is heard at the table. When the group assembled, there wasn't anyone above the rank of lieutenant colonel. Most of them were majors. That's indicator number one, CINCs don't care."[24]

Representatives of the CINCs assembled in late February, says Connolly. "The meeting was conducted in great secrecy," but "one of my people was involved" and "I got a readout from his [Shalikashvili's] charge to the group, which was, I want you to lock yourselves in the room...and I don't want you to come out until the smoke is white. You pick the position, and you bring it to me, and we'll run with it."[25]

The group concluded that antipersonnel mines, while still useful, were no longer integral to US war plans in any theater, including Korea. "The feedback I got is that nobody could articulate a requirement for them. The Korea guy came closest and it was the standard one, we need them to defend Seoul," says Connolly. At one point, the deputy chief of staff for operations proposed that they get rid of all antipersonnel mines. He polled representatives of all the CINCs. Not one objected.[26] Jan Lodal disputes that. "That's not my memory," he says. "I don't think anything [like that] got to OSD, much less all the way up to the secretary." Instead, he says, they concluded that "we did not need dumb old-fashioned antipersonnel mines."[27]

THE FIGHT GOES PUBLIC

Tim Connolly tried hard to convince other civilians that Shalikashvili was acting as though a ban was attainable without a revolt in the ranks. "At this point, I remember talking to an NSC guy," says Connolly, and telling him, "You've got to look at the indicators. If the military was against this, Shali would call the president. He would not be reticent." That was not all. "The CINC representatives were all lower-grade officers. They didn't send the deputy CINCs to say, I've got to have these thing or I'm going to fall on my sword. Or I'm going to the *Washington Times* with the story.... There would be a heavy lobbying campaign, a whispering campaign, officers talking about how the Clinton administration is undercutting our ability to fight." In 1997, a year after the joint chiefs had made their decision, the military would exhibit just such behavior, but not in the spring of 1996. "You don't see any of that. That tells you, all they're looking for is political cover. They want the president to act like the commander-in-chief and order them to do what they are inclined to do."[28]

Officials at the White House did not see it that way. "That's what these meetings were all about...Tony sitting down with Shali and Perry and saying we want to do this, but we're not going to order something the military can't do," says a senior NSC staff member. "You can't just have the president wave a magic wand.... There would have been such a backlash." Unfamiliarity was a factor. "You can't just pop in with no education on an issue and say, this is what we're going to do," the official says. "All of this is an educational process. You never know how hard you can push back on the Pentagon."[29] Connolly had little patience for the gradual slope of the learning curve or the excess of caution at the White House. "I could get no traction over there when I would talk to people I knew from the campaign who worked on the NSC," he says. "Nobody gave a shit."[30]

Connolly's entreaties had gone unheeded, so he took his fight outside. In conversations with Robert "Bobby" Muller and Tim Rieser, Senator Leahy's aide, "I made the point that the way that the chairman was reacting," he says, "and the lack of people setting their hair on fire and running into the hallways screaming, as I had seen them do on other issues, led me to believe that we had an opportunity here."[31] VVAF, in turn, encouraged Raymond Bonner of the

New York Times to contact Connolly at the Pentagon, says Mark Perry. "He was our deep throat there."[32]

Bonner's story appeared on March 17. General Shalikashvili, it reported, had told the joint chiefs that he was "inclined to eliminate all antipersonnel landmines," according to a senior Pentagon official.[33] The story went on to report that Connolly was pressing for a ban with a limited exception for situations such as Korea. Rejecting a compromise that would have permitted "smart" mines, Connolly said, "There is no evidence in the United States that we are capable of building a device capable of working 100 percent or nearly 100 percent of the time." Likening mines to chemical weapons, which were already banned, Connolly said, "Some day, and that day has to be sooner rather than later, we are going to reach that same conclusion about antipersonnel landmines."[34]

Bonner's source was Connolly. The target of his leak was Clinton. According to Connolly, "The moment around Ray Bonner's article was the point at which a fairly low-risk intervention by the president" would have enabled Shalikashvili to deliver the chiefs. Connolly had also been the main source for John Mintz's February 4 story in the *Washington Post* about the Pentagon's "acrimonious and table-pounding debate" over landmine policy. On April 14, as the Pentagon was backing away from a ban, Connolly would be forced out of office for his outspokenness.[35]

Meanwhile, girding for the coming struggle, campaigners tried to provide political cover for the commander-in-chief by lining up high-ranking Army retirees behind a ban. One stellar recruit to their cause was General H. Norman Schwarzkopf, who had commanded US forces in the 1991 Gulf War. Frank J. Fahrenkopf, Jr., who had been chairman of the Republican National Committee during the Reagan years, wrote Schwarzkopf asking him to sign an open letter to President Clinton endorsing a ban. "I very much oppose antipersonnel landmines," Schwarzkopf replied, "because they are indeed indiscriminate in their killing and maiming." His desire to have landmines "forever eliminated from warfare," he said, was based on his own experience of "having seen hundreds of my own troops killed or maimed by them," as well as being "keenly aware of the devastating effects" on civilians. He asked for more time to consider signing a letter to the president.[36]

General Colin Powell, chairman of the Joint Chiefs of Staff during the Gulf War, shared Schwartzkopf's sentiments. "I abhor mines. I saw what they did in Vietnam and I know what they are doing around the world." Yet Powell was unwilling to go as far as Schwarzkopf. He begged off joining in a public appeal, "I want to give Shali time to conduct this review."[37]

The generals' letter was Bobby Muller's idea. "My wife and I were having dinner with Bobby and his wife in December of 1995 and he told me the landmine issue was dead," says Mark Perry of the Vietnam Veterans of America

Foundation. "Bobby said, why don't you call your general friends" and get them to support the ban "and we'll put an ad in the paper." Perry, who had developed close contacts in the officer corps while writing a book on the Joint Chiefs of Staff, had lunch with a friend of his, Colonel Bob Sorley. "He asked, does this ban you're talking about prohibit command-controlled devices," Perry recalls, "and I said, no, it doesn't." Sorley agreed to draft a letter favoring a ban, have Perry edit it, and then contact his fellow West Point graduates to see who would sign it. "He did and I got it to Tim [Rieser], who re-edited it," says Perry. "It went out to 38 generals. There was dead silence." At long last Perry got a late-evening phone call from General Volney Warner. "He asked me, what does your organization do?" Perry recalls. "I said, we're a humanitarian organization. We have prosthetic clinics around the world. We put limbs on people." In Vietnam?, he asked. Yes, Perry replied. "Goddammit, he said, any organization that does that for those poor people, I'll sign anything you want."[38] At Perry's urging, Warner called his fellow officers and soon the campaigners had firepower of their own to throw into the battle for a ban.

VVAF ran an ad on March 28 that called on President Clinton to ban antipersonnel landmines now. "No one paid any attention," says Perry. "A week later we ran the ad with the names. It was as if a 5-megaton bomb had gone off."[39] Joining Schwarzkopf, Warner, and nine other retired generals and admirals in signing the open letter to the president were General David Jones (former chairman of the Joint Chiefs of Staff), General John R. Galvin (former commander of US forces in Europe), General Frederick F. Woerner, Jr. (former commander of US Southern Command), and perhaps less notable but most noteworthy of all, General James Hollingsworth (a former I Corps commander in South Korea and architect of the Hollingsworth line). Published in a full-page ad in the New York Times on April 3, the letter put antipersonnel landmines "in a category similar to poison gas. They are hard to control and often have unintended consequences (sometimes even for those who employ them)." It endorsed the ban as "not only humane, but also militarily responsible."[40]

VVAF's ads had an unintended effect in the administration: they drove the landmine issue deeper underground. "The public side of it was moving so far to an immediate ban that it was putting us in an impossible situation," says Nancy Soderberg, third-ranking member of the NSC staff. As the ban campaign caught on outside, policy making inside gravitated into fewer and fewer hands. "It got very high level and intense toward the end where it was really among Tony, Shali, the chiefs, and the president," she says. "All the outside groups were cut out of it at that time because we had to figure out what we were doing. We already had all the input from them."[41] That put the White House on a collision course with the campaigners.

THE WHITE HOUSE BACKS DOWN

The CINCs' representatives had provided an opening to get rid of antipersonnel landmines. Still expecting Clinton to opt for a ban and order him to comply, Shalikashvili was waiting for a presidential directive before sounding out the CINCs in person and then taking up the issue with JCS.

In an interview with the *Washington Post* on April 2, a day before the generals' ad appeared, Shalikashvili was careful not to tip his hand. "Where do I want to come out on that issue?" he mused aloud. "I think where everyone else wants, that we stop the use of landmines producing all the tragedy, those young lives snuffed out and limbs torn off. It's absolutely something that has to be brought to a halt. But I don't think I get paid to just look at it from that aspect without also understanding what impact it will have on American youngsters on some battlefield tomorrow who might lose their lives because they don't have protective mines. I owe it to them and their parents."[42]

As Shalikashvili was girding to charge up policy hill for the president, administration officials, anticipating intense military opposition to a ban, sounded retreat. Secretary of Defense William Perry chose not to go to the mat on landmines, says a senior Pentagon official. "The question was, 'Is this the issue on which we want take on the military?' The answer came down, 'No'."[43] A White House official agrees, "OSD did not play a strong role."[44]

The White House was wary as well. Nancy Soderberg was just one of the civilians on the NSC staff who favored a ban but assumed that the armed forces would resist it. "I think they made a fairly convincing case that the removal of landmines without some kind of alternative to delay attacking troops on the ground was just something they were not going to support," she says. "If the president had mandated a ban on landmines, there would have been such an uproar. I don't know whether they could have gotten a voting majority to override a veto. It was never seriously discussed so I don't know what the numbers would have been."[45] As a result, no presidential directive to ban landmines ever materialized.

Instead, the White House settled for less. "We were feverishly trying to come up with a policy that would make good on the president's pledge to eventually get rid of landmines," says Soderberg. "We finally said, all right, we recognize that you need to find alternatives and they're not there now. We'll give you time to come up with them."[46]

If it was left up to the Army to come up with alternatives, "eventually" could turn out to be a very long time. "The fight we had was not so much, are we going to get rid of landmines, but how quickly and how far we were going to push [it] to develop an alternative," says Soderberg. "I started out wanting to find a way to ban them more quickly and was pretty committed to doing it." Setting a date for the military to end landmine use was critical. "You had to give the Pentagon a deadline to force the Army or they'd never do it," she says. "The date certain was also the only way we thought we'd get [Senator] Leahy on board." The deadline proved contentious. "They came back with some really long timetable," she says, "and we pushed back. We initially tried to make it 2005 and ended up having to negotiate."[47]

By the second week in April, Shalikashvili knew that Clinton was not about to order a ban. Only then did he poll the CINCs by telephone. All but one confirmed what the chairman already knew, that they could do without antipersonnel landmines. The lone holdout was General Gary Luck, who, as combined forces commander in Korea, would have to take operational control of ROK troops, along with their landmines, in the event of war. Due to retire in July, he had been in command during the nuclear crisis after North Korea had removed spent fuel containing five or six bombs' worth of plutonium from its nuclear reactor at Yongbyon in May 1994. When the United States asked the UN Security Council to impose sanctions and decide to send reinforcements to Korea, the crisis came to the brink of war. As Shalikashvili expected, and Nicholas Katzenbach would have predicted, Luck, having lived through that dire time, was in no mood to take chances. He wanted ROK forces under his command in wartime to be free to use dumb antitank mines and the antipersonnel mines that kept the barriers to Seoul from being breached quickly. He also wanted the United States to be able to transfer mines to the South Koreans and to deploy its own smart mines by air and artillery. "The standoff in Korea was the only scenario left—there was no Fulda Gap—where you would potentially have to stand behind a barrier for a long period of time and wait for the war to start," says Jan Lodal. "Shali got all the other CINCs to agree that there were no scenarios anywhere else in the world that had this characteristic."[48]

That allowed the armed forces to get rid of most, but not all, of their pure antipersonnel landmines, along with a lot of other mines as well. "Basically, by that time we had pretty much agreed, with the exception of Korea, to a new policy statement which said we would not have any more dumb mines and we wouldn't have any more antipersonnel mining," says Lodal, "but that there would be antipersonnel mines used in these mixed packages of self-destruct/self-deactivating systems."[49]

Lodal and other civilians in the Department of Defense were acting under the misapprehension that the US Army still had responsibility for the barrier defense of Seoul. "There was also the fact that some of our units," he says, "had in their war plan the mission to go emplace some antipersonnel mines." Lodal would eventually learn just how ancillary that mission was for defending Seoul. "What happened later when we finally agreed that we could get out of the business in Korea, it was concluded in negotiations with the Koreans that our role was minor. We could turn it all over to the Koreans and we didn't have to do it any more."[50]

Tim Connolly's recollection differs from Lodal's. Connolly thought "a way for us to be able to eliminate the antipersonnel landmines from the US stockpile and to make that affirmative statement" was to "transfer ownership of the mines that are currently in the Korean peninsula to the Koreans so that they're not on our books—admittedly a smokescreen." He had broached the idea to Stephen Goose of the ICBL. "I had this conversation with Steve. The NGOs always understood that Korea was a sticking point, because of the belief that [US landmines] were integral to the defense of the South" he says, "so they were pragmatically open to this idea." Connolly even recalls "a back-channel from the South Koreans that said, if the United States will officially ask us, do we believe we need you to use antipersonnel landmines to defend us, we do not." He passed along the message: "We moved that to State and the United States refused to ask the question. The Defense Department essentially did not want to ask the Koreans the question because they did not want to hear the answer that they knew they were going to get." Why didn't he raise the issue with Undersecretary of Defense Walter Slocombe? "I don't think in the entire time I dealt with this I had one conversation with Walt on the issue of antipersonnel landmines."[51]

On April 13, National Security Adviser Anthony Lake sent a decision memorandum to the president. General Shalikashvili, with the support of Perry and the concurrence of the DOS, ACDA, and UN Ambassador Albright, recommended that he "commit to a complete ban by a date certain in 2010," according to an NSC official, because the armed services "need time." That was a lot more time than they needed. As if that were not enough, the recommendation also had generous exemptions for use of antipersonnel landmines. Use would "stop now," says the NSC official, "except to defend US and allies from armed aggression" and "facilitate where necessary, combat search-and-rescue operations or escape and extraction of special operations forces."[52] The loopholes were arguably broader than the ban. They also went beyond the limits on use in Senator Leahy's moratorium bill that the president had signed into law on February 12.

Leahy reacted even before the decision memorandum landed on the president's desk. He wrote to Lake on April 11 expressing concern about reports of a draft policy that would permit use "for another 10 years."[53] His opposition mattered to President Clinton, who wanted somehow to get Leahy and Shalikashvili to accept a common landmine policy. Lake was trying to broker just such a policy. "All through this process if you could get Leahy and Shali to agree on an option, Perry and Lake would sign on in a second," says a senior NSC staff member. "They're trying to find something that meets the political imperative from Leahy but doesn't do something irresponsible to our troops."[54] An April 18 memorandum from the NSC staff to Harold Ickes, a White House political operative who handled the tough issues on Capitol Hill, flagged the problem. "We are far off what Leahy can support. 2010 is way out of the ballpark," it read.[55] Leahy was not swayed by the administration's willingness to go beyond his legislation and eventually eliminate antipersonnel landmines, not just ban their use, and in the meantime have any military requirement for landmines subject to annual certification starting in 2001.

Ban campaigners got wind of the recommendations even before the president had approved them. "Connolly called me," recounts VVAF's Mark Perry, "and said we got everyone on board but Gary Luck just vetoed what you wanted." Perry got in touch with Hollingsworth, who telephoned General Luck and urged him to back the ban. "They had a tension-filled talk," says Perry, in which Luck "told him you're not here now. I am." Hollingsworth also tried to get General Henry Emerson to call Luck, who had served in the 2nd Division under his command, but Emerson refused.[56]

VVAF leaked the recommendations to the press on April 17.[57] Caught off guard by the premature disclosure, Pentagon officials tried to put the best face on the proposed policy by redirecting attention from how long it would take to eliminate landmines to where the armed forces might need to deploy them. Responding to a student's question after a speech at Georgetown University on April 18, Defense Secretary Perry spoke of "the terrorist nature of these landmines," adding, "We should seek ways of eliminating them." Yet he was careful to keep options open. "Landmines do provide essential protection, perimeter defense, to American troops, particularly today in Korea," he went on. "Until we can find a way of replacing that military capability, we have to somehow keep those in service. So the question is one of timing and developing the proper transition plan so that we can get rid of them."[58] In an interview with the *Washington Post*'s defense correspondent Bradley Graham, a Pentagon official said, "What's new is, the military chiefs have stated their bottom-line needs for the use of antipersonnel landmines and would like to focus the debate on protecting those needs in the short term." Those "bottom-line needs" were spelled out by a senior defense official who briefed reporters, "In our planning, the use of what we call 'dynamic obstacles' is an important force multiplier" in Korea and the Persian Gulf. "Dynamic obstacles in open terrain channelize, delay, and temporarily block an enemy force, protect the flanks of a friendly force, and, in the final stages of a campaign, serve to cut off the retreat and repositioning of an enemy force."[59]

Senator Leahy remained unpersuaded. Within days, his aide, Tim Rieser, telephoned Nancy Soderberg to complain about the NSC staff's signing off on a policy that "betrayed serious lack of understanding" and had "substantive problems."[60] Rieser had already voiced his misgivings to reporters. "If the United States continues to make exceptions on use, it will have no impact in persuading other countries to renounce landmines," a Senate staffer and ban advocate was quoted in the *Washington Post*. He also objected to the delay in banning their use. "Setting an early deadline is central, since it, more than anything else, will send a message that we're serious."[61]

VVAF kept up the pressure on the president. At that point, says Perry, "it was clear to us he was not going to give the armed forces an order." Unable to get an appointment with Clinton, Muller arranged to attend a mid-April dinner at the White House to honor the memory of Eleanor Roosevelt. "He bought a table—like $5,000 a chair," says Perry, and invited some of the signers of the generals' ad to join him. Two did, David Jones and Robert Gard. At the dance after dinner, Clinton was standing alone when Muller rolled onto the dance floor. Gard and Jones followed, says Perry. "Bobby had to shout over the band, 'I'm here to tell you, you can ban these landmines. We need to talk.' Clinton said I'd like to do it. Clinton turned to Jones and asked, 'Dave, can I do this?' Jones said, 'Mr. President, I think you can'." Clinton turned to Gard, who nodded. Clinton, unpersuaded, shook his head.[62] Muller picks up the story. "I said to the president, what more can we do?" and Clinton replied, "'I can't afford a breach with the joint chiefs. Get the joint chiefs off my ass.' That's literally what he said." Muller disclosed his encounter with the president to *Washington Post* columnist Mary McGrory along with the Albright letter.[63] "We told McGrory that," says Perry, "which set Clinton up as a guy who caved in to the military."[64]

The administration tried to tighten some of the loopholes in the April 13 recommendations. On April 23, the NSC staff canvassed the interagency community on a proposal for President Clinton to announce at the UN General Assembly that fall, seeking a ban on use, transfer, production, and stockpiling in the Conference on Disarmament. In the interim the United States would press for a protocol in the CCW with tighter restrictions on use, urge other countries to adopt their own moratoria on use, and abide by a ban on use "except in cases of armed aggression in Korea or the Persian Gulf." General Wesley Clark, the JCS representative, was "receptive" to the proposal but reserved judgment until the joint chiefs discussed it in the tank later that day. Rick Inderfurth, representing Albright, liked the idea of the CD and the General Assembly resolution, but noted that Leahy would insist on a date certain. Seconding Inderfurth, Jan Lodal said OSD did not oppose to negotiating an international treaty but needed an early date for elimination of antipersonnel landmines. Defense Secretary Perry, he reported, "thinks he can deliver the chiefs on a date for elimination of all APL as early as 1999 with prohibition on use effective now," assuming a presidential waiver for Korea and the Persian Gulf.[65] His assessment erred on the side of optimism.

That evening Shalikashvili took up the ban in "the tank" with Army Chief of Staff Dennis Reimer, Marine Commandant Charles Krulak, Chief of Naval Operations Jeremy Boorda, and Air Force Chief of Staff Ronald Fogleman. Korea was hardly mentioned. General Reimer rested his case on grounds sure to enlist the sympathies of his fellow chiefs: We have a good set of weapons that we've already paid for. Nobody is going to give us anything to replace them—we know that. Once the NGOs forced the Army to get rid of landmines, he wondered aloud, which service would be the next to be disarmed?[66] Reimer's appeal to Army autonomy carried the day. As a result of the discussion, the joint staff's conclusions were toughened up, making them more supportive of landmines. A date certain for elimination of landmines was one casualty of the chiefs' deliberations. As a result, PDD-48 would set no deadline for the Army to divest itself of landmines.

Policy in hand, Shalikashvili began telephoning signers of the generals' letter. The chairman could be very compelling, to judge from General Henry Emerson's reaction. "He backed down Emerson," says Mark Perry of VVAF, "who called me [and] said, I'm not going to renounce my position on this ad, but I want you to know I'm not going to be an active participant." Perry had James Hollingsworth telephone Emerson, to no avail. That a general of Emerson's caliber felt compelled to retreat after a call from the chairman impressed Perry: "This is a gunfighter. He killed 22 guys single-handedly in Vietnam and ran some of the best tactical operations in that war."[67] Shalikashvili got to Schwarzkopf as well. "Immediately after the letter came out," says Robert Sherman, "Schwarzkopf started telling friends that wasn't what he meant. He thought the ad had been directed against persistent mines, but for reasons I don't understand he refused to comment publicly on that. It wasn't until we were actually in the Oslo conference that Tom Bowman of the *Baltimore Sun* somehow talked to him and got him to say, I favor a ban on dumb mines. The smart mines are ones we can use. If he had called a press conference the day after the ad appeared to say that, there might never have been an Ottawa Convention. But as it was, a perception was created both at home and abroad that the US military itself thought APLs should be banned."[68]

As difficult as it was to withstand a personal appeal from the chairman of the Joint Chiefs of Staff, some signers did. One was James Hollingworth. "Hollingworth was pretty adamant," says Perry. "He had had two sergeants die in Korea in peacetime playing golf. One hit a ball out of bounds. They went to retrieve it and tripped a mine." Harold Moore and Frederick Woerner stood their ground as well. "Hal Moore was tough and Fred Woerner was toughest of all," says Perry. "His searing experience in Vietnam coupled with his intelligence means he's not easily impressed by some four-star." According to Perry, "Shalikashvili called him and said, I really need your help on this. I know you signed the ad but we just can't do this." Woerner expressed appreciation for the call but stood firm. "Not only are you going to ban these things," he told Shalikashvili, "but when you're done, you're going to ban cluster bombs, too."[69]

The generals' ad also set off a row inside the ban campaign. "We hadn't told Jody [Williams] about it, of course," Perry says. "She came steaming in here about a week after the ad ran, yelling and screaming at me and Bobby, what the hell are you doing? You're consorting with the enemy. How could you do this?"[70] While VVAF was still trying to coax the United States into accepting a ban, Williams and others in the ICBL were using the United States as a foil to rally support for the ban elsewhere in the world. It was not the first time that campaigners clashed over the merits of an insider versus outsider strategy. Nor would it be the last.

WHAT WAS THE NEW POLICY?

The joint chiefs' recommendations did not satisfy President Clinton's goal of a landmines policy that both Shalikashvili and Leahy could accept. In a memo to Lake on May 1, the NSC staff tried once more to frame alternatives. One issue was the geographic scope of the loophole on interim use of landmines. The memo laid out three variants. One would make an exception for Korea only, which the staff thought was "likely to be accepted by Leahy and opposed by JCS." A second would exempt both Korea and the Iraqi border with Kuwait from the ban on use, which "might be acceptable to JCS but to date had been rejected by Leahy." A third would exempt Korea and allow the use of self-destruct/self-deactivating APL as a "last resort to save lives," which "might fly with JCS and would put opponents on the defensive." The second alternative might be extended to "capture a DMZ other than Korea and the Iraq–Kuwait border." Among the "likely candidates" were Cyprus, the Western Sahara, India–Pakistan, and Israel's borders with Lebanon, Syria, and Egypt, but no "definitive answer" was possible "without involving State legal experts." The memo opted for negotiating a global ban on antipersonnel landmines in the Conference on Disarmament. DOD would begin preparing now "to conduct all military operations without APL" and do a study within 1 year that "will identify critical paths to these adjustments in the interim period."[71] The memo made no mention of a date certain for ending use.

The president had not yet signed on, however. Aware of his desire not to antagonize Leahy, NSC staffers prepared the ground carefully. Among those they contacted was one of the signers of the generals' letter, David Jones, who had sounded out Leahy and reported that the third option would be a "hard sell" and that Senator Robert Dole, the likely Republican nominee for president, "might preempt" it by announcing his backing for a ban. Bobby Muller, he added, would even be "harder than Leahy" to sell on the change. Jones expressed willingness to act as a "go-between" with the other signers of the generals' letter.[72]

Top advisers were scheduled to see Clinton on May 10 in the Oval Office to seek approval for the new policy. In preparation for that meeting, Robert Bell, NSC senior director for defense policy and arms control, sent a memorandum to Lake. "JCS," he wrote, "can live with a five- to ten-year transition for all cases except Korea." Focusing on what to do in the interim, he listed the three options of May 1, none of them yet "endorsed by Leahy or Shali." Option 1, an exemption for Korea only, "Shali can't accept." Option 2, precluding smart mines outside Korea and the Persian Gulf, raised "concern" in the military "because smart antitank mines were prepackaged" with antipersonnel mines. The chiefs raised an objection to option 3 as well: it was "so narrowly worded" that it would bar use outside Korea in all but limited circumstances.[73]

A *New York Times* news story by Philip Shenon datelined May 10 revealed that the joint chiefs, in a "proposal which was presented to President Clinton in a White House meeting today," recommended "a broad exception" that "would allow the use of mines indefinitely in Korea and in other potential war zones where the United States and its allies patrol a demilitarized area recognized by the United Nations."[74]

The campaigners promptly gave vent to their displeasure. Bobby Muller told the press, "Last week the president stressed his personal concern over landmines by describing the hours he has committed to addressing this problem, and by noting that he keeps an antipersonnel landmine on his desk in the Oval Office. This proposal would make a mockery of the president's concern, and would run a dagger deep through the heart of our international campaign to ban this weapon."[75] Decrying the lack of advanced consultation, the USCBL urged President Clinton to reject the recommendation.

To try to placate them, Nancy Soderberg held a last-minute meeting at the NSC with Muller and other ban campaigners. "It was one of the toughest meetings I ever had in my life," says Soderberg. "Bobby Muller was absolutely outraged and insulted that we didn't inform him of the policy before it leaked and that the policy was the wrong one."[76] The late-night session added injury to insult, further fueling Muller's outrage. "We're trying to get the administration to do the right thing," he recalls, "and she's saying we're going to take all these views into consideration, when a guy opens the door, sticks his head in and says the president just signed off on the landmine directive." Feeling "scammed," Muller told Soderberg, "I guess this meeting is over."[77]

The NSC staff did think through how to notify Leahy. The president himself would call the senator no later than 24 hours before the policy was to be made public. The NSC staff circulated talking points highlighting the "international effort to conclude a ban in 5–10 years," the administration's pledge to "destroy dumb mines by 1999 except those needed for use in Korea or training," and its commitment to "identify alternatives" and to "mine detection and clearing." Jan Lodal added two points. "This is a two-track policy: negotiations and some unilateral moves on the first track" and the "program" to replace antipersonnel landmines on the second, which "eventually gets rid of APL." Lodal's second point addressed the sensitive matter of why no deadline was set for ending use: "The issue in Korea is not how dependent we are today, but that it takes considerable time, some new technology, and lots of money to rebuild our force structure without mines, to redo the war plans" in place "since the 1950s," and "retrain tens of thousands of affected US troops and 500,000 ROK troops." The Army is "a big complicated machine. It takes time to redesign it without APL as one of the parts of the machine."[78] Yet the prime mover was himself unmoved. As an NSC internal memo notes, "Leahy blasted the Pentagon proposal to continue use" in an interview with the *Boston Globe* on May 15.

On May 16, 1996, President Clinton announced the new policy. The announcement was overshadowed by the suicide that morning of Admiral Jeremy Boorda, chief of naval operations. Jan Lodal picked up Secretary Perry at Andrews Air Force Base and drove him to the White House, where they were scheduled to brief the president. "We ended up talking to Clinton mostly about Boorda," says Lodal. "Clinton then went across to the Executive Office Building to announce the new landmines policy."[79] It was a missed opportunity to head off some embarrassing misstatements.

The president seemed to accept the central premise of the campaigners at the start and follow it to its logical conclusion, a ban on antipersonnel landmines. "Boys and girls at play, farmers tending their fields, ordinary travelers—in all, more than 25,000 people a year are maimed or killed by mines left behind when wars ended," he began. "To end this carnage, the United States will seek a worldwide agreement as soon as possible *to end the use of all antipersonnel landmines.*"[80]

The problem was, this statement was literally not true. As the new policy made clear, the United States was prepared to give up all but a few purely antipersonnel landmines, including self-destructing and self-deactivating ones, but it intended to retain its stockpile of mixed munitions, which combined antipersonnel mines with antitank mines—"old mines in new bottles," Leahy called them.[81] To maintain the pretense, White House officials contended that mixed munitions did not contain antipersonnel mines, which was a deceptive, if not downright deceitful claim.

To compound the confusion, the president added a second commitment, "I will propose a resolution at the 51st United Nations General Assembly this fall, urging the nations of the world to support *a worldwide ban on landmines.*"[82] The new policy committed him to get rid of some antipersonnel landmines but to retain the rest, along with antitank mines.

In his most significant undertaking, the president noted, "I am directing that, effective immediately, our armed forces discontinue the use of all so-called dumb antipersonnel mines" and to have them "removed from our arsenals and destroyed by 1999."

Not in Korea, however: "The only exception will be for those mines required to defend our American troops and our allies from aggression on the Korean Peninsula."[83] That wording played fast and loose with the dumb mines in Korea and why they were being retained. "We don't have any mines in the ground in Korea," says Robert Sherman. "The Koreans do."[84]

"Until an international ban takes effect," the president continued, "the United States will reserve the right to use so-called smart mines or self-destructing mines as necessary."[85] That statement was somewhat disingenuous. The president had given the armed forces unlimited time to come up with an alternative, postponing the day that the United States would ban antipersonnel landmines, possibly forever.

The president glossed over that problem a moment later, "While the exceptions I have mentioned are necessary to protect American lives, I am determined to end our reliance on these weapons completely. Therefore I am directing the secretary of defense to begin work immediately on research and development of alternative technologies that will not pose new dangers to civilians."[86]

The bind the administration had put itself in was all too apparent in a briefing after the president's remarks. Secretary of Defense Perry told reporters that "we are prepared to give up the smart mines as part of any agreement. And we believe that may be necessary to get the international agreement."[87] The haves would sacrifice some smart mines in order to get the have-nots to limit dumb ones.

Sherman blames the NSC staff for what he calls "that nonsensical statement," which was never cleared with other agencies. "The NSC wrote it," he says. "They never sent it around."[88]

One casualty of the policy review, in Sherman's view, was the distinction between self-destruct and persistent landmines. "In April 1996, I found out later, NSC looked at the possibility of resting our case on the self-destruct distinction and decided it was too technical to sell to the American people. Somehow—this is really bizarre, don't ask me to explain it—they decided that, rather than telling the world that short-duration mines aren't the problem, we would tell the world that APL in mixed systems really aren't APL, and this would be more persuasive and easier to understand. This was a total failure, of course. There were some members of the US government who were expert on selling the self-destruct distinction—that is the CCW team, and yours truly in particular. We were not consulted.... No one said, let's try a focus group and see if it works. The decision making was strictly amateur hour, the Peter principle personified. The NSC staff put garbage in and got pig-swill out. They did President Clinton a severe disservice."[89]

Tim Connolly could not have disagreed more. "That, I felt, was my contribution to the process, to use whatever cachet my title and my biography had to make the...point whenever they stupidly put me in front of the press: there is simply no evidence we can achieve 100 percent reliability on self-destruct, self-neutralizing, and absent 100 percent, we are no better off [with a smart mine] than we are with a dumb mine."[90]

On June 17, Secretary Perry signed a Defense Department directive to implement the president's decision, but Presidential Decision Directive 48 was not issued until June 26, 9 days later. The documents differ on two points. PDD-48 contains a section entitled "Background" that the DOD directive does not. "The policy," it reads, "has been established pursuant to a principals' level review, which included a thorough study of US military requirements conducted by the joint chiefs of staff, with the involvement of the services and the combatant commands." It "sets forth a concrete path to a global ban on APL, but ensures that as the United States pursues this ban, essential US military requirements and commitments to our allies will be protected."[91] It was a transparent attempt to drape PDD-48 in military authority.

The other difference is that, while both documents affirm, "The United States will aggressively pursue an international agreement to ban the use, stockpiling, production, and transfer of antipersonnel landmines with a view to completing the negotiation as soon as possible," PDD-48 adds a sentence, "The United States should seek to initiate such negotiations as soon as feasible." It does not designate a venue for negotiations, but instead directs the chairmen of the Arms Control Interagency Working Group and the Landmine Control and Demining Interagency Working Group, Robert Bell and Eric Newsom, respectively, to prepare options for review by the Principals Committee by July 19, a sign that the issue had been too contentious to resolve in time.[92]

Both documents stipulate that dumb mines will be eliminated, except for stocks set aside for Korea: "Effective immediately, the United States will unilaterally undertake not to use and to place in inactive stockpile, with intent to demilitarize by the end of 1999, all nonself-destructing APL not needed for (a) training personnel engaged in demining and countermining operations, and (b) to defend the United States and its allies from armed aggression across the Korean demilitarized zone."

Both documents also say, "Between now and the time an international agreement takes effect, the United States will reserve the option to use self-destructing/self-deactivating APL, subject to the restrictions the United States has accepted in the Convention on Conventional Weapons."

PDD-48 directs the secretary of defense to "undertake a program of research, procurement and other measures needed to eliminate the requirement for these exceptions."[93] His directive turned over that responsibility to the undersecretary of defense for acquisition and technology. Neither directive set a date for meeting the objective, however. Among the "other measures" cited in the DOD directive, the JCS chairman was told to "direct changes in war plans, joint doctrine and training to reduce and eliminate the reliance on APLs, consistent with the president's new policy," and to "direct the services to begin development of tactics and service doctrine eliminating the need to rely on self-destructing APLs in anticipation of prompt international agreement to ban all antipersonnel landmines." He was ordered to "initiate steps to remove all nonself-destructing APL from unit basic ammunition loads," except in Korea.[94]

Both documents ordered the JCS chairman, starting in 1999, to certify annually to the president and secretary of defense whether "a military requirement for the exceptions" remained and assess "the status of the search for alternatives to APL."

The Department of Defense was also ordered to expand training in humanitarian demining and to develop mine detection and clearing technology and share it with other countries.[95] Until now the Army had invested much more in landmines of its own than in technologies to detect and detonate mines or even breach minefields. US troops, mostly from special operation forces, would not help in humanitarian demining, but would train others to perform this delicate mission.

Pentagon press briefings made the key changes public. "We can look for devices that do the specific job that antipersonnel mines do without the residual and very undesirable side-effects," Defense Secretary Perry told reporters, "and the most promising techniques in that area fall in the category of nonlethal technologies—technologies which slow and disrupt an infantry advance without killing." Beyond that, he mentioned "generic ways of shaping the battlefield differently than you shape it with mines...changes across the board in the way we fight battles—in tactics and doctrine as well as in systems."[96]

To the NSC staff, the administration never got the credit it deserved for its decision to end the use of all but a few pure antipersonnel mines and get rid of all dumb landmines outside of Korea. "That was a very dramatic move," says a White House official, "but it was not necessarily recognized as such because public expectations had been built, rightly or wrongly, by all of the various leaks."[97] Prior expectations were not the only problem, however. The president's statement was unclear and Army officers kept blurring what had been decided. "The Army was its own worst enemy," says Jan Lodal. It "couldn't make a clean statement, we don't need and won't keep and will get rid of all of the antipersonnel landmines."[98]

Once the president had accepted the recommendation of the joint chiefs against a ban, those in the military who wanted to hold onto antipersonnel landmines were free to resist any change in policy. "Our military people did personalize and emotionalize this issue to a degree that I had not seen before," says Eric Newsom. "To an important extent they saw this as essentially a litmus test of this administration's determination to stand up for the troops."[99] By 1997 the Monica Lewinsky affair and the threat of impeachment would lend passion to military resistance to a landmines ban. It would also make civil-military relations more fractious than at any time since 1951, when President Truman cashiered General Douglas MacArthur for open insubordination.

QUEST FOR THE HOLY GRAIL

One form that military opposition took was lobbying by the armed services to repeal Leahy's legislation imposing a 1-year moratorium on use. "They were calling all their friends on the Hill," says an NSC official. The provision was inserted into a defense authorization bill that passed the House. Secretary Perry took up the issue at breakfast with Leahy on June 20, but Leahy reaffirmed his stance later that day: "the only exception to a complete ban by 1999" could be the DMZ in Korea—subject to "annual certification by the president" of continuing need for antipersonnel landmines. On June 28 the NSC designated DOD to be the administration's agent on the legislation. Lake decided that the "administration will not lobby, but if asked, DOD will say it supports" repeal.[100]

A more important form of military opposition was determined resistance to devising alternatives to landmines. The president may have been committed to seek alternatives, but the Army was not. Ban opponents saw the commitment as a sop to Leahy and other ban proponents.

Overseas, others interpreted the commitment to mean that alternatives were feasible. "They presume, as many countries do, that any technological problem the United States sets out to solve, it can," says ACDA's Robert Sherman. "That's not the case here."[101] Yet the point man on landmines policy in the Pentagon was not as pessimistic as Sherman. "I was always a believer that you could make technology so that you could have [mines] that were remotely deactivated," says Jan Lodal. "If you wanted to go another step, rather than make them remotely deactivated, make them remotely activated."[102] Others had pet alternatives of their own—sensor-triggered Hornet wide area munitions, Brilliant antiarmor submunitions for delivery by surface-to-surface missiles, and Maverick and Longbow air-to-surface missiles.[103]

In canvassing for alternatives, however, the joint chiefs deferred to the Army and the Army in turn deferred to the combat engineers, whose idea of an alternative was another variant of a landmine. Abandoning landmines altogether would require the Army to change doctrine, which the combat engineers did not want to do, as well as to rely more on the Air Force for close air support, which the Army was even more reluctant to do. Devising another alternative would require the Army to set aside funding in a tight budget for new, more expensive, and untried technology—something it preferred to avoid. "The politics are against a new system," says Lodal. "Nobody ever looked at the cost-effectiveness of a better system because it just isn't very high on anybody's list. This is a mission that only works against vehicular columns, armored or unarmored. We just don't have that many cases in the world where we're going to fight these kinds of wars. Korea is sui generis." The threat there can be met "by just keeping a bunch of old stuff that you've already got."[104] Politics and technology conspired to frustrate a search for alternatives.

One possibility was to remove the antipersonnel mines from the mixed munitions. "There was a briefing on that," says Eric Newsom. "They said it was an extremely delicate and dangerous thing to disassemble mixed munitions. We asked, was it possible to do it? Can't you just take these antipersonnel landmines out and use other means of protecting the antitank mines, like artillery? They said removing the APLs can be done, but it would be very expensive and it wouldn't be as effective."[105] Officials in PM concluded that the Army did not want to.

Lodal could scarcely contain his exasperation with the Army. "They came up with this scheme. They said, okay, we'll get rid of these mixed packages. The only time we'll have anything that's antipersonnel, even by its original design, is antipersonnel protecting the anti-tank [mines]," says Lodal. "Then you look at the fine print." The price was prohibitive, "a billion dollars," by Army estimates. "That got everyone to focus on it." Once they did, they discovered it was "another trick." The Army was "going to take all the self-destruct antipersonnel things and dilute them with a few antitank things and call them a mixed package," says Lodal. "We said, wait a minute, we're not going to do that, and Shali got really pissed."[106]

The search for alternatives consumed considerable time and energy, much of it wasted, according to Lodal. Because Claymore mines, which have a man in the loop, were permitted in the draft treaty, "people focused on trying to come up with one or another cockamamie scheme to put a man in the loop. They weren't likely to work, they weren't likely to distinguish combatants, and they were going to be very costly." In one scheme, Lodal recalls, "The gunner is some guy sitting in a command center in the Pentagon or wherever looking at a monitor and he's noticing that people are stepping on the mines, at which point he turns them all on and they blow everybody up. He has no ability to tell whether the people are kids or what." Delivering mines with sensors was also fraught with difficulty. "You don't have time," says Lodal, "to have people set up their little TV cameras. If you need them, you have to call in aircraft and deploy them in 5 minutes—how are you going to drop little TV cameras out of an airplane?" To Lodal, the search for alternatives was fruitless: "A lot of guys were coming out of the woodwork who stood to make money out of it, so they'd come up with all these nutty ideas."[107] Nutty ideas were a dime a dozen, some more memorable than others. "My favorite was the ultrasound device that caused the victims to lose control of their bowels," says Michael Matheson. "I do like the spectacle of hundreds of thousands of North Korean troops losing control of their bowels as they invaded the South."[108]

The Army also thwarted Lodal's quest for a command-detonated device. Such a device should have appealed to the Army, he says. "It solves the problem of fratricide," running over mines it had laid, "because if you turn them on you could probably turn them back off again." The Army did not buy the idea, however. "They'd say you could jam them," he says, but "if we can build a lot of cheap GPS receivers that pick up stuff from a satellite, for god's sake, we can get a lot stronger signal than that in there and we can encode it in a way that makes it very hard to jam." Lodal was unimpressed with the seriousness of the search: "I thought that our guys who looked at this stuff were just horrible. They wouldn't look at anything worthwhile." The way the draft treaty defined antipersonnel landmine also proved to be an impediment: "The definition did not have any exemption for the mechanism by which you turn them on or off." It put Lodal between a rock and hard place: "None of the peaceniks would support it because it didn't get you into Ottawa anyhow, and the military didn't support it because they didn't want to spend money on it. They don't have enough precision-guided munitions. Why are they going to spend money on replacing systems that they don't think they'll use very often—that are way down the list of priorities?"[109] That was a billion-dollar question. The Army had a money-saving answer: no way.

Army resistance was a source of endless frustration for Nancy Soderberg of the NSC staff as well. The Army's position was, "If you can't come up with an alternative, we're not going to get rid of them," she says. "So that's where the sticky foam nerf ball came in. We said, tell us what you need and we'll make sure you'll get the money to do research, but we're serious about this timeline." Without a deadline, however, the Army took its time. "I would meet with them every 6 months and very quickly it became clear they were doing zippo," she says. "We had a little working group where I'd sit there and say, where are we on the alternatives? They were totally blowing it off. They never were serious."[110]

In April 1997, the commandant of the Army Engineering School would circulate a draft white paper calling for alternatives. Warning of a potential "operational void" in warfighting if the United States were to renounce all antipersonnel mines, he wrote, "Unless we build powerful arguments for investment of scarce dollars, the operational capabilities of antipersonnel mines may well be gone before acceptable alternatives are in place." Yet he acknowledged, "There is general agreement that antipersonnel mines contribute to U.S. warfighting capabilities. There is *not* uniform agreement on the magnitude of the contributions."[111]

Military resistance to an alternative was one more sign that PDD-48 would not meet the political need to outflank the ban campaign. "We tried to put together a package which would allow us to regain the initiative," says Eric Newsom. "We were going to displace what came to be called the Ottawa process." In his view, some contents of the package were "quite helpful"—he cites the elimination of all dumb mines, the search for alternatives to mixed munitions, the expanded demining effort—"but the thing that tied our hands was the CD decision."[112]

"TAKE OTTAWA SERIOUSLY"

To liberal institutionalists, international institutions facilitate cooperation among states. Yet, far from a boon to cooperation, the Conference on Disarmament was an impediment to it. Left unresolved in the May 16 announcement was whether the administration would seek to negotiate on landmines in the CD. The choice of venue was mired in an "internal dispute," says a White House official. "ACDA wanted to do this in the CD." So did OSD and JCS as well as "folks in State who had the lead in the CD," the legal adviser's office.[113] PM dissented vigorously. "ACDA, not surprisingly reflecting its institutional imperatives, said CD forever," according to Newsom. "We in State said the CD will never ever produce one meaningful thing in this field, and we will have forfeited our chance for leadership if we go the CD route." PM offered two alternatives: "We strongly advocated that the United States promptly decide to reassume the leadership of the international landmines movement—that either we move into the Ottawa process and lead it or we marginalize it by creating a stand-alone forum into which we draw off all the significant countries."[114] Michael Matheson in the legal adviser's office sided with ACDA on the Landmines Control Regime: "It was not our project. We would provide technical assistance, but it was PM's project." He was even more standoffish toward PM's preferred option, joining the Ottawa process. "I didn't get immersed in it, which was, from my point of view, good," he says. "I could see a loser from a mile away."[115]

Ambivalence about US participation was not confined to Washington. Canada's diplomats were "divided among themselves," says Lee Feinstein of the policy planning staff in the State Department. "There is a foreign ministry wing which very much likes to define itself in opposition to the United States and a foreign ministry wing which thinks this is completely nuts and it is their enlightened self-interest to be a bridge to get the Americans to do better things."[116] The split made it hard, says Eric Newsom, "to know what the Canadians' game was."[117]

Canada's foreign minister, Lloyd Axworthy, sided with the wing that wanted to bring the United States along. In a letter to Secretary of State

Christopher, he invited US cooperation with Canada to ensure that the Ottawa strategy session would advance international agreement. Christopher agreed, and over the summer Canadian officials made several trips to Washington to meet with Newsom. When US officials objected to the commitment in the draft of the Ottawa declaration to "zero by 2000"—to cease all new deployment of landmines by the year 2000—Canada tried to address the concern by excising the language. In return, the United States agreed to reconsider participating in Ottawa. When US officials voiced doubts about giving the ICBL a seat at the negotiating table, the Canadians prevailed on the NGOs to close some meetings to anyone but governments.

If the United States was opposed to full participation by the NGOs at Ottawa, that feeling was reciprocated by the NGOs. Canadian official Robert Lawson consulted weekly by telephone with the ICBL, who wanted to set higher barriers to entry and to keep ban opponents like the United States out instead of trying to win them over.

The US Campaign to Ban Landmines was still pressing the Clinton administration "to take the upcoming meeting seriously," but in meetings with her, recalls USCBL coordinator Mary Wareham, US officials dismissed Ottawa as a "pep rally" and "an exercise in symbolism," by a "coalition of angels" out to get the United States.[118] Yet the campaigners were hamstrung because the choice of negotiating forum was hardly the stuff of mass protest. According to Lora Lumpe, director of the Arms Sales Monitoring Project of the Federation of American Scientists, "The action message to the grassroots at this time asking them to call the White House hotline and urge that the US-led negotiations not go [to] this dead forum called the Conference on Disarmament was such an obscure sell."[119]

Senator Leahy weighed in on the venue question in a letter to Secretary of State Christopher a month later. "Although I was disappointed by the president's May 16 announcement" stopping short of a comprehensive ban on landmines, Leahy began, "I take seriously his commitment to negotiate an international agreement to ban antipersonnel mines as soon as possible." Leahy expressed concern about the CD, noting that "only eight of the 41 states that support an immediate, total ban are members." In addition, he argued, the CD's "calendar is taken up with other matters at least until sometime next year" and "it is widely regarded as an exceptionally cumbersome process where months and years are spent haggling over even the most insignificant details." At the same time, he said, "a newly established forum has the disadvantage of requiring time and money to get up and running." With that in mind, Leahy urged the administration "to postpone making a final decision on the forum for negotiations until after the conference on landmines in Ottawa."[120] Leahy reiterated his appeal for delay to National Security Adviser Lake on August 6.[121] Leahy's stance seemed compelling to PM, but other officials remained unmoved.

The Arms Control Interagency Working Group chaired by Robert Bell, NSC senior director for defense policy and arms control, dealt with the issue of venue. "Bob Bell took charge and there were repeated meetings in which this was hotly debated," says PM's Eric Newsom. "The joint staff, after a lot of internal agonizing and haggling, came down in support of ACDA on the CD because we had a veto there. OSD went along, although I think by this time some of them knew this was going to be a loser."[122] NSC went along. Bell's view was "let's see what happens in Ottawa," says a White House colleague.[123] Against that lineup PM was overmatched. To the CD they would go.

Determined to make one last try, Newsom appealed to higher authority, starting with his immediate superior: "It was just clear that this was a recipe for isolation and embarrassment for the United States, so I asked to see Lynn Davis and went through it chapter and verse." He recalls her response: "You don't understand the influence of the United States. We will go into the CD and we will get what we need. You guys stop sounding like Jeremiahs and get on board." Newsom shot back, "We are in for a diplomatic disaster and the president is going to be very unhappy. We simply have to reconsider this decision." Davis relented and arranged for Newsom to see the third-ranking member of the NSC staff, Nancy Soderberg. "I was not able to persuade her," says Newsom. "The bottom line was, she talked it over with DOD, she talked it over with Bob Bell, and they all decided to stay with the CD. They did agree, however, that we would reevaluate our strategy early in the summer."[124]

A Principals Committee meeting to settle the issue took place July 19. The CD carried the day. It would allow the United States "to enter into negotiations as soon as feasible." The CD was due to convene in January, before negotiations could begin in a stand-alone forum. The CD was "slow," officials conceded, but it "has broad participation and a track record" while "a free-standing forum can't assure that the problem states—Russia, China, etc.—would ever sign." Cost was also a consideration: it was "cheaper to use an existing location." Yet speed was not an imperative to those who argued that the CD would "protect the US requirement to use all CCW-compliant APL in Korea until an alternative was available or the risk of aggression was removed." If anyone thought the CD would bury the ban, they did not say so, says an NSC official who referred to contemporaneous notes of the discussion. "Leahy I'm sure is convinced that we went to the CD to slow it down. We had those debates and I'm personally convinced we thought it was a better way to get the big powers on board."[125]

Lee Feinstein disagrees, "The president of the United States has said he wants a global ban on landmines." Yet his own administration decides "to favor a negotiated ban through the CD—on its face, a completely crazy approach." The basis for that choice, says Feinstein, was an "assumption of the key operational people working this issue that until the United States comes to the table, there would not be an agreement on landmines." It reflected "their experiences accumulated over many years of arms control negotiations."[126] That assumption proved wrong.

It was nonetheless a watershed moment for the landmines issue inside the US government. Although President Clinton had expressed an interest in the issue, until then what to do about it had never percolated up the interagency process to a full-dress Principals Committee meeting. "That was the first time it got in the principals' sight," says Feinstein. "The main energy—to the degree that the word 'energy' can be used about arms control in that period—is on the [nuclear] test ban."[127]

By August 1, the NSC staff reported to Lake that the British, Germans, Belgians, and Australians were "on board" for the CD. Even so, the NSC staff decided on September 19 "not to include a reference to the CD" in President Clinton's address to the UN General Assembly, at a time when "DOD was generating an appeal opposing Leahy's landmine use legislation." As it lobbied to repeal the moratorium and have Congress classify antipersonnel mines as a "legitimate weapon of war," says an NSC staffer, "we were trying not to get in Leahy's face. It was Hill politics."[128]

On January 17, 1997, the White House announced it was taking the issue to the CD. At the same time the administration made the moratorium on exports of antipersonnel landmines permanent and capped its inventory of smart mines at current levels. It was already committed to destroy its stock of 3 million mines.

In a conference call with the USCBL, Bell defended the decision, but noted, "if we're wrong about the CD and experience shows that it's going nowhere, we will reassess and are prepared to switch to a more promising venue."[129] A White House official says, "As part of the January decision, we said we'd come back to it. Bob put a lot of it out there."[130] Speaking to reporters on background, Bell made the case against Ottawa: "Our fear is that when you have simply like-minded states joining, you're missing the problem. The problem is not with the like-minded states. It's with the others out there who are producing and transferring...and they have already said they're not interested in Ottawa. We want to engage them very quickly and make progress with them as quickly as we can on this issue."[131] This begged the question why unlike-minded states like China and Russia would be more willing to make progress in the CD than at Ottawa.

Campaigners believed that once a ban was negotiated, it would establish an international norm, endorsed by the vast majority of states, making it easier to single out nonsignatories and put political pressure on them. Bell tacitly acknowledged that: "I would say we are looking at the Canadian bandwagon. We hope many people jump on it, and if the right people jump on it, we would consider it as well."[132]

By not jumping aboard before the ban wagon picked up speed, however, the United States was missing a chance to slow it down or help steer it.

CAMPAIGNERS TAKE OFF THE GLOVES

Military opposition to a landmines ban had been decisive in turning the Clinton administration away from a comprehensive ban, campaigners believed. In a contest confined to lobbying, pitting pressure politics against information politics, the insiders had defeated the outsiders. The campaigners would have to enlarge the scope of conflict if they were to get a global ban on landmines.

Until now, the US campaigners had played the inside game. "We had a lot of people in the White House, at the UN, in the State Department, and even in the Defense Department who were listening to us," says Stephen Goose, "and we perceived a great deal of movement in US policy in 1993, 1994, 1995, and 1996. We had talked about it from time to time, but we had never made a conscious effort to develop a grassroots constituency on this issue." Indeed, there was no national campaign in the United States. "We had an inside-the-beltway approach which produced a lot of dividends, but ultimately didn't succeed."[133]

Bobby Muller, point man of the lobbying campaign, was not quite ready to give up, but he did call time out. "In May 1996 we got to what we felt was a critical mass," he says. "When Clinton said no, we said it's time to take a break. We've got an election coming on. We'll give it a breather." Instead of rejecting the inside game, however, Muller decided to learn how to play it better. He consulted a former chairman of the Republican National Committee, Frank Fahrenkopf, Jr., "How do you lobby in this town?" He was told, "Put a consortium together, a stable of consultants, Republicans and Democrats." Muller chose Pat Griffiths, who had handled congressional relations for the Clinton White House, to "put a team together" that included Tony Podesta, whose brother John was a close aide of Clinton's, and Stanley Greenberg, a pollster who did a lot of work for the White House, along with well-connected Republican lobbyists. By 1997, says Muller, "we built a substantial legislative effort" that lined up support on both sides of the aisle. "We really went back and forth on whether to drive the legislation and call the question or take the chance that we could still work with the administration and get some sort of buy-in to the Ottawa process." In the end, "we said let's hold the legislative process and try to get the administration...because we had a load of people who were talking to the White House and the president."[134]

As Muller was moving to play the ultimate inside game, the US affiliate of the International Campaign to Ban Landmines was moving outside. Until now, even as the ICBL had been putting the ban in the public eye, the USCBL had functioned largely as a lobbying arm of Senator Leahy without ever attempting to organize a mass base.

Having set up a steering committee and named a coordinator in March, the USCBL did not organize its first demonstration until May 7, 1996, just 9 days before the administration announced its new policy. The target was Alliant Techsystems in Hopkins, Minnesota. Alliant was the leading land-mine manufacturer in the country, according to a report, *Exposing the Source*, by Stephen Goose of the Arms Project at Human Rights Watch. Goose iden-tified 47 firms in 23 states engaged in production and sale of landmines or components. Before issuing the report in April 1997, the USCBL had con-tacted firms to ask them to "voluntarily renounce" production or else be stig-matized in public. The timing was fortuitous: no US firm had a contract to make mines. Moral suasion helped convince 17 of the more public relations-conscious corporations to renounce mine making, among them, Motorola, Kemet, Hughes Aircraft, and Olin Ordnance, but 13 others did not reply and 17 firms refused, including Alliant Techsystems, Lockheed Martin, Raytheon, and General Electric ("We bring good things to life"), and became the targets of demonstrations or pointed questions at stockholder meetings.[135]

Long a staple of American populists and the traditional left, flaying the arms merchants appealed to antimilitarist sentiment in the grassroots—some 250 protesters showed up at the May 7 rally at Alliant headquarters. As sym-bolic politics, however, stigmatizing the minemongers was not a compelling way to draw much media attention or to build much of a mass movement.

The US campaign made little headway with accountability politics, either. Getting the administration to live up to its pretensions by exposing the gap between the president's words and its deeds required that he have a policy to hold it to. "Part of the problem for the USCBL throughout," recalls coordina-tor Mary Wareham, "was the lack of a clear administration policy on antiper-sonnel mines other than a rhetorical call for their eventual elimination." That changed with the May 16 announcement, she says. "Now the challenge for the USCBL was in explaining a complicated policy to the public and the media."[136] That wasn't easy. The USCBL called on the administration to demonstrate its commitment by turning its export moratorium into a permanent ban, extend-ing the moratorium to production of antipersonnel mines, and pressing for a global registry for such mines.

President Clinton's call for "a worldwide agreement as soon as possible to end the use of all antipersonnel landmines" also left the timing up to the US government. Momentum for a ban was building overseas, both on the diplo-matic and the public fronts, and the campaign did not want that momentum to dissipate. Governments and campaigns have different temporal horizons. Delay is a time-honored tactic of defenders of the status quo and "now is not the time" is a mantra of bureaucrats everywhere. If negotiations on a ban could be prolonged, the campaign would have trouble sustaining media atten-tion, allies in the coalition would drift away to other concerns, and pressure group politics could determine the outcome. Antiwar groups had faced a comparable predicament in 1969 when President Nixon pursued a policy of phased withdrawal from Vietnam and negotiations to end the war. "Out now" became the rallying cry of the Vietnam Moratorium. When commentators like Eric Sevareid of CBS criticized it as a "practical impossibility," the antiwar movement's rejoinder was, "Be realistic. Demand the impossible."[137] The ban campaigners' response to the Clinton administration's newly announced policy on landmines was similar. The USCBL, says coordinator Mary Wareham, "demanded that it ban landmines *now*!"[138]

In May 1997, playing accountability politics, the USCBL marked the first anniversary of the president's pledge to ban landmines by asking, "Where's the ban?" It also stimulated the mailing of thousands of postcards to the president asking him to keep his promise to ban antipersonnel mines. At the Capitol, the campaign presented Senator Leahy with the results of a petition drive—110,680 signatures of Americans demanding a ban. It capped the anniversary with a rally outside the White House.

Yet the USCBL's strategy of leverage politics was in deeper trouble, in the view of some campaigners. "The ethics of the landmine situation made no difference to the president or to many of his advisers, such as the vice president, except where they could get cheap credit for it," complained Joe Volk of the Friends' Committee on National Legislation. "So shaming Clinton doesn't do a damn thing."[139]

What modest success they did have at leverage politics could be explained by the administration's effort to keep up appearances in an election year. In the Fall 1996, the United States and 83 co-sponsors introduced a resolution in the UN General Assembly calling on states "to pursue vigorously an effective, legally-binding international agreement to ban the use, stockpiling, production and transfer of antipersonnel landmines with a view to completing the negotiation as soon as possible."[140] Despite lobbying by Canada and other members, the resolution made no mention of the Ottawa process. On December 10, it was adopted 156–0 with 10 abstentions.

On January 17, 1997, 3 days before the Conference on Disarmament was scheduled to open in Geneva, the White House decided to make the moratorium on exports permanent. President Clinton, the announcement read, "has decided that the United States will observe a permanent ban on the export and transfer of antipersonnel landmines" and "cap our antipersonnel landmines stockpile at the current level of inventory."[141]

From the campaigners' perspective, however, banning exports instead of use ran the risk of letting the administration off easy. Instead of a stepping stone to a comprehensive ban, they saw it as a way for the United States and others to avoid a ban.

Concluding that lobbying and shaming had failed to move Washington, most American campaigners gave up on the inside game. They took an adversarial tack instead, trying to convince other countries to adopt a ban by capitalizing on US opposition to it. Mary Wareham, coordinator of the ban campaign in the United States, put it this way, "With hopes dashed, the gloves were now off."[142]

That strategy would find many willing collaborators around the globe. Some, such as South Africa, were developing countries eager to leave their mark on world affairs. Others, such as Canada and Austria, were middle powers long used to playing a role on the global stage, some allied with the United States and others neutral.

While the outside strategy played well abroad, however, it had significant disadvantages at home. Once President Clinton had embraced the joint chiefs' landmines policy as his own, the campaigners, unaware of disagreements within the armed services, turned the military into their enemy. They did so just as Robert Dole, an internationalist and a key source of bipartisan backing for the ban, had resigned as Senate majority leader to run for president, leaving the unilateralist right wing of the Republican Party in control of the party caucus in both houses of Congress.

8

The Ban Wagon Starts to Roll

All forms of political organization have a bias in favor of the exploitation of some kinds of conflict and the suppression of others because
organization is the mobilization of bias.

E.E. Schattschneider[1]

Canada's railway stations are imposing stone structures, Victorian monuments
to railroading that make a vivid impression on those who travel across the country. In an age of air travel, a few no longer serve passengers. The Wellington
Street station in Ottawa, for one, has been converted into a conference center,
but its original use was not lost on delegates who convened there to negotiate
a landmines ban. To proponents of a ban, it conjured up the image of a train
leaving the station. To opponents, it evoked a sense of being railroaded.

Six months after the Ottawa gathering was conceived out of frustration
with the CCW Review Conference, 74 states—50 participants and 24 observers, among the latter, the United States—met October 3–5, 1996, for what con-
veners billed as an "exercise in unconventional diplomacy."[2]

The Ottawa process would soon take root and burgeon into the venue
for completing a comprehensive ban on production, sale, stockpiling, and use
of antipersonnel landmines. In little over a year, 122 states would return to

Ottawa to sign the ban treaty. It was testament to the political efficacy of the normative approach.

BOARDING AT WELLINGTON STATION

Unlike the CCW, the strategy conference had a name that made its purpose plain even to a casual observer, "Towards a Global Ban on Antipersonnel Mines." That was not the only way it parted company with arms control as usual.

The conference was premised on a new conception of security—human security—in contrast to national security with its preoccupation with state sovereignty and territorial integrity. Human security, as Canada's Minister of Foreign Affairs Lloyd Axworthy had spelled out in a September 24, 1996, address to the UN General Assembly, "includes security against economic privation, an acceptable quality of life, and a guarantee of fundamental human rights," as well as "the rule of law, good governance, sustainable development and social equity."[3] Human security encompassed safety from both nonviolent and violent threats—freedom from want and freedom from fear. Later, Axworthy would make the challenge to national security explicit. "With the end of the Cold War, the threat of major conflicts between states has lessened," he told the Mines Action Forum on December 2, 1997. "Threats to human security—human rights abuses, inter-ethnic tension, poverty, environmental degradation and terrorism—have grown, fueling recurring cycles of violence. Civilians are their primary victims."[4] That definition was elastic enough to be stretched into meaninglessness, but if construed narrowly to mean "freedom from pervasive threats to people's rights, safety or lives," the idea of human security was a normative counterpoint to national security—and a critical standard for challenging the need for landmines.[5]

The most unconventional part of the Ottawa strategy session, in the view of its hosts, was the diversity of its participants: "ministers and officials sharing plenary and workshop platforms with mine victims, parliamentarians, and representatives from international and non-governmental organizations active in advocacy for the ban, mine clearance, and victim assistance."[6] It was the essence of what the Canadians would later call "the new multilateralism."[7]

Accused by some states of "selling out to the NGOs," Canada did bow to diplomatic tradition by closing some sessions to the NGOs, but that made little practical difference.[8] Twenty NGO participants, many of them affiliates of the ICBL and Mines Action Canada, were privy to all of the proceedings because they were on the official delegations of a dozen countries.

The campaigners made their presence felt, inside as well as outside the conference room. They could be quite undiplomatic in exposing diplomatic pretense, as the French discovered to their dismay. Just days before France's presidential election in 1995, Handicap International had wrung a promise from candidate Jacques Chirac of "his full support to all efforts which will be made internationally to ban the use of landmines as quickly as possible."⁹ With a moratorium on the export and production of antipersonnel mines already in place, France had begun drawing down its stockpile of mines. During the October 2 session in Ottawa, France's chief delegate, Michel Duclos, announced two initiatives by the new center-right government in Paris. It was introducing legislation in the National Assembly to ban mine exports and production and to require an annual accounting of its stocks of mines. It was also ready to ban use of antipersonnel landmines, except "in the case of absolute necessity to protect its forces."¹⁰ The ICBL had been alerted in advance by Handicap International, which was represented on the French delegation. Instead of the polite applause that might have greeted Duclos' disclosure in the Conference on Disarmament, the ICBL's Jody Williams took to the floor in Ottawa in an exercise of what she called "in-your-face diplomacy" and denounced it. "Your policy is contradictory," she told Duclos. "You are saying that you want to ban landmines, except when you want to use them. I suppose this is better than a stick in the eye, but it is not what we are looking for here."¹¹ Her frontal attack shocked some delegates, but others, Senator Patrick Leahy among them, rose to her defense. Stung by the criticism, the French government did not bother to bring up the legislation for a vote before the National Assembly was dissolved on May 9 for new elections.¹²

Leverage politics eventually had the desired result: Duclos would become a staunch supporter of the Ottawa process. But not yet. In Ottawa, France, seconded by Italy and the United States, urged that landmines negotiations be held in the CD.

Unwilling to bury the ban in the CD, Canada's diplomats came up with an alternative. Chairing the conference on the morning of October 4, Ralph Lysyshyn, director-general of the international security bureau, became convinced that most delegates would go along with France on the question of venue. He surmised that half of the 50 participants had little interest in the landmines issue and were not committed to a ban. Yet the breadth of pro-ban sentiment impressed him. So did the extensive coverage of the proceedings in Canadian news media. Lysyshyn recalled his experience negotiating the Open Skies agreement, which provided for unimpeded aerial reconnaissance over NATO and Warsaw Pact countries. After Prime Minister Mulroney had broached the idea with President Bush in 1989 of holding talks outside the usual arms control channels, Ottawa hosted the negotiations, which yielded an accord in only 3 months. Then, as now, political leaders were under public pressure and looking for a way to say yes. Why not take the Open Skies route on the landmines ban?

At noon, Lysyshyn telephoned his boss, Assistant Deputy Minister Paul Heinbecker, to try out his idea. The issue was ripe, he said, and Foreign

Minister Axworthy had shown interest in it, but some states wanted to bury the ban in the CD. Belgium had already announced it would host a follow-up meeting that June in Brussels. If Canada did not seize the initiative in banning landmines, Belgium would. Canada could instead take the lead by hosting follow-up talks to complete an international ban by the end of 1997. He had not discussed the idea with anyone else, he said, and he would not put it to the foreign minister unless he could come up with the money to host the talks. How much? asked Heinbecker. Recalling an earlier discussion with Mark Gwozdecky, deputy director of nonproliferation, arms control, and disarmament, about a stand-alone forum for negotiating a ban, Lysyshyn guessed $2 million. Three hours later, Heinbecker called back to say that he had secured the $2 million from Deputy Foreign Minister Gordon Smith and would brief Axworthy.[13] Lysyshyn had Jill Sinclair, director of the nonproliferation, arms control, and disarmament division, and Gwozdecky insert the idea into Foreign Minister Axworthy's speech closing the conference the next day.

That evening, Sinclair sat down at a computer with Robert Lawson of her staff and Jody Williams and Stephen Goose of the ICBL to draft Axworthy's speech. Concerned from the outset that conferees would be unable to agree on a common plan of action without watering it down, the Canadians had decided even before the strategy session opened to draw up one of their own. They had canvassed delegates for a list of follow-up actions for governments and NGOs to take. High on the list was passage of Resolution 51 in the UN General Assembly, calling on member states to implement at the earliest possible date moratoria, bans, and other constraints of their own on the use and transfer of antipersonnel mines; rapid entry into force of Protocol II of the CCW; regional action to ban landmines such as mine-free zones; and assistance for mine clearance and mine victims. Now they turned the list into a "chairman's agenda for action."[14] They concluded the speech with Lysyshyn's idea of a signing conference in Ottawa next year. The next morning, they faxed the draft to Michael Pearson, Axworthy's senior policy adviser, for the foreign minister's approval.

Lysyshyn did not notify other diplomats. Few could have committed themselves without consulting their governments first, but it was Saturday and ministries throughout Europe, Africa, and Asia would already be closed. Under the circumstances, letting the delegates know would only have alerted opponents before he could line up support. Williams and Goose did pass the word to some NGOs. The Canadians told Peter Herby of the International Committee of the Red Cross and asked him to get a statement of support from its president, Cornelio Sommaruga. Mary Fowler, who worked in the Department of Humanitarian Affairs at the United Nations and was married to Canada's ambassador to the United Nations, offered to seek the UN secretary-general's endorsement. Lysyshyn then briefed Foreign Minister

Axworthy, underscoring the need for bold action but noting the risk that by failing to consult other delegations, Canada would leave itself open to the accusation of not playing by the rules. Axworthy gave his assent, "It's the right thing. Let's do it."[15]

Eschewing the usual closing remarks by a host nation bidding the delegates au revoir and thanks for their help, Axworthy stunned all but a knowing few by announcing that Canada planned to work with the ICBL on a treaty to ban landmines and inviting them back to Ottawa a year hence. He saved the best for last: "I have one final point to add to your action plan. The point comes in the form of both an invitation and a challenge. The challenge is to see a treaty signed no later than the end of 1997."[16]

It was catalytic diplomacy, a plan of action with a deadline, intended to jump-start states into acting instead of waiting for consensus to crystallize. The campaigners leapt to their feet and gave Axworthy a standing ovation. Most diplomats sat stone-faced, applauding politely, if at all. A few were infuriated. The US delegation was caught off base. "It was a total surprise to us," says Robert Sherman of ACDA. "In fact, until that point, the whole October meeting seemed like a total waste of time and money."[17] Expecting nothing more of consequence to transpire and hoping to be home for the weekend, "a lot of us had left," says another member of the delegation.[18]

Reaction was swift. Delegates rose to berate Canada for defying diplomatic convention and acting unilaterally. Within days the State Department made a stinging *démarche* in Ottawa and summoned Canadian diplomats in Washington to express displeasure with Axworthy's action.[19] Despite the criticism, the "ban wagon" had left Wellington Station bound for Brussels.

A DIPLOMATIC ALLIANCE PAVES THE WAY TO BRUSSELS

To the Canadian diplomats, the criticism was expected. Of much greater concern to them was the skepticism of potential signatories, who wondered how a landmines treaty backed by a small group of middle powers over the opposition of the United States, Russia, China, and India could be negotiated in less than 14 months to ban a weapon that they and dozens of other states still used.[20]

After the strategy conference, the Canadians undertook an assessment of the views of governments around the world about antipersonnel landmines. They concluded that "given the right conditions, potential support for the AP mine ban treaty could peak at somewhere over 100 states."[21] Conditions were far from right, however. Opponents resented Canada's "grandstanding" and supporters doubted the ban's chances of success. "We never talked publicly about how shaky it was in those first couple of months after Ottawa," says Jody Williams. Instead, to allay supporters' skepticism, "we kept up the smoke and mirrors routine" about unstoppable momentum behind a ban.[22] Canada's diplomats phrased it more diplomatically, "The international community was moving decisively towards the ban and states could not afford to wait before taking action. The most frequently used metaphor was that of a train leaving the station."[23]

Canada also made another attempt to coax the United States on board. To do so, the Canadians were ready to reopen a central issue that the campaigners thought was closed. Starting in January 1996, Austrian diplomats had been drafting the text of a comprehensive convention to ban landmines. The Canadians knew that a single convention would "force states to make a single difficult choice—either you supported a total ban on the production, stockpiling, transfer, and use of AP mines or you did not. How many states would be willing to make such a choice, and would this group include those states that would be essential to the operational success of a ban?" In talks with the United States, Canada floated an alternative, "four separate protocols for bans on the production, stockpiling, use, and transfer of AP mines, each of which, in theory, could be signed and implemented independently of the others." The Canadians recognized the disadvantage of this approach: "Providing states with the flexibility to pick and choose which of the ban elements they would adopt and when they would adopt them would effectively remove most of the political pressure for states to move quickly towards a total ban." Nevertheless, some states were only ready to move part-way toward a total ban and the Canadians felt "the four-protocol model would provide a more inclusive framework for diplomatic action within the Ottawa process." In particular, they hoped to draw in Washington—to no avail: "The four-protocol model failed to attract the support of the United States, which would turn to the Conference on Disarmament as the alternative to the Ottawa process."[24]

The Deputies Committee revisited the issue on November 18. As the NSC staff reviewed the state of play 3 days before, "OSD, JCS and ACDA want the CD. State wants an alternative." There is "no agreement on interim use restriction. JCS, OSD, probably ACDA" favor the "CCW Protocol only," while State wants "no first use" of antipersonnel mines and, beginning in 1999, a UN ban except at internationally sanctioned demilitarized zones or borders. OSD and JCS are in agreement that they "will require a provision to allow transfer of APL in time of war"—to allies in NATO as well as South Korea.[25]

When the CD convened on January 20, 1997, the head of the US delegation, Ambassador Stephen Ledogar, read a personal appeal from President Clinton for "prompt conclusion of a ban on producing fissile material for use in nuclear explosives" and "negotiation as soon as possible of a comprehensive, global ban on antipersonnel landmines."[26] As the difference between "prompt" and "as soon as possible" implied, a ban on production of fissile material, not a ban on landmines, was Washington's top priority in the CD.

Nor was timely CD action on a landmines ban likely. Mexico, Indonesia, and others preferred that the CD focus on nuclear disarmament by the United States and others before turning to the fissile material ban. The CD also included outspoken opponents of a landmines ban who could exploit the rule of consensus to delay its consideration. Even proponents of action were divided, with Austria, Belgium, and Ireland in favor of a comprehensive ban and France and Britain in favor of a phased approach, starting with a ban on exports. With this lineup, the CD quickly deadlocked on whether even to include landmines in its work program.[27] "The Ottawa proponents stopped us cold in Geneva," says Eric Newsom, principal deputy assistant secretary of state for political-military affairs, "We tried, but we got totally stiffed by almost everybody other than countries we didn't want to have anything to do with"—those, like Iraq, that wanted to be free to use landmines.[28]

Six months later, according to a senior US official, the pace was still "glacial."[29] Landmines were not yet on the agenda. The CD had managed to name a coordinator on landmines, but he was empowered only "to conduct consultations on a possible mandate on the question of antipersonnel mines"—in plain English, to hold talks about having talks.[30] Even that modest proposal was adopted by consensus only after the Syrian delegate was persuaded to leave the room. On June 12, Mexico, which had come out in favor of a ban, blocked negotiations in the CD on landmines.[31] In the view of some delegates, after the difficult birth of the Comprehensive Test Ban Treaty, the CD had lapsed into postpartem depression.[32]

Meanwhile the Ottawa process was chugging along, picking up steam. A driving force in that process was concerted action by the core states. All were middle powers, some of them allies of the United States, others neutral, who had played important roles in the wings in the cold war, but were now taking center stage.

Even in the Cold War years, middle powers were occasionally able to constrain superpower freedom of action or draw the superpowers into serving their ends. The Jaruszelski government in Poland could dissuade the Soviet Union from invading to crush the Solidarity trade union movement in 1980–1981. So, too, after Jaruzelski declared martial law and suppressed Solidarity, NATO allies and neutrals withstood US pressure to curtail work on a gas pipeline to the Soviet Union. With the waning of the Cold War, the emptiness of the US claim to deference as the "sole superpower" was exposed by middle powers like Canada and Austria who were willing to act on their own in defiance of US wishes in seeking a landmines ban. Some Canadian diplomats viewed this prospect with considerable enthusiasm. "The end of the Cold War has opened up exciting possibilities for middle-power diplomacy," wrote Robert Lawson, "and restored faith in the conviction that countries like Canada can make a difference."[33]

NATO and the Warsaw Pact may have been military alliances on paper, but they acted more like diplomatic alliances in practice, co-sponsoring resolutions in international forums like the UN General Assembly, plotting common strategy, coordinating their lobbying of other governments for votes, even working out common talking points. Alliance membership was a shared identity. Now, in the wake of the Cold War, Austria, Belgium, Canada, Ireland, Mexico, the Netherlands, Norway, the Philippines, South Africa, and Switzerland, though not all members of the same club, were forging a common identity and a diplomatic alliance of their own. Austria, Canada, and Norway were accustomed to working hand in hand on humanitarian issues, says an Austrian diplomat, and the "personal chemistry" among the officials strengthened these bonds.[34] "Proposals developed in Ottawa, Vienna, Oslo, Brussels, and Pretoria were quickly shared with capitals throughout the world through joint or reinforcing diplomatic *démarches* using common speaking notes," according to Canadian diplomats—but with a difference. "Embassies were also instructed to coordinate their actions with local NGOs and delegates of the ICRC. Diplomatic correspondence, usually reserved exclusively for national use, was often shared to provide insights into the challenges facing core partners within regional contexts."[35]

The core group met in Geneva in late 1996 to shape the Ottawa process. Austrian and Canadian officials were guided by two lessons from their experience at the CCW Review Conference: "The first was the importance of maintaining a clear message—based on principles of international humanitarian law, AP mines should be banned. Second, the focus would be on norm-building by a coordinated group of like-minded states rather than attempt to reconcile humanitarian and military considerations in a forum that included major mine-users or mine-producers, such as the CCW Review Conference or the Conference on Disarmament."[36]

Implicit in the actions of an alliance of like-minded states was a third lesson that the officials did not mention: the end of the Cold War made it easier for middle powers, operating multilaterally and in concert with NGOs, to assemble a winning coalition for a ban over US, Russian, and Chinese opposition. That had been Canada's experience during the Cold War, on those occasions when it had acted as a broker of compromises within NATO, allying with others to restrain US unilateralism. That had also been Sweden's experience when, ostensibly neutral but tacitly allied with the United States, it had acted as an East-West go-between to ease hostility. That had also been the traditional stance of Mexico, so close to the United States that it had kept its diplomatic distance, asserting its independence both within the Organization of American States and as a leader of the nonaligned movement. The end of the East-West divide expanded the maneuvering room for such middle powers.

To prepare for the June 24–27 conference in Brussels, the core group would hold two meetings of experts, in Vienna on February 12–14 and in Bonn on April 24–25. Its aim was to draft the convention. Its starting point was the Austrian text, completed before the Ottawa strategy conference and circulated to governments by Austria's embassies soon after. It was brief and to the point. "A simple text," recount two of its authors, Thomas Hajnoczi, head of the disarmament department in Austria's foreign ministry, and Thomas Desch, senior legal adviser in its defense ministry, "was less likely to open a Pandora's box of questions regarding the intricacies of verification mechanisms or trigger a North-South conflict on the questions of assistance and responsibility for mine clearance." The draft ran just over a thousand words in all, many of them appropriated from other documents. "To facilitate the acceptance of the text and minimize the duration of future negotiations," they say, "language from other treaties was taken over wherever possible."[37] Grafting a new norm onto existing norms made it easier to accept.

Article 1 stipulated that the convention "shall apply in all circumstances including armed conflict and times of peace." That included civil wars.

In what would prove to be a source of unending controversy, Article 2 retraced the wording of Protocol II of the CCW, which defined "antipersonnel mine" as "a mine *primarily* designed to be exploded by the presence, proximity, or contact of a person." That differed from the definition in the ICBL's draft text: "any munition placed under, on or near the ground or other surface area and designed to be detonated or exploded by the presence, proximity or contact of a person." The difference was critical, because it exempted mines equipped with antihandling devices and other hybrid mines—such as the mines possessed by Austria, as well as by Belgium, Britain, the Czech Republic, Germany, Spain, Norway, and Sweden.

Article 3 outlawed the use of antipersonnel mines and obliged parties to the convention "never to develop, produce, otherwise acquire, stockpile, retain or transfer, directly or indirectly antipersonnel mines to anyone." Article 4 exempted the acquisition or retention of "small amounts" of mines "if they are exclusively used for the development and the teaching of mine detection, mine clearance, or mine destruction techniques" but mandated a registry of the amounts and types of such mines. Article 5 allowed parties up to 2 years from the time that they ratified the convention to destroy their stockpiles and up to 7 years to destroy their deployed mines.

Article 6 stipulated that any act or omission in armed conflict, "if committed willfully or wantonly and causing death or serious injury, shall be treated as a grave breach" of the Geneva Conventions of August 12, 1949. It obliged parties to adopt laws imposing penal sanctions for breaches by persons within their jurisdiction.

Article 7 required parties, at the time they gave notice of their formal accession to the convention, to supply complete information on the number, type, use, type of fuse, and lifetime of mines stockpiled or deployed and maps of deployment areas. It also provided for challenge inspections of suspect sites. At the request of any contracting party, a Board of Eminent Experts appointed by the UN secretary-general "may decide not later than 24 hours after receiving the inspection request" to order such an inspection if it found the evidence warranted one.

Article 8 provided for ratification; and Article 9 for entry into force 6 months after the 40th instrument of ratification had been deposited, or for subsequent signatories, 6 months after they ratified the convention.

In a diplomatic departure, Article 10 barred signatories from attaching reservations to the convention in the course of ratifying it. Article 11 provided for withdrawal by any party upon 90 days' notice if "extraordinary events, related to the subject matter of this convention, have jeopardized [its] supreme national interests," but required the withdrawing party to spell out the "extraordinary events" in a statement to all other parties. The text said nothing about assistance for landmine victims or for demining.[38]

THE AUSTRIAN DRAFT ATTRACTS STANDING

The Austrian draft lacked political or legal standing. "It is not enough for a paper to be distributed by a state for it to become the main proposal in a treaty negotiation," note two of its authors. "It is only when states participate in a drafting exercise and are able to identify themselves with the text that it makes sense to convene formal negotiations."[39] The Austrians' aim at Vienna was thus to "start the speedy elaboration of a draft text that can serve as the basis of negotiations."[40] The Austrians' idea that states would come to "identify themselves with the text" is consonant with the normative approach.

US officials took scant notice of the Austrian draft. A White House official working on the landmines issue recalls not even bothering to read it: "We weren't that interested."[41] At State, PM and the legal adviser's office did review the draft, says Eric Newsom. "Actually we sent informal comments from a technical treaty-drafting point of view," but did not comment on the substance.[42]

The Vienna session was billed as an "Experts Meeting on the Text of a Total Ban Convention." Working with the Austrians, Canadian diplomats formulated a concept paper for discussion and came up with common talking points for joint *démarches* in capitals around the world urging states to attend. To increase turnout, Canada, with contributions from others in the core group, arranged to defray the travel costs for delegates from developing countries. As a result, 111 states attended.

The ICBL and Belgium circulated draft texts of their own before the Vienna meeting, but for Canada and the rest of the core group, the Austrian text served as the basis of the experts' deliberations. To finesse its doubtful diplomatic status, the Austrian chair of the meeting stated that Austria was providing the text "only for the purpose of discussion (and would not bind any delegation)." The challenge was "how to get states to comment on the text and incorporate their suggestions without putting the integrity of the draft treaty text at risk."[43]

The Austrian text met that challenge. Prior to the meeting, the Austrians received about two dozen comments on their draft. At Vienna they got many more. In the process the draft acquired diplomatic standing. To the Austrians' delight, even the United States, Britain, and France, which had intended to endorse the CD as the sole negotiating forum without addressing the substance of the Austrian draft text, were drawn into the discussion lest they "leave the impression that the positions of the core group commanded the general support of the meeting."[44]

No such impression could be drawn from the discussion of compliance and verification, which proved so contentious that Germany offered to host an experts meeting in Bonn to address it.

At a meeting of their own in Vienna in March, the core group decided to address a number of the objections by rewriting the text. Their emendations and qualifications loosened some of the treaty's provisions and doubled its length. They extended the time allowed for parties to get rid of their landmines—to 3 years from 2 to destroy stockpiled mines and to 10 years instead of 7 to destroy those deployed in minefields. Mines deployed outside minefields had to be removed and destroyed "as soon as possible." They added a provision mandating assistance for mine clearance, but not for mine victims. They eased the exemption for "small amounts" of mines retained for training by omitting the word "small." They relaxed a requirement to identify the location of minefields by adding the phrase "to the extent possible." They qualified the unlimited duration of the treaty by providing for a review conference 5 years after its entry into force. At the same time they toughened the provision on withdrawal by requiring 1 year's notice instead of 90 days—they would eventually settle on 6 months—and stipulating that if a party was at war when the period of advanced notice expired, its "withdrawal shall not take place before the end of the armed conflict."[45] That was a break with diplomatic custom, which allowed states to withdraw from a treaty when they judged their supreme national interests were in jeopardy.

DEVIATIONS FROM THE NORM

Except for the provisions on compliance, the definition of antipersonnel mine had drawn the most intense fire at the meeting of experts. The core group wanted the definition to conform to Protocol II, both to attract signatories that wanted to use antitank mines and to minimize the negotiating over wording. Just as they had at the CCW Review Conference, however, the ICRC and the ICBL took issue with the definition, contending it would exclude not only antivehicle mines with antihandling devices, but also "hybrid mines" with antipersonnel use and would tempt states to play semantic games in order to reclassify their antipersonnel mines.[46] "The Ehrlich draft and the subsequent Austrian draft," says the ICBL's Stephen Goose, "talked about 'primarily.' We spent 1996 and early 1997 saying that this was unacceptable to us" and could jeopardize "ICBL support for whatever emerged" from the Ottawa process.[47]

The core group relented and redrafted the definition, dropping the word "primarily" and adding explicit language to exempt antivehicle mines: "Mines designed to be detonated by the presence, proximity or contact of a vehicle as opposed to a person, that are equipped with antihandling devices, are not considered antipersonnel mines as a result of being so equipped." It also defined antihandling device as "a device intended to protect a mine and which is part of, linked to, attached to or placed under the mine and which activates when an attempt is made to tamper with the mine." The language reflected "what had happened in CCW at the very end," says Goose, when "Germany and other nations stood up and said it was their understanding that the word 'primarily' was intended to mean that antitank mines with antihandling devices were not to be considered as antipersonnel landmines." Once again, these definitions had the effect of permitting mines used by Austria, as well as Belgium, Britain, the Czech Republic, Germany, Spain, Norway, and Sweden. "We were worried about that," says Goose, "but we were also worried that 'primarily' would be an excuse for all kinds of futuristic weapons. It was just a huge loophole. So the compromise that governments came up with was to take 'primarily' out and stick in the CCW understanding."[48] In this instance, the norm of no mines yielded to the interest of some states in keeping some of theirs.

The changes did not sit well with some ICBL affiliates. A few NGOs like Medico International wanted the ban to cover antivehicle mines as well. Such mines endangered NGOs that delivered humanitarian aid by putting their trucks at risk. Some NGOs opposed any loophole for antihandling devices. In an e-mail to other ICBL affiliates, Caleb Rossiter posed the question, "Does the antihandling exception turn the Ottawa Treaty into another CCW? (And if so, should we fight it the way we would any 'killer' provision?)" The Pentagon, Rossiter argued, "would eventually take advantage of the loophole and build, sell, and use small...and therefore cheap antivehicle weapons, both short- and long-lived, with a wide variety of antihandling devices, starting the AP humanitarian problem all over again." He noted that the ICRC, in a paper it presented to the experts meeting in Vienna, had objected to the original Austrian draft on grounds that the word "primarily" in the definition of anti-personnel mine would exempt "anti-handling devices on small scatterable A/T [antitank] mines which equip them with A/P [antipersonnel] functions."[49]

Rossiter laid out three options: accepting it as a compromise "that moves us toward our goals," coming out "against the Ottawa process if the exception isn't removed," or "strongly denouncing the exception, supporting the Ottawa Treaty, and stating that our new campaign goal will be to eliminate it in a review conference." He argued that "the present, rather than the future, offers the best chance to remove the exception because of Canada and other allies' dependence on the ICBL and ICRC for the legitimacy of their effort."[50] Rossiter's e-mail did not convince the ICBL, but the ICRC and other NGOs continued to object to the definition. "In the negotiations," says Goose, "we were faced not so much by improving the definition as by having it opened up by the United States. This was somewhat of an eye-opener for some of the campaigners who said we shouldn't support the treaty because it had this anti-handling device exception in it."[51]

The dissident NGOs had a point, according to Robert Sherman. The definition had left a larger loophole than intended. "They fucked up the language," he says. The definition of antihandling device should have read "which activates only when an attempt is made to tamper with or otherwise intentionally disturb the mine." By omitting the word "only," the definition permitted antitank mines with magnetic fuzes sensitive enough to be tripped inadvertently by a passerby. Of the two challenges the NGOs made to the definition, he says. "on the sensitive magnetic fuzes, I think their case was very strong substantively." On "the antihandling device," which the NGOs wanted to classify as an antipersonnel landmine, "I think their case was very weak."[52] Later on, at Oslo, the ICBL would try to patch the loophole with another understanding, "Antihandling devices that explode from the unintentional act of a person are considered antipersonnel landmines and are therefore banned." Goose says, "We had a number of countries stand up and say what that means is certain types of antihandling devices are de facto antipersonnel mines and captured by this definition of this treaty and are therefore illegal."[53] Not all signatories accepted that interpretation, however.

The Pentagon's reaction to the reworded definition was even more hostile than the NGOs'—but because of what it covered rather than what it exempted. "People in our acquisition and technology community" came to a "horrifying" conclusion when they were asked "which systems could this definition be stretched" to prohibit, according to a Department of Defense briefer. "Not only do they capture our four or five landmines that we expected; it caught a total of 35 systems, some as far afield as ATACMs [the Army's new tactical missiles] and various types of bombs and many munitions that have nothing to do with landmines," among them, "a number of high-tech systems that our military is really depending upon with our reduced forces."[54] They reportedly included cluster bombs with delayed action, 155-millimeter howitzer projectiles, submunitions used to prevent airfields from being easily repaired after they were bombed, and grenade launchers of the Multiple Launch Rocket System.[55]

The Defense Department's fears were exaggerated, to judge from the ICBL's willingness to grant exceptions. For instance, the definition exempted Claymore mines. Claymores are usually command-detonated, but they can also be rigged with a tripwire. That is why Stephen Goose had first tried to ban them in CCW, but later heeded Tim Connolly's advice to exempt them. "The NGOs, in a pragmatic move in my view, decided to turn a blind eye to the use of Claymores," says Connolly. "They're so ubiquitous that Steve and his guys were smart." The average soldier "doesn't know anything about FASCAMs and ADAMs, but he knows a Claymore. When he goes to basic training, he gets to fire a Claymore." Banning Claymores would have triggered "an emotional response." Nor did exempting Claymores pose much of a humanitarian risk. "If you were to go to the HALO Trust or Mines Advisory Group and ask how many tripwire-detonated Claymores have you demined, the answer would be zero, so this is not a problem weapon."[56] The decision to exempt Claymores "was and continues to be a contentious item within the campaign," Goose acknowledges, but "one had to become more exacting about what was going to be banned and what was not going to be banned," and "I could not find any way to seriously argue that a command-detonated Claymore would meet the definition of AP mine" or was "indiscriminate by nature." Still, the ICBL asked that Claymore mines be modified to prevent the installation of a separate fuse for the tripwire. "What we've done through the mine ban treaty is try to force governments to make technical modifications to existing mines and report on it."[57]

It was not the only US landmine "that was going to become a deal breaker" whose use the ICBL decided not to contest, says Tim Connolly. Another was the pursuit deterrent munition. "It's a landmine in the special operations inventory that is basically designed to be thrown behind you as you're running. Its tripwires go out and if someone hits one, it blows up," says Connolly. "We had a debate on it with Steve [Goose] and Human Rights Watch and those guys. I advised against making an issue of it because it was a prototype device [for use] only by special operations and they buy a couple of thousand. This is not a humanitarian issue."[58] In these instances, as in the exemption for European mines with antihandling devices, the norm of no antipersonnel landmines gave way to the interest of some states in keeping some of theirs, and the ICBL went along.

VALIDATING THE TEXT

At the core group meeting in March, the Canadians also circulated a road map for turning the Ottawa process into a formal negotiation. Concerned about countering accusations of "illegitimacy because of its birth outside normal diplomatic channels," the Canadians got the Norwegians to host the treaty negotiations in Oslo. This satisfied the need for an alternative venue to the CD other than Ottawa. "The establishment of a recognized diplomatic conference, grounded in precedence and traditional diplomatic practice," the Canadians thought, would impart legitimacy to the Ottawa process. Moreover, "as a stand-alone forum, there would be tremendous scope for flexibility in Oslo."[59] Norway took the lead in drafting rules of procedures for the negotiation. The core group also decided to approach a South African diplomat and senior official of the African National Congress, Ambassador Jacob Selebi, to serve as chair.

The redraft of the Austrian text was circulated to states before the April 24–25 Experts Meeting on Possible Verification Measures in Bonn. Of the 120 states in attendance, 70 expressed a preference for the Ottawa process over the CD. They showed much less enthusiasm for the draft provisions on compliance, however. "That meeting served an important purpose—to consider in concrete terms the applicability of traditional verification measures for the various obligations," wrote Austrians Thomas Hajnoczi and Thomas Desch and Canadian Deborah Chatsis, who were involved in the negotiations. "While some progress was achieved, no convergence of minds was in sight."[60]

Based on comments from some 70 states, the core group met later that month to produce a third draft, which was circulated on May 13, 1997. It rejected compulsory universal jurisdiction sought by the ICRC for serious violators.[61] In deference to objections from developing states sensitive to any infringement on their sovereignty, it dropped the references to "verification" and "on-site challenge inspection." Instead, it empowered a panel of experts to conduct a fact-finding mission that would report to an annual meeting of the parties, or to a special session if one was requested by the party lodging the complaint and approved by one-third of the members. Given the millions of mines in arsenals around the world, a breakout from the treaty by one party using a few thousand mines was thought to be of less consequence than testing a nuclear weapon in violation of the Comprehensive Test Ban Treaty. "[It] is a question of how important hot pursuit is," said one Western negotiator. "The focus is on use as the real problem and this points the finger of international opinion against widespread use."[62] In this respect, the humanitarian norm took priority over disarmament.

While it was trying to meet objections from participants, Canada did not give up trying to woo the United States. In Washington for an April 7–9 state visit, Prime Minister Jean Chretien again urged the United States to participate fully in the Ottawa process. He also issued an invitation for substantive bilateral discussions. Foreign Minister Axworthy and Secretary of State Albright followed up the invitation, and a US delegation went to Ottawa for closed-door talks on June 12.[63]

As a sendoff, that day Senator Leahy introduced the "Landmine Elimination Act" to prohibit US forces from deploying any more antipersonnel landmines after January 1, 1999. Among the bill's 56 co-sponsors was Senator Chuck Hagel, a centrist Republican from Nebraska who had been wounded twice by landmines in Vietnam, and four other Vietnam combat veterans in the Senate. That same day, more than 160 House members, 18 of them Republicans, sent a letter to President Clinton drafted by Representatives Lane Evans (D-IL) and Jack Quinn (R-NY) urging him to join the Ottawa process.[64] In private Leahy indicated that if the administration did so, he would withhold action on his bill.

Even though the president favored a ban, neither Secretary of State Albright nor any other top official stepped forward to take the lead on his behalf, leaving lower-level officials little elbow room to break new ground in Ottawa. Without high-level involvement in Washington, the talks made little headway. "At that point," says Lee Feinstein of the policy planning staff, "the Canadians are not believing. They don't have an interlocutor they can deal with. They can't get anybody's attention."[65]

"We were trying to get them to accept self-destruct mixed munitions and Korea," says Robert Sherman, who was on the US delegation. "There was no meeting of the minds," he says, just "some give-and-take on a transition period" that would allow the United States more time to adjust militarily.[66] When the US officials insisted Seoul could not be defended without using landmines, Axworthy tried to be accommodating. "We can look at how you can put some codicils" in the convention to permit an "exception for Korea," he told them.[67]

The NGOs had been shut out of the talks, but when this exchange became public, Mines Action Canada issued an action alert to others in the ICBL opposing any erosion in the treaty.

It was easy for the campaigners to rally many countries to their cause by stigmatizing the United States. Canada's foreign minister saw it differently: having the United States remain outside the treaty would make it more difficult to stigmatize landmines. It was the first sign of open discord between the diplomats who preferred to bring the Americans into the Ottawa process and the campaigners who wanted to keep them out.

BARRELING OUT OF BRUSSELS

The Brussels Conference on Antipersonnel Mines opened on June 24. For the core group, mobilizing political support for the Austrian text, not revising it, was the core business of the gathering. By then, according to the drafters, "it appeared as though the chances for another draft being put forward to compete with the Austrian draft were slim." Instead of wordsmithing the text in Brussels, "the level of discussion was kept general to ensure that the negotiations began only in Oslo."[68] Yet, if the Brussels conference hall was not a forum for negotiating, there was plenty of hard bargaining in the corridors.

The chief US negotiator, Ambassador Thomas "Ted" McNamara, was confined to quarters. "The Pentagon objected to our attending as actual participants," according to Eric Newsom, who prepared McNamara's briefing book but did not accompany him to Brussels. "The joint staff, backed by OSD, was against it."[69] OSD let the joint staff have its way because, compared to intervention in the Balkans or the Comprehensive Test Ban Treaty, a wrangle over landmines was not worth the effort. As a result, a mid-level US official sat in as observer while McNamara met with delegations one-on-one in his hotel to press for an explicit exemption in the treaty to use mines in Korea and smart mines anywhere.

The campaigners were having none of that. At the opening session, ICBL coordinator Jody Williams was invited to give a keynote address along with Belgium's foreign minister and Canada's chief delegate. She used the occasion to demand a comprehensive ban with "no exceptions, no reservations, no loopholes."[70] That became the campaigners' battle cry.

The Canadians had come up with a way to "lock in" wavering states and put the ban on a fast track.[71] Even before the Ottawa conference, the ICBL had started keeping a "good list" of states that supported the ban. Now the Canadian diplomats turned it into a way for states to identify themselves with the ban. Before the conferees left for Brussels, Canada had circulated a declaration for them to "affirm their objective of concluding the negotiation and signing of...an agreement banning antipersonnel landmines before the end of 1997 in Ottawa." The "essential elements" of that agreement, it read, would be "a comprehensive ban on the use, stockpiling, production, and transfer" of such mines, international aid for mine clearance in mine-strewn countries, and destruction of mines stockpiled or uprooted from the ground. Special mention was reserved for the Austrian text alone.[72] To commit the uncommitted, Canada stipulated that only states that signed the Brussels declaration would be allowed to participate fully in the Oslo negotiations. Others could attend as observers. Some 97 states signed. The United States was not among them.

Support for the Brussels declaration emerged in unexpected places. By late spring, elections had brought new governments to power in Britain,

France, and Australia that reversed course on a ban. New Labour led by Prime Minister Tony Blair was dominated by Scottish Presbyterians prone to preachment about the "ethical dimension" of foreign policy who promised to put "human rights at the heart of our policy."[73] For exponents of the "third way," a landmines ban was one way to appease Labour's left wing, long discomfited by the arms trade, who had pushed for a pro-ban plank in the party's election manifesto. Princess Diana's backing for a ban did not hurt, either. Her mistreatment by the royal family had won her sympathy among Labourites who regarded the throne as a relic of a bygone era. So did Tory fury over her backing for a ban. On May 21, the government announced "a complete moratorium on their operational use" and an accelerated "phasing out of stocks of antipersonnel landmines" to eliminate them "by 2005 or when an effective international agreement to ban their use enters into force, whichever comes first."[74]

In France the opposition Socialists gained a parliamentary majority in elections on June 1. The new prime minister, Lionel Jospin, in an interview with Handicap International 2 years earlier, had pledged to defend "without hesitation the total banning" of antipersonnel landmines and to fight for a shutdown of production in France. Three weeks after taking office, the government announced it would stop using antipersonnel mines by the end of 1999 and sign the Brussels declaration.[75]

In contrast to Britain and France, elections in Australia had brought a conservative government to power, but it, too, did an about-face and supported a ban. It "was getting so much flak for its other policies—treatment of aborigines and so forth—that it decided this was one battle it didn't need," says Robert Sherman, a ban opponent. "We lost on both ends"—on the left in Britain and France and on the right in Australia.[76] The normative approach was attracting governments of varying political hues. Still, Canada's diplomats wondered "how many of these states would be prepared to sign a legally binding international convention as opposed to a political declaration."[77]

The campaign had a related concern. In October the ICBL had worried that "action in the CD could derail the Ottawa process," Jody Williams e-mailed colleagues on July 1. "But now, with such limited movement in the CD, particularly when compared with the dramatic movement of the Ottawa process...the possible detrimental impact of work in the CD is minimal."[78] The United States and others that still preferred to negotiate in the CD were sounding a new refrain, however, that the CD was not in competition with Ottawa, but complementary to it.[79] That sparked new concern in the ICBL. "How would complementarity work?" Williams wondered. In draft talking points intended for use with governments, she posed a series of questions: "If the CD were able, for example, to negotiate a global export ban treaty in a step-by-step approach to a comprehensive ban, what would the impact be of having three separate landmine treaties: the Ottawa treaty, the CD export ban treaty, and the CCW Landmine Protocol? How would having three such instruments contribute to the creation of a new international norm?"[80] She did not raise a more troubling question: if the three treaties did not conform, and each had a different set of signatories, how many states would feel bound to observe the most restrictive of them? Would legal obligation trump normative power?

The ICBL would take a less sanguine view after the Ottawa Convention was signed. Negotiating an export ban in the CD would be "counterproductive," Goose contended, providing states with "an alternative to moving toward signing the comprehensive Mine Ban Treaty, or more bluntly, as an excuse not to sign."[81]

US officials had already reached the same conclusion, but were no longer as confident of it. Brussels made a profound impression on US negotiator McNamara, who, when he was not in his hotel consulting one-on-one with other governments, would slip into the conference to check out the proceedings. "As an observer it was fascinating to watch as these governments were being dragged by the NGOs in directions that they had not imagined heading before the conference began," he says. In the bilaterals "I'm trying to find out how far everybody is willing to go—or how far they think they are going to be driven."[82] To McNamara and other US officials, Brussels was synonymous with NATO, where the United States was used to getting its way. Now Brussels had a very different connotation.

A few days after returning to Washington, McNamara tried to relive his experience for an Interagency Working Group meeting chaired by NSC senior director Robert Bell. "I remember coming home and telling people that governments weren't running Brussels. NGOs were," he says. In the past the United States might have worked its will on the allies in the bilaterals. Once outsiders were inside, however, it was more difficult for private covenants to be privately arrived at. "It was the new diplomacy in which NGOs had virtually equal status inside the delegations and you had NGO delegations sitting around the table. It was a free-for-all," he told others at the IWG. "It was the first I'd seen governmental delegations in which the nongovernmental elements were in charge. The Belgians had, in effect, turned the conference over to the NGOs." The landmine issue was getting out of control. "The Canadians, the Belgians, and the Austrians have gotten on the back of a tiger, but they're certainly not guiding it at all." His audience was unimpressed, McNamara says. "I don't think many people believed me."[83] There were exceptions, however. "Our experience was traditional arms control," says a White House official. "The idea that someone would leak a diplomatic note was unusual."[84] The official's recollection about the prevalence of leaks may have been faulty but the basic conclusion that the Brussels conference had not functioned like a traditional international institution was correct.

A "seismic change in diplomacy," Eric Newsom calls it. Yet the shock wave passed through Washington without disturbing it. "At this stage, no one in the Department of Defense, in OSD or the joint staff, no one in the Department of State above Ted [McNamara], no one at NSC," he says, "seemed to understand this was anything other than an arms control issue that could be dealt with in a normal manner." Newsom thought otherwise. Because of his work in Senator Leahy's office and his previous contacts with the NGOs, "even given my conservative professional mindset, I had gained some sense of the emotiveness of this issue." So had his aide, Dave Appleton, "who interacted with these people himself as the issue caught fire." In the aftermath of Brussels, says Newsom, "We kept trying to explain that this is not an arms control issue. This is not even a diplomatic issue any more. This is a political issue. Foreign ministries and defense ministries are not going to do this in the standard way."[85] Long accustomed to getting their way with allies and imbued with a faith in realism that states always act to preserve or enhance their military power, US officials paid little heed to Newsom's warning that normative force was propelling the landmines issue toward a ban.

"We pleaded for the United States to seize control of this issue while there was time," says Newsom. "We said, given our stature, our power, our standing, we can lead this issue into directions that would be consistent with US interests as long as we are prepared to move...toward the eventual elimination of these landmines. It may be like the NPT and the elimination of nuclear weapons some day, a thousand years from now, but we have to have that as an open goal and we have to move toward it."[86] PM's solution held little appeal for other agencies.

"After Brussels the issue became, should we become part of the Ottawa process or not? If we become part of the Ottawa process, where do we want to take it?" For months, says Newsom, "The debate swirled around these questions. All the while we kept warning that this issue is getting out of control. The longer we took to make up our minds, the less likely we would be able to reassert leadership."[87] The core group's strategy would make it ever more difficult for the United States to take the lead.

9

Think Globally, Act Locally

Some issues are organized into politics while others are organized out.

E.E. Schattschneider[1]

Brussels was just one stop in a globe-spanning strategy to round up backers for a ban. That strategy had crystallized at a core group meeting in Vienna in March 1997. "The group recognized," Canadian diplomats recall, "that global reach would be the key to achievement of a ban, and thus the core group members would have a role to play in bringing along their own subregional and regional communities."[2] Canada mapped out a geographic division of labor. Mexico would lobby members of the Organization of American States; the Philippines would take the lead in Asia; Ireland and the Netherlands, each slated to hold the presidency of the European Union for 6 months that year, would work with Austria and Belgium to bring their European neighbors on board.

The Canadians and the campaigners concentrated on developing states, paying special attention to mine-devastated countries. In the assessment of the ICBL, "A key failure of the CCW had been the lack of participation by mine-affected countries and the developing world in general."[3] Their involvement would highlight the humanitarian rationale for a ban.

In the 11-month run-up to the Oslo conference, regional conferences were held in Stockholm, Sydney, Manila, Ashgabat, New Delhi, Maputo, Harare, and

Kempton Park. Their purpose, according to the Canadians, was "to combine state-led diplomatic activism with NGO-led advocacy through the media and a growing number of prominent supporters of the ban movement."[4] It was one form of what would become known as "track two diplomacy," collaborations of nonofficials and officials acting in an unofficial capacity.

The rationale for the regional approach was laid out by the Canadian diplomats who devised it: "What was clearly needed and was soon developed by Canada was a comprehensive 'critical path' that would break down the blizzard of ICBL, ICRC, and government-sponsored events into a coherent 'track two' for the Ottawa process—bilateral and multilateral opportunities for Canada and its coalition partners to highlight the AP mine problem and emphasize the Ottawa process solution."[5]

The developing world was not only where most landmines lay, but also where the best prospects for support of a ban were to be found. Support there would help muster support elsewhere, in the view of the Canadians:

> This approach would also facilitate the engagement of mine-affected regions in the march towards the ban. In addition to getting states that had already deployed mines to halt any further deployments, the active participation of southern mine-affected states would also be critical to the coalition's efforts to prevent the emergence of a North-South split on key issues related to the AP mine ban.[6]

By homing in from the periphery to the core, the Canadians and the campaigners took advantage of the permeability of states unaccustomed to civic activism or outside involvement.[7] In some countries, the ICBL set up campaigns staffed mostly by indigenous NGOs but with organizing and funding help from abroad. In others, the ICBL confined itself to publicizing and lobbying for the ban.

The outside-in strategy played particularly well in political settings where distrust of the United States was endemic and where US opposition to the ban might be a reason to support it.

The strategy had an unintended consequence: it exposed a rift within the ICBL. Affiliates whose main mission was the care and rehabilitation of mine victims or the removal of landmines had chafed at the low priority the ICBL placed on their concerns. Making common cause with poor mine-afflicted countries in desperate need of assistance, these NGOs succeeded in putting mine victims and demining near the top of the Ottawa agenda. That met with resistance from ICBL leaders who, though sympathetic to the plight of states and people victimized by mines, worried that the United States and others opposed to a ban would try to divert the impetus for a ban into aid for mine victims and demining.

The regional strategy was part of "the chairman's agenda for action" put forth by Canada's foreign minister, Lloyd Axworthy, at the close of the

October 1996 strategy conference in Ottawa. "Actions at the subregional and regional levels," it read, "will be instrumental in catalyzing the development of political will for a global ban on AP mines." Among the actions that Axworthy mentioned was creating "the world's first regional AP mine-free zone" and "increased funding for mine clearance and victim assistance for those regions and subregions which have taken concrete steps to create 'AP mine-free zones'."[8]

Creation of mine-free zones was a brainchild of the ICBL. In May 1996, as the CCW was winding down, campaigners casting about for ways to generate global support for a ban latched onto the idea of nuclear-free zones, where the possession, development, testing, and deployment of nuclear arms were prohibited, and applied it to landmines. The mine-free zone was a tool, say ICBL's Jody Williams and Stephen Goose, "to build regional blocs in support of a ban."[9] In September 1996 the six states in Central America, notably El Salvador and Nicaragua which had experienced indiscriminate use of mines, embraced the idea. Two months later the nations of the Caribbean Community followed suit. The ICBL selected Africa as the next likely locale for a mine-free zone.

STRIKING PAYDIRT IN SOUTHERN AFRICA

Nowhere was the outside-in strategy more successful than in southern Africa. Unique circumstances made that outcome possible. Thirty years of strife had left it the most mine-afflicted region in the world; since 1961, when the first known landmine casualty fell in Angola, mines had claimed over 250,000 victims across the region.

Nelson Mandela's rise to power was also a major impetus in moving the region and the rest of Africa toward a ban. The old South Africa had helped destabilize Angola and Mozambique and its surrogates had sowed many of the 20 million mines that littered the region's landscape. The new South Africa, led by Mandela and other veterans of the antiapartheid struggle, was determined to overcome that legacy and redress the grievances of mine-afflicted neighbors. Human rights was the watchword of South Africa's new foreign policy and civil society was accorded a special place in the formulation of that policy—in contrast to the pariah state diplomacy and the closed and insular policy process under the old regime.

Starting in 1995, the International Committee of the Red Cross, in cooperation with the Organization of African Unity (OAU), tried to generate a regional response to the landmines crisis on the continent by convening four seminars: two in Addis Ababa, one in Harare, and one in Yaounde. Participants in the Harare seminar on March 2–3, 1995, agreed that states "seriously consider working toward a total ban of antipersonnel landmines."[10] As a measure of the dramatic shift in attitude wrought by the regional strategy, only 3 months later on June 22–23, the OAU Council of Ministers endorsed "the total ban on manufacture and use of mines" as an "African common position" at the upcoming CCW Review Conference.[11]

That is how norms work. Disarmament is, in essence, a political act by states in which security and economic interests are not the only values that affect their behavior. Ideas of right and wrong come into play as well. Ever so gradually, states with quite disparate interests came to embrace the norm that antipersonnel landmines were not a proper instrument of war. Once they did, the words came easily, in the form of private pledges and public declarations. Would deeds follow?

Southern Africa was fertile ground for a regional campaign. Seeded by skilled organizers and a little money from the outside, support for the ban could sprout quickly. The ICBL, according to Williams and Goose, engaged in "capacity-building," identifying indigenous talent and conducting workshops on campaigning skills throughout the region.[12] Between September 1996 and February 1997, ICBL organizers created ban campaigns in Zambia, Zimbabwe, Angola, and Somalia. With ICBL help, the campaign in Mozambique was launched in November 1995, hired a full-time coordinator, attracted 70 affiliates, and mounted a petition drive that gathered over 100,000 signatures in little more than a year.

Delegates to the ICBL's third international conference in Phnom Penh began a similar effort in South Africa in July 1995. Reconstituted in early 1996 with a coordinating committee that included Oxfam-UK and Ireland and the Anglican Church, among others, the South African Campaign to Ban Landmines leveraged a few sympathizers in parliament and a small band of volunteers, many of whom had been active in the antiapartheid struggle, into a loose network of more than a hundred affiliates, mostly religious and community groups, student movements, and NGOs active in environmental, disability, and human rights causes. While the campaign focused on lobbying parliament and working groups of the African National Congress, recalls staff member Neil Stott, it "took advantage of its unprecedented access to senior state officials and the desire of the new South African government to re-enter international society as a recognized progressive force" to advance the ban.[13] To take on the defense ministry, still a bastion of the old South Africa, the campaign mustered allies from the new South Africa, veterans of both the army and antiapartheid forces in the South African Council of Military Veterans, Azanian People's Liberation Army, and Umkhonto we Sizwe, who questioned the military utility of mines and sent an open letter to President Mandela calling for a ban.

In August 1996, the ICBL sent a conference organizer to the region. By November, plans were put in motion for the ICBL, along with the ICRC, to hold major conferences on landmines in Maputo, Mozambique, and Harare,

Zimbabwe, in February and April 1997. Canada's consultations with the Organization of African Unity led South Africa to host an Africa-wide conference in Kempton Park in late May, just weeks before the OAU summit in Harare.

The first of these conferences, the fourth annual gathering of the ICBL, a 4-day affair, opened in Maputo on February 25, 1997, with 400 representatives from 60 countries in attendance. Although the conference was originally destined for Zimbabwe, it was relocated to Mozambique, say Williams and Goose, because "organizers believed it to be extremely important that the conference be held in a seriously mine-contaminated country."[14]

Mozambique was a fitting site, having suffered from nearly unremitting war—and indiscriminate use of landmines—since its struggle for independence from Portugal began in 1964. Victorious in 1975, the Front for the Liberation of Mozambique (Frelimo) had ruled the country with an iron fist, brooking no opposition and exploiting ties with kindred Marxist-Leninist parties in power elsewhere. In retaliation for Frelimo's aid to guerillas fighting minority white rule in neighboring Rhodesia, Rhodesia's Central Intelligence Office founded the Mozambique National Resistance (Renamo) in 1977 to wage war on Frelimo. In 1980, with white-ruled Rhodesia on the verge of morphing into black-ruled Zimbabwe, South Africa's Military Intelligence Directorate took control of Renamo. Renamo fought on, relying on a supply of South African arms and intelligence, even as Frelimo shed its Marxist-Leninist past and improved relations with many states in the West. The flow of South African arms, including landmines, continued unabated even as Renamo weaned itself from Pretoria's tutelage and committed more and more atrocities, killing civilians by the thousands. Only in late 1989, after President F.W. de Klerk took power in Pretoria, did its arms aid taper off. Peace talks opening in July 1990 concluded with the signing of an accord on October 4, 1992, but Mozambique was left littered with as many as 3 million mines. Not only had Renamo and Frelimo sowed mines with abandon there. So had Portuguese, Rhodesian, and Tanzanian forces. Those from Zimbabwe and Malawi may have, as well.

Mozambique was not the only neighbor of South Africa to be victimized by landmines supplied by Pretoria. South African-made mines have turned up in Angola, Eritrea, Rwanda, Somalia, and Zambia.[15] So it was appropriate that, 5 days before the start of the Maputo conference, South Africa would give the landmines ban an unexpected boost. The de Klerk government had imposed a moratorium on exports in 1994, which the government of national unity under President Mandela had turned into a ban in 1996. At that time it suspended, but did not ban, its use of mines, while keeping its stockpile of 160,000 mines and continuing to produce "smart" mines. South Africa had also signed a "declaration of intent" with Mozambique in 1995 to cooperate in demining and was training Angolans in that dangerous duty. Now Pretoria announced it would "ban the use, development, production, and stockpiling of antipersonnel landmines—with immediate effect"—and destroy all but "a very limited" number of stockpiled mines, for use in training and research in demining.[16] Perhaps the ultimate change of heart was the romance between South Africa's president, Nelson Mandela, and Graca Machel, widow of Mozambique's president and a strong advocate of a ban. They would later marry.

On the second day of the conference, Mozambique followed South Africa in announcing it was banning the use, production, importation, and export of antipersonnel mines. The conferees endorsed the Ottawa process as "the most clear expression of the will of the international community as stated in the December 10, 1996 United Nations General Assembly resolution calling for the conclusion of an international ban treaty 'as soon as possible'," and noted that "other negotiating fora, such as the Conference on Disarmament, will not fulfill that will in a timely fashion." African states were not well-represented in the CD. The conferees also called on all states to commit themselves publicly to signing a landmines ban treaty in December 1997 and to take unilateral and regional steps to ban antipersonnel mines.[17]

The next regional conference, in Harare on April 21–23, was attended by all 12 states in the Southern African Development Community. They pledged to establish a mine-free zone in southern Africa, stop deploying antipersonnel mines "immediately," enact "national prohibitions" on production, stockpiling, transfer, and use, and "declare, at an early date, that they will participate actively in the Brussels conference," where they would officially endorse conclusion of a "new treaty comprehensively prohibiting" antipersonnel mines.[18]

The regional effort culminated in May 1997 at the First Continental Conference of African Experts on Landmines hosted by South Africa and chaired by Ambassador Jacob Selebi—"very skillfully," Jody Williams reported to her ICBL allies. Of the 41 African states in attendance, 38 dispatched delegations from capitals, unusually good by OAU standards. Canada and four other core states sent observers, as did the United States. Archbishop Desmond Tutu opened the conference with a "moving" appeal for a ban. UN Secretary-General Annan, who had previously voiced support for the CD, sent a statement noting "the increasing momentum towards a ban in the seven months since the convening of the Ottawa conference." In Williams' unvarnished opinion, Annan, "as the keeper of the UN, had to be seen "supporting processes within the UN, but clearly he has recognized that the CD eats shit and it is time to throw the weight of his office behind the Ottawa process."[19] Botswana, Burundi, Cape Verde, Guinea-Bissau, Lesotho, Mauritius, Sierra Leone, Tanzania, Uganda, and Zimbabwe made statements for the first time pledging full support for a total ban. Of the 12 states in southern Africa, just three—Angola, Namibia, and Zambia—remained on the ICBL's list of holdouts. On the final day, South Africa gave delegates a noisy sendoff by blowing up one-fourth of its landmine stocks.

The regional strategy worked in Africa partly by using the United States as a foil. Identifying the "sole superpower" with opposition to a landmines ban inspired others to favor it. A case in point occurred in Kempton Park: when a resolution calling for all of Africa to become a mine-free zone was under consideration, the US observer took the floor to oppose it. That outraged the ICBL's Williams, who e-mailed campaigners, "How can the US government make comments in an OAU-wide meeting and not be seen as the 600,000-pound gorilla it too often is?" Its diplomatic intervention had limited effect, however. Egypt alone opposed the consensus. The United States tried to make a closing statement to the effect that, had it been an OAU member, it would have blocked consensus, only to be blocked from making the statement by chairman Selebi, who had obtained a copy in advance. He conferred with the US delegates and, in Williams' hyperbole, "read them the riot act."[20] By the close of the conference, the one-two punch of core group diplomacy and NGO activism had scored a knockout: of the 53 members of the OAU, 43 pledged their active support for the Ottawa process.[21]

SURVIVORS SPEAK FOR THEMSELVES

The regional strategy drew attention to countries that had experienced the devastating impact of landmines. ICBL affiliates specializing in demining and victim assistance seized the chance to bring to the fore questions of mine awareness, mine removal, and the care and rehabilitation of mine victims— much to the dismay of other campaigners.

In so doing one NGO provided a platform for total outsiders to voice their concerns in person—people twice victimized by landmines, first disabled by the blast and then, because of their wounds, treated as outcasts in their own societies. The Landmine Survivors Network was founded in April 1996 by two Americans, Ken Rutherford and Jerry White, with that very purpose in mind.

Rutherford was working for the International Rescue Committee, a private voluntary agency that provides relief and resettlement for refugees, when his car ran over a landmine near the Ethiopian border in Somalia in December 1993. He has a stark recollection of seeing his foot on the floorboard of the car: "I thought, 'Is it mine?' I kept trying to put it back on. I dragged myself out of the car and called for help on my radio." Evacuated by air to a hospital, he went on to the United States for medical care. "Needless to say, most victims are not so lucky."[22] Some bleed to death before help arrives. Very few can afford the nearly $400,000 he spent on medical care and rehabilitation. Others survive but face a life of pain and social ostracism.

White was a 20-year-old American student on his junior year abroad in 1984 who was hiking in Israeli-occupied territory when his right foot tripped a mine. "We don't have landmines in this country, so no one can even fathom what they are," he says. "It's only the freak like myself who goes off camping in Israel...and walking in the footsteps of the prophets not realizing that it was a deadly thing to do."[23] The blast was stark evidence of the long-lasting menace posed by antipersonnel landmines. "I was only 4 years old when Syrian soldiers, retreating during the 1967 Arab-Israeli War, laid Soviet-supplied mines in the Golan Heights," he says. The minefield, like many, was unmarked. "There were no fences and no signs to keep me out," says White. "All the talk about fencing and marking minefields is a distraction from the real problem: how to stop the proliferation of landmines. Even in a small, security-conscious state like Israel, fences break down, signs fade, fall, or are stolen, and mines shift."[24]

After pain-filled months of rehabilitation, White finished college and took a job tracking nuclear proliferation. That made him aware of "the limits of arms control treaties and how much better it would be if we could create a humanitarian framework for solving the problem."[25] A decade later, in September 1995, he was assistant director of the antinuclear Wisconsin Project, but spending more time on landmines, when he and Rutherford were invited to tell their stories at the CCW Review Conference in Vienna. They received a "respectful" hearing from delegates, but as the conference unfolded, "disabled participants felt they were being relegated to the sidelines." Even worse, they sensed, "no one quite knew what to do about the needs of survivors."[26]

White was struck by the contrast between survivors and the "policy wonks" from the NGOs. "I learned that I was among secular missionaries, people who were so engaged, so passionate, who had lived around the world fighting the good fight." Being a survivor gave him a different perspective. "The rest of them might rotate out to the next policy assignment or next disaster tour," but he would remain a survivor. "They liked victims who are also silent. That's an awful way of putting it. Yes, landmine survivors are victimized. Here's the nasty, gnarly picture of the blown-up child. That's what the weapon does." White was determined to do more. "I wasn't going to allow the survivors to be mere window dressing, or literally, poster children, in this cause. They were going to be participants and taken seriously."[27]

Their reception in Vienna led Rutherford and White to found the Landmine Survivors Network in April 1996, just as the CCW was reconvening in Geneva. In their words, "One of the slogans of the international campaign had been 'to speak for those who cannot speak for themselves.' Perhaps the time had come for landmine survivors to start speaking on their own behalf."[28]

White wanted to turn victims into survivors—to empower them. "My passion was acknowledging the survivors' voice," he says. "Those most affected by the weapon are among the most powerful spokespersons for the ban. The idea that you get rid of a weapon that scarred your body and killed your loved ones—it doesn't get any more raw than that." The very rawness made others uncomfortable, he knew: "Because of the nature of the grotesque injury, because of people's fear of mortality and disability and stumps, I realized early on that I had to navigate a message that didn't scare people away with the anger of the survivors. I would play up their outrage, but still remind them to be polite," he says. "So it was controlled rage, packaged theatrically for media effect to make sure we got on the map of policy."[29]

In the first of their public acts, they tried to put "a human face on the mass suffering." They dedicated a "wall of remembrance," covered with photographs of people victimized by landmines in Cambodia's Battambang province between the close of the conference in Vienna and its resumption in Geneva. In that brief period, the province, with fewer than 250,000 inhabitants, had experienced 230 mine accidents. Behind the display in the conference center was an electronic counter that tolled another mine victim around the world every 22 minutes. Tun Channareth, a Cambodian who had lost both legs to a landmine near the Thai border in 1982, introduced the exhibit along with Rutherford. Later, White and fellow survivors from Afghanistan, Bosnia, Britain, Cambodia, and Mozambique held a press conference in the main lobby of the conference center. One by one, they removed their prosthetic limbs and described their own encounters with mines to dramatize the need for a ban and for victim assistance. In their recollection, the diplomats remained unmoved, "Our landmine-disabled friends had travelled a great distance to Geneva, only to discover apathy concerning their needs."[30]

The campaigners' response was scarcely an improvement over the diplomats'. "Victim assistance and demining were secondary goals of the ICBL," say White and Rutherford. Before the October 1996 Ottawa conference, "the LSN approached the ICBL coordinator to determine whether its leadership would object to the LSN's efforts to promote effective victim assistance in Ottawa. There was no response, so the LSN took matters into its own hands and prepared to fight for the rights of survivors."[31] The experience was "eye-opening," says White. "The fact that our friends inside the campaign were reluctant incensed me. How dare we all talk about this and put up posters of suffering victims and not do something about it." That summer, "I was just an awful person to be dealing with. There was no appeasing my position," he says. "There were e-mails back and forth, why wouldn't I work with the campaign" and "funnel language suggestions through Steve Goose and the negotiators of the treaty, and they would address my needs. But I had never experienced that."[32] Goose concurs, "In retrospect, I think that we probably hadn't done as much politically on victim assistance as we should have done from the early days."[33]

Acting on its own initiative, the LSN began by defining "victim" broadly to include not only those impaired by mine explosions and their families, but also those impeded from pursuing their lives and livelihoods by the menace of uncleared landmines. By victim assistance, the LSN meant much more than "care and rehabilitation provided for the immediate and long-term needs of mine victims, their family members and/or dependents, and mine-affected communities." It meant social and economic reintegration of outcasts stigmatized by their injuries. That encompassed not only emergency and medical care, access to prosthetics, wheelchairs, and other devices, and psychosocial services, but also legal services, employment opportunities.[34]

By embracing mine awareness and accident prevention programs among its goals, the LSN was able to make common cause with NGOs seeking support for demining. The ICBL remained unpersuaded. Aid for mine victims had been a divisive issue for the ICBL since its inception. Even as the six founders were drafting the call for a ban in Fall 1992, says Stephen Goose, "there was some back and forth about adding other things. Some European groups wanted to mention reparations," their term for assistance to individuals victimized by landmines, but "it never became a central part of the ICBL message."[35] By summer 1997, Goose and Williams had "enough on their plate without worrying about victim assistance," says White. "I got some chiding e-mails from the campaign."[36]

Victim assistance might prove diversionary, campaigners worried. The United States and other ban opponents were arguing that a ban was impractical and more should be done for victims and demining instead—in White's words, "some sugar-coating to a bad policy." Assistance was also expensive: estimates ranged from $3,000 to $5,000 per victim. Having the treaty mandate aid for victims and demining might be an inducement for some states to sign but cause others to back away. "If you're trying to get third world countries to become part of a convention," says Goose, "that's the first thing they want. They'd like to have it legally binding, but the donors always say, 'those in a position to do so'."[37]

The deeper difference was that as the survivors began taking matters into their own hands and experiencing a sense of empowerment, the ICBL was still trying to make the most of "the poor victims," say White and Rutherford. "One of the biggest challenges was to convince other campaigns that survivors were more than just 'poster children' for the ban movement."[38]

"I was confused that we didn't have more allies than the survivors and the deminers, but also emboldened by that," says White. "I was alone."[39] But the LSN did find an ally in Canada's Department of Foreign Affairs and International Trade, Jill Sinclair. She arranged for White to address a plenary session of the October 1996 Ottawa conference where he told the delegates, "Despite all the talk about the human suffering of mine victims, it seems that we still have trouble putting our money where our mouth is. What is really being done to help these victims? Very little I'm afraid."[40] By the end of the conference, inclusion of victim assistance in the treaty had received at least rhetorical support from the US and Irish delegations. Knowing that it could ill-afford to alienate mine-infected states in need of victim and demining assistance, Canada was willing to do more. As Canada's diplomats put it, "States such as Cambodia, Angola, Mozambique, and Afghanistan, which were producing the majority of mine victims, should be among the first to sign the Convention."[41] In January 1997 Foreign Minister Axworthy hosted a Humanitarian Demining and Victim Assistance Conference.

Asked to bring landmine survivors to the Maputo conference the following month, White and Rutherford came "with high hopes." Again they were disappointed, "While eager to embrace the survivors, conference participants seemed unsure of how best to include their disabled guests in the dialogue on the treaty and the role of victim assistance." At a dinner organized by the LSN, survivors vented their frustration at the role they were cast to play in the campaign: "Survivors were shown almost exclusively as 'victims,' many photographed only at their worst moments of pain and anguish. By showing the horrible effects, the media had assigned to mine victims an aura of tragedy and helplessness." The discussion convinced survivors of the need to change that depiction: "Extraordinary strength is required to overcome disfiguring injury and sometimes ostracism. Somehow, that message needed to come out, as well as a realistic portrayal of the human suffering."[42]

Empowerment of mine-affected people became one of the LSN's aims. The survivors were determined to secure a provision in the treaty on victim assistance by their own effort. In campaign strategy sessions they pressed for a stronger commitment to victim assistance in the ICBL platform. "At the very least, we argued, the issue deserved its own bullet, instead of being lumped in an inconspicuous clause together with the issue of demining efforts," White and Rutherford recount. Nor did they confine their effort to the impersonal plane of policy: "The LSN privately urged the ICBL members to help landmine survivors get proper care instead of just flying them around the world to speak at international landmine conferences."[43]

Yet the LSN itself did not shy away from its own high-profile exploitation of mine victims to attract news media attention to the need for victim assistance. In January 1997, the British Red Cross and HALO Trust, a British NGO engaged in demining, had invited Diana, Princess of Wales, to tour minefields in Angola and meet with disabled victims. Wherever Diana went, cameras were sure to follow. Poignant pictures provided the backdrop for her call to ban landmines. The waspish reactions of Britain's Conservative government and Tory sympathizers ranged from snide to venomous. A junior defense minister dismissed Diana as a "loose cannon." A Tory MP compared her concern for landmine victims to "Brigitte Bardot and cats," adding, "she was not up to understanding an important, sophisticated argument." The *Spectator* accused her of using "Angola as a catwalk." It alleged that "even in the children's wards, the Princess would regularly emit a light giggle, at once nervous and insincere, while her eyes flickered constantly towards the photographers. The first emotion came when she was told that she had been described as a 'loose cannon.' That makes me want to burst into tears, she replied. Can they not see that I am a humanitarian, always was, always will be? So she will, at the drop of a camera shutter."[44] Diana was stung. "It was a state visit," says Jerry White, "and it left a bitter taste in her mouth, she told me later." It gave her the impetus to turn against the establishment. Diana "was coming into her own and realizing that she could call her own shots," White feels.[45]

Diana's eye-catching appeal to the tabloids was not lost on Rae McGrath of the Mines Advisory Group, a British demining NGO and a founding member of the ICBL. "I always had this real frustration that we could always get stories in the *Guardian*, but you were preaching to the converted. We wanted to have stories on the front page of *Sun*, the *Mirror*, and the *Mail*."[46] McGrath had Diana address a seminar on demining and victim assistance co-hosted by the LSN and the Royal Geographical Society on June 12.

Invited to appear at a luncheon in Washington sponsored by the American Red Cross a few days later, she asked White and Rutherford to accompany her on the trans-Atlantic flight. En route, "she asked me, how was her speech," White recalls, "and I said, Americans are much denser. We're hard of hearing when it comes to the subtleties of the English accent and the way you described the landmine issue, so you really have to turn up the volume in the United States and use explicit language regarding the ban. So she did that." It did not go over well with Elizabeth Dole of the American Red Cross. "You could tell that Mrs. Dole was not so pleased with Diana's performance, which was an all-out call for a ban," says White, "and Diana's experience with Mrs. Dole was less than warm, in her own words." The ban was not the only difference they had. The LSN had arranged for a Cambodian landmine survivor to come to Washington for the occasion. "The American Red Cross said there's really no extra ticket for this gala event," says White, and asked "whether she could wear a traditional Cambodian dress for the press conference and maybe present Elizabeth Dole or Diana a gift from Cambodia—the bastards. This was a peasant girl who had lost her leg." Diana, he later learned, "was fighting the Red Cross folks," telling them "if she comes, I want to meet her, give her a gift and have her be my guest at the lunch."[47]

What impressed White was that "Diana identified with the survivors." He and Rutherford had just gotten a grant from AID "to look at landmines as a potential peace and reconciliation project for the warring parties in Bosnia," and he wrote Diana asking her to accompany them there. She invited them to

Kensington Palace to talk it over. She wanted the visit to be private, says White. "It was Diana doing antiestablishment. She's saying it's not the Red Cross. It's not even British. It's two cowboy American survivors from a group that nobody's ever heard of because I like them and they have a story I want to tell and they're asking me for my advice." She even kept the trip secret from the Foreign Office. White recalls a telephone call he received from the British ambassador 2 days before her arrival in Bosnia. "He was apoplectic. What were you thinking? A private visit from the Princess of Wales, are you insane?" White recounts sheepishly. "He was really helpful. It was becoming a media circus—300 photographers chasing her through the minefields of Bosnia. It would have been a disaster if the UK Embassy hadn't stepped in and protected her."[48]

White and Rutherford were novices about protocol. "We didn't know that actually we were supposed to pay for Diana when she came," says White. "The day I'm flying to London to go pick up Diana and fly to Sarajevo, Ken Rutherford is going around with her bodyguards to walk in the footsteps of where we'd be going. I had reserved a whole floor of this inn and Ken asked, how does this work? Do you have a palace gold card or something? The bodyguard just laughed and said, people would pay hundreds of thousands of dollars to be in your shoes right now. There's no palace gold card. We don't have any money. So I went begging." White managed to borrow some, he recalls, "but we'd get these bills for 20 security people for lunch. I'd say, there's only eight of us. I don't know these people."[49]

In the glare of publicity, Diana did not lose sight of the point the LSN was trying to make. "I hope that you felt all your hard work was worthwhile in raising awareness of the plight of the survivors and helping to ensure that they are not forgotten in the framework of negotiations for a ban on antipersonnel landmines," she wrote to Rutherford on her return. "You should be justifiably proud of the wonderful work you are doing to bring hope and a sense of personal values to those who have suffered so much at the hands of these terrible weapons."[50] It was, wrote Rutherford and White, "her last public act of charity."[51]

Instead of applauding the favorable publicity generated by Diana, the ICBL was miffed at the LSN for using the Bosnia trip to spotlight the survivors' plight. "I was criticized for not getting out a press release or telling the ICBL enough so that they could have used it," recalls White. "The e-mail that came after the trip with Diana said the LSN was just running off with Diana and doing things on its own. Why weren't we negotiating with them? Why weren't we a team player?" Of the campaigners, he says, "The only person who congratulated me for the...Bosnia trip was Bobby Muller." The displaced attention was also a source of resentment: "This was a threat to the heads of the ICBL because they didn't know the Princess of Wales. As a NGO activist you think your hard work is getting it done, but without having the Princess of

Wales, you do not have the tipping point. It was about Diana's ability to attract the spotlight to the issue."[52]

Yet the campaigners managed to suppress their differences in ways that a more centralized organization might not have. "The key to success was the loose structure that let groups do what they wanted to do and say what they wanted to say, while at the same time insisting that things are not being said on behalf of the ICBL or described as being ICBL positions unless they have been agreed to by the steering committee," says Stephen Goose.[53] "How we did hang together," White agrees, "says a lot about the nature of the coalition."[54]

EXPANDING THE NORM TO ACCOMMODATE SURVIVORS

Norms have a natural tendency to grow. Once grafted onto the norm against "weapons of ill repute" and propagated around the globe, the taboo on landmines sprouted new tendrils that some groups nurtured. If landmines were wrong, people who were wronged by them deserved recognition and redress. The taboo on landmines legitimated the demands of the survivors, much to the discomfort of some in the ICBL who tried to nip that growth in the bud.

Shortly before the Brussels conference opened in late June, the LSN belatedly saw the Austrian draft and was dismayed to discover that it did not contain one word about victim assistance. The dozen survivors in attendance issued a statement of protest, "To this day, the real needs of mine-affected communities are not being addressed. Survivors remain an afterthought. Their numbers grow each day, but without your help they have little hope of ever receiving proper medical attention or rehabilitation."[55] The statement drew a heartening response. "At that point," recalls White, "there was sort of a groundswell from developing countries like South Africa and Thailand saying we aren't going to be part of a treaty that doesn't address the needs of survivors."[56] The survivors also won backing from the ICRC as well as the two ICBL founders engaged in victim rehabilitation, Medico International and Handicap International, but another ICBL steering committee member expressed displeasure at being "surprised" by the survivors' statement and others opposed a commitment on aid.

The LSN enlisted a Washington-based law firm, Arnold & Porter, to do a *pro bono* brief on the legal precedents for the duty to compensate victims of violations of humanitarian law and to draft language on victim assistance to insert in the treaty. The survivors discussed the idea with Canadian diplomats, who faxed them contact information so that they could approach other countries directly. With the encouragement of Canadian diplomats Jill

Sinclair and Robert Lawson, they circulated the brief to the core group prior to the Oslo meeting. "Again, this independent initiative was not well received by some in the campaign leadership," wrote White and Rutherford. "The LSN was accused of pursuing its own agenda rather than that of the campaign."[57]

In the run-up to Oslo, the International Committee of the Red Cross joined the LSN in calling for a treaty provision on victim assistance. In its comments on the third draft of the Austrian text, the ICRC raised two objections: obliging states to clear all minefields "as soon as possible" was too "open-ended" and it was difficult in practice to distinguish "minefields" from "mined areas." It proposed, instead, that all antipersonnel mines be cleared within 10 years, but allow severely mine-contaminated states to apply for an extension of up to 10 years. The ICRC also sought a proviso that committed signatories to provide care and rehabilitation of landmine victims and promote their economic and social reintegration. The ICRC would be a direct beneficiary of this effort: the convention would expressly suggest that aid be channelled through it and the Red Crescent Movement.[58]

The ICBL was still wary of any binding commitment to victim assistance. "The concern that I had coming into Oslo was opening up the text to major new subjects that we hadn't already wired the language on, because once you open up one big issue area, sometimes others will want to open up other big issue areas," says Stephen Goose. "I was also nervous about what that language might be. If you tried to put in language that implied legally binding obligations to do things, that could scare countries off." Which ones? "The poorer countries that might have to spend a bunch of money to get mines out of the ground or get rid of stockpiles or help others."[59]

White was scheduled to come to Oslo early but his arrival was delayed by Diana's death. Asked by officials in Kensington Palace for survivors to join in the funeral procession, he agreed. "If Diana hadn't died, more victim assistance language would have gotten into the treaty."[60]

The LSN did succeed in having two subsections on victim assistance inserted into Article 6 of the treaty. The first reads:

> Each State Party in a position to do so shall provide assistance for the care and rehabilitation, and social and economic reintegration, of mine victims and for mine awareness programs. Such assistance may be provided, *inter alia*, through the United Nations system, international, regional or national organizations or institutions, the International Committee of the Red Cross, national Red Cross and Red Crescent societies and their International Federation, nongovernmental organizations, or on a bilateral basis.

The second reads:

States Parties may request the United Nations, regional organizations, other States Parties or other competent intergovernmental or non-governmental fora to assist its authorities in the elaboration of a national demining program to determine, *inter alia*,...assistance to mine victims.

These provisions are the first in any arms control treaty to recognize the needs of victims, but they stop well short of mandating aid.

In the end, little aid was forthcoming. When the LSN sent a letter to 122 treaty signatories signed by more than 20 NGOs urging them "to commit significant resources to help rehabilitate the growing number of landmine victims worldwide," fewer than ten governments bothered to reply.[61] Victim assistance ran a distant second to aid for demining and did not meet the range of victims' needs for rehabilitation and social and economic reintegration.

Still, had Canada and the campaigners not adopted the regional strategy of building support for a ban from the outside in—from the periphery to the core—the survivors would not have been able to capitalize on it. The strategy also gave a more prominent role to states most devastated by landmines, which may have increased aid for demining. The growth of a norm is not easy to control, however much ICBL campaigners tried.

The regional strategy made the ICBL seem more like a global movement. In Africa, where few resources went a long way, it used outsiders to set up indigenous campaigns that gained relatively easy access to governments. Opposing the United States was also good politics in much of the developing world. The outside-in strategy enabled Canada and others, with help from South Africa, to convince African states, underrepresented in the Conference on Disarmament and unused to international attention, to join the Ottawa process. As a result, almost all of Africa was primed to support a ban once the sole superpower came out against it.

10

From Oslo Back to Ottawa

Visibility is a factor in the expanding of the scope of conflict.

E.E. Schattschneider[1]

The oppressive summer heat had long ago led the British diplomatic service to classify Washington as a hardship post, grounds for granting higher pay to the suffering souls sent to work there, but in August 1997 the diplomats and US officials who dealt with landmines policy stayed at their desks instead of abandoning the sweltering capital for the beaches or mountains. Diplomacy in Europe usually takes a holiday in August as well, but 1997 was an exception for those working on landmines.

The core group met in Vienna in early August to make last-minute revisions in the Austrian draft in the hope that it would become the sole negotiating text at Oslo. Diplomats and legal experts spent "a great deal of time" plotting strategy for Oslo, Canadian participants recall, "with bottom lines and alternative language on issues from definitions to entry-into-force provisions to compliance mechanisms. The positions of other players were also discussed and fallback positions planned."[2]

The biggest player of all was still on the outside looking in and US officials were divided over what to do about that. So were diplomats and campaigners who favored a ban. Antipersonnel landmines would be more difficult to ban if the United States did not sign the treaty. US moral suasion and media attention could help stigmatize and outlaw mines. Without the accession of the United States, it would also be easier for China, India, Pakistan, Russia, and others to withstand pressure to abandon their export and use of landmines. That is why Canada had tried to bring the United States on board in June by offering to seek an exemption for some US mines. That is also why Canada renewed its offer in August.

Some campaigners agreed with Canada and were lobbying the US government to participate at Oslo and sign the treaty. Organizers in the International Campaign to Ban Landmines were not among them. Instead, they sought to capitalize on US standoffishness to line up global backing for a ban.

US officials on all sides assumed that President Clinton was still looking for a way to sign the treaty. Many doubted his chances of success. "We recognized that when our top guy said, let's see if we can work it out, that in itself solved nothing," says Robert Sherman of ACDA.[3] Ban proponents shared his dark assessment. "There's no way we can ask for a treaty that has one standard for the United States and another for the rest of the world," said Senator Patrick Leahy. "You don't have to be much beyond Diplomacy 101 to know the US negotiating position is not going to work."[4] As the ban campaign picked up steam, says Eric Newsom, principal deputy assistant secretary of state for political-military affairs, "it was dawning on people" in Washington that "foreign ministries and defense ministries were not responding in their customary way."[5] Allies were paying much less deference to the United States.

Still, Canada's willingness to accommodate the United States persuaded officials at the State Department and the National Security Council staff to give Oslo a try. "Their view," says Sherman, "was that we had to go to the Oslo conference and try to negotiate something. They believed that the Ottawa people wanted the United States in there so badly that they would compromise on the question of banning all antipersonnel landmines if we gave them a fig leaf to do it."[6] Newsom remembers "arguing that there was still a last chance. It was late in the game, but if we could do it right, we could still influence the outcome of Ottawa."[7]

In retrospect, that may seem like a long shot. At the time, though, "fear that the United States was actually going to participate" was the prevailing sentiment among campaigners, says Jerry White of the Landmine Survivors Network. "With the United States coming, the whole thing was at risk. It was going to be fraught with power politics and superpower bullying."[8] Newsom sensed it, too: "People don't realize there was a great deal of trepidation among the Ottawa proponents that the United States would come in and take over their conference. This was something to work with if we were half-way subtle and sophisticated, but by now clearly we'd have to swallow some things we didn't like."[9] Subtlety, sophistication, and a tolerance for swallowing anything distasteful were in short supply in Washington in August 1997.

The Oslo conference was due to open on September 1. Having turned down Canada's earlier invitation, the United States announced on August 18 it would go to Oslo and try to rewrite the draft treaty to exempt many of its mines from the ban. If you can't beat the Ottawa process, join it, was the administration's conclusion. "The decision to participate was a knock-down drag-out [fight] requiring the secretary of state to weigh in," according to Lee Feinstein, deputy director of policy planning at the State Department. "We finally prevailed on getting the United States to participate but, of course, it was extremely late."[10] The administration also decided at this late date that if others had inserted loopholes in the treaty to accommodate their landmines, why shouldn't the United States? The administration decided to seek exemptions for all US mines in Korea and for smart mines anywhere whose "primary function is something else, such as protecting a particular location from jeeps or tanks," as State Department spokesman James Rubin phrased it.[11]

Reaction to the US decision was divided. A Canadian diplomat made the best of it, "Our position has been we would not want a treaty that allowed continued use. But, that said, we want this treaty to be as inclusive as possible. It is better to have people participating in the process than have them sniping from the outside."[12] The campaigners, in contrast, regarded the United States as a Trojan horse. "For the ICBL," recalled Jody Williams and Stephen Goose, "it was clear that the United States was not in Oslo as a 'like-minded' participant in the negotiations, but rather to put its full weight behind modifying the treaty to accommodate existing US policy."[13] Even Robert Muller, who had lobbied long and hard to draw the United States in, sounded wary. "The only apparent interest of the United States in going," he said, "is, one, to be able to say they actually tried and, two, to try to weaken the treaty."[14] The reaction of Cecilia Tuttle of Mines Action Canada was tart: "It would be nice to have the United States in, but do you kiss every frog, hoping it'll turn into a prince?"[15]

Any exemption, campaigners argued, would contravene their effort to stigmatize landmines. The broad exemptions sought by Washington gave the campaigners an opening to stigmatize the United States, instead. To US officials, the campaigners' uncompromising stance smacked of unfairness: loopholes had already been written into the treaty to exempt some Europeans' mines. To the campaigners, Washington's last-minute decision to participate was an act of inherent bad faith. They opposed any amendments that would have made it easier for the United States to sign the treaty. The ICBL's intransigence put the campaigners at odds with their erstwhile ally, Canada. It also threatened to sunder the NGO coalition.

WASHINGTON DRAWS THREE RED LINES

By refusing to sign the Brussels declaration, the United States had relegated itself to the sidelines of a negotiation in which it had substantial stakes. Now, with the Ottawa process on a fast track, some US officials did not want to be left behind. Nor were Senator Leahy and Representative Evans inclined to let that happen. They threatened to enact legislation barring further US deployment of antipersonnel landmines after 1999 unless the administration joined the negotiation.

Opposition to Leahy's bill soon surfaced. On June 27 Jesse Helms of North Carolina, a right-wing Republican who chaired the Foreign Relations Committee, circulated a letter to his fellow senators attacking it. He enclosed letters critical of the bill from the chairman of the Joint Chiefs of Staff, the Army chief of staff, and Secretary of Defense William Cohen, who, as a senator from Maine, had been one of the Republican supporters of previous legislative efforts by Leahy. Criticism from another front was made public on July 10, a letter signed by all the chiefs of staff and every regional commander. Dubbed "the 64-star letter," it deplored the new legislation: "Passing this bill into law will unnecessarily endanger U.S. military forces and significantly restrict the ability to conduct combat operations successfully."[16] This warning shot was followed by another on July 21, aimed at the ban treaty itself, an open letter to President Clinton from 24 retired generals, including a chairman of the Joint Chiefs of Staff, three Army chiefs of staff, six Marine commandants, two commanders-in-chief in Korea, and former Secretary of State Alexander M. Haig, Jr. It expressed "strong opposition to U.S. participation in any international agreement that would prohibit the defensive use by American forces of modern, self-destructing antipersonnel landmines and/or the use of so-called 'dumb mines' in the Korean demilitarized zone."[17]

Under hostile fire and the press of events, the Clinton administration began to reconsider participating in the Ottawa process. Immediately after the CD adjourned in late June, "we had full-fledged interagency meetings at the assistant secretary level," says Eric Newsom. "Everybody was showing up. It was meat axes and Bowie knives."[18]

The turning point came in early August. "We decided to sound out our closest allies. A group of us, including Robert Bell of the NSC staff, went to Bonn and met the British, the Germans, and the French," says Newsom. "The four delegations convened in a beautiful room overlooking the Rhine." It was "a decisive meeting," in his assessment, "because essentially our allies told us, this is heading for a ban on landmines, the CD is a dead letter, and the options open to you are either to get in and try to influence the process or stand outside and be isolated. Our closest allies told us bluntly what we in State had been saying for months. The question was, was it already too late?"[19]

On August 15, President Clinton met with Secretary of State Madeleine Albright, Defense Secretary William Cohen, and National Security Adviser Samuel Berger to decide whether to join the negotiations. Albright favored participating. Cohen insisted that some issues were non-negotiable. Clinton, as was his wont, agreed with both.

The belated decision to participate but demand significant revisions in the Austrian draft was the result of an interagency decision-making process that had relegated landmines to lower reaches of the bureaucracy for too long, says Lee Feinstein. "By the time the issues dribbled up to the principals, they were so fucked up there was almost nothing you could do about them."[20]

The process was, if anything, even messier inside the Pentagon, where work had continued on landmines policy following PDD-48. "A lot of the more difficult refinements happen after that," says Jan Lodal, the senior civilian official in the department working on the issue.[21]

Undersecretary of Defense Walter Slocombe spearheaded the opposition to entering the negotiations. "The Pentagon opposed our participation because Slocombe understood what would happen," says Feinstein, who favored a ban. Robert Bell, special adviser to the president for defense policy and arms control, wanted to see if there was a way for the United States to sign the treaty. "I believe Bell's position was not so much that he wanted to give up mines," says Robert Sherman, "but that he wanted to be a part of Ottawa."[22] So did Newsom, who would lead the negotiating team in Oslo.

JCS did not take a firm stand on whether or not to go to Oslo, but it did feel strongly about what stance to take if the United States went. It put down three negotiating "red lines." Until they were accepted, says Newsom, "the joint staff and OSD refused to concur on attending."[23] JCS wanted to be free to use self-destructing, self-deactivating antipersonnel landmines. It wanted an exemption for Korea that covered the use and transfer of mines: "We would be bringing additional landmines out of storage and deploying them and there would be a requirement to transfer them to the Koreans," says Lee Feinstein. It also had "a search-and-rescue red line."[24] Rescuing downed pilots and other captives was one of the missions performed by special operations forces, such as the Army's Delta Force and the Navy's SEALs, which operated in small units and planned to use antipersonnel mines if they found themselves outmanned or outmaneuvered.

OSD backed JCS. "Their position was, if we go, we should go with this," recalls Sherman, who was against joining the negotiations at all. "My view was there was no way we could or should win with the pretense that APL in mixed munitions stop being APL." He recalls telling ACDA director John Holum, "'This will be a major embarrassment to the United States and to the president, and we should go to Oslo just as a friendly observer, help with the drafting and verification, and make clear we can't sign.' That became the ACDA position."[25]

"It did not prevail interagency," says Sherman, "because NSC and Eric Newsom and Lee Feinstein were not willing to accept that we would not come out of Oslo with something and that we wouldn't at least try. But what we had to try with was a cheeseburger without the cheese and without the burger."[26] Feinstein concurs with Sherman's last point, but disputes his reasoning, "The red lines were nuts. As nuts as they were, had we gotten in early in the [Ottawa] process, we could have gotten them, but it was too late."[27] By now, such a proposal was no longer negotiable.

Newsom considered appealing to Secretary of State Albright to weigh in against the red lines: "I concluded it was hopeless because we were isolated. Bob Bell told me it was pointless to fight for more flexibility." Newsom consoled himself with the thought that once the United States became engaged at Oslo, the joint staff's red lines would be crossed: "I felt that Bell's thinking might be similar to mine, which was, they can have all the red lines they want. Let us get the negotiating dynamic going and then engage the president of the United States and who knows what will happen." The same thought crossed the minds of Pentagon officials, he surmised: "They were all worried that that's what would happen, which is why they insisted on the red lines."[28]

By the Pentagon's own analysis, however, none of the three red lines were necessary. That was particularly so for the Korea exception. "By that time, several of us had pushed everybody in the building with a lot of help from Shali [General John Shalikashvili, JCS chairman] that we didn't need mines in Korea partially because people paid more attention to the mines that were already there," says Jan Lodal. "We didn't actually have any mines in the ground out there. As far as the ones that we were going to deploy, we could live with self-destruct things in a real crisis."[29] The United States no longer needed an exemption for dumb mines in Korea because the barriers belonged to South Korea and so did the mines to emplace in them.

Transferring the remaining US stocks in California still posed a problem. In the run-up to Oslo, recalls Newsom, "We had Steve Solomon, a brilliant lawyer, work on this because we learned that it was actually the South Koreans who possessed most of the nonself-destructing landmines there. We were looking for some legal way of saying we didn't control the mines in Korea," says Newsom. "We tried to work out come kind of gimmick." He sounded out others on the idea of transferring mines to South Korea so that the United States could sign the treaty: "In fact, [Tim] Rieser [of Senator Leahy's staff] and I had a couple of back-channel conversations about whether it could work. But it didn't fly. It was too clever by half and the lawyers couldn't make it work."[30] The shell game troubled Pentagon officials. "Nobody was too happy with a trick," says Lodal. The need for one proved superfluous, however. "Now between the first decision memorandum and the Oslo conference there was some more effort put into this. I didn't do it directly. I just got the results reported to me." It turned out that the mines already belonged to the Koreans. "It wasn't as if we were giving them away at the last minute."[31]

The Army needed time to transfer dumb mines stockpiled in the United States to the ROK Army. How much time was worked out by Lodal and General Wesley Clark, director for strategic plans and policies on the joint staff. "Wes Clark and I figured out how fast we could phase out all of this stuff," he says. That was done by March, when Clark left to take command of US forces in Europe, says Lodal. "So that's how we came to believe that with a little timing we could get past the Korea [problem]."[32]

That left the issue of how the United States could sign the treaty without South Korea. "We are such close allies," says Lodal, "that just hanging this on the Koreans" was "not a fair outcome." Talks with their South Korean counterparts led Pentagon officials to "conclude we could do it without it being a trick, that in fact it [the barrier] is really their responsibility, and they would not join the treaty no matter what, so it's not like we're asking them to make believe," says Lodal. "So it looked like Korea could be dealt with in the Ottawa negotiations and therefore we were down to these other things."[33]

Working out the Korea problem opened the way for the Defense Department to get rid of all its pure antipersonnel mines, which would obviate the need for another of the red lines. That sparked "a little opposition in some of the military circles," Lodal says. "The special forces carry around some stuff that was not self-deactivating or self-destruct—things for very narrow uses." The "stuff" Lodal refers to, pursuit deterrent munitions, were not deemed much of a military requirement. "Nobody anywhere except for a couple of little pockets of special forces guys and so forth," he says, "thought that outside of Korea there was any mission anywhere for true antipersonnel landmines."[34] Nor did the armed services deem special operations missions essential enough to spend money to replace them with smart versions. Nevertheless, when Deputy Secretary of Defense John Hamre directed that the few thousand in inventory be destroyed, he failed to get his way. "Apparently some people in the Pentagon did not want to obey that order," says Stephen Goose, "and got to [Senator Jesse] Helms, who said, sorry, we're not going to do that. Helms wrote into the CCW ratification that we've got to hold onto pursuit deterrent munitions. You can't destroy those."[35]

The Korea exemption was unnecessary. Yet JCS insisted on it and OSD went along. As the subsequent US negotiating position at Oslo would confirm, military requirements could be met by a transition period to phase out antipersonnel mines, which the draft treaty already provided. Yet JCS wanted more time for the transition, 9 years, and again, OSD went along. JCS deferred to the special operations forces who wanted an exemption from the ban, and again, OSD went along. JCS wanted to delete a provision barring signatory states from attaching reservations to their instruments of ratification and to insert a provision allowing states to withdraw from the treaty if their "supreme national interests" were in jeopardy. These changes would bring the ban into conformity with most other arms control treaties, which had similar withdrawal clauses, not "no reservations" clauses. Again, OSD went along.

The upshot was that United States would participate at Oslo but demand five changes in the draft treaty, three of which were unnecessary, one of which was indefensible, and none of which were negotiable. The United States sought to exempt Korea from the ban on use and transfer of mines, reword the definition of antipersonnel landmines to exclude mixed munitions from coverage, delay the treaty's entry into force for a 9-year transition period, nullify the "no reservations" clause to permit a state to sign the treaty but enumerate the parts it refused to accept or comply with, and permit a party to withdraw when that party's "supreme national interests" were threatened.

The Pentagon's bottom line was that mixed munitions were a military requirement for now. To protect that requirement, the NSC staff came up with the expedient of exempting all mixed munitions on the grounds that they were not antipersonnel mines. That was patently absurd. Mixed munitions combined antitank with antipersonnel mines. US officials had said as much on numerous occasions on the public record and in testimony to Congress. As a Pentagon spokesman phrased it at an August 19 press briefing, "We also believe that there needs to be an exception for antitank and antivehicular landmines, which have a sub-munition component which is antipersonnel in nature."[36] Diplomats at Oslo were well aware of such public statements. So were the NGOs. "That fig leaf, that mixed munitions are not APL, was created by the NSC," says Sherman. "They thought [it] was something the Ottawa people would latch onto." Sherman's is unsparing in his criticism, "What they thought of as political heavyweights pulling off political master strokes was just Olympic-level political incompetence."[37]

On August 18 at the president's vacation site on Martha's Vineyard in Massachusetts, the White House press office announced the decision to participate at Oslo and to seek exemptions for US landmines. The daily press briefing at the State Department dwelt on the exception for Korea, where, as spokesman James Rubin put it, "our defense officials believe that antipersonnel landmines are required in order for us to fulfill this, frankly, United Nations responsibility to protect the Korean Peninsula."[38] Rubin confirmed more of the details in his August 21 daily briefing. The United States would be seeking "an exception for the Korean Peninsula" and also "an exception by virtue of a new definition." He went on, "We are going to seek a definition in the treaty that ensures that a weapon primarily designed not to kill people but to stop a tank or a jeep, but a weapon that might also have antipersonnel aspects to it, would not be covered by the treaty."[39]

All five changes were listed by Secretary of State Albright in a letter cabled to US embassies for delivery to key foreign ministers on August 20. "PM had the lead," recalls Feinstein. The letter was drafted "by people at the assistant secretary level" and cleared at a Principals Committee meeting.[40] It took only days for an NGO representative on one country delegation to slip Albright's letter to the ICBL, which made its contents public.

The August 20 cable was not so much an invitation to diplomatic give-and-take as a substitute for it. "That showed, I think, how little diplomacy at important levels took place on this issue," says Feinstein. "The reason you put out a cable is basically to make everybody in the US delegation feel good about what's going on. You don't put out a cable as a negotiating position. It's not a serious way to do business. If you're on the receiving end of something like this, you think, my God, these guys can't get it together."[41]

Yet Eric Newsom did what any good diplomat does—try to make the most of his instructions. Accompanied by Robert Bell, and Richard Kelly, a Marine general representing the Defense Department, he flew to Geneva, where the core group was holding a last-minute strategy session. His aim was "to take our exceptions and see if they can be shoved into the Ottawa treaty," according an official. "He's going to see what the traffic will bear."[42] Newsom did most of the talking. "In 2 days, one after another until we got utterly sick of having to repeat the same lines, we had approximately 40 bilaterals," he says, "to let people know we were going to Oslo, we were going to have a proposal, we had red lines we would not cross, we were seeking to come out of it with a treaty that the United States could sign, and we wanted to gauge the responses." Afterwards, "We wrote a report and brought it back with us. We didn't cable it because it was so unnerving. Essentially we said we have almost no support, other than some sympathy for the special case of Korea."[43]

Perhaps because their report was so closely held, others had more hopeful impressions. "They came away from the bilaterals," recalls a White House official, "thinking there was some chance, however low, that we could get what we needed to be able to sign the treaty."[44] Pentagon officials had a similar impression. "We thought he was making some headway and was going to get the definitions straight," says Jan Lodal, "and therefore we could join the treaty."[45]

After returning to Washington to report on the results of the bilaterals, Newsom flew to Oslo, where he was joined on the US delegation by four generals and two "minders" from Senator Helms' staff.

Foreign Minister Lloyd Axworthy of Canada welcomed the US decision to participate at Oslo as "a very positive step that further legitimizes the process and makes this into a very significant event."[46] Ban campaigners, by contrast, were spoiling for a fight. "The fact that the United States is seeking all kinds of exceptions represents an attempt to negotiate in bad faith," Goose told reporters. "It would have been better if they stayed away."[47]

TURNING OSLO INTO AN US-OR-THEM AFFAIR

The campaigners had had time to organize for Oslo. They also exploited two advantages they had lacked at Geneva: access to the conference and attention from the news media. The ICBL and other NGOs had observer status at the negotiations, giving them entree to all sessions, even working group meetings. And some NGOs were more privy than others, like Mines Action Canada and Handicap International, which were represented on their countries' official delegations. A Norwegian affiliate arranged for the ICBL to have an office across the hall from the conference room, well-situated for buttonholing delegates or barraging them with a slogan a day.[48] Even though NGOs were formally precluded from proposing treaty language, they could still circulate their suggestions informally. They were also denied a vote, but disenfranchisement proved no impediment: no votes were ever taken.

The ranks of reporters swelled at Oslo, both because of the US decision to participate and because of the death of Princess Diana on the eve of the conference. Diana had put landmines on television and tabloid news around the world. The media coverage enabled campaigners to play up the human interest angle of the landmines story. By framing the story as a David-and-Goliath struggle, the news media allowed the ban campaigners to use the United States as a foil and shine a spotlight on delegations that wanted to alter the treaty.

The United States bore the brunt of ICBL opprobrium at Oslo. Alerted in advance to the US-proposed changes, the ICBL was armed with language of its own. In response to the US bid to redefine "antipersonnel landmines" in order to exempt its smart mines from treaty coverage, the ICBL deployed the slogan, "When is an AP mine not an AP Mine? When it's American." In response to the US attempt to classify antipersonnel mines placed "near" antitank mines as antihandling devices, the slogan of the day became, "Near Is Too Far."[49] Protesters took to the streets to challenge a US proposal for a "transition period" to allow it to use mines in Korea until it came up with alternatives. Being represented on the Canadian delegation did not keep Mines Action Canada from distributing a press release in the parliament building in Ottawa accusing the prime minister of "selling out" the treaty "to US policy" after he ventured to say that some exceptions on use of antipersonnel mines might be acceptable.[50]

The ICBL placed exhibits inside the conference center and festooned the square outside with banners and posters, many of which bore the same slogan as the masthead of its newsletter: "no loopholes, no exceptions, and no reservations."[51]

Public rhetoric is often used by political movements to reassure the faithful that ideological purity is being preserved while pragmatic bargaining goes on behind the scenes. In this case, the ICBL was deploying rhetoric to cloak deals it had made in the past and to forestall any future bargaining that might threaten to divide the campaigners. The slogan papered over fault lines within the ICBL between NGOs that insisted on accepting the treaty as it stood and NGOs that wanted it changed. Some sought a more stringent ban. A handful of others were ready to relax the ban somewhat in order to accommodate Washington.

The ICBL's willingness to go along with treaty language exempting some European mines with antihandling devices and permitting antivehicle mines did not sit well with some NGOs. These fissures would erupt into open disagreements after Oslo. At Ottawa in December, Rae McGrath, director of Mines Advisory Group, which specialized in demining, accused ICBL organizers of "caving in" by not opposing the exemption for antihandling devices. Mark Perry of the VVAF recalls his outburst, "He said, have you read this treaty. Really read it? Read this paragraph! This allows antipersonnel mines." The campaign's first imperative, Perry countered, was to "stigmatize the weapon." Once the treaty establishes "the norm, we can go back and fix it." That did not satisfy deminers like McGrath who had the delicate job of disabling antihandling devices in order to remove mines. Nor did it satisfy NGOs that delivered humanitarian aid to war-torn countries. McGrath spoke for them as well, "Let me tell you, humanitarian operations cease when a Red Cross truck runs over an antitank mine. We've got to ban the whole thing. This treaty's junk." The argument became so heated, says Perry, "we had to clear the room."[52]

Just as troubling to other NGOs were the transition periods for getting rid of stockpiles and clearing minefields. "We were under great pressure to indicate what level of compromise—delays—we would accept," says an ICRC representative, who was willing to compromise only so far and no further to satisfy potential signatories. He expressed the unease felt by some NGOs that they were nearing "the limit of the role" they could play without giving up their independence: "We were on the verge, in spite of collaboration, of having a treaty that would have been very difficult for the ICRC to bless."[53]

Most affiliates agreed with the ICBL and adamantly opposed accommodating Washington at Oslo. Not the Vietnam Veterans of America Foundation. Disagreements between Robert Muller of VVAF and Jody Williams of ICBL would later turn into open hostility. "There was a fight before Oslo," recalls Perry. "We were trying to get the United States on the treaty. Bobby was very angry afterward. He said, this is about the $3.50 Saturday night specials and we're keeping the United States off because of smart mines. This is a disaster for the treaty. He just couldn't move his colleagues." Muller had aimed his efforts at Washington, while Williams had turned her back on Washington and, using the United States as a foil, mobilized support in the rest of the world. His base of support was firmest among the founders of the ICBL, while Williams had built a global network by drawing in a host of foreign affiliates. "We had the core," says Perry. "She had the Jamaica campaign, the Colombia campaign." Distrust of the United States was endemic among many affiliates.

"Her priority," he says, "was not to get the United States on the treaty but to stigmatize the United States as a way of getting other countries on the treaty."[54] The political soon became personal. "Because of the position she had, she'd get fêted in national capitals around the world, being treated like a fucking ambassador," says Muller. "You get a Norma Nobody and all of a sudden they get treated like they're somebody and they internalize it." In parts of the campaign, he says, "the conversations we had were, should we fire her because she just became impossible." He decided not to. "We had such a hard time keeping that rapidly broadening coalition together. Knowing that we had an end point in Ottawa in December, the idea was, don't rock the boat."[55]

Yet even VVAF, the NGO that had tried hardest in private to bring Washington on board, lent support to the ICBL's public call to stigmatize the United States. It was the response of a spurned suitor. "From the moment that Shalikashvili turned around on this," Perry acknowledges, "our organization's relationship with the military was really strained and we were not inclined to believe anything that they said. So when the Ottawa Convention was negotiated in Oslo and they came in with five interlocking demands, we thought this was just stupid." VVAF has since had second thoughts. "When Clinton and the military objected," Perry notes, "and said, our allies are deploying antipersonnel mines disguised as antitank mines because they have antihandling devices. That's not fair. Our mines are safer than theirs. You guys just don't get it. Ottawa is a hollow shell. We said you just want to keep your weapons." In retrospect, "We didn't know the weapons that well," Perry says. "I think we were dead wrong. I think the military knew we were wrong and just looked at us as another bumbling NGO."[56] To others in the ICBL the VVAF's regrets sounded like sympathy with the aggressor.

The ICBL did not want to accommodate Washington in hopes of getting it to sign the ban. Its adversarial stance toward the United States played well abroad, and not just in the developing world. Perry recalls talking to Canadian diplomat Dan Livermore 2 years after Oslo. Livermore, who had witnessed the results of landmine use first-hand when he was ambassador to Guatemala and El Salvador, spoke for a faction within Canada's foreign ministry when he told Perry, "That was always our strategy. We knew if we could keep the United States off the treaty, we could make the argument to Gabon, Jamaica, South Africa that this is something the United States wouldn't do and we could make the United States look bad."[57] Livermore was not alone, according to Robert Muller. "We were told by Robert Lawson that he used the same argument."[58]

It played well in some parts of Europe, too. In Oslo, says Philippe Chabasse of Handicap International, "France became one of the key players to resist the American attempts to influence the negotiations."[59] When VVAF, as a way to get the United States to sign the Ottawa Treaty, tried talking France into refusing to cooperate on the use of landmines by NATO, a stance similar to the one it had taken on NATO nuclear strategy, Mark Perry recalls the reaction of one French defense ministry official, "We don't want the United States on Ottawa. Every time the Americans show up at a NATO meeting, the French delegation gets to point the finger at them because they still have landmines. I said, you don't understand. If we don't get the United States on Ottawa, Ottawa is going to die. He said, you don't understand. We don't give a fuck about the treaty."[60]

Many Oslo participants were convinced that the United States had a similar view. That made it easy for the campaigners to line up opposition to American proposals to amend the draft treaty.

"HITTING THE OTTAWA WALL"

On September 1, the Oslo conference opened with 87 states participating and 33 observing. They endorsed the core group's nominee for presiding officer, Jacob Selebi, the South African diplomat who had chaired the Africa-wide experts conference in May. Selebi was an inspired choice. A veteran of the struggle against apartheid, he was an appealing figure to Africans and other developing countries well-represented in Oslo—a target audience for the core group, who hoped his prominence would blur the perception of the landmines campaign as Western-dominated. Campaigners fervently hoped that the independent Selebi would stand up to the United States.

Selebi moved the proceedings along expeditiously. Later that first day, conference rules were approved providing for decisions to be taken by a two-thirds majority if no consensus could be reached. Most important of all, the conferees swiftly adopted the Austrian draft as the basis for negotiation.

Working groups of South African delegates and five "friends of the chair"—Austria, Brazil, Canada, Ireland, and Mexico—were set up to resolve disputes about definitions and other contentious drafting issues. How much time to allow for removing deployed mines was one. That fell to the Austrians to resolve. As they framed the question, "How could the convention prescribe a certain period for mine-clearing in heavily mine-infested states, while knowing that in all likelihood this objective could not be achieved?"[61] Their answer was not to dispense with a time limit, which would only delay mine-clearing everywhere. An earlier draft had distinguished between areas that could be cleared quickly and heavily mined areas. The Austrians dropped the distinction and instead allowed up to 10 years for mine-clearing while allowing mine-infested states like Angola and Mozambique that needed more time to apply for an extension of up to 10 additional years and seek assistance for completing the task.

Canada was the "friend of the chair" chosen to settle the contentious question of noncompliance. Canadian diplomats did so by melding two competing models: one, intrusive verification common in arms control treaties;

and the other, fact-finding, the practice in international humanitarian law. The compromise, a far cry from the short-notice, on-site inspections of the Chemical Weapons Convention, was noticeably vague about sanctions for noncompliance. The crux of the matter was whether a fact-finding mission could take place only with the consent of a state accused of noncompliance or whether the parties to treaty could authorize a mission without its consent. Also at issue was the scope of fact-finding. Article 8 tried to square the circle by allowing time for an accused party to clarify whether or not it was complying before a fact-finding mission could be authorized. States would submit a "request for clarification" through the UN secretary-general. The offending party would have 28 days to respond. If the complainant was dissatisfied by the response, it could refer the matter to next year's meeting of states parties, or else request a special meeting. If, within 14 days of such a request, one-third of the states agreed, then a special meeting would be held within the next 14 days. At that meeting, if the majority was not satisfied, it could authorize a nine-member, fact-finding mission, to be appointed by the UN secretary-general after consulting with the offending state. Given at least 72-hours notice, that state would have to grant access to the areas in question and to all relevant persons who could provide information. The mission could remain on its territory for just 14 days, no more than 7 days at any one site, and then report its findings through the secretary-general to the meeting of states, which could decide, by two-thirds vote, on appropriate action.

The main bone of contention at Oslo was how to deal with the US proposals. Campaigners who preferred to freeze out the United States prevailed over Canada and others who wanted to bring it in. Washington's insistence on seeking approval of all five of its amendments as a package made that easier. As Canadian diplomats put it, "The central fault-line of the Oslo conference quickly formed along the three most problematic U.S. proposals—the Korean exception, the deferral of [entry into force], changes in the antipersonnel mine definition—the core of what US negotiators repeatedly stated was an 'all-or-nothing package'."[62]

Some US officials accuse Canada, not just the campaigners, of deliberately setting up the United States in order to rally international support for a ban rather than forge the compromises needed to secure Washington's accession to the treaty. "Many people who worked the issue much more closely than I still say that the United States would have liked to sign that agreement depending on how certain very technical definitions were handled—antihandling devices and the like," says a military officer who became deeply engaged in the issue after Oslo. "I still believe that certain signatories to that agreement frankly did not want the United States to sign it because they wanted the United States to be isolated from the world community—several of whom have long borders with the United States."[63]

The evidence suggests, however, that the United States isolated itself by its own uncompromising stance.

The US delegation proposed some relatively uncontroversial changes to treaty provisions on the destruction of stockpiles and deployed mines, transparency, and implementation, but five other US amendments provoked intense opposition. One singled out Korea in all but name, according to Robert Bell of the NSC staff. It referred to a "a military command (operating) under the auspices of the United Nations overseeing a UN armistice for a war that is not officially over."[64] The permanent exemption it sought for US and South Korean mines stockpiled on the Korean peninsula and deployed along the DMZ was a nonstarter. It was supported by just one delegation, Japan, and opposed by 32.

Amending the definitions of antipersonnel landmine and antihandling device would have permitted the United States to exempt mixed munitions, much as the Europeans had exempted some of their mines, but it also would have widened a loophole in the treaty to allow devices designed to harm people, weapons that may have been smart enough to self-deactivate eventually but not smart enough to distinguish combatants from noncombatants while operational. Again, only Japan spoke in favor of changing the definitions.

The Austrian draft required removal of all antipersonnel mines within 10 years of signing and destruction of stockpiles within 4 years. A US attempt to defer the treaty's entry into force by 9 years was calculated to appeal to some mine-infested states and make it easier for holdouts like Russia to sign, but allowing signatories an additional 9-year delay ran the risk of codifying noncompliance, diluting the stigma that the ban was designed to cast. Australia, Ecuador, Japan, and Poland spoke in favor while Canada lent tacit support, but the amendment met with firm opposition led by several African delegations.

Making it easier for states to attach reservations to the treaty, however much it appealed to unilateralists in the Senate, would have let states object to and not comply with parts of the treaty even though they signed it. Not a single delegation spoke in favor of deleting the "no reservations" clause.

Australia, Brazil, Britain, Ecuador, and Spain supported the US effort to allow parties to withdraw from the treaty if they judged their "supreme national interests" were endangered and to drop a provision requiring them to give reasons in writing as well as shortening the period of advanced notice for withdrawal to 90 days from 6 months. Canada, France, and Italy led the charge to defeat these changes.

Each of the US proposals, in short, had significant opposition. By insisting on all five as a package, the United States made any accommodation much more difficult and polarized the proceedings, turning Oslo into a US-or-them affair.

The US delegation soon sized up the situation. "I felt that the organizers of the conference, the most powerful NGOs and the little inner circle of eight or ten countries that ran things," says Newsom, "were only worried about what we might do until the end of the first day after I made my opening statement in which I laid out the five red lines. Then they knew that they were in charge, that we had blown any chance we had of changing the atmosphere. The rest of the conference was, in a way, anticlimactic."[65] Robert Sherman shares Newsom's assessment. "Initially, our position was supported out of loyalty by the Japanese and the Poles, no one else," he recalls, "and they rapidly left us, too." Even the Australians, who had stood shoulder to shoulder with the Americans on the landmine issue generally, parted company over the package proposal. Sherman says Ambassador John Campbell told him, "Bob, this is bloody ridiculous."[66]

To Sherman it was confirmation that the United States never should have participated in Oslo. "Eric Newsom had a spectacular conversion," he says, but perceptions back in Washington were not nearly as pessimistic. "Lee Feinstein was telling people that the delegation is making significant progress. Eric was really steamed at that, and rightly so. He knew we had made no progress at all," by Sherman's account. "About halfway through I heard that Bob Bell was saying in Washington, maybe it's time to show a little ankle," or hint at a compromise. Sherman phoned ACDA director John Holum, "That is totally out of it. Showing ankle will get us nowhere. We've got two choices: we stand pat or we do a world-class blow job. There is nothing in between."[67] A decade earlier, Sherman, then a Congressional aide, had helped secure passage of legislation backing a nuclear freeze. Now he was doing his best to stop the United States from signing a landmines ban.

The transition time that the United States said it needed remained limitless. That hamstrung the US delegation when other countries asked, "How long will it take you to find a solution in Korea and how long will it take you to find a replacement for mixed munitions?" says a senior US official. "We don't know what either of those can be and there was no way we could answer. To find a replacement for mixed munitions is more a matter of decades than it is years. Is that what they wanted to hear?"[68] When a reporter put the question to a Pentagon spokesman, he replied, "I can't give you a time constraint on all of this because at this point I'm not sure.... We do have a program underway to develop alternative measures—but we are not talking about delaying in order to develop alternative measures." His tortured reply led the Pentagon to issue a clarification that did not clarify much: The "US position is there must be a transition period, the length of which has not been clarified."[69] Asked about the US amendment to defer the treaty's entry into force for 9 years, Robert Bell spoke of 9 years as an "educated estimate" of how long it would take to develop and field alternatives.[70] Signatories would then have another 10 years after entry into force to remove the banned landmines.

The prolonged delay was unnecessary. "I think we knew we'd have to give a few more years on the timing," says Jan Lodal, "and everyone was prepared to do that." The Korea exemption was also unnecessary: "We could get rid of the Korea stuff because by this time we'd gotten everybody to agree it wasn't a trick. So it was only [a matter of] timing on Korea." There was no impediment elsewhere, either. "We'd already started getting rid of the other stuff. It had already been our policy not to use the other stuff. We were already well on our way to demining even Guantanamo." Both demands could be finessed, according to Lodal. "It was not that these things were not issues, but they were workable issues. They could have played out over time."[71]

The sticking point for the Pentagon was mixed munitions. "We had to keep these Gators and other deployable systems. We had to have something that would not render them illegal because we were not going to get rid of them," says Lodal. "This was the issue we couldn't compromise on."[72]

By now "it was clear that the basic definition had gone against us," says Lodal. "It was put to bed and Newsom had lost." But he was not done trying. "Even though we'd lost on the basic definition, he said we can work it through the fine print."[73] When the core group introduced its language on antihandling devices at a working group meeting, "I excoriated them for hypocrisy," Newsom recounts. "I drew the obvious distinctions between the device which they had now rendered legal and the device which they were making illegal— the fact that ours would self-destruct after a matter of hours and was far safer for civilians, while their device would remain a threat to civilians indefinitely, the fact that the devices served the same purpose, just that ours was more effective. Essentially, I said we're going to protect our troops. If that means we don't sign this treaty, then we won't sign it." He says ruefully, "I doubt it will enter the annals as one of the more diplomatic statements ever made."[74]

Having made it, however, Newsom soon had second thoughts. "The first reaction was to be angry at the double standard," but on reflection, "we said maybe we could use this as leverage," he recalls. "We said, you need antitank mines and you want to protect them with these antihandling devices. Well, in principle, there's no difference whatever between your antihandling devices and our protective munitions. By then, we didn't call them antipersonnel mines. We coined a new term"—mixed munitions.[75]

Lodal credits Newsom with figuring out that the "Ottawa definitions already permitted antitampering devices that might be themselves dangerous to civilians. That is effectively what we're doing in these mixed packages. We're including devices that might be dangerous to civilians, but only for a short period of time because they self-destruct and self-deactivate." That was not all. "Newsom also figured out that there were other loopholes in the definitions. For example, antitank mines with tripwires," says Lodal, "were actually permitted because they were big enough to be clearly antivehicular and because the tripwire was an antitamper device. It would blow anyone to smithereens if they touched it." Newsom tried to exploit the loopholes to exempt the antipersonnel mines integral to US mixed munitions: "Newsom's idea seemed so good to lard it in through the antitampering [language] because the Europeans wanted to allow tripwires on theirs and we thought, aha, now they see, they do have to protect antitank mines because otherwise all you have to do is send soldiers in and dig them up. That's the only reason we have for these things and since they're self-destruct, they ought to be willing to agree that that's a reasonable exemption, and in many ways more reasonable than theirs, which don't self-destruct."[76] Pentagon officials, says Lodal, were heartened by Newsom's effort to exploit the loopholes for European landmines to exempt US mixed munitions. "We thought, clever man, clever man."[77]

Lodal was also heartened by what he took to be signs that Newsom was making headway. "He reported back that he was making some progress. The Canadians wanted us on board, and so did the Europeans."[78] Newsom himself was much less upbeat about his chances of convincing the core group. "These countries had done their deal," he says. "They had reached their understandings and they were going to stick by them, no matter what we said."[79]

Had the United States joined the Ottawa process earlier, it might have succeeded in amending the definitions to exempt its own mines, or else it might have reinterpreted the definitions in a way that other countries found acceptable. Instead, it insisted on rewriting the definitions at the last minute. Lodal believes even this stratagem might have succeeded if the president had personally intervened sooner: "The Clinton administration has got to take responsibility for it because if [National Security Adviser Samuel] Berger had gotten the president fired up and he called up [Foreign Minister Axworthy] and said we're going to do it this way, I'm absolutely convinced that no way was Axworthy going to turn it down." Did the United States have any evidence of that? "No," says Lodal, "What we know is that Newsom got close without any high-level help." In any event, the belated attempt to persuade others that US mines were less likely to harm noncombatants was unsuccessful. "We could never get that point across," says Lodal. Even some US officials "didn't understand that the Ottawa definitions were goofy." Lodal's frustration is still palpable: "What we were asking for is so utterly reasonable and their definition is so utterly unnecessary and we were so close to having a huge consensus which would have been vastly in the US interest."[80]

Preparing for the worst, Newsom opened a back channel with the chair of the conference, Jacob Selebi. "The second day I went to see him. I made crystal clear that I did not want the United States humiliated." Selebi "could have called for a vote that day," he says, "and we would have been bashed. He told me he would give us time to make our best case. He and his inner circle would not force a vote." Newsom is grateful to Selebi to this day. "He promised me we would not be humiliated and, as much as we criticized his dominance of the conference, he lived up to his promise. He did not force a vote."[81]

That gave Newsom time to try on his own to salvage what he could from Oslo. "Discussions in the first few days made clear to any of us who did not know already that our five red lines were utterly out of the question," he says. Newsom reached out to US allies. "Virtually all of our friends, even those who privately sympathized with our views, were paralyzed by the politics of the ban campaign and the death of Princess Diana," he says. "A few delegations, actually tried to work with us, the Germans, the Canadians, and two or three others."[82]

Toward the end of the first week, Newsom and Larry Dodgen, an Army brigadier general who represented OSD and was deputy head of the delegation, sent a cable back to Washington. "It was titled something like 'Hitting the Ottawa Wall'," says Newsom. "Our message was that Washington needed to prepare itself now for a total ban on antipersonnel landmines with not a single one of our five red lines." The cable "apparently caused consternation in Washington" because "it was in the second week that higher-ups got involved."[83]

REDRAWING THE RED LINES

If the US delegation was preparing for defeat, Princess Diana's death revived Canadian hopes for a compromise. At a luncheon after Diana's funeral on September 5, Foreign Minister Axworthy had a chat with Hillary Clinton, who asked how she could help. Axworthy suggested she telephone her husband, which she did.[84] With that encouragement, Prime Minister Chretien wrote President Clinton on September 8, "The negotiators in Oslo are prepared to exercise flexibility and ingenuity to accommodate [Washington's] legitimate security interests," but Chretien put down a diplomatic marker that compromise had its limits: "There is a clear danger that any open-ended exception will lead to demands for other exceptions and would fundamentally weaken the treaty we are seeking."[85]

September 8 was a busy day in the White House mail room. Another missive came from Senator Jesse Helms, chairman of the Senate Foreign Relations Committee, putting down a marker of his own. Having bottled up many a treaty in committee to preclude a Senate vote, Helms provided his personal advice and consent to the president: the United States should say in no uncertain terms that its negotiating positions in Oslo were "bottom lines," not a "starting point for debate."[86] It was a demonstration of aggressive unilateralism.

Five days later, General Henry Shelton, commander-in-chief of US special operations and soon to replace John Shalikashvili as chairman of the Joint Chiefs of Staff, weighed in. Responding to a query from Senator James Imhofe (R-OK), Shelton described antipersonnel landmines as "integral to the defense of the Republic of Korea." Then he removed the NSC's fig leaf from mixed munitions. An "accurate definition" of antipersonnel landmines was "essential to prevent the banning of mixed munitions under the treaty," he insisted. "I firmly believe that our antitank (AT) and antivehicle (AV) munitions—which are mixed systems composed entirely of smart AT *and* AP mines that self-destruct or self-deactivate in a relatively short period of time—are vital to the protection of our men and women in the field." That was not all. "Nonself-destructing (NSD) or 'dumb' mines," he added, "are essential to our commanders in the Republic of Korea."[87] That could have applied not only to the barrier mines controlled by the South Koreans but also to pursuit deterrent munitions, the pure antipersonnel mines used by special operations forces. In short, Shelton was digging in his heels, insisting on all the JCS red lines.

Entrenched opposition from JCS and influential Republicans in Congress put the administration in a bind. "By the second week in Oslo," write the Canadian diplomats, "it appeared that the inability of the U.S. team to break open their package reflected a policy stalemate in Washington."[88] Immobility in Washington reinforced intransigence in Oslo, which played into the campaigners' hands.

After consulting with Canada and others, the administration came up with other ways to amend the draft treaty and satisfy JCS. The new language, quickly leaked to the press, was confirmed by a State Department spokesman on September 15. One change would allow a party to withdraw from the treaty if it or an ally was "a victim of armed aggression in violation of the UN charter." The second change would permit a state to defer compliance with the treaty for 9 years from the time it signed the treaty, instead of 9 years from the time the treaty entered into force.[89] That meant that the United States or any other signatory could take as long as it wanted to come into compliance. The third changed the definition of "anti-handling device" in Article 2, "a device intended to protect a mine and which is part of, linked to, attached to or placed under the mine and which activates when an attempt is made to tamper with or otherwise intentionally disturb the mine," by adding the words "or near." That would allow the United States to reclassify mixed systems like Gator and Volcano that it dispersed near antitank mines and to exempt some of its antipersonnel mines as antihandling devices.

"That was unenforceable and unworkable because how do you define what is 'near'," objected Tim Rieser. "We felt that would open it up to all kinds of interpretations that could potentially undermine the treaty." Rieser recognized, however, that mixed systems posed "a much bigger problem than Korea" for the Pentagon. "The fact was that this treaty, which was an antipersonnel mine ban, was going to make illegal most of the US antitank mines. That was not fully appreciated during the negotiations." It put him at odds with the campaigners. "We argued with the NGOs about that, at least insofar as saying that this was not a contrived issue. It was a real issue. As much as we wanted to solve that one, we could not solve it in the way the administration was proposing." He saw two ways out. "One was to remove the APLs from the mixed systems, which was a solution that was developed within the Pentagon and costed out." The other was "a phase-out plan," which might have been negotiable "had the administration become involved in the Ottawa process a lot earlier."[90]

Washington hoped to attract support by no longer insisting on a specific exemption for Korea but instead extending the withdrawal clause to cover aggression against parties to the convention and their allies, by allowing more time to comply for parties that subsequently signed the treaty, and by permitting not just smart antipersonnel mines located near an antitank mine, but dumb ones as well.[91] The revisions did not have the desired effect. Trying to insert the words "or near," says Newsom, "basically provoked laughter."[92] Even though it received tacit support from Canada, the US amendment on Korea was too transparent to fool—or convince—anyone. Canada and a few others were also willing to accommodate the United States on a "transition" period. "Any convention needs a certain phasing-in period," noted Foreign Minister Axworthy of Canada. Japan alone spoke in favor of the US attempt to reword the definition of antipersonnel landmine to allow mixed munitions; all of the core group spoke out against the change.[93]

The proposed revisions drew immediate fire from the ICBL which denounced them as "killer amendments" intended to "maim" the treaty.[94] When Canada indicated it was amenable to compromise on the question of a transition period, Williams of the ICBL accused Ottawa of "carrying the water" for Washington. "The Canadian prime minister is calling other governments around the world. What signal is that giving when the father of this ban treaty is calling governments [to] help the United States?"[95]

US negotiators were almost as unhappy as the campaigners. Newsom had contempt for the "or near" proposal: "I didn't want to do it. I was embarrassed. That's the sort of desperation stuff they were coming up with back in Washington. They seemed to have no grasp of what it was like in Oslo."[96] Washington was far away, insulated from heat in Oslo. "We had three demonstrations against us and we were just looking stupid," says Sherman. "The feeling in the delegation went past resentment into active hatred of the NSC and the upper levels of State that were handling this thing so incompetently." The breaking point came when the delegation was instructed that as a fallback position, it could drop the requirement for mixed munitions to self-destruct to qualify for exemption. "NSC decided that while we had specified that mixed munitions had to be self-destructing, that wasn't a firm decision and we could fall off of that," says Sherman, "so the final proposal we were handed by the NSC would have exempted a mixed munition that had a 30-year lifetime, maybe one that was nonmetallic, and had every evil property a landmine could have. This was morally unconscionable and politically stupid." The campaigners' reaction was predictable, says Sherman. "The NGOs stuck it to us hard on that one, as I would have done if I were in their place."[97]

Some officials who wanted the United States to sign the ban now proposed that instead of seeking to reword the definition of antipersonnel landmines, the United States simply reinterpret the words to exempt its mines. That occasioned "a gigantic fight," says Feinstein. "We argued that you could choose on a unilateral basis to define the ban on landmines to permit us to deploy mixed munitions." Reinterpreting the definition contradicted the stance taken by the United States in CCW, where US negotiator Michael Matheson "had said this would ban mixed munitions." Although that stance was clear from the negotiating record of CCW, acknowledges Feinstein, that was "before anybody could envision what was going to happen." Now Matheson "insisted that we can't change our view on the subject, which I find hard to understand. Then the deputy assistant secretary for politico-military affairs [Newsom] reiterated the position and opposed any effort to reexamine our previous position on what the definition is, which was complete madness."[98]

Matheson sees it differently, "Some at the very last minute said, why can't we say 'linked to' means linked in a functional sense, that is, it's part of the same overall weapons system." Having tried and failed to insert the words "or near" into the definition of antihandling device, "it was almost impossible at that point to interpret 'linked to' as meaning anything other than physically linked." Matheson's brief was strong: "The main problem was, you had a text in the Ottawa negotiation and the United States tried to modify it to exempt our mixed munitions and that attempt was soundly rejected. The record clearly shows what seems obvious from the text, namely, that our devices are not exempted. So as both a legal and political matter that made it almost impossible to maintain later, notwithstanding all of that, our stuff is okay."[99] Matheson's brief did not sway Feinstein. In negotiating treaties and persuading the Senate to ratify them, as those familiar with the history of the 1972 Anti-Ballistic Missile Treaty may recall, "you try to squeeze as much as you can out of the language," says Feinstein. "It's not fun. You have to hold your nose."[100] Matheson demurs, "We couldn't possibly go to Jesse Helms and say, Jesse, you don't really have to worry about this because we've decided to reinterpret the provision." Matheson discussed the issue with Newsom "and Eric had to agree that there was nothing there."[101] The gambit was a "nonstarter" in Tim Rieser's view, too. "The definition in the treaty was unambiguous and we felt it would have been a dishonest interpretation of the language." It also would have opened up a big loophole because the antipersonnel mines and antitank mines, "while they are packaged together, are scattered separately."[102]

At a breakfast in Oslo, Sherman says, Senator Leahy asked him where things stood. "I told him, 'Basically nowhere.' And he said, Does the president know that we're not going to be signing at Ottawa?" In Sherman's view, Leahy "had the belief that, faced with this fact, the president would make a major change in US policy rather than have us not be part of Ottawa." Clinton "had always kept the door open, but now we were at the point where you no longer could just keep the door open. You either had to walk through it or you had to close it."[103] Unbeknownst to all but a few officials, the president was poised to walk through it.

LEFT IN THE LURCH

Newsom had still not given up his quest for a compromise that would allow Washington to sign the treaty. Invited to dinner by the core group during his second week in Oslo, he phoned home for instructions. "I was authorized by Bob Bell to go in and tell the group that we would compromise—drop our transition period from 9 to 7 years and consider some constraints on our exemption for Korea," says Newsom. The United States was now down to two demands: "We'd dropped the other three."[104]

At dinner with Selebi and representatives of the core group, Newsom recalls, "There were about ten core group countries there, and I figured, what the hell, and told them like it was. I said, you people have boxed in the United States. You're going to make it impossible for us to sign this treaty. No formal decision has been made yet but you are going to have a treaty that will not have the United States in it. You're going to have to ask yourselves, what is that worth, when you can have us in it for so little." It was a case calculated to appeal to the Canadians. "I may be exceeding my instructions. There was dead silence." He plowed ahead, "We're asking no more than to be able to honor our security commitments to other countries." Then he spelled out Washington's new bottom line: "We're asking that you allow us a period of time in Korea to develop alternatives and that you give us a transition period for the rest of the world, that's all."[105]

"We might be able to get one of the two, either a time-limited exemption for Korea or a transition period—not 9 years, maybe 5," Newsom thought. "So I was telling them, we'd drop the other demands. They were immovable," he says. "I reported back that while there were over 100 countries, only six or eight, working with the NGOs, were calling the shots and Jacob Selebi was running it like he was Mayor Daley. That's when they said, get a suspension of the conference," he says, "because they wanted to go all-out at political levels in capitals."[106] It would take more authoritative US officials than Newsom to move the core group.

At the end of the second week, Newsom consulted with the Canadians and with Selebi, who agreed to allow time for a last-ditch try by the United States to climb on board—much to the dismay of pro-ban campaigners. In a dramatic moment, Newsom rose in plenary session to request a 3-day recess. Afterward, some US delegates made no secret of their unhappiness with the draft treaty. "As it stands now," Sherman told reporters, "we cannot sign it."[107] Some observers took that as a threat to boycott the conference unless the United States was granted key concessions.

By now top officials in Washington were fully engaged. "I was told the president was getting briefed frequently," says Newsom. "They were having daily PCs [Principal Committee meetings]. I was absolutely exhausted. I was spending all day at the conference and then the phone would keep ringing until 3 or 4 in the morning."[108]

Over the weekend President Clinton phoned Prime Minister Jean Chretien of Canada, Prime Minister Tony Blair of Britain, President Jacques Chirac of France, and President Nelson Mandela of South Africa, to line up support for the two US conditions. National Security Adviser Berger and Secretary of State Albright also called their counterparts. The revised conditions, these conversations showed, would fare no better than the ingoing US position. Clinton and Mandela had "a very polite conversation," recalls Lee Feinstein, who has read the transcript. "This was an important moment in history when the president of the United States asked for something, didn't get it, and there were no negative consequences for the people who didn't give him what he asked for."[109] Retaliating against South Africa, however, might have accomplished little; Mandela was hardly alone in telling Clinton that the revised conditions were insupportable.

The White House drew the correct conclusion: the United States would have to settle for a lot less if it wanted to sign the ban.

During the recess, Newsom discussed the transition period with the Canadians and one or two other delegations, who in turn consulted others. "They came back and said, we think there is a chance that you could get a 5-year transition, but with a half-dozen restrictions that essentially rendered it useless."[110]

After the recess, Newsom got a phone call from Bell. "As usual, it was very late at night," recalls Newsom. "He said, Eric, I'm about to go in with the president, the secretary of state, the secretary of defense, and the national security adviser to do a final assessment. I need your best judgment as the negotiator on the scene. Do we have any reasonable chance of getting either an exception for Korea or a 7-year transition period? You talk about being put on the spot." Based on his consultations, Newsom replied, "No, I don't think we do. My gut feeling is, we might still get a 5-year transition period but with constraints on it so severe that it would be almost useless to us, and we won't get an exception for Korea. There will be nothing else and I can't guarantee we'll even get that. He said, all right. Thank you."[111]

Newsom's recollection of that pivotal moment is revealing. "Clinton wanted to sign that treaty," he says. "Bob Bell had made that clear to me.

Those red lines had vanished. They would have settled for one thing. I think he would have told the joint staff to swallow it if we could just have gotten the 7-year transition."[112]

The administration's frantic efforts had come up short. "Senator Leahy," says Sherman, "had successfully fostered the presumption that at the end of the day somehow a rabbit was going to be pulled of this hat, but by the second week in Oslo it was clear that there was no rabbit."[113] Leahy's own postmortem is more revealing. It was "a genuine attempt to break the impasse," he said, but the landmines ban "proved to be an issue that could not be solved by the kind of frenzied all-night, eleventh-hour scramble that sometimes has been raised to an art form in this administration. There simply are too many countries involved, and the issues are too serious for that."[114]

Why did the Clinton administration wait so long to get fully engaged? Lodal points the finger at NSC and the Department of State. "Nobody really committed the diplomatic strength of the United States to try to get this to come out right," he says. "You had a whole bunch of guys in the State Department, driven by the NGOs and their own misunderstanding and lack of trust in the Defense Department, who believed that at the end of the day the United States would be forced to go along with the treaty and that would be a good thing."[115] Yet civilians in the Pentagon were slow to determine how limited the need for landmines was and slower to acknowledge it, allowing the joint staff to insist on unnecessary red lines like the Korea exemption and a prolonged transition period. There is plenty of blame-passing and more than enough blame to share.

A more fundamental reason for the late start was the widely shared assumption in Washington that nothing ever happens without the United States. "The truth of the matter was that none of us quite believed that at the end of the day Oslo would end up signed," says Jan Lodal. "It literally was only in the last few days or week that we realized we lost." The mindset at the time, he recalls, was that somehow a way would be found to finesse the differences and allow the United States to sign the treaty. "We thought that either the president would intervene or Madeleine would intervene, or Newsom would be successful without us, or we'd get a delay, or the British would come to our aid." Something would turn up. It was as if Micawber had materialized in Washington, fresh from Dickens' pen. "It just seemed so unreasonable that we couldn't get it."[116] By then it was too late.

WITHDRAWING IN CONFUSION

President Clinton decided against banning landmines for now. "About 7 in the morning, the phone rang," says Newsom. "It was Bob Bell saying, the president had made a decision. We are not going to sign this treaty. But you are not to announce it there. The president wants to announce it here." While Washington prepared, says Newsom, "I had to do a diplomatic fandango for about a day and a half."[117]

When the conference resumed the next day, Newsom formally proposed the three new amendments to the draft treaty as a package—"reject one, reject all." Then he requested a 1-day extension of the conference, giving Washington time to prepare for the inevitable. The interlocking amendments attracted little additional support. On September 17, with talking points cleared from Washington, he addressed the plenary. "I announced that we were withdrawing all our proposed amendments to the treaty text, that the United States did not seek a recorded vote, and that the United States would not pose an objection to adoption of the treaty by acclamation."[118]

"Needless to say, I had already rigged it with Selebi, who was all set to gavel this through," notes Newsom. He had told the conference chairman, "I do not want a vote in which the United States is by itself with one or two others and I do not want to have our friends walk the plank"—have to vote for or against the United States. Selebi, says Newsom, "was as good as his word. A couple of delegations tried to get the floor to demand a roll call vote. They wanted to humiliate us. They wanted the vote to be 120–1. But Selebi banged it through."[119] The extra day had passed with the draft treaty intact.

The motion to adopt the treaty by voice vote evoked "a roar," Newsom recalls, with "everyone standing on tables, people throwing papers in the air," and amid the uproar "the US delegation sitting like the Politburo, stone-faced." As cameras focused on him, Newsom thought to himself, "This one I botched. I should have rigged it beforehand so we had a chance to get out of the room before they did this. But I did not want to pull a Khrushchev and walk out."[120] Ambassador Karl F. "Rick" Inderfurth recalls, "When I saw clips of him on television, I told him that he should have been wearing a helmet."[121] Afterwards, Newsom met the press. There was little he could say. "I went into an absolutely packed room and did one of my best wooden-headed bureaucrat routines," he says. "I stonewalled for about 45 minutes and then left."[122] Newsom was not alone in his discomfort.

Later that day, a visibly distressed President Clinton held a press conference at the White House to say he could not "in good conscience" sign the treaty because it did not provide an adequate transition period to develop alternatives to antipersonnel mines and "would have banned the antitank mines our troops rely on from the outskirts of Seoul to the desert border of Iraq and Kuwait." He dwelled on Korea, where, as he put it, "our antipersonnel mines there are a key part of our defense line." He declared, "As commander-in-chief, I will not send our soldiers to defend the freedom of our people and the freedom of others without doing everything we can to make them as secure as possible." Trying to put the best face on the decision, he told reporters, "I called for the global elimination of landmines in 1994." That was a generous rendering of the phrase "eventual elimination of antipersonnel landmines" that he had used at the United Nations. He then announced a unilateral initiative to "eliminate all antipersonnel landmines from America's arsenal"—another exaggeration. He was directing the Defense Department "to develop alternatives to antipersonnel landmines," specifying that they "be ready by 2006," and naming General David Jones, former JCS chairman, as personal adviser to him and the secretary of defense to "help us make sure the job gets done."[123]

The statement was "flat out wrong," says Sherman. He raised the matter with a member of the NSC staff soon after the president had spoken. "When I asked Ann Witkowsky how did that happen, she said, we did it at the last minute and didn't have time to check it. So much for the clearance process."[124] Pentagon officials who saw an advance copy of the president's text had tried and failed to correct the error.

Defense Secretary Cohen issued a partial retraction the same day, noting that the United States "will continue to deploy" antipersonnel mines in the form of submunitions used with antitank mines. NSC senior director Robert Bell walked back the statement further in a White House briefing, "These explosive devices that protect our antitank mines are not antipersonnel landmines. They are not being banned under the president's directive because they are not antipersonnel landmines. These things are explosive devices, just like the explosive devices that protect our allies' antitank mines. They are built into this munition. It's sealed at the factory. It's an integral unit." The Gator was one such mixed munition. "In the canister, which is sealed at the factory, you have 72 antitank mines. And in that same canister you have 22 of these explosive devices that are designed to keep infantry off the antitank mine," Bell insisted. "We don't consider those explosive devices in those canisters to be antipersonnel landmines for the purposes of this treaty or for the purposes of the president's directive today."[125] The misstatements that the treaty banned US antitank mines and that US antipersonnel mines were essential to the US defense of Korea were allowed to stand. So was the commitment to eliminate all landmines.

The campaigners were quick to jump on the misstatements. VVAF helped inspire a September 24 news story in the *Washington Post* by Dana Priest, calling into question President Clinton's commitment to "eliminate all antipersonnel landmines" from US stockpiles. Under the lead, "When is an antipersonnel landmine...no longer an antipersonnel landmine? When the president of the United States says so," Priest reported that, contrary to President Clinton's statement that the United States would "eliminate all antipersonnel landmines" from its arsenal, the Pentagon was retaining mixed munitions in the stockpile by reclassifying antipersonnel landmines as antihandling devices.[126]

VVAF ran two ads quoting Priest's lead and attacking President Clinton for his misleading September 17 statement. One ad was headlined, "Would a rose by any other name smell as sweet? Would a landmine by any other name be as deadly?" and the other, "Bill Clinton's landmine dodge."

On September 18, 1997, the draft treaty banning landmines, more formally, the Convention on the Prohibition of the Use, Stockpiling, Production and Transfer of Antipersonnel Mines and on the Destruction, was adopted by acclamation in plenary session and the Oslo conference closed with a prolonged standing ovation. The US delegation was noticeably absent.

ANTICLIMAX IN OTTAWA

A hundred countries had already pledged to sign the convention when it opened for signature in Ottawa on December 3. Among the holdouts were the United States, Russia, China, India, Israel, Greece, Turkey, Pakistan, Egypt, Iran, Iraq, Syria, Libya, Sri Lanka, North and South Korea, and the rump republic of Yugoslavia. All except Turkey and Libya were members of the Conference on Disarmament. In all, more than half of the CD's 61 members had yet to say whether they would sign, a point made by US officials in justifying their refusal to sign.

A Canadian resolution at the UN General Assembly calling on states to sign the convention in Ottawa became the focal point of a coordinated lobbying campaign. Canada teamed up with its partners in the core group to conduct joint regional *démarches* to coax the fence-sitters into signing.

The most visible public phase of the landmines campaign had been launched in the wake of Oslo. A "Ban Bus to Ottawa" wended its way from California, stopping en route to protest in front of landmines producers' plants and headquarters and to conduct more than 100 presentations in 75 American cities, many in pivotal congressional districts. It arrived a day before the conference convened. A series of public service announcements by the International Committee of the Red Cross tracked a young mine victim's pilgrimage from her hut in Cambodia to Ottawa to highlight the message, "the people of the world want a ban on antipersonnel mines—now it's the governments' turn." Save the Children USA and the Afghan Campaign to Ban Landmines delivered more than 25,000 postcards to the White House with drawings by Afghan children depicting their desires for a mine-free world.[127]

Publicity about the landmines ban surged after October 10, when Jody Williams and the ICBL were named co-winners of the 1997 Nobel Peace Prize. Canada's foreign minister, Lloyd Axworthy, and the ICRC had been among the finalists. The prestigious prize lent international legitimacy to the NGOs, but did little to allay suspicion in the US government. The Nobel decision would become a source of disappointment, even resentment, for some campaigners after Jody Williams decided to pocket her share rather than plow it back into NGO efforts.

On the day of the Nobel Prize announcement, following talks with Prime Minister Chretien, President Boris Yeltsin pledged to sign the treaty as economic conditions in Russia permitted. The White House greeted his tepid commitment warmly. When Foreign Minister Keizo Obuchi announced the next day that Japan, having steadfastly backed the United States, would now sign the treaty, the administration reaction to the about-face was decidedly more ill-tempered. "Senior US officials bluntly reminded Japan of its defense obligations yesterday and make little effort to conceal their annoyance," reported Toronto's *Globe and Mail*.[128] Undaunted, Australia soon became the next US ally to reverse itself and sign the treaty, although it would later attach reservations to its ratification exempting from criminal liability "anything done by way of mere participation" in joint military operations with a state that was not a party to the treaty, such as the United States.[129]

The 2-day Ottawa conference drew over 500 journalists, but generated little news. It was just another instance of the media habit of paying attention after the fact. There was little left for the 2,400 participants to do. The time for negotiating was over. States had all decided whether or not to sign the treaty—122 did—so the delegates' speeches were mostly posturing.

What made the conference more than a mere formality was the passionately expressed concerns of victims and of mine-strewn lands. To address those concerns and head off potential trouble, the Canadians decided to use the occasion to launch what they would call Ottawa Process II, featuring 20 mine action roundtables with panels of experts to address various aspects of the landmines crisis. Drawing on the conclusions, Canada compiled *An Agenda for Mine Action*, a comprehensive list of initiatives to turn the Ottawa treaty into reality.

The highlight of the conference was the December 3 signing ceremony. Afterward Rick Inderfurth, who represented the United States at Ottawa, went to see the treaty book, accompanied by two members of his staff. "Knowing that I very much wanted the United States to be able to sign the treaty, they asked, half jokingly, if I would turn over any pens that I had with me before I went into the room, which I did," he recalls. "When I came in, the Canadian officials in charge were very much taken aback." Inderfurth quickly explained that he was not there to sign. "We know that at some point you will," replied one of the Canadians, who then handed him a commemorative pen and a copy of the convention that was "bound nicely in some Cambodian cloth made by landmine survivors."[130]

Soon thereafter Inderfurth was named special representative of the president and assistant secretary of state for global and humanitarian affairs. His job was to redirect attention from banning landmines to removing them.

Newsom had a hand in his appointment. During the 3-day recess at Oslo, he recalls, assuming the United States would not sign the treaty, he and his deputy, Larry Dodgen, addressed the question, "How do we recover from this disaster?" Their answer was, "By making ourselves the world's leader in a campaign to rid the world of landmines already in the ground." They cabled home, strongly recommending that Washington announce a doubling of the amount it was spending on demining, organize an international conference to launch a global demining campaign, and name a special representative of the president to lead it. On his return from Oslo, Newsom met with Albright's closest aides, Counselor Wendy Sherman and Special Assistant Elaine Shocas. "We asked ourselves, who should it be?" Sherman suggested Inderfurth, assistant secretary for South Asian affairs, who had worked the landmines issue for Albright in New York. Newsom and Shocas agreed. "Wendy called him up while I was in her office," says Newsom, "and he joined us and accepted on the spot."[131]

"Demining 2010," announced with the usual fanfare by Secretary of State Albright on October 31, pledged to increase US spending for demining to $77 million a year, up from $68 million, and to host a donors' conference aimed at boosting worldwide spending to $1 billion a year, a fivefold increase. The $1-billion target, Inderfurth told reporters, was not a firm calculation of the cost, but an attention-getting device for the aim of clearing the world of mines that endanger civilians by 2010. The administration announcement prompted the same question from Senator Leahy that had inspired the ban movement in the first place, "Why spend billions of dollars to get rid of the mines if they are only going to be replaced with new mines?"[132]

YET ANOTHER LANDMINES POLICY

The 1-year moratorium on landmines use whose passage Senator Leahy and Representative Evans had secured in 1996 was due to take effect in February 1999. No sooner had it been signed into law by President Clinton than House Republicans, with behind-the-scenes backing from the Army, tried to nullify it. They inserted a provision in the defense authorization bill for fiscal year 1997 to bar the moratorium from taking effect as mandated unless the secretary of defense, after consulting with the chairman of JCS, "certifies to Congress that (1) the moratorium will not adversely affect the ability of U.S. forces to defend against attack on land by hostile forces; and (2) the armed forces have systems that are effective substitutes for antipersonnel landmines."[133]

To head off Senate action, Leahy struck a deal with the administration that would provide the basis of a new landmines policy, Presidential Decision Directive 64. Leahy was uncertain if he had the votes to defeat repeal or waiver. "We were concerned," says Tim Rieser, "so Senator Leahy negotiated that agreement, which was enshrined in PDD-64." For his part, the president did not want an open fight to undo what he had previously signed. "What happened was they were going to seek a repeal or waiver of that law," says Rieser, "and we knew they could probably win, but they didn't want to take on Senator Leahy if they could avoid it, so he had some leverage."[134] Leahy, who had so far successfully blocked adoption of the waiver provision in the Senate, agreed to stand aside.[135] In return, National Security Adviser Berger made five commitments to Leahy, which he later reaffirmed in writing:

> The United States will destroy by 1999 all of its non-self-destructing APLs, except those needed for Korea.

> The United States will end the use of all APLs outside Korea by 2003, including those that self-destruct.

> The United States will aggressively pursue the objective of having APL alternatives ready for Korea by 2006, including those that self-destruct.

> The United States will search aggressively for alternatives to our mixed anti-tank systems by (a) actively exploring the use of APL alternatives in place of the self-destructing antipersonnel submunitions currently used in our mixed systems and (b) exploring the development of other technologies and/or operational concepts that result in alternatives that would enable us to eliminate our mixed systems entirely.

> Finally, the United States will sign the Ottawa Convention by 2006 if we succeed in identifying and fielding suitable alternatives to our antipersonnel landmines and mixed anti-tank systems by then.[136]

Inasmuch as President Clinton could not bind his successor, only the first of these commitments was certain to be carried out.

The accord mostly reaffirmed existing policy. PDD-64 "does build on what they've already committed to," says Rieser, but the Berger letter broke new ground in two key respects. "The earlier agreements don't speak to signing Ottawa and the earlier agreements did not set the dates of 2003 and 2006."[137]

Berger worked out the details with General Joseph Ralston, vice chairman of JCS. "They closed the doors and said, this is a matter of such political sensitivity that only the adults are going to play, and the adults were defined as Ralston and Berger," says Robert Sherman, who found out from his contacts in JCS. "I was able to get enough leaks so I knew what was happening, but we were not allowed to have any input."[138] PM was left on the sidelines as well. "We were involved in it to some extent, but that was really a White House–run operation," says Eric Newsom. The biggest fight erupted over a phrase that "sounded committal, that we would eventually sign the convention." PM entered the fray at that point. "We and others, like Rick Inderfurth, weighed in very strongly that that phrase had to be in there and it was adopted," says Newsom. "I had a number of conversations with Bell about it and behind the scenes with Rieser, too."[139]

Officials agree that the landmines issue was taken out of the hands of lower-level experts at this stage, but disagree whether or not doing so was beneficial. Some find the banishment of expertise excusable. "The process was difficult," says a White House official. "Papers could not be put on the table because stuff was getting leaked all over. So the issue had to be worked at the senior level. That doesn't necessarily lead to optimal solutions."[140] The outcome was a bitter disappointment to many of those left out. Lee Feinstein agrees the issue was handled at the very top, but within narrow constraints previously set below. "This is a story of a policy question that was handled at a very very low level for a very very long time," he says "and by the time it got to serious people, the options had narrowed too greatly to change what happened."[141] It was "the Peter principle" in action, in Sherman's judgment. "The decisions were being made by people who didn't know the issue."[142]

As with PDD-48 of June 1996, PDD-64 conditioned the ban on finding an alternative to landmines, which gave the Army a hook to prevent any change in policy. The administration's commitment to a ban was disingenuous, says Sherman. "Clinton policy never included an unconditional promise to comply with the Ottawa Convention. It only committed to sign Ottawa in 2006 if suitable alternatives to antipersonnel mines had been fielded by that time. That is not technologically feasible and never was."[143]

How committed the Pentagon was to a search for alternatives to mixed munitions was open to question. It had found none and was not looking hard, Jan Lodal reported in a memorandum to Secretary of Defense Cohen on November 29. Prompted by Senator Leahy's expressed "concern that we are not searching for an alternative to the use of self-destructing APL in mixed systems with the objective of eventually signing Ottawa," Lodal noted, "Sandy Berger, along with some officials in State, are questioning us on this point, asserting that the President's decision implied that we would continue to look for an alternative." The Pentagon was no closer to finding one. "In the run-up to the Oslo meeting," he wrote, "the military...argued persuasively that there is no alternative to the use of APL in mixed systems. The studies carried out... had not even identified a workable concept for an alternative." That should have come as no surprise to the White House or the State Department: "We believe that the situation was fully appreciated when the president decided to permit mixed systems. NSC-approved talking points included this explanation, as have our discussions worldwide with allies." The Pentagon was not about to conduct a serious search for an alternative: "To reopen this issue now would be a terrible mistake. It would break faith with the JCS, who reluctantly agreed to give up all APL in favor of mixed packages. It would put us on a path to spend billions of dollars on alternative munitions that would in all likelihood be both less effective and less humanitarian. Our mixed systems provide essential tactical capabilities for our ground forces and pose absolutely no threat to noncombatants. The problem is not with these systems, but with the words of the Ottawa Convention."[144] Coming up with an alternative would require taking on landmine enthusiasts in the Army, a war of attrition that had ground down Lodal and that he was not eager to renew.

PDD-64 did not put an end to efforts to bring the United States into the fold. Canada and Norway "were uncomfortable" with "the idea of leaving the United States outside. Leahy also didn't like where he was," says Lee Feinstein. They knew that the US commitment to sign the treaty by 2006 was liable to lapse once President Clinton left office. "So there was an effort to see whether we could put the toothpaste back in the tube." The idea was for Canada "sotto voce, to reinterpret the language without amending the treaty so that the United States could then climb aboard." The effort "did not get very far," says Feinstein. "The politico-military affairs bureau and the legal adviser's office opposed the effort." Although "Secretary Albright was interested, nobody wanted to do it unless it could really happen."[145]

In the waning days of the Clinton administration, Senator Leahy and other ban proponents made a last-ditch effort to get President Clinton to sign the treaty before he left office, once again, without success. The ban would take effect without the United States.

It took the Bush administration 3 years to undo PDD-64. On February 27, 2004, it announced a new landmines policy banning long-lived antipersonnel or antitank landmines, but perpetuating the use of self-destructing, self-deactivating mines. It set a date certain of 2010 for eliminating all persistent mines from US stockpiles, as well as all mines that could not be detected because they contained less than the metallic equivalent of 8 grams of iron ore. It pledged to develop alternatives to such mines. It committed the United States to seek a global ban on nonself-destructing mines.[146] While noting that the new policy had "some positive aspects," Senator Leahy said, "on the whole, it is a deeply disappointing step backward."[147]

11

Campaigners and Officials

The outcome of every conflict is determined by the extent to which
the audience becomes involved in it.

E.E. Schattschneider[1]

The United States was pivotal in establishing the postwar world order. It was a
world order built on realist and liberal foundations: a network of alliances that
counterbalanced and contained the Soviet Union and fostered conditions for
the liberal political, economic, and legal arrangements of today to flourish.

As the world's most powerful nation, the United States benefits mightily
from today's international regime, the rules and institutions that help govern
the interactions of states. International norms and law are less of a limit on US
freedom of action than on others because the United States had a major hand in
writing most of the rules. International organizations enable the United States
to mobilize political support for its aims and round up posses of the willing to
enforce the rules, again, because it was instrumental in setting up these organizations and because it remains the predominant player in them—politically
and economically, as well as militarily. That puts Washington in an advanta-
geous position to get what it wants through diplomatic give-and-take.

Yet the international norms, law, and organizations put in place over the
past half-century are under dual challenge today, first, from nonstate threats

to peace and security like disease, pollution, and terrorism that require cooperative responses but that existing norms, laws, and organizations were not designed to meet; and second, from American unilateralists who believe that the United States should go it alone in the world, unfettered by allies and unbound by treaties.

The unilateralist challenge was manifest throughout the Ottawa process, especially at Oslo. To many diplomats there, US negotiating tactics smacked of "bossism," Stanley Hoffmann's apt word for the US impulse to use international institutions to impose its will on others rather than to cooperate with them.[2] Making others choose sides—with us or against us—may have worked well during the Cold War, but since then it has proved less useful to the United States in getting its way.

US allies and others are usually willing to cooperate with the United States, but not wholly on American terms. That point seems lost on many in Washington, where a decent respect for the opinions of mankind, never mind a willingness to accommodate others, has been in short supply in recent years. In the thrall of unilateralists, the United States is acting less like a status quo power than a revisionist one. That is the starting point for understanding why it did not sign the global landmines ban and why the Bush administration has since rewritten US landmines policy to prolong their use.

THE CAMPAIGNERS' ACHIEVEMENTS

In the face of opposition from the United States and the other major powers, how did the International Campaign to Ban Landmines succeed in banning a weapon that many countries deemed useful?

The ICBL's signal achievement was to define the landmines issue in normative terms. The indiscriminate use of antipersonnel mines in communal violence around the world, campaigners repeated time and again, had caused a humanitarian crisis. Attempts to regulate their use had failed. Nothing short of a global ban on production, transfer, stockpiling, and use of such mines was the solution.

The ICBL helped put the ban on the international agenda. Governments usually define issues and set that agenda, especially on matters of security, and none has a greater capacity to do so than the US government. Its word carries weight in the world. To get its message out, it has more embassies in more countries than other governments and, even after post Cold War budget cuts, the most propaganda resources. Its briefings are more widely covered than any others around the world, thanks to the dense concentration of globe-spanning news media in the United States. Yet the NGOs managed to overwhelm it, in no small part, because of its message—and theirs.

The US arsenal of mixed munitions, US officials never tired of repeating, did not pose the humanitarian problem that cheap, long-lasting plastic antipersonnel landmines did. Persistent or not, antipersonnel mines kill indiscriminately, the NGOs retorted. An antipersonnel mine was an antipersonnel mine, no matter who made it or how sophisticated its design. The United States, they added, ignored the potential for smart mines to fail to perform as designed. Antitank mines, some NGOs noted, could also be set off by noncombatant vehicles. The best way to address the humanitarian menace posed by antipersonnel landmines, the ICBL insisted, was a universally applicable norm to ban them.

The human rights approach antagonized military officers by stigmatizing weapons that they considered legitimate implements of war and no more likely to inflict gratuitous harm than others in their arsenal. Yet reframing the landmines issue as one of human security, not national security, broadened the political appeal of the ban campaign. By emphasizing the physical harm that landmines caused to noncombatants, campaigners turned the ban into a moral cause, making it easier to attract affiliates and motivate activists.

Morality mattered. It motivated the founders of the campaign to become involved in banning landmines. It helped recruit other campaigners to the cause. It helped sustain their activism and hold the disparate affiliates of the ban campaign together. It attracted media and public attention. It moved even tough-minded politicians, diplomats, and generals. The ban campaign used moral language and symbolism to break down the walls of silence and euphemism with which officials shielded themselves from the consequences of their indifference. It brought them face to face with victims, transforming landmines from a remote abstraction into something up-close and personal.

The campaigners were adept at attracting media attention for their message. They used Princess Diana and landmine victims to reframe an international arms negotiation into a human interest story that the news media found compelling. They devised visually engaging ways of getting the issue on television.

The ICBL was indispensable in selling the ban to countries in Africa and Asia. The countries, many of them autocracies or fledgling democracies with limited exposure to civic activism, proved permeable to a campaign by outside NGOs. Knowing that the United States was opposed to a ban made it easier for some of these countries to favor it.

Yet, for all the ICBL's achievements, many campaigners were dismayed by its failure to bring the United States into fold. One was Senator Leahy's aide Tim Rieser: "If we can't get rid of this indiscriminate weapon, with all the commitments by the US government including the president's, the Nobel Peace Prize, Princess Diana, all the publicity, what we have seen in Bosnia,

Afghanistan, and elsewhere, the money we are spending to clear mines, and the recognition that these weapons are a relic of the past, what can we do?"[3]

Jerry White of the Landmines Survivor Network shares this disappointment: "I was one of the few people who did not think the Nobel Prize was a good idea, especially in 1997. It was premature to raise champagne glasses in celebration of something that was remarkable, but we were the victims of our own success." In White's assessment, "Landmines spiked so fast offshore that it never really penetrated the dialogue of national security here."[4]

Whatever the campaign's shortcomings, however, without the ICBL to define the problem and the solution, a global treaty to ban landmines never would have been adopted.

THE NETWORK IS THE SOLUTION

The ICBL's success calls into question the contention that the ban campaign, and NGOs in general, are democratically suspect because they are not politically accountable. Their pivotal role in mobilizing legislative and popular support for outlawing antipersonnel landmines suggests that NGOs were a democratizing force, whose existence depended on their ability to manifest, if not mobilize, popular will. Indeed, military bureaucracies in the United States, Italy, and other democratic polities are often less subject to democratic control than the NGOs.

The ban campaign proved more successful abroad than in the United States. The campaign fared better in countries that had had little experience with democracy or indigenous NGOs than in countries that had strong states, well-developed civil societies, and deeply-rooted democratic traditions. Even France, Italy, and other Western democracies with robust ban campaigns grandfathered their own landmines into the treaty. Only Canada renounced all its mines. Still, the ICBL's outside-in strategy of moving other states that would in turn move the United States failed. Why?

Despite polls that registered substantial popular support for a ban and congressional votes for moratoria on exports and use, the campaign had little sway over leaders of the right wing of the Republican Party and no base among their constituents.

The campaigners did not help their cause, either. Unaware of internal differences over landmines within the armed services until after the ban was negotiated, they deliberately made the US military their foil. Some ban proponents preferred another strategy. "There were a lot of people in the NGO community who wanted to paint the military as the bad guys," says Tim Connolly, principal deputy assistant secretary of defense in the Office of Special Operations and Low-Intensity Conflict. "I'm not one of them."[5] Had the campaigners chosen to work with, not against, the military, they might have found a compromise to allow the United States to sign the treaty. Instead, they turned the military into their enemy.

Only a handful of US firms manufactured landmines and none made much money doing so. They, too, became targets of the campaign. Taking on the military-industrial complex is seldom the way to advance a cause in Washington, but it does have resonance in some parts of the country.

Yet the ban campaign never did mobilize much of a grassroots following in the United States. It organized its first public demonstration in May 1996, just days before the administration came out against a ban. Instead, the US affiliate of the International Campaign to Ban Landmines functioned mostly as a lobbying arm of Senator Patrick Leahy's, engaging in information politics and accountability politics, with mixed success. So long as landmines remained an insiders' game, domestic politics could not trump Congressional politics or bureaucratic politics.

The ICBL had greater impact elsewhere. It organized national campaigns from Italy to Cambodia. It mounted successful signature drives in polities as disparate as Canada, France, Cambodia, and Mozambique and gained privileged access to governments from South Africa to France. Still, other landmine-afflicted countries like Angola or Zimbabwe exhibited apathy rather than revulsion. China, India, and Russia, with well over half the world's population, did not sign the ban.

Campaigners fostered the impression of a mass movement that transcended borders by forging coalitions of NGOs, but most of them were letter-head organizations. Everywhere, the campaign was a virtual mass movement with few rank-and-file members and less grassroots support than it would have liked. Affiliates did stage spirited demonstrations at various negotiating sites in Europe, but they seldom drew large crowds like those that turned out for antiwar, antiglobalization, or environmental causes. Although polls registered majority support for a ban throughout much of Western Europe and North America, that popular support was largely passive.

Campaigners found it easier to enlist existing groups and hold them together than to recruit individual activists and sustain their participation. At the core of these coalitions were human rights groups and NGOs specializing in removal of mines and rehabilitation of mine victims. In the next circle were peace and disarmament groups and NGOs, both faith-based and nonsectarian, engaged in humanitarian work. For these groups the landmine issue was a minor digression from their usual missions. For other NGOs, such as those working on development assistance, social justice, or care for the disabled, the landmines ban was more of a stretch. By involving NGOs, many with their own cross-border connections, the campaign was able to extend its reach around the globe.

Yet a common sense of direction among ICBL affiliates with such diverse purposes was difficult to sustain. So was the morale of isolated activists scattered around the world. How did the ICBL keep such a disparate coalition on a common path to a ban?

The network was the solution. New communications technology linked the dispersed nodes of the landmines network, allowing the ICBL to reach out and touch someone anywhere around the globe. "In order to hold together NGOs of such diverse interests," ICBL's Jody Williams and Stephen Goose wrote, "these organizations would have to feel an immediate and important part of developments within the campaign." Taking advantage of modern communication technology to maintain connectedness across time zones, they weaved the ICBL's diverse parts into a seemingly seamless whole: "The fax was relatively new—it was 'exciting.' Information arriving almost instantaneously by fax was perceived to be more important—and thus more deserving of an immediate response—than regular mail." In the early years of the ICBL, when it was focusing its efforts on the industrialized world, it relied on the fax and the telephone, but these technologies were less reliable and more expensive elsewhere. In the developing world, e-mail came in handy: "It was not until the ICBL was able to broaden its work from largely mine-producing countries to mine-affected countries that its members began to make the shift to [e-mail]— a switch that was not fully achieved until late 1995 and early 1996."[6]

The network was loose enough for the ICBL to let dissident affiliates such as the landmine survivors go their separate ways yet maintain a common front. It suppressed most of its internal differences, keeping them from becoming public until after the ban was negotiated in Oslo. Given the depth of those differences, that was quite a feat.

The ICBL accomplished this feat by turning itself into the public face of the ban campaign. When reporters wanted an authoritative pro-ban view, they turned to the ICBL. Casting itself as David against Goliath, it framed the issue as getting the world to ban landmines over the opposition of the United States, especially its military. That took advantage of journalistic conventions that conflict is deemed newsworthy and that, once a story line is set, it is slow to change. That story line was pro-ban versus anti-ban. NGOs that differed with the ICBL usually aired their disagreements in private, but when they did go public, the news media tended to ignore or downplay the differences because they did not fit the script.

NOT CAPTIVES BUT ALLIES

The campaigners also made common cause with some officials in the United States and abroad. Canadian diplomat Robert Lawson has coined the term "new multilateralism" to describe the Ottawa process. What was new, according to Lawson, was an alliance of diplomats and NGOs: "The driving force behind this process was a coalition of like-minded states and NGOs such as the ICRC and the ICBL." In negotiating the landmines ban, "the secret to success would be to maintain [Foreign] Minister Axworthy's deadline for action, combined with a series of multilateral meetings during which NGO and media pressure could be brought to bear directly on officials and their political leaders."[7]

Critical to that process was the unusual role played by the NGOs in the diplomatic process—the extent to which they were brought inside. NGOs had representatives on some delegations, received invitations to address diplomatic conferences, and took part in core group strategy sessions. Their access gave them advanced notice of negotiating moves and allowed them to involve other outsiders. It also allowed them to express their moral and humanitarian concerns to diplomats face to face.

Lawson cites three other features of this new diplomacy. One was the transnational network facilitated by new communications technologies: "International public opinion, transnational NGOs, and revolutions in telecommunications and the mass media have eroded the traditional boundaries and prerogatives of diplomatic praxis." A second was the outside-in strategy of the core group, working in concert with the ICBL, which was employed to greatest effect in southern Africa: "The process provides a dramatically expanded diplomatic tool kit for officials developing strategies to influence key decision makers at state, regional and global levels. The Ottawa process effectively combined public diplomacy efforts by key foreign ministers and senior officials with NGO-led civil society advocacy campaigns." A third was the challenge to American unilateralism posed by the core group: "Multilateral diplomacy remains a contested terrain where middle powers such as Canada often have a home-field advantage."[8] How far the new multilateralism can go without the participation of the United States remains to be seen, but it will continue to make headway, the longer Washington sticks to its unilateralist course.

Lawson's thesis was taken a step further by Jessica Tuchman Mathews in a 1997 article that contended, "National governments are not simply losing autonomy in a globalizing economy. They are sharing powers—including political, social, and security roles at the core of sovereignty—with businesses, with international organizations, and with a multitude of citizen groups, known as non-governmental organizations (NGOs)."[9] One reason Mathews adduces for the change is the ease of communications brought about by satellites, faxes, personal computers, the Internet, and e-mail: "Widely accessible and affordable technology has broken governments' monopoly on the collection and management of large amounts of information and deprived governments of the deference they enjoyed because of it."[10] The democratizing effect of the new technologies was evident in the landmines campaign, at least to the extent that they empowered some groups in civil society to use information to influence some governments. Mathews is at her most provocative in discussing the growing influence of nonstate actors—she has in mind NGOs, not multinational corporations. Transnational networks facilitated by the new technologies give NGOs the "clout" to "push around even the largest governments," Mathews contends. "NGOs' easy reach behind other states' borders forces governments to consider domestic public opinion in countries with which they are dealing, even on matters that governments have traditionally handled between themselves."[11] The Ottawa process would seem to be a case in point, but was it?

A quango or quasi-governmental NGO, the International Committee of the Red Cross, was instrumental in exposing the humanitarian crisis caused by indiscriminate use of antipersonnel landmines around the world. The ICRC was soon joined by three NGOs that would later help to found the ICBL, Vietnam Veterans of America Foundation, Human Rights Watch, and Physicians for Human Rights. Their work, starting in the early 1990s, drew attention to the rising civilian casualty count and the persistent impact of landmines laid long ago, which lent urgency to a ban.

The ban campaign did not make much headway, however, until a a seasoned, entrepreneurial politician, Senator Patrick Leahy, saw a chance to do some good by working with it. Similarly, a Canadian affiliate of the ICBL, Mines Action Canada, caught the attention of two enterprising foreign ministers, André Ouellet and Lloyd Axworthy, looking for an issue on which to make a name for themselves. Unlike in Canada, where it was easier to do well by doing good, especially with party backing and US opposition, the landmines issue was never much of a vote-getter or attention-grabber in US politics. Yet Leahy managed to charm Congress into enacting an export moratorium, then used his power of the purse to get the State Department to promote it abroad. Leahy's idea of a moratorium on exports was soon picked up by Italy, France, and other governments in Europe as a way to head off pressure from campaigners for a more far-reaching ban.

The middle powers in the core group, Austria, Belgium, Canada, Ireland, Mexico, the Netherlands, Norway, the Philippines, South Africa, and Switzerland, were willing to take the issue further. What is striking about their role, however, is that it was not driven by the NGOs. Only in Belgium, Canada, and Norway were well-organized ban campaigns under way when the core group first convened in January 1996.

The ICBL had global reach, but little local penetration. Some of the ICBL's affiliates were politically well connected, as in South Africa, or politically adept, as in France, but few could mobilize masses of adherents to demonstrate in the streets or the corridors of power. As outsiders trying to dramatize the tragic impact of landmines, publicize the limits of arms control, or lobby or shame governments into backing a ban, the campaigners seldom forced the hands of officials. They were most effective where they joined with them in an alliance of convenience or found prominent politicians willing to embrace their cause.

What made a critical difference was Canada's decision to involve the campaigners in the work of the core group. Although the insider role caused considerable unease about cooptation among campaigners in Canada and elsewhere, the campaign might never have achieved a ban by remaining outsiders. Only when they began to work in tandem with officials did the campaigners' strategy of symbolic politics, leverage politics, accountability politics, pressure politics, and linkage politics pay off. The campaigners kept enough distance from the insiders to attract affiliates yet held officials' feet close enough to the fire to dissuade the core group from compromising the ban too much.

Relationships between campaigners and officials ran the gamut from antagonism to collaboration. Officials occasionally briefed NGO representatives, an increasingly common practice in the United States and elsewhere. Officials also found it useful to have NGOs provide political backstopping by making public what they could not and by serving as go-betweens with legislators. Some dissident officials went well beyond that to conspire with the campaigners. Some states took that practice further by including NGO representatives on their delegations, where they were privy to much, if not all, of the behind-the-scenes maneuvering.

Such forms of cooperation have long been a staple in trade talks, where trade associations and ad hoc business coalitions play these roles. They were also found in arms control talks, among NGOs like the Arms Control Association, the Heritage Foundation, and the Chemical Manufacturers Association. In the past, some delegations have become captive of NGOs, typically industry lobbies. For example, US representatives at meetings of the International Telecommunications Union were referred to as the "delegation from Motorola," according to one observer.[12] On occasion, mini-states have even allowed NGOs to represent them at international conferences, as Nauru did at the London Dumping Convention, because they could not afford to send delegations of their own. That did not happen in the landmines case, but pro-ban campaigners and core group diplomats did exert considerable sway over a number of delegations from developing countries.

On past occasions, NGOs have engaged in track two diplomacy involving nonofficials, former officials, and officials acting in an unofficial capacity. Private citizens, typically ex-officials, have served as go-betweens or extra-governmental channels of communication with other governments. One example was former President Jimmy Carter's June 1994 mission to Pyongyang, which headed off the imposition of sanctions by the UN Security Council and thereby opened the way to a negotiated freeze of North Korea's nuclear program, a turning point in US relations with the North. The ICBL's involvement in the core group goes far beyond track two.

The UN Economic and Social Council seats NGOs like the International Chamber of Commerce and allows NGO representatives to address plenary sessions. That practice is the basis of UN Secretary-General Boutros Boutros-Ghali's oft-quoted statement, "Nongovernmental organizations are now considered full participants in international life."[13] His statement obscures the difference between the formality of a seat alongside diplomats or invitations to address plenary meetings and an equal place at the negotiating table. To judge from the Ottawa process, which accorded extraordinary access to the campaigners but still excluded them from some diplomatic councils, the ICBL exercised only marginal influence on diplomacy independent of the core group's.

Allegations arose during the Ottawa process that Canada, France, and other delegations had become captives of the NGOs. Campaigners often voiced unease that they would be coopted. Yet captivity and cooptation mischaracterize the relationship between campaigners and officials. That relationship was an alliance in which NGOs and governments used each other to advance their own goals.

The campaigners may have exerted a subtler social influence on officials from some countries. It is common to conceive of institutions in contractual terms as a set of norms or rules that constrain states or the officials who act on their behalf, much as markets and regulations constrain corporations and their managers. Yet institutions are also social environments, and the Ottawa process was a very different social environment from the CD, which was dominated by diplomats who shared the belief that treaties should be the handiwork of professionals and experts, insulated as much as possible from the push and pull of politics. Despite national differences, diplomats tend to identify with one another as professionals and to view NGOs as outsiders, never to be invited inside, or a source of pressure to be ignored or resisted. A very different esprit de corps developed in the Ottawa process, where campaigners were treated more like insiders, whose views, while not always accepted, could not be denied a hearing or dismissed out of hand.

The close social interaction may have made a critical difference in quite another way, as well. It is one thing to be criticized in the press and quite another to be criticized in person. Cognitive dissonance can be poignant and diplomats are no less thin-skinned than people in other walks of life. By shaming them in face-to-face encounters, exposing the contradictions between their professed beliefs and negotiating behavior, campaigners discomfited the diplomats. They helped inculcate the norm that antipersonnel landmines were taboo. Some states had ulterior motives in accepting a ban, but many did not, and even those who refused to go along felt the need to pay lip service to the norm, not only in the words they used to justify themselves, but also in the deeds they committed themselves to undertake, such as aid for demining and landmine survivors. Norms are social constructs and evolve with changes in social interaction.[14]

Yet socialization is not a one-way street. Some campaigners were willing to tolerate exceptions to the landmines ban that met the needs of officials with whom they worked closely.

That may explain why some US officials regarded pro-ban delegations as captives of the NGOs and campaigners bristled at the charge of being coopted by governments. Yet neither officials nor campaigners were captives. In a setting that reduced the social barriers between them, they became allies, which made the ban campaign more effective.

Did the success of the ban campaign imply that civil society is displacing the state as the lead actor on the international stage? No. Indeed, the very question is misleading, premised as it is on a false dichotomy between a state-centered international system and a society-centered one—an academic artifact of the theory wars in international relations between realism and other schools of thought.[15]

NGOs like the ICBL do constitute evidence of an emerging international civil society that transcends national identities and challenges the primacy of states as a source of world order, but it is premature to make too much of that. The ICBL was more international than transnational. It was an alliance of mostly national groups, only some of which had connections across state boundaries. While the NGOs agreed on some goals, they did not share others.

Perhaps better evidence of at least a nascent international civil society was the widespread acceptance of humanitarian norms that stigmatized landmines. Yet the concept "international civil society" implies a global public that shared some values. The humanitarian norms undergirding the ban were embraced by peoples from disparate cultures, but those norms were shared, not by the general populace, but by indigenous activists in the ban movement and diplomats, who can be said to constitute international civil society only in a narrow sense.

NGOs have succeeded in articulating and propagating norms that changed behavior in the past. The anti-slavery movement is a case in point. So too is the work of the Red Cross in gaining acceptance for treating wounded soldiers and prisoners of war as noncombatants. What began as the moral cause of a few became the expected behavior of all nations. Breaches of norms do occur—slavery persists in parts of Africa today, prisoners of war are mistreated, and the wounded are left to die—but they are exceptions. Nor can self-interested behavior wholly account for widespread adherence.

COMMANDER-IN-CHIEF?

The power of norms is something politicians appreciate, and President Clinton was a consummate politician. More than most officials in his administration, he grasped the appeal of the ban campaign and tried to embrace it. Yet he meant well weakly.

On October 6, 1999, 6 days before the Senate rejected the Comprehensive Test Ban Treaty, President Clinton spoke of an earlier defeat on another treaty that he had favored: "One of the biggest disappointments I've had as president, a bitter disappointment for me, is that I could not sign in good conscience the treaty banning landmines." His explanation was a variation on his usual themes: "I couldn't do it because the way the treaty was worded was unfair to the United States and to our Korean allies in meeting our responsibilities along the DMZ in South Korea and because it outlawed our antitank mines while leaving every other country's intact." That said, he then spoke with palpable feeling, "But it just killed me. All of us who are in charge of the nation's security engage our heads as well as our hearts. Thinking and feeling lead you to the conclusion that this treaty should be ratified."[16]

If the president wanted to sign the ban landmines that much, why didn't he? Congressional politics and bureaucratic politics are two reasons. The election of 1994 gave Republicans control of both branches of Congress. Perhaps more important, it gave the right wing a commanding majority within the Republican caucus in the House of Representatives and a near majority in the Senate caucus. Many on the Republican right, if they gave much thought at all to foreign affairs, were unilateralists by conviction. They were also passionate partisans, disinclined to give Clinton any quarter. They opposed most of his foreign policy initiatives—especially any that smacked of multilateral cooperation. The partisan divide in Congress did not prevent President Clinton from signing the Comprehensive Test Ban Treaty. Nor was that divide evident in 1993 when the Senate voted 100–0 to impose a moratorium on US export of landmines or when Congress enacted a moratorium on use in 1996. Senate Majority Leader Robert Dole was instrumental in the latter's passage, but when he resigned his post to run for president in 1996, he was succeeded by Trent Lott, who sympathized with the unilateralists. With the right wing now firmly in control of the Republican party caucuses in both houses of Congress in 1996, the ban's fortunes on Capitol Hill faded.

The political landscape had changed in other ways by then. Partisanship had heated up in Congress with the election of 1996 and reached a fever pitch over impeachment of President Clinton. The erosion of presidential power made the bureaucratic impediments to a landmines ban more difficult to overcome.

The chief impediment, however, was not implacable opposition in some military circles, but timid high-level civilian support for a ban within the administration. Unlike nuclear arms, which the armed services no longer deemed essential, antipersonnel landmines did have some enthusiasts in military ranks. Among the most dedicated were Army combat engineers, who stood to lose the most from a ban. Faced with a major threat to their roles and missions and their morale, they dug in and fought hard to hold onto mines. Yet the rest of the military did not close ranks with ban opponents. The combatant commands were lukewarm about antipersonnel mines, and so were the service chiefs. In the view of most, mines were useful but hardly a military requirement. The armed forces could win without them. The case for landmines was mostly anecdotal and historical. It was based on outmoded doctrine—what the Army would call with a touch of contempt, "legacy warfighting."[17] Only the CINC in Korea opposed a ban—not because landmines were integral to US forces stationed there, but because a ban would have precluded him from transferring them to South Korean forces under his command. Military opposition to a ban was largely interest-driven, but military interests were much more varied than top administration officials or ban campaigners believed.

Military opposition did not prevent JCS from approving President Clinton's September 1994 address to the UN General Assembly committing the United States to the "ultimate goal of the eventual elimination of antipersonnel landmines." Nor did it motivate the CINCs' representatives to insist that such mines were a military requirement to be protected at all costs. Nor did it keep General John Shalikashvili, chairman of the Joint Chiefs of Staff, from exploring the option of waging war without such mines in the expectation that his commander-in-chief would order a ban in 1996 and ask the armed services to comply.

Yet Shalikashvili acted alone. The unwillingness of President Clinton to issue that order and the reluctance of most top civilian officials in the Pentagon or anywhere else to exert much leadership on landmines kept him from fulfilling his wish. Concern about a deepening civil-military divide at times predisposed top military officers, sometimes against their better judgment, to accommodate the president on landmines, but that same concern also made civilians wary of pushing for a ban in the belief that they would have to take on the military. That belief may have been warranted by 1997, once the joint chiefs had decided against a ban, but it was exaggerated in 1996, when the chiefs' stance was still in flux.

Getting the armed services to deny themselves a weapon is never easy. They prize their autonomy and resent deferring to civilians, especially rank outsiders like the ban campaigners. Yet there is a darker side to military autonomy—insularity. Civil-military relations may have been especially parlous under President Clinton, but no more so than they became under his successor. With the rise of a professional army, military life is more and more a world apart, not a healthy development in a democracy.

Had President Clinton or his top aides fully engaged the armed services on this issue, they might well have discovered what those opposed to a ban did not want them to know: that US forces had no requirement for antipersonnel landmines anywhere in the world. That included Korea, where ROK forces had taken possession of all the landmines deployed in the barrier defense of Seoul. The United States did have some landmines stockpiled in Korea for its own use, but US plans called for using these mixed munitions in an offensive against North Korea, not for the defense of Seoul, and the Pentagon's own assessment raised doubts about using them even for that purpose.

Why were White House officials unaware of this in 1996? "When you are lied to, or when you're denied information that is only in the possession of the armed forces, then it is very difficult to question or challenge or to advance another point of view," says Tim Rieser. "The White House never figured out how to effectively challenge the information they were getting from the Pentagon, and neither did we."[18] Why the civilians' reluctance to probe? Most participants cite the White House's political estrangement from the armed services dating back to differences over gays in the military and intervention in Somalia, Haiti, and Bosnia at the start of the administration. Robert Muller has a different explanation. He detects in Clinton a strain found in the Vietnam generation, "a difference between those who didn't serve and those who did. Psychologically as time has gone on, I find it amazing that guys feel guilty about not having participated in a bullshit war," he says, "and I think Clinton carried that feeling to an extreme. He was more deferential to the military than most." Deference to the military may have kept civilians from probing. Estrangement from the military contributed to the White House's failure to pick up their ambivalence about landmines.

Had he sensed that ambivalence, President Clinton could have ordered a ban on antipersonnel landmines in 1996. That would have given General Shalikashvili the political cover he needed to seek military compliance. Once that moment had passed, top civilians in the Defense Department still could have done what other administrations did to overcome armed service objections to its negotiating proposals: carefully review military requirements with the service chiefs to try to narrow their objections, then negotiate to accommodate requirements they still had. This, the administration did only belatedly.

Fearful of taking on what they believed to be entrenched opposition in the military and among Republicans in Congress, top officials did not become engaged in the Ottawa process until just weeks before the Oslo conference opened. At that late date, the United States demanded sweeping exemptions for its landmines that were militarily unnecessary and politically unattainable. Only in the waning moments of Oslo did they finally redraw the negotiating red lines. The last-gasp try would become the basis of the president's claim, "We went the extra mile and beyond to sign this treaty."[19] It was not far enough.

Had the United States negotiated in the months following the Ottawa strategy conference of October 1996, the core group might well have agreed to exempt US mixed munitions, much as it did the mines used by Austria and other European countries. Canada was willing to accommodate the United States and may well have carried its confrere. Any exemption would have been contentious within the ban campaign, as was the exemption for European mines, and may have led the ICBL to oppose it. Had the exemption been incorporated into the Austrian draft early on, however, removing it would have been difficult.

Stephen Goose of the ICBL thinks so. "If some of our opponents had taken the ban a little bit more seriously, then the United States could have done any number of things, starting with the CCW and moving forward to the days of what become the Ottawa process, to affect [the outcome] greatly, as was shown by how close they came, despite having bungled it for years, to having it radically altered in their favor in Oslo. That shows if they had a little foresight, done a little compromising, they could have gotten a lot more," he says. "During the CCW, if they had made clear that antitank mine systems have these things in them that we called antipersonnel mines in the past but really aren't antipersonnel mines and if they had agreed in the CCW on that, then it would have been carried forward to the mine ban treaty, but they never thought it would be necessary. If they had decided early on that they wanted to push for a global ban on dumb mines, they could have gotten that, too." Even the campaigners would have gone along. "If they had started talking about that in 1993, 1994, or 1995, then they would have had a lot of NGOs buy into it as a first step, just as we bought into export moratoria as a first step," says Goose. "We always tried to maintain the high ground, but we also promoted a whole series of interim measures by any number of governments as ways they could move toward a ban."[20] Had the United States achieved a global ban on dumb mines, the wheels just might have come off the ban wagon.

Some officials doubt an accommodation was ever possible. ACDA's Robert Sherman is one. "Once the Ottawa process began, it was clear to anyone who understood the issue that the ICBL had an inflexible political requirement to have a total ban on APL and that the US armed forces had an inflexible military requirement to use self-destructing APL. There was no way that square peg could fit into that round hole." He dismisses the idea that other countries could have ignored the ICBL. "There was a historical revisionist school after Oslo that said if we had just done this earlier, we could have carried the day," he says. "As I confirmed with the Ottawa Convention principals afterward, that is, was, and always will be delusional. As one of them said to me, 'How could you have APL use in an APL ban?'"[21] The answer others might give is that the treaty as negotiated allowed it.

Other officials do not share Sherman's certainty. "We should have made the decision more quickly. It dragged on too long," says NSC staffer Nancy Soderberg. "Had we taken the initiative earlier, before we got the international movement, we could have looked like we were leading it, instead of getting dragged kicking and screaming into it by the landmine groups." Jan Lodal, principal deputy undersecretary of defense for policy, agrees, "Nobody really committed the diplomatic strength of the United States to try to get this to come out right." He lays responsibility for that failure on President Clinton. "What he didn't do was call the secretary of state up and tell her, look, Madeleine, you've got to get this straight. Go up there yourself if you have to and explain to these people why the United States needs to be part of this, you need the United States to be part of this, and don't keep screaming at each other and listening to the NGOs. Nobody did that."[22]

When the Oslo conference was over, US negotiator Eric Newsom wrote a five-page after-action report to Secretary of State Madeleine Albright. "I remember posing the basic question," he says, "How did it happen that the United States found itself isolated and defeated on an issue on which the senior leadership, the president and the secretary of state, wanted a positive outcome?" In Newsom's view, "There were many reasons why we were unsuccessful—inability to make timely decisions, lack of understanding of the nature of the issue, mistrust among the agencies, bureaucratic vested interests—but the decisive factor was the inability to engage at political levels on what had become a political issue until it was too late."[23]

That was just as much the case in the State Department as it was in the White House and the Pentagon. "I thought when Madeleine Albright became secretary of state that we were going to have an involved advocate," Newsom says. "She did move in and out of it, but she, like all secretaries, was overwhelmed with decisions and crises and couldn't spend much time on a secondary issue like this." A fleeting attention span is an occupational hazard for all top officials. Yet "without sustained high-level attention, the landmines issue was fought out in the bureaucracy where all sorts of institutional imperatives prevailed."[24]

Most lower-level officials were more attuned to bureaucratic politics than to the domestic political mood generated by the ban campaign. "The problem that bedeviled us throughout was the inability of key people to grasp the unusual nature of this event," says Newsom. "They just would not accept that it wasn't a standard issue to take to the CD, massage for 3 or 4 years and get our way by quietly working our friends and allies. They couldn't see it as a political movement that we forfeited leadership of."[25]

The Ottawa process dethroned, at least momentarily, the reigning assumptions in the executive branch that no multilateral treaty could be negotiated without US participation and that the United States could block agreement if and when it chose to—assumptions of US indispensability and unilateralism. In the aftermath of Ottawa, a treaty to outlaw child soldiers was under negotiation, and the Pentagon was initially disinclined to participate, says Morton Halperin, director of policy plans in the State Department, but the Clinton administration decided to become involved early on, rather than stand aside in the hopes that no treaty could emerge. Instead of trying to prevent any agreement, it had language inserted in the treaty to permit ROTC for 17-year-olds and the drafting of 18-year-olds, two provisions the armed services wanted.[26]

General Shalikashvili did what he could for the president to sign the ban, but there was a limit to how much he could do on his own. He got the armed forces to get rid of dumb mines and pure antipersonnel mines, but not mixed munitions. A president, recognizing the limited utility of landmines, might have helped him go that one step further—but not President Clinton. Had he done so in Spring 1996, he might have succeeded. In Spring 1997, the administration could have launched an all-out diplomatic effort to exempt US mixed munitions from a ban, much as the Europeans had done. By Oslo it was too late.

NORMS AND THE POLITICS OF A LANDMINES BAN

It was a widely shared view among US officials that the landmines ban was "a feel-good treaty" which is likely to prove ineffective, that the norm against antipersonnel landmines will not stop countries from using them, and that US adherence to this or any other international norm or law has no bearing on the behavior of others. Officials who disparage the landmines ban and doubt its effectiveness also underestimated the effectiveness of the ban campaign. Their beliefs and misperceptions stem from a common source—realism.

Realists believe what counts in international politics is military force, not norms, and the interests of the state, not domestic or bureaucratic politics. Realists assume that states pursue enduring national interests, narrowly defined in terms of security or power, and that other values do not matter.

For realists, it follows that the norm of international politics is normlessness. International law is circumscribed, in their view, because law is rooted in morality and norms that are not widely shared across cultures and societies and because the powerful will not pay the price of enforcing it.

Realists overlook what seems obvious to ethicists like Michael Walzer, that "no limit is accepted simply because it is thought that it will be useful." Rules of war "must first be morally plausible to large numbers of men and women; it must correspond to our sense of what is right. Only then will we

242 • Negotiating Minefields

recognize it as a serious obstacle to this or that military decision, and only then can we debate its utility in this or that particular case."[27]

Just as ethicists evaluate the international order, holding it to a standard of justice, so lawyers reach judgments to uphold the rule of law—judgments about aggression and self-defense and who bears responsibility for initiating a war (*jus ad bellum*), as well as judgments about whether the use of force follows the rules of war (*jus in bello*). These judgments are not just idle musing. They influence state behavior. As a leading realist, E.H. Carr, notes, "It is an unreal kind of realism which ignores the element of morality in any world order."[28] Order does not rest on power alone; it needs to be legitimated. Realists who take a cynical view of the world dismiss morality as immaterial, mere justification for actions motivated by interests. Yet hypocrisy is a tribute paid to morality.

Military force has an inherently moral dimension. "Strategy, like morality, is a language of justification," wrote Michael Walzer.[29] Strategy is a language of interpretation and explanation as well, in which morality has a place. Scholars who ignore the moral dimension of antipersonnel landmines have trouble accounting for the outcome of the controversy over the ban. To realists the security interests of the powerful should have carried the day against a landmines ban. They did not.

Realists believe that the aim of foreign policy should be national security. Human security, defined as freedom from pervasive threats to people's rights, safety or lives, offers an alternative normative metric for evaluating foreign policy results, one that has a number of advantages as a guide to US policy makers under current global conditions. It redirects attention from the balance of power to the underlying conditions that give rise to instability, improving policy makers' ability to anticipate threats to world order and take prudent action to counter them. It demands a deeper understanding of the domestic structures of states, not just relations among states, to bring about a change for the better. It puts a premium on nonmilitary means of influence for achieving US aims abroad. It points to the inappropriateness of some weapons, whatever their military utility, because of their net effect on people's security. It gives proper place to norms in international affairs. It is a useful corrective to a realism that all too often blinds US officials to the larger ends and means of US policy.

That narrowness of vision and its perverse consequences are evident in the controversy over the landmines ban. The cavalier attitude taken by some US officials toward a ban is contrary to US interests. The Ottawa convention codifies a humanitarian norm that landmines are simply too indiscriminate and too horrific to be used as weapons of war. For the United States to ignore or disparage this norm and the international law that embodies it calls into question its support for related norms and law that undergird its efforts to prevent the spread of nuclear, chemical, and biological arms and the missiles to deliver them. That is particularly imprudent when international norms and law have been vital to mobilizing political support for dissuading countries like Argentina, Brazil, Belarus, Ukraine, Kazakhstan, Libya, and North Korea from nuclear arming.

Norms are a motive force in politics. The ban campaign's effectiveness in rapidly mustering global acceptance for a ban cannot be explained without reference to its normative appeal.

Antipersonnel mines were normatively suspect because of the harm they posed to noncombatants. It inspired activists to campaign for a ban and was critical to politicizing the weapon in ways that led states to make them taboo.

It is arbitrary to single out landmines as the target for such odium. After all, armed forces can be just as indiscriminate in their use of other weapons, with similarly atrocious effects, for instance, the firebombing of cities. Yet indiscriminateness and the potential for harm to noncombatants were critical to the development of taboos against chemical, biological, and nuclear weapons, not just landmines.

The horrific effects of use against noncombatants do not have to be demonstrated before weapons are outlawed, but it helps. Biological weapons were banned even before the revolution in biotechnology made designer germs feasible. So, too, chemical weapons were banned even before they were developed. Initiating the use of "projectiles, the object of which is the diffusion of asphyxiating or deleterious gases" was outlawed in the Hague Declaration of 1899, but that taboo was slower to take hold. International law ran ahead of international norms and proved ineffective at preventing the use of gas during World War I. No state used chemical weapons to target population centers, only enemy combatants on the battlefield. Even so, fear of their use against civilians helped strengthen the taboo against any use at all after the war. In 1925, the Geneva Protocol outlawed the use of chemical weapons, though not stockpiling, producing, and transferring them. Despite expectations that gas warfare would be used extensively in World War II, it was not. Even states like the United States that did not ratify the protocol accepted the taboo, which contributed to the marginalizing of chemical warfare within the US Army. The taboo did not preclude all use, but it led states that did use chemical weapons, like Japan against China in the 1930s or Italy against Ethiopia in 1935–1936 or Iraq against Iran and the Kurds in the 1980s, to deny or cover up their transgressions rather than try to justify them or to overstep those limits only at the margin, such as the US use of tear gas, napalm, and herbicides in Vietnam.[30]

Unlike the case of chemical weapons, where international law initially ran ahead of normative practice, the taboo against antipersonnel mines has marched in lockstep with international law. By contrast, the norm against military use of nuclear arms has held firm since 1945 even without a treaty to codify nonuse or nonpossession.

The United States preferred to regulate mines rather than ban them. It tried to direct attention to the uncivilized use of landmines in communal strife, where their impact on noncombatants was demonstrably most profound. Sophisticated mines, especially self-destructing, self-deactivating ones, were not the problem, US officials insisted. Cheap mines were. Making normative distinction between civilized and uncivilized conduct has a hoary tradition. Use of "weapons of the weak" by technically backward peoples of the world is deemed indefensible. Adherence to norms was bound up with one's identity as a civilized country.[31] Civilized countries were marketing landmines to uncivilized combatants and that had to stop.

Norms can be politicized in more or less inclusive ways, but they are inherently expansive. As US officials learned to their dismay, it proved difficult to confine the odium to mines sown by uncivilized combatants and not those stockpiled by supposedly more civilized Europeans or Americans. Similarly, as ICBL leaders learned to their chagrin, the norm against antipersonnel mines empowered some of the most marginalized people in the world, landmine survivors, legitimating their demands for rehabilitation and reintegration.

The norm against landmines was sufficiently potent that even though the United States did not sign the Ottawa convention, it did take steps to limit transfer, manufacture, and stockpiling of antipersonnel landmines. It has not used them since. It also offered tortured rationales for continuing to do what the treaty prohibits, evidence that the effect of the taboo extended even to treaty outliers. Similar evidence comes from the first ever summit meeting between North and South Korea, where the sides decided to carve a landmine-free corridor through the barrier defenses north and south of the Demilitarized Zone in order to permit construction of rail and road links. The time has come for the United States to take the next step: to acknowledge it has little military need for antipersonnel landmines and to join most of the nations of the world in signing the ban.

The ban campaign propagated a new norm that is influencing states to shun landmines. Production and trade are dramatically down and so is use. In time that norm may rid the world of landmines. If some old soldiers never die, they just fade away, perhaps the same may be said of some old weapons.

Endnotes

CHAPTER 1

1. E.E. Schattschneider, *The Semi-Sovereign People* (Hinsdale, IL: Dryden Press, 1960), p. 7.
2. Interview with Robert Muller, March 4, 2002.
3. Ibid.
4. Interview with Stephen Goose, May 15, 2002.
5. Lydia Monin and Andrew Gallimore, *The Devil's Gardens: A History of Landmines* (London: Pimlico, 2002), p. 7.
6. Stephen Goose, Arms Project director, Human Rights Watch, Conference on Landmines: How Global is the Ban? Center for the Study of Human Rights, New York, Columbia University, December 2, 1999.
7. Jody Williams, "David with Goliath: International Cooperation and the Campaign to Ban Landmines," *Harvard International Review*, 22 (2000): 88.
8. Thomas Risse-Kappen, ed., *Bringing Transnational Relations Back In: Non-State Actors, Domestic Structures and International Institutions* (Cambridge: Cambridge University Press, 1995), p. 3.
9. By 1914, some 460 international NGOs existed, according to F.S.L. Lyon, *Internationalism in Europe, 1815–1914* (Leiden: A.W. Sijthoff, 1963), p. 14.
10. Peter J. Spiro, "New Global Communities: Nongovernmental Organizations in International Decision-Making," *Washington Quarterly,* 18, 1 (Winter 1995): 46–47. See also Peter Willetts, ed., *The Conscience of the World: The Influence of Non-Governmental Organizations in the U.N. System* (Washington, DC: Brookings Institution Press, 1996), pp. 31–62.
11. Todd Gitlin, *The Whole World Is Watching* (Berkeley: University of California Press, 1980), chs. 4–5.

12. Theda Skocpol has referred to such cause-oriented advocacy groups run by professional activists as "associations without members." *American Prospect* (July/August 1999): 66–73.

13. Leon Gordenker and Thomas G. Weiss, "Pluralizing Global Governance: Analytical Approaches and Dimensions," in Thomas G. Weiss and Leon Gordenker, eds., *NGOs, the United Nations, and Global Governance* (Boulder, CO: Lynne Rienner, 1996), pp. 32–36.

14. Jessica T. Mathews, "Power Shift," *Foreign Affairs*, 76, no. 1 (January/February 1997): 50–66.

15. The best recent statements of realism are Kenneth Waltz, *Theory of International Politics* (Reading, MA: Addison-Wesley, 1979); John Mearsheimer, "The False Promise of International Institutions," *International Security*, 19, no. 3 (Winter 1995): 5–49; and John Mearsheimer, *The Tragedy of Great Power Politics* (New York: Norton, 2001).

16. The classic formulation of bureaucratic politics is Graham T. Allison, *Essence of Decision* (Boston: Little Brown, 1971). The concept of organizational interest owes much to Morton H. Halperin, "Why Bureaucrats Play Games," *Foreign Policy*, 2 (Spring 1971): 70–90; and *Bureaucratic Politics and Foreign Policy* (Washington, DC: Brookings Institution Press, 1974), ch. 3.

CHAPTER 2

1. E.E. Schattschneider, *The Semi-Sovereign People* (Hinsdale, IL: Dryden Press, 1960), p. 35.

2. Richard H. Johnson, "Why Mines? A Military Perspective," in Kevin M. Cahill, ed., *Clearing the Fields: Solutions to the Global Landmines Crisis* (New York: Council on Foreign Relations/Basic Books, 1995), p. 25; and Lydia Monin and Andrew Gallimore, *The Devil's Gardens: A History of Landmines* (London: Pimlico, 2002), p. 45.

3. Monin and Gallimore, *The Devil's Gardens*, pp. 47–49.

4. Alva Myrdal, *The Game of Disarmament: How the United States and Russia Run the Arms Race* (New York: Pantheon, 1976), pp. 263–264.

5. Hans-Peter Gasser, "Agora: The U.S. Decision Not to Ratify Protocol I to the Geneva Conventions on the Protection of War Victims," *American Journal of International Law*, 81, no. 4 (October 1987): 910–925; and Abraham D. Sofaer's response, *American Journal of International Law*, 82, no. 4, (October 1988): 784–787.

6. Interview with Michael Matheson, January 23, 2002.

7. International Committee of the Red Cross statement, "Summary of the law regulating the use of mines and proposals for change," April 15, 1993.

8. The Arms Project of Human Rights Watch and Physicians for Human Rights, *Landmines: A Deadly Legacy* (New York: Human Rights Watch, 1993), p. 408.

9. Thomas W. Lippman, "Sen. Leahy Continues Crusade Against Export of Landmines," *Washington Post*, August 8, 1993.

10. Interview with Eric Newsom, March 4, 2002.

11. Lippman, op. cit.

12. Interview with Eric Newsom, March 4, 2002.

13. Ibid.
14. Ibid.
15. Interview with Robert Muller, March 4, 2002.
16. Ibid.
17. Interview with Tim Rieser, February 13, 2002.
18. Jody Williams, "Notes on meeting with Tim Rieser, Leahy's aid[e]," memorandum to Robert Muller, John Terzano, Tom Cardamone, and VVAF Staff, December 5, 1991. Cf., Mary Wareham, "Rhetoric and Policy Realities in the United States," in Maxwell Cameron, Robert Lawson, and Brian Tomlin, eds., *To Walk Without Fear: The Global Movement to Ban Landmines* (London: Oxford University Press, 1999), p. 213.
19. Letter from Robert Muller to Patrick Leahy, July 6, 1992.
20. Interview with Robert Muller, March 4, 2002.
21. Ibid.
22. The Arms Project of Human Rights Watch and Physicians for Human Rights, *Landmines: A Deadly Legacy* (New York: Human Rights Watch, 1993), p. 36.
23. Ibid., p. 69.
24. Interview with Eric Newsom, March 4, 2002.
25. Interview with Robert Muller, March 4, 2002.
26. Interview with Tim Rieser, February 13, 2002.
27. Interview with Eric Newsom, March 4, 2002.
28. Patrick Leahy draft text.
29. Robert Muller to Patrick Leahy, July 29, 1992.
30. Interview with Eric Newsom, March 4, 2002.
31. Among those she had already enlisted were Aryeh Neier, executive director of Human Rights Watch; Rae McGrath of the Mine Advisory Group; Ambassador Charles Flowerree, who had helped negotiate the chemical weapons ban; and Bishop Walter Sullivan from Richmond. Jody Williams to Patrick Leahy, July 30, 1992. On October 1, Leahy agreed to let them use his name.
32. Among those writing were VVAF, the Church World Service and Lutheran World Relief, Neighbor to Neighbor Action Fund, Central America Working Group of the Church of the Brethren, Coalition for Peace and Reconciliation in Cambodia, and InterAction (a coalition of the American Friends Service Committee, American Refugee Committee, Bread for the World, CARE, International Medical Corps, Oxfam America, U.S. Committee for Refugees, and World Vision).
33. Interview with Tim Rieser, February 13, 2002.
34. Jody Williams and Stephen Goose, "The International Campaign to Ban Landmines," in Cameron, et al., op. cit., p. 26.
35. U.S. Department of State, Bureau of Politico-Military Affairs, Office of International Security Operations, "Hidden Killers: The Global Problems with Uncleared Landmines," p. ii, excerpted in The Arms Project, op. cit., Appendix 5, p. 394.
36. Patrick Leahy, "Landmine Moratorium: A Strategy for Stronger International Limits," *Arms Control Today,* 23, no. 1 (January/February 1993): 13.
37. Interview with Eric Newsom, March 4, 2002.
38. Ibid.

39. Interview with Robert Sherman, August 6, 2001.
40. Letter from Senator Patrick Leahy and Representative Lane Evans to Acting Director Thomas Graham, Jr., October 6, 1993.
41. Letter from Frank G. Wisner to Patrick Leahy, October 27, 1993.
42. The Arms Project, op. cit., p. xii. The preface came in response to a request from Stephen Goose and Kenneth Anderson, March 5, 1993.
43. Interview with Rick Inderfurth, February 13, 2002.
44. Ibid.
45. Ibid.
46. Letter from Madeleine Albright to Patrick Leahy, October 6, 1993.
47. Letter from Patrick Leahy to Madeleine Albright, October 25, 1993.
48. Letters from Ambassadors Boris Biancheri of Italy, November 8, 1993, and Robin Renwick of the United Kingdom, November 15, 1993, replying to Patrick Leahy's of October 27, 1993.
49. Letter from Patrick Leahy to Rick Inderfurth, October 26, 1993.
50. Letter from Tim Carstairs to Patrick Leahy, October 28, 1993.
51. Letter from Madeleine Albright to Patrick Leahy, January 21, 1994.
52. Letter from Patrick Leahy to President Clinton, December 23, 1993.
53. Letter from Madeleine Albright to Patrick Leahy, January 21, 1994.

CHAPTER 3

1. E.E. Schattschneider, *The Semi-Sovereign People* (Hinsdale, IL: Dryden Press, 1960), p. 68.
2. Interview with Lee Feinstein, September 5, 2001.
3. Mary Wareham, "Rhetoric and Policy Realities in the United States," in Maxwell Cameron, Robert Lawson, and Brian Tomlin, eds., *To Walk Without Fear: The Global Movement to Ban Landmines* (London: Oxford University Press, 1999), p. 14.
4. Ibid.
5. On the norm against use and its effect on chemical warfare in the US armed forces, Frederic Brown, *Chemical Weapons: A Study in Restraint* (Princeton: Princeton University Press, 1968). For application of Brown's thesis about normative restraints and its limits, Leon V. Sigal, *Fighting to a Finish: The Politics of War Termination in the United States and Japan, 1945* (Ithaca: Cornell University Press, 1988), ch. 4. For a constructivist interpretation of the development of this norm, Richard Price, *The Chemical Weapons Taboo* (Ithaca: Cornell University Press, 1997); and Price and Nina Tannenwald, "Norms and Deterrence: The Chemical and Nuclear Weapons Taboos," in Peter J. Katzenstein, ed., *The Culture of National Security: Norms and Identity in World Politics* (New York: Columbia University Press, 1996), pp. 114–152. For a critique of this view, Paul Kowert and Jeffrey Legro, "Norms, Identity, and Their Limits: A Theoretical Reprise," in Katzenstein, op. cit., pp. 451–497.
6. The Arms Project of Human Rights Watch and Physicians for Human Rights, *Landmines: A Deadly Legacy* (New York: Human Rights Watch, 1993), pp. 36, 57, 106, 109.

7. Thomas Franck, *The Power of Legitimacy Among Nations* (New York: Oxford University Press, 1990), p. 184. Richard Price, "Compliance with International Norms and the Mines Taboo," in Cameron, et al., op. cit., ch. 17, elaborates this point with respect to landmines.

8. The concept of "grafting" comes from David A. Snow, E. Burke Rochford, Jr., Steven K. Worden, and Robert D. Benford, "Frame Alignment Processes, Micromobilization and Movement Participation," *American Sociological Review*, 51 (1986): 473. The International Committee of the Red Cross played a comparable role in propagating the Geneva Conventions regulating war. See also Martha Finnemore, *National Interests in International Society* (Ithaca: Cornell University Press, 1996), ch. 3.

9. To Friedrich Kratochwil, *Norms, Rules, and Decisions* (New York: Columbia University Press, 1989), p. 11, "rules and norms influence choices through the reasoning process" in which reasonableness, fairness, appropriateness, and other value considerations, not just instrumental means-ends calculations, figure prominently. In *National Interests in International Society*, Finnemore (op. cit.) conceptualizes the spread of norms in terms of socialization, "teaching," and "learning" and writes about politics as a matter of "persuasion" and "debate." Richard Price, "Reversing the Gun Sights: Transnational Civil Society Targets Landmines," *International Organization*, 50, no. 3 (Summer 1998): 621, 639, following in Finnemore's footsteps, views the spread of norms more in pedagogical than in political terms. "Teaching," he writes, "does encompass the critical pedagogical ingredients of information, persuasion, shame, and discipline that... account for crucial developments of an anti-mine norm that are not captured by other approaches," (p. 617) which seems to conflate teaching with preaching. "Networks provide the classroom," (p. 627) he contends, but he does not establish just who "learned" what. His idea of politics boils down to elections: "Few if any politicians or governments that have agreed to a ban on AP landmines," he writes, "adopted the new norm directly for instrumental reasons of domestic political pressure—in other words, elections of leadership struggles would not be won or lost because of the landmines issue" (p. 631).

10. William T. Sherman, *Memoirs of William T. Sherman*, vol. 2 (New York: D. Appleton and Company, 1875), p. 194.

11. W. Michael Reisman and Chris T. Antoniu, *The Laws of War: A Comprehensive Collection of Primary Documents on International Laws Governing Armed Conflict* (New York: Vintage, 1994), p. 36. Some of these limits had already been spelled out in the Hague Conference of 1899, in adopting a declaration "to abstain from the use of projectiles the sole object of which is the diffusion of asphyxiating or deleterious gases." Chemical weapons had yet to be developed. Price, op. cit., p. 15.

12. U.S. Army, *The Law of Land Warfare*, Field Manual 27-10, (1956), p. 3.

13. Ibid., p. 19.

14. The Arms Project, op. cit., p. 350. Cf., pp. 306-15 for a brief on "how international law supports a ban on landmines."

15. Interview with Stephen Goose, May 15, 2002.

16. Human Rights Watch/Arms Project, Memorandum, "Landmines in International Law: Why Is a Complete Ban Required?" March 4, 1994, pp. 2–3.

17. Ibid., pp. 9–10.
18. Patrick Leahy to Conrad Harper, March 15, 1994.
19. U.S. Department of State, Legal Adviser, Non-Paper.
20. American Law Division, Congressional Research Service, Library of Congress, "Landmines and Customary International Law," April 18, 1994, p. 3.
21. Margaret E. Keck and Kathryn Sikkink, *Activists beyond Borders: Advocacy Networks in International Politics* (New York: Cornell University Press, 1998), pp. 26–27.
22. Interview with Stephen Goose, May 15, 2002.
23. Thomas C. Schelling and Morton H. Halperin, *Strategy and Arms Control* (New York: The Twentieth Century Fund, 1961), p. 1.
24. Report of the ICRC for the CCW Review Conference, "Results of the Symposium of Military Experts on the Military Utility of Antipersonnel Mines," January 10–12, 1994, Annex II, p. 50.
25. Ibid., p. 51.
26. Ibid., pp. 55–56.
27. Interview with Stephen Goose, May 15, 2002.
28. "A Joint Call to Ban Antipersonnel Landmines," in The Arms Project, op. cit., p. 360.
29. Report of the ICRC for the CCW Review Conference, Geneva, February 14, 1994, p. 4.
30. Ibid., p. 12.
31. Ibid., p. 10.
32. Memorandum from Françoise Hampson, Department of Law, University of Essex, to Ken Anderson, Monica Schurtman, Stephen Goose, March 30, 1994, p. 2.
33. Memorandum from Ken Anderson, Stephen Goose, and Monica Schurtman to Françoise Hampson and Jody Williams, "Draft Provisions for Revised Weapons Convention/Landmines Protocol," April 8, 1994, p. 2.
34. Interview with Stephen Goose, May 15, 2002.
35. Memorandum from Françoise Hampson, p. 2.
36. Memorandum from Ken Anderson, Stephen Goose, and Monica Schurtman, pp. 1–2.
37. Memorandum from Françoise Hampson, p. 1.
38. Ibid., p. 3.
39. Interview with Tim Connolly, March 28, 2002. US "smart" mines were said to be 99.9994 percent reliable. White House Fact Sheet, Anti-Tank Munitions, September 17, 1997.
40. Philippe Chabasse, "The French Campaign," in Cameron, et al., op. cit., pp. 60–61.
41. Ibid., p. 62.
42. Letter from Dr. Philippe Chabasse and Tim Castairs to Senator Patrick Leahy, February 17, 1993.
43. Interview with Tim Rieser, February 13, 2002.
44. Chabasse, op. cit., p. 62. A three-year moratorium replaced the indefinite one on September 29, 1994.

45. Jody Williams and Stephen Goose, "The International Campaign to Ban Landmines," in Cameron, et al., op. cit., p. 28.
46. Stenographic record of the 39th session of the Senate, August 2, 1994, Department of State trans., p. 2.
47. Human Rights Watch, *Off Target: The Conduct of the War and Civilian Casualties in Iraq* (New York: Human Rights Watch, 2003), pp. 70–72, documents their use by Iraq in 2003.
48. Ambassador Boris Biancheri to Senator Patrick Leahy, November 8, 1993.
49. Williams and Goose, op. cit., p. 29.
50. Joseph Vandrisse, "Le Vatican condamne la proliferation des armes," *Le Monde*, June 22, 1994.
51. Fax from Jody Williams to Tim Rieser and Tom O'Donnell, "Italian defense minister calls for complete ban of landmines," June 23, 1994.
52. Fax from Nicoletta Dentico to Jody Williams, containing a translation of the letter, June 29, 1994.
53. Fax from Jody Williams to Tim Rieser, Stephen Goose, and Robert Muller, "Italy; the US," September 27, 1994. Cf., Williams and Goose, op. cit., pp. 29–30.
54. Memorandum from Jody Williams to Robert Muller, Stephen Goose, Tim Rieser, Stuart Maslen, September 4, 1994, p. 4.
55. Foreign Ministry Statement, "Italian Moratorium on the Export of Antipersonnel Landmines," September 29, 1994.
56. Fax from Jody Williams to Tim Rieser, Tom O'Donnell, Robert Muller, and Stephen Goose, "Italy," October 5, 1994.
57. His talking points are contained in a memorandum to Senator Patrick Leahy from Tim Rieser, "Meeting with Italian officials on landmines," September 9, 1994.
58. Text of the resolution, letter from Deputy Emma Bonino to Senator Patrick Leahy, December 8, 1994, and Leahy's reply, December 10, 1994.
59. Jody Williams to Emma Bonino, January 16, 1995. This prompted Senator Ronchi and a colleague to ask for a report on Italy's stance at the experts' meeting from Stuart Maslen of UNICEF. Fax from Senator Eduardo Ronchi and Giovannio Campo to Maslen, January 18, 1995.
60. Letters from Patrick Leahy to Alan Simpson and John McCain, May 16, 1994; and McCain reply of June 8, 1994.
61. Interview with Thomas McNamara, August 14, 2001.
62. Letter from Secretary of State Warren Christopher and Secretary of Defense William Perry to Senator Patrick Leahy, June 28, 1994, reprinted in U.S., Congress, Senate, *Congressional Record*, July 1, 1994, p. S8174.
63. U.S., Congress, Senate, *Congressional Record*, July 1, 1994, p. S8174.
64. Interview with Nancy Soderberg, June 6, 2002.
65. Ibid.
66. Interview with Eric Newsom, March 4, 2002.
67. Ibid.
68. Ibid.
69. Interview with Lee Feinstein, September 5, 2001. In signing protocols of the African Nuclear-Free Zone Treaty, the United States, in order to secure Senate ratification, reserved the right to use nuclear arms against any state using

chemical or biological weapons—in violation of its obligations under the Non-Proliferation Treaty not to threaten or use nuclear arms against a non-nuclear state.

70. Interview with Eric Newsom, March 4, 2002.
71. Interview with Thomas McNamara, August 14, 2001.
72. Interview with Eric Newsom, March 4, 2002.
73. Interview with Thomas McNamara, August 14, 2001.
74. Ibid. Cf., Thomas McNamara, "The U.S. Approach Toward Landmines: A Realistic Policy for an Evolving Problem," in Kevin M. Cahill, ed., *Clearing the Fields: Solutions to the Global Landmines Crisis* (New York: Council on Foreign Relations/Basic Books, 1995), p. 64.
75. Interview with Thomas McNamara, August 14, 2001.
76. Interview with Eric Newsom, March 4, 2002.
77. Ibid.
78. Interview with Thomas McNamara, August 14, 2001.
79. Interview with White House official, August 6, 2001.
80. Ibid.
81. Ibid.
82. Interview with Eric Newsom, March 4, 2002.
83. Interview with Tim Rieser, February 13, 2002.
84. Interview with Rick Inderfurth, February 13, 2002.
85. Interview with Robert Sherman, August 8, 2001.
86. Interview with Rick Inderfurth, February 13, 2002.
87. Ibid.
88. Ibid.
89. Interview with Tim Rieser, February 13, 2002.
90. Interview with Rick Inderfurth, February 13, 2002.
91. Interview with Lee Feinstein, September 5, 2001.
92. Interview with Eric Newsom, March 4, 2002.
93. Ibid.
94. Wareham, op. cit., p. 221.
95. Interview with Stephen Goose, May 15, 2002.
96. Interview with Thomas McNamara, August 14, 2001.
97. Ibid.
98. Ibid.
99. "U.S. Urges International Action to Combat Landmine Crisis," News conference at International Conference on Mine Clearance, Geneva, July 6, 1995.
100. Ibid.
101. Ibid.
102. Interview with Thomas McNamara, August 14, 2001.
103. E.H. Carr, *The Twenty Years' Crisis, 1919–1939* (New York: Harper and Row, 1964), pp. 177–78. For a more recent restatement of this position, see Robert J. Art and Kenneth Waltz, "Technology, Strategy, and Uses of Force," in *The Use of Force: International Politics and Foreign Policy*, 2nd ed. (Lanham, MD, University Press of America, 1983), p. 6.
104. Among the exponents of this view are John G. Ruggie, "International Responses to Technology: Concepts and Trends," *International Organization*, XXIX, 3

(Summer 1975): 557–584; Stephen Krasner, "Structural Causes and Regime Consequences: Regimes As Intervening Variables," *International Organization*, 36 (1982): 186; Stephen D. Krasner, ed., International Regimes (Ithaca: Cornell University Press, 1983); Robert Keohane, *After Hegemony: Cooperation and Discord in World Political Economy* (Princeton: Princeton University Press, 1984), chs. 5–6; Robert Keohane, *International Institutions and State Power: Essays in International Relations* (Boulder, CO: Westview Press, 1989); and John G. Ruggie, ed. *Multilateralism Matters: The Theory and Praxis of an Institutional Form* (New York: Columbia University Press, 1993).

105. This view is found in John G. Ruggie, "International Regimes, Transactions, and Change: Embedded Liberalism in the Postwar Economic Order," in Krasner, op. cit., pp. 195–231; Kratochwil, op. cit.; Ernst Haas, *When Knowledge Is Power: Three Models of Change in International Relations* (Berkeley: University of California Press, 1990); Barry Buzan, *People, States and Fear: The National Security Problem in International Relations*, 2nd ed. (Chapel Hill: University of North Carolina Press, 1991); Alexander Wendt, "Anarchy Is What States Make of It: The Social Construction of Power Politics," *International Organization*, 46 (Spring 1992): 391–425; Audie Klotz, *Norms in International Relations: The Struggle Against Apartheid* (Ithaca: Cornell University Press, 1995), esp. ch. 2; Yosef Lapid and Friedrich Kratochwil, eds., *The Return of Culture and Identity in International Relations Theory* (Boulder, CO: Lynne Rienner, 1995); Katzenstein, op. cit.; Martha Finnemore, op. cit.; Robert Latham, *The Liberal Moment: Modernity Security, and the Making of Postwar International Order* (New York: Columbia University Press, 1997); Ann Marie Clark, *Diplomacy of Conscience: Amnesty International and Changing Human Rights Norms* (Princeton: Princeton University Press, 2001); and Ward Thomas, *The Ethics of Destruction: Norms and Force in International Relations* (Ithaca: Cornell University Press, 2001).

106. Interview with Thomas McNamara, August 14, 2001.

107. Interview with Eric Newsom, March 4, 2002.

CHAPTER 4

1. E.E. Schattschneider, *The Semi-Sovereign People* (Hinsdale, IL: Dryden Press, 1960), p. 16.

2. Interview with Stephen Goose, May 15, 2002.

3. Frame bridging denotes linking of two or more ideologically congruent but structurally unconnected frames by individuals or groups. David A. Snow, E. Burke Rochford, Steven K. Worden, and Robert D. Benford, "Frame Alignment Processes, Micromobilization, and Movement Participation," *American Sociological Review*, 51 (1986), pp. 467–468.

4. Interview with Stephen Goose, May 15, 2002.

5. David A. Snow, E. Burke Rochford, Jr., Steven K. Worden, and Robert D. Benford, "Frame Alignment Processes, Micromobilization and Movement Participation," *American Sociological Review*, 51 (1986): 464–481; Sidney Tarrow, *Power in Movement* (New York: Cambridge University Press, 1994), pp. 10, 15–23; Doug McAdam, John McCarthy and Mayer Zaid, eds., *Comparative Perspectives on*

Social Movements, Political Opportunities, Mobilizing Structures, and Cultural Framings (New York: Cambridge University Press, 1996).

6. David Knoke, *Political Networks: The Structural Perspective* (Cambridge: Cambridge University Press, 1990), pp. 65, 68, 72–73; Doug McAdam, *Freedom Summer* (New York: Oxford University Press, 1988); John McCarthy and Mayer Zald, *The Trend of Social Movements in America: Professionalization and Resource Mobilization* (New York: General Learning Press, 1973); John Lofland, *Protest: Studies of Collective Behavior and Social Movements* (Piscataway, NJ: Transaction Publishers, 1985); and Luther P. Gerlach and Virginia H. Hine, *People, Power, and Change: Movements of Social Transformation* (Indianapolis: Bobbs-Merrill, 1970).

7. Interview with Stephen Goose, May 15, 2002.

8. Jody Williams, "David with Goliath: International Cooperation and the Campaign to Ban Landmines," *Harvard International Review*, 22 (2000): 87.

9. The antiwar movement faced a similar problem in the 1960s. Cf., Todd Gitlin, *The Whole World Is Watching* (Berkeley: University of California Press, 1980), ch. 5.

10. Interview with Jan Lodal, January 23, 2002.

11. Interview with Lee Feinstein, September 5, 2001.

12. Interview with Robert Sherman, August 6, 2001.

13. Interview with Tim Connolly, March 28, 2002.

14. Ibid.

15. Interview with Michael Matheson, January 23, 2002.

16. Ibid.

17. Interview with Robert Sherman, August 6, 2001.

18. Description of the landmines is drawn from the National Research Council, Office of International Affairs, Commission on Engineering and Technical Systems, *Alternative Technologies to Replace Antipersonnel Landmines* (Washington, DC: National Academy Press, 2001), Appendix C.

19. Interview with Robert Sherman, August 6, 2001.

20. Ibid.

21. Ibid.

22. Interview with Michael Matheson, January 23, 2002.

23. Ibid.

24. Interview with Robert Sherman, August 6, 2001.

25. Ibid.

26. Interview with Michael Matheson, January 23, 2002.

27. Notes of a briefing by Michael Matheson for Senator Patrick Leahy, undated.

28. Fax from Jody Williams, Kenneth Anderson, and Stephen Goose to Sohrab Kheradi, secretary of the Review Conference, February 22, 1994.

29. "UNICEF Participation in the Group of Intergovernmental Experts Preparatory to the Review Conference of the 1980 Inhumane Weapons Convention," p. 3. Cf., cover note from Jody Williams to Tim Rieser, June 10, 1994.

30. Memo to Steve [Goose], Ian [?], and Jody [Williams] from Tim [Rieser], April 28, 1994.

31. Ibid.

32. Memorandum from Stephen Goose to Ken Rutherford, Jody Williams, Tim Rieser, Tom [Cardamone], Ken Anderson, "Landmine Meeting," August 3, 1994.

33. Interview with Robert Sherman, August 6, 2001.

34. Memorandum from Stephen Goose to Kenneth Anderson, Jody Williams, Tim Rieser, and Tom Cardamone, March 29, 1994.

35. Interview with Robert Sherman, August 6, 2001.

36. Interview with Michael Matheson, January 23, 2002.

37. Interview with Stephen Goose, May 15, 2002.

38. Memorandum from Stephen Goose to Ken Rutherford, Jody Williams, Tim Rieser, Tom [Cardamone], Ken Anderson, "Landmine Meeting," August 3, 1994.

39. Ibid.

40. Memorandum from Jody Williams to Tim Rieser and Stephen Goose, September 7, 1994.

41. International Committee of the Red Cross, "Statement on Antipersonnel Mines and Proposed Amendments to Protocol II," January 9, 1995.

42. Interview with Robert Sherman, August 6, 2001.

43. Interview with White House official, August 6, 2001.

44. International Committee of the Red Cross Briefing Paper, "Landmines and Blinding Weapons from Expert Group to the Review Conference," Geneva, March 17, 1995.

45. Memorandum from Stephen Goose to Jody Williams, Stuart Maslen, Tim Rieser, Tom Cardamone, "Meeting on Thursday 1-26-95," January 30, 1995.

46. Ibid.

47. Interview with Michael Matheson, January 23, 2002.

48. Mary Wareham, "Rhetoric and Policy Realities in the United States," in Maxwell Cameron, Robert Lawson, and Brian Tomlin, eds., *To Walk Without Fear: The Global Movement to Ban Landmines* (London: Oxford University Press, 1999), p. 215.

49. Ibid.

50. Jody Williams and Stephen Goose, "The International Campaign to Ban Landmines," in Cameron, et al., op. cit., p. 28.

51. Ibid., p. 30.

52. Philippe Chabasse, "The French Campaign," in Cameron, et al., op. cit., p. 64.

53. Interview with Tim Connolly, March 28, 2002.

54. Interview with Stephen Goose, May 15, 2002.

55. Interview with Tim Connolly, March 28, 2002.

56. Interview with Stephen Goose, May 15, 2002.

57. Interview with Rick Inderfurth, February 13, 2002.

58. "Landmine section of John Holum's letter to Chinese Deputy Foreign Minister Li," undated. The nonpaper specified a 95 percent reliability for self-destruction within 30 days and a 99 percent reliability for self-deactivation within 90 days. "U.S. Non-Paper on Landmines and the Convention on Conventional Weapons," faxed on February 21, 1996.

59. Interview with Stephen Goose, May 15, 2002.

60. Ibid.

61. Ibid.

62. Ibid.

63. Ibid.

64. In modified form, these distinctions draw on those in Margaret E. Keck and Kathryn Sikkink, *Activists beyond Borders: Advocacy Networks in International Politics* (New York: Cornell University Press, 1998), pp. 16–25.

65. Williams and Goose, op. cit., pp. 31–33.

66. Stuart Maslen, "The Role of the International Committee of the Red Cross," in Cameron, et al., op. cit., p. 87.

67. Interview with Rick Inderfurth, February 13, 2002.

68. Statement of the United States delegation to the Meeting of Governmental Experts, March 3, 1994.

69. Letter from Senator Patrick Leahy and Representative Lane Evans to Warren Christopher, William Perry, and John Holum, April 11, 1995.

70. Ambassador Johan Molander to Senator Patrick Leahy, April 21, 1995.

71. Memorandum, "Certification Requirement on AP Landmines Moratorium in the FY97 DOD Authorization Act," July 17, 1996.

72. Interview with Rick Inderfurth, February 13, 2002.

73. Interview with Robert Sherman, August 8, 2001.

74. Interview with Rick Inderfurth, February 13, 2002.

75. International Committee of the Red Cross, "Informal Comments on the Chairman's Rolling Text," Review Conference of the 1980 Convention on Certain Conventional Weapons, Vienna, 25 September–13 October 1995, May 24, 1995, p. 1.

76. Ibid., and Chairman's Rolling Text, article 1.

77. Ibid., pp. 3, 6–7.

78. Ibid., pp. 5-6.

79. Williams and Goose, op. cit., p. 32.

80. Interview with Michael Matheson, January 23, 2002.

81. Ibid.

82. Ibid.

83. Ibid.

84. Stephen Goose, e-mail, April 15, 1996, "Notes from the meeting with Matheson."

85. Interview with Michael Matheson, January 23, 2002.

86. Interview with an NSC official who drew on contemporaneous notes, March 18, 2003.

87. Ibid.

88. Text of Jody Williams's statement to the opening plenary session, Review Conference of the CCW, Geneva, April 22, 1996.

89. Jim Wurst, "Closing in on a Landmine Ban: The Ottawa Process and U.S. Interests," *Arms Control Today*, 27, no. 4 (June/July 1997): 15.

90. CCW Review Conference Results, adopted by the plenary on April 30, 1996, as presented by Peter Herby of the ICRC.

91. State Department Fact Sheet 740, "U.S. Proposes Improvements to Landmines Protocol of CCW," September 27, 1995.

92. Transcript of press conference by Michael Matheson, May 3, 1996. Cf., U.S. Department of State, Office of the Spokesman, "Adoption of the Revised Protocol on Landmines," May 3, 1996.

93. Interview with Robert Sherman, August 6, 2001.

94. Maslen, op. cit., pp. 86, 92.

95. International Committee of the Red Cross statement, "The New Protocol—Not a Step out of the Minefield," May 2, 1996.

96. Stephen D. Biddle, *Landmine Arms Control* (Alexandria, VA: Institute for Defense Analyses, 1996), pp. 5, 48.

97. Statement of Secretary-General Boutros Boutros-Ghali, May 7, 1996, UN Department of Public Information, DC/2556. The ICBL put the figure at 41, up from 11. Williams and Goose, op. cit., p. 33.

98. Interview with Robert Sherman, August 6, 2001.

99. Interview with Stephen Goose, May 15, 2002.

100. Williams and Goose, op. cit., p. 32.

CHAPTER 5

1. E.E. Schattschneider, *The Semi-Sovereign People* (Hinsdale, IL: Dryden Press, 1960), p. 56.

2. Brian W. Tomlin, "On a Fast Track to a Ban: The Canadian Policy Process," in Maxwell Cameron, Robert Lawson, and Brian Tomlin, eds., *To Walk Without Fear: The Global Movement to Ban Landmines* (London: Oxford University Press, 1999), p. 186. Cf., Norma Greenaway, "The Anatomy of a Landmines Agreement," *Ottawa Citizen*, November 29, 1997, p. B-1.

3. Paul Koring, "Arm's Length Friends," *Time*, 149, no. 15 (April 14, 1997). In a revealing moment, Chretien, unaware he was at an open microphone, confided with two fellow prime ministers, Jean-Luc Dehaene of Belgium and Jean-Claude Juncker of Luxembourg, as they awaited President Clinton's arrival at a NATO summit meeting. What if "we started without them?" asked Juncker. "To prove that we know what to do without them," chimed in Dehaene. "To prove we're independent. He [Chretien], he's used to not doing what they want," rejoined Juncker. "I make it my policy," acknowledged Chretien. "But it's popular." Wolf Blitzer, "Open Microphone Catches Chretien's Criticism of Clinton," CNN, July 9, 1997.

4. International Institute for Strategic Studies, *The Military Balance*, 1996–97 (London: Oxford University Press, 1996), p. 50.

5. U.S. Arms Control and Disarmament Agency, *World Military Expenditures and Arms Transfers, 1996* (Washington, DC: US Government Printing Office, 1997), p. 41.

6. Statement by Christopher Westdal, Ambassador for Disarmament, Ninth Session of the UN General Assembly, Item 22: Assistance in Mineclearing, October 1994.

7. U.S. Secretary of Defense, Report to Congress, *Allied Contributions to the Common Defense*, March 1997, Charts III-4, III-13, III-25. The figures are in 1995 US dollars.

8. Tomlin, op. cit., p. 191.
9. Ibid.
10. Ibid., p. 192.
11. Maxwell A. Cameron, "Democratization of Foreign Policy: The Ottawa Process as a Model," in Cameron, et al., op. cit., p. 434.
12. Greenaway, op. cit.
13. Cameron, op. cit., p. 432.
14. Valerie Warmington and Celina Tuttle, "The Canadian Campaign," in Cameron, et al., op. cit., p. 48.
15. Cameron, op. cit., p. 433.
16. Canada, Department of Foreign Affairs and International Trade, *Canada in the World: Government Statement* (Ottawa: Canada Communications Group, 1995), pp. 48–49.
17. Ibid.
18. Warmington and Tuttle, op. cit., pp. 50–51.
19. Ibid., pp. 51–52.
20. Tomlin, op. cit., p. 209n25.
21. Cameron, op. cit., p. 433.
22. Warmington and Tuttle, op. cit., pp. 49–50.
23. Cameron, op. cit., p. 434.
24. Tomlin, op. cit., p. 194.
25. News release no. 5, "Canada Announces Antipersonnel Landmines Measures," January 17, 1996.
26. Tomlin, op. cit., p. 194.
27. Ibid., p. 199.
28. Ibid., pp. 194–195, 200.
29. Cameron, op. cit., pp. 435–436.
30. Ibid., p. 435.
31. ICRC Briefing Paper, "Landmines and Blinding Weapons from Expert Group to the Review Conference," Geneva, March 17, 1995.
32. Cameron, op. cit., p. 435.
33. Ibid., p. 436.
34. Robert Lawson, "Towards a New Multilateralism: Canada and the Landmines Ban," *Behind the Headlines*, 54, no. 4 (Summer 1997): 19.
35. Williams and Goose, "The International Campaign to Ban Landmines," in Cameron, et al., op. cit., p. 34.
36. Interview with Stephen Goose, May 15, 2002.
37. Williams and Goose, op. cit., p. 32.
38. Greenaway, op. cit. Australia, Germany, the Netherlands, New Zealand, Peru, and Sweden joined the original eight, along with a representative of the Vatican.
39. Interview with Robert Sherman, August 6, 2001.
40. Greenaway, op. cit.
41. ICBL, "Meeting of States and Select NGO Representatives Supportive of a Comprehensive Ban on Antipersonnel Landmines 29 April," *Report of the Second Session of the Review Conference*, Geneva, 1996, pp. 97–98.
42. Interview with Stephen Goose, May 15, 2002.

43. Conversation with an Austrian official, December 14, 2001.
44. Thomas Hajnoczi, Thomas Desch, and Deborah Chatsis, "The Ban Treaty," in Cameron, et al., op. cit., p. 293.
45. Craig Turner, "Ottawa Is Flushed with Success as Its Longshot Crusade for a Ban Pays Off," *Los Angeles Times*, August 30, 1997, p. A-11.
46. Peter Herby, "Future Landmines Negotiations," Internal note, June 17, 1996. Senator Leahy was quick to echo this concern in a letter to Secretary of State Warren Christopher 3 days later.
47. Mark Gwozdecky and Jill Sinclair, "Landmines and Human Security," in Rob McRae and Don Hebert, eds., *Human Security and the New Diplomacy: Protecting People, Promoting Peace* (Montreal: McGill-Queens University Press, 2000), p. 37.
48. Tomlin, op. cit., p. 195.
49. Lawson, op. cit., p. 20. The announcement also drew the displeasure of the minister's office because Lawson received media attention instead of his minister. The displeasure was short-lived. A few days later, when Germany's foreign minister, Klaus Kinkel, visited Ottawa, Lloyd Axworthy and he appeared at a media event staged on Parliament Hill. The news coverage showed them standing in front of another mountain of shoes. Tomlin, op. cit., p. 196.
50. Greenaway, op. cit.
51. Robert Lawson, Mark Gwozdecky, Jill Sinclair, and Ralph Lysyshyn, "The Ottawa Process and the International Movement to Ban Antipersonnel Mines," in Cameron et al., op. cit., p. 161.
52. Tomlin, op. cit., p. 199.
53. Ibid.
54. Ibid., p. 200.
55. Ibid., p. 203.

CHAPTER 6

1. E.E. Schattschneider, *The Semi-Sovereign People* (Hinsdale, IL: Dryden Press, 1960), p. 18.
2. Bernard E. Trainor, "Landmines Saved My Life," *New York Times*, March 28, 1996, p. A-25.
3. White House press briefing, May 16, 1996.
4. Richard H. Johnson, "Why Mines? A Military Perspective," in Kevin M. Cahill, ed., *Clearing the Fields: Solutions to the Global Landmines Crisis* (New York: Council on Foreign Relations, 1995), p. 33.
5. Department of the Army, Headquarters, *Information Paper: Landmine Arms Control*, June 8, 1994, p. 1.
6. ICRC, "Antipersonnel Landmines—Friend or Foe? A Study of the Military Use and Effectiveness of Antipersonnel Mines," March 1966, par. 11.
7. Ibid., ch. 9, point 1.
8. Ibid., ch. 9, point 4.
9. Interview with Tim Connolly, March 28, 2002.

10. Stephen D. Biddle, Julia L. Klar, and Jason Rosenfeld, *The Military Utility of Landmines: Implications for Arms Control* (Alexandria, VA: Institute for Defense Analyses, June 1994), p. 70.
11. Interview with Tim Connolly, March 28, 2002.
12. Interview with Eric Newsom, March 4, 2002.
13. Interview with Jan Lodal, January 23, 2002.
14. Interview with US Army officer, October 22, 2001.
15. Interview with Lee Feinstein, September 5, 2001.
16. Interview with NSC official, March 18, 2003.
17. Interview with Lee Feinstein, September 5, 2001.
18. Human Rights Watch Report, "Civilian Deaths in the NATO Air Campaign," vol. 12, no. 1 (February 2000).
19. Human Rights Watch, *Off Target: The Conduct of the War and Civilian Casualties in Iraq* (New York, December 2003), p. 20.
20. Interview with Robert Sherman, August 6, 2001.
21. Interview with Lee Feinstein, September 5, 2001.
22. Johnson, op. cit., p. 35.
23. Department of Defense Background Briefing on the New US Landmine Policy, May 16, 1996.
24. Background Briefing by Senior Military Official, Subject: Landmine Policy, January 17, 1997.
25. Interview with Jan Lodal, January 23, 2002.
26. White House, Office of the Press Secretary, "U.S. Requirements for Landmines in Korea," September 17, 1997. Emphasis added.
27. Interview with Thomas McNamara, August 14, 2001.
28. Interview with Jan Lodal, January 23, 2002.
29. The data are drawn from a briefing book by Lt. Gen. Robert Gard and Maj. Edwin Deagle, Jr., consultants to VVAF, based on a US Forces Korea briefing, December 11, 2000.
30. Interview with Jan Lodal, January 23, 2002.
31. Interview with Thomas McNamara, August 14, 2001.
32. Interview with Lee Feinstein, September 5, 2001.
33. Interview with Robert Sherman, August 6, 2001.
34. Interview with Jan Lodal, January 23, 2002.
35. Interview with Maj. Edwin Deagle, Jr., May 3, 2001.
36. Ibid.
37. Capt. Mike Doubleday, deputy assistant secretary of defense for public affairs, Department of Defense press briefing, January 15, 1998.
38. Interview with Maj. Edwin Deagle, Jr., May 3, 2001.
39. Interview with US Army officer, October 22, 2001.
40. Ibid.
41. Interview with Maj. Edwin Deagle, Jr., May 3, 2001.
42. General Accounting Office, *Information on U.S. Use of Landmines in the Persian Gulf War*, GAO-02-1003, September 2002, p. 2.
43. Ibid., pp. 8–9, 11. The Army said it was unsure whether records of use may remain undiscovered in its Gulf War archives.
44. Ibid., p. 21.

45. Ibid., pp. 2–3.
46. Ibid., pp. 23–26. Cf., ICRC, op. cit., par. 100.
47. General Accounting Office, op. cit., p. 3. Cf., discussion on pp. 14–16, 67.
48. Quoted in David H. Hackworth, "One Weapon We Don't Need," *Newsweek*, April 8, 1996, p. 29.
49. Interview with Maj. Edwin Deagle, Jr., May 3, 2001.
50. John F. Troxell, "Landmines: Why the Korea Exception Should Be the Rule," *Parameters*, XXX, no. 1 (Spring 2000): 82–83.
51. Ibid. Troxell would later see the ban campaign as an example of "netwar" in which "networked enemies" are made up of "dispersed nonstate, paramilitary, and other irregular forces, including peaceful social activists" that use "media measures to attract rather than to coerce."
52. Interview with US Army general, May 4, 1999.
53. Interview with Tim Connolly, March 28, 2002.
54. Interview with senior Defense Department official, May 4, 1999.
55. Interview with US Army officer, October 22, 2001.
56. Interview with Tim Connolly, March 28, 2002.
57. Ibid.
58. Morton H. Halperin, "The President and the Military," *Foreign Affairs*, 50, no. 2 (January 1972), pp. 314, 322–323.
59. Interview with US Army officer, October 22, 2001.
60. Wesley K. Clark, *Waging Modern War* (New York: Public Affairs, 2001), p. 313. The withholding of the Apaches was one of a number of differences Clark had with the chiefs. On the differences and on Goldwater-Nichols, see pp. xxx–xxxi, 19, 47, 65–66, 69–70, 119–120, 126–127, 131–132, 164–165, 178–179, 181–182, 223–233, 246–247, 278–279, 302–305, 310–313, 319–321, 332–333, 338, 340–342, 349–350, 364, 367, 451–455.
61. Interview with senior Defense Department official, May 4, 1999.
62. Interview with Tim Connolly, March 28, 2002.
63. Ibid.
64. Ole R. Holsti, "A Widening Gap Between the US Military and Civilian Society?" *International Security*, 23, no. 3 (Winter 1998-99): 13. Few in the military were registered Democrats but by the 1990s the number who called themselves Independents had dropped markedly and those who said they were Republicans had doubled from 1976 to 1996, from 33 percent to 67 percent.
65. Interview with Lee Feinstein, September 5, 2001.
66. Ibid.
67. Interview with Nancy Soderberg, June 6, 2002.
68. Interview with Thomas McNamara, August 14, 2001.
69. Interview with Eric Newsom, March 4, 2002.
70. Interview with Tim Connolly, March 28, 2002.
71. Ibid.

CHAPTER 7

1. Interview with former Under Secretary of State Katzenbach, July 13, 1970, by John B. Henry II, "February 1968," *Foreign Policy*, 4 (Fall 1971), p. 12.
2. Interview with White House official, August 6, 2001.

3. Department of Defense Background Briefing, May 16, 1996.
4. John Mintz, "A Global Bid to Ban Mines," *Washington Post*, February 4, 1996, p. A-1.
5. Raymond Bonner, "Pentagon Weighs Ending Opposition To a Ban on Mines," *New York Times*, March 17, 1996, p. 1.
6. Interview with Jan Lodal, January 23, 2002.
7. Interview with Nancy Soderberg, June 6, 2002.
8. Telephone interview with a senior administration official, March 8, 2002.
9. Mary McGrory, "Clinton's Duty to Command the Pentagon," *Washington Post*, April 21, 1996, p. C-1.
10. Interview with Robert Sherman, August 6, 2001. Cf., Mary Wareham, "Rhetoric and Policy Realities in the United States," in Maxwell Cameron, Robert Lawson, and Brian Tomlin, eds., *To Walk Without Fear: The Global Movement to Ban Landmines* (London: Oxford University Press, 1999), p. 223.
11. McGrory, op. cit.
12. Interview with Robert Muller, March 4, 2002.
13. Interview with Mark Perry, May 3, 2001.
14. Interview with Nancy Soderberg, June 6, 2002.
15. Ibid.
16. Interview with Karl Inderfurth, February 13, 2002.
17. Interview with Tim Connolly, March 28, 2002.
18. Interview with Jan Lodal, January 23, 2002.
19. Interview with Tim Connolly, March 28, 2002.
20. Mintz, op. cit.
21. Interview with NSC official who drew on contemporaneous notes, March 18, 2003.
22. White House press briefing, May 16, 1996.
23. Department of Defense, Background Briefing, May 16, 1996. Asked whether he was aware of the IDA study, he replied, "We're aware of lots of studies."
24. Interview with Tim Connolly, March 28, 2002.
25. Ibid.
26. Ibid.
27. Interview with Jan Lodal, January 23, 2002.
28. Interview with Tim Connolly, March 28, 2002.
29. Interview with NSC official, March 18, 2003.
30. Interview with Tim Connolly, March 28, 2002.
31. Ibid.
32. Interview with Mark Perry, May 3, 2001.
33. Raymond Bonner, op. cit., p. 1.
34. Ibid.
35. Caleb Rossiter, "Winning in Korea without Landmines," *VVAF Monograph*, 1, no. 3 (Summer 2000), p. 49.
36. Bonner, op. cit.
37. John Mintz, "Shalikashvili Awaits Study on Banning Land Mines," *Washington Post*, April 4, 1996, p. A-16.
38. Interview with Mark Perry, May 3, 2001.

39. Ibid.
40. "An Open Letter to President Clinton," *New York Times*, April 3, 1996, p. A-11.
41. Interview with Nancy Soderberg, June 6, 2002.
42. Mintz, "Shalikashvili Awaits Study on Banning Landmines," op. cit.
43. Interview with senior Defense Department official, May 4, 1999.
44. Interview with White House official, August 6, 2001.
45. Interview with Nancy Soderberg, June 6, 2002.
46. Ibid.
47. Ibid.
48. Interview with Jan Lodal, January 23, 2002.
49. Ibid.
50. Ibid.
51. Interview with Tim Connolly, March 28, 2002.
52. Interview with NSC official, March 13, 2003.
53. Ibid.
54. Interview with NSC staff member, March 18, 2003.
55. Interview with NSC official who drew on contemporaneous notes, March 18, 2003.
56. Interview with Mark Perry, May 3, 2001.
57. Neil A. Lewis, "U.S. Has Plan to Ban Landmines, but Not Yet," *New York Times*, April 18, 1996, p. A-7. Wareham, op. cit., p. 224.
58. Linda D. Kozaryn, "DOD Plans to Use Self-Destructing Landmines," Armed Forces Press Service, April 23, 1996.
59. Bradley Graham, "Pentagon Prepares to Forgo Most Landmine Use Except in Korea, Persian Gulf," *Washington Post*, April 19, 1996, p. A-26.
60. Interview with NSC official who drew on contemporaneous notes, March 18, 2003.
61. Graham, op. cit.
62. Interview with Mark Perry, May 3, 2001.
63. Interview with Robert Muller, March 4, 2002.
64. Interview with Mark Perry, May 3, 2001.
65. Interview with NSC official who drew on contemporaneous notes, March 18, 2003.
66. Interview with Maj. Edwin Deagle, Jr., May 3, 2001.
67. Interview with Mark Perry, May 3, 2001.
68. Interview with Robert Sherman, August 6, 2001. Schwarzkopf called "smart" mines a "military capability we can use" in the *Baltimore Sun* on September 8, 1997, p. A-2.
69. Interview with Mark Perry, May 3, 2001.
70. Ibid.
71. Interview with NSC official who drew on contemporaneous notes, March 18, 2003.
72. Ibid. The conversation with David Jones took place on May 2.
73. Interview with NSC official who drew on contemporaneous notes, March 18, 2003.
74. Philip Shenon, "Joint Chiefs Weaken Proposal for Land Mine Moratorium," *New York Times*, May 11, 1996, p. A-4.

75. Statement of Robert O. Muller, Vietnam Veterans of America, "Pentagon Proposal to Continue Landmine Use Denounced," May 10, 1996.
76. Interview with Nancy Soderberg, June 6, 2002.
77. Interview with Robert Muller, March 4, 2002.
78. Interview with NSC official who drew on contemporaneous notes, March 18, 2003.
79. Interview with Jan Lodal, January 23, 2002.
80. "Remarks on the Antipersonnel Landmines Initiative," May 16, 1996, in U.S., *Public Papers of the Presidents, William J. Clinton—1996*, 1 (Washington, DC: U.S. Government Printing Office, 1997), pp. 754–756. Emphasis added.
81. Wareham, op. cit., p. 226.
82. "Remarks on the Antipersonnel Landmines Initiative," op. cit. Emphasis added.
83. Ibid.
84. Interview with Robert Sherman, August 6, 2001.
85. Ibid.
86. Ibid.
87. White House press briefing, May 16, 1996, in American Forces Information Service, *Defense Viewpoint*, Defense Issues, 11, No. 40.
88. Interview with Robert Sherman, August 6, 2001.
89. Ibid.
90. Interview with Tim Connolly, March 28, 2002.
91. Presidential Decision Directive NSC-48, June 26, 1996.
92. Ibid.
93. PDD-48. Cf., White House, Office of the Press Secretary, Fact Sheet: U.S. Announces Antipersonnel Landmine Policy, May 16, 1996.
94. Memorandum for Secretaries of the Military Departments, Chairman of the Joint Chiefs of Staff, et al., Subject: Implementation of the President's Decision on Antipersonnel Landmines, June 17, 1996.
95. PDD-48. Cf., White House, Office of the Press Secretary, Fact Sheet: U.S. Announces Antipersonnel Landmine Policy, May 16, 1996.
96. White House press briefing, May 16, 1996.
97. Interview with White House official, August 6, 2001.
98. Interview with Jan Lodal, January 23, 2002.
99. Interview with Eric Newsom, March 4, 2002.
100. Interview with NSC official who drew on contemporaneous notes, March 18, 2003.
101. Letter to the editor, *Los Angeles Times*, August 3, 2001, e-mailed to the author.
102. Interview with Jan Lodal, January 23, 2002.
103. Eventually a committee of the National Academy of Sciences conducted an independent evaluation of a list of alternatives. Cf., the National Research Council, Office of International Affairs, Commission on Engineering and Technical Systems, *Alternative Technologies to Replace Antipersonnel Landmines* (Washington, DC: National Academy Press, 2001).
104. Interview with Jan Lodal, January 23, 2002.
105. Interview with Eric Newsom, March 4, 2002.
106. Interview with Jan Lodal, January 23, 2002.

107. Ibid.

108. Interview with Michael Matheson, January 23, 2002.

109. Interview with Jan Lodal, January 23, 2002.

110. Interview with Nancy Soderberg, June 6, 2002.

111. Major General Clair F. Gill, Commandant, U.S. Army Engineering School, Fort Leonard Wood, "White Paper: Operational Capabilities of Antipersonnel Mines," April 4, 1997.

112. Interview with Eric Newsom, March 4, 2002.

113. Interview with White House official, August 6, 2001.

114. Interview with Eric Newsom, March 4, 2002.

115. Interview with Michael Matheson, January 23, 2002.

116. Interview with Lee Feinstein, September 5, 2001.

117. Interview with Eric Newsom, March 4, 2002.

118. Wareham, op. cit., p. 226. For the phrase, "coalition of angels," see Philip C. Winslow, "Landmine Usefulness in Dispute 40 Years," *Baltimore Sun*, August 10, 1997.

119. Wareham, op. cit., p. 217.

120. Letter from Senator Patrick Leahy to Secretary of State Warren Christopher, June 20, 1996. Leahy forwarded a copy to National Security Adviser Anthony Lake on August 6.

121. Letter from Senator Patrick Leahy to National Security Adviser Anthony Lake, August 6, 1996; and interview with NSC official who drew on contemporaneous notes, March 18, 2003.

122. Interview with Eric Newsom, March 4, 2002.

123. Interview with White House official, August 6, 2001.

124. Interview with Eric Newsom, March 4, 2002.

125. Interview with NSC official, March 18, 2003.

126. Interview with Lee Feinstein, September 5, 2001.

127. Ibid.

128. Interview with NSC official who drew on contemporaneous notes, March 18, 2003.

129. Wareham, op. cit., p. 228.

130. Interview with White House official, August 6, 2001.

131. Background briefing by senior military official, Subject: Landmine Policy, January 16, 1997.

132. Ibid.

133. Interview with Stephen Goose, May 15, 2002.

134. Interview with Robert Muller, March 4, 2002.

135. Human Rights Watch Arms Project Report, "Exposing the Source: US Companies and the Production of Antipersonnel Mines," 9, no. 2 (April 1997).

136. Wareham, op. cit., p. 217.

137. Eric Sevareid commentary, CBS Evening News, October 15, 1969.

138. Wareham, op. cit., p. 215.

139. Interview with Joe Volk, executive director of the Friends' Committee on National Legislation, April 9, 1998, quoted in ibid., p. 238.

140. Statement to the UN First Committee by Ambassador Madeleine Albright, November 4, 1996.

141. White House Statement, January 17, 1997, in prepared text of address to the CD by Ambassador Stephen Ledogar.
142. Wareham, op. cit., p. 226.

CHAPTER 8

1. E.E. Schattschneider, *The Semi-Sovereign People* (Hinsdale, IL: Dryden Press, 1960), p. 71.
2. Robert J. Lawson, Mark Gwozdecky, Jill Sinclair, and Ralph Lysyshyn, "The Ottawa Process and the International Movement to Ban Antipersonnel Mines," in Maxwell Cameron, Robert Lawson, and Brian Tomlin, eds., *To Walk Without Fear: The Global Movement to Ban Landmines* (London: Oxford University Press, 1999), p. 162.
3. Lloyd Axworthy, Address to the 51st General Assembly of the United Nations, September 24, 1996, Department of Foreign Affairs and International Trade, Canada. Cf., "Canada and Human Security: The Need for Leadership," *International Journal*, 53, No. 2 (Spring 1997), p. 184. Sara Edson, "Human Security: An Extended and Annotated Bibliography" (Centre for History and Economics, King's College, University of Cambridge, UK, June 1, 2001), p. 7, attributes the concept to Lincoln Chen, then at the Center for Population and Development Studies at Harvard, and given currency by Emma Rothschild in "What Is Security?" *Daedalus*, 124, no. 3 (Summer 1995): 53–90. They both were involved in the Common Security Forum, established in 1992 to build on the work of the Independent Commission on Disarmament (Palme Commission) a decade earlier. In 1994 the concept was embraced by the United Nations Development Program, which construed it broadly to cover economic, food, health, environmental, personal, community, and political security: "Human security can be said to have two main aspects. It means, first, safety from such chronic threats as hunger, disease and repression. And second, it means protection from sudden and hurtful disruptions in the patterns of daily life—whether in homes, in jobs or in communities." UNDP, *Human Development Report 1994* (New York: Oxford University Press, 1994), p. 23. By redefining security, in the traditional sense of safety from armed conflict, out of existence and appropriating it for an even more ambitious agenda of political and economic development, the concept went too far. Its very breadth made it an unwieldy policy instrument in the view of Axworthy, who tried to construe human security more narrowly as "freedom from pervasive threats to people's rights, their safety, or even their lives." Not only did that definition keep the focus on the person, not the state, but by including people's rights, not just their lives, it also posed a direct challenge to the traditional preoccupation with state sovereignty and territorial integrity. Axworthy, "Human Security: Safety for People in a Changing World," April 29, 1999, Department of Foreign Affairs and International Trade, Canada. Yet it is still quite broad insofar as it extends protection to economic as well as political rights, or the right to "life, liberty, and the pursuit of happiness."
4. Lloyd Axworthy, Address to the opening of the Mines Action Forum, Ottawa, December 2, 1997, p. 2.

5. That definition was the one adopted by Canada's foreign ministry by 1999. http://www.humansecurity.gc.ca/menu-en.asp

6. Lawson, et al., op. cit., p. 162.

7. Robert Lawson, "Towards a New Multilateralism: Canada and the Landmines Ban," *Behind the Headlines*, 54, no. 4 (Summer 1997): 21.

8. Maxwell A. Cameron, "Democratization of Foreign Policy: The Ottawa Process as a Model," in Cameron, et al., op. cit., p. 437.

9. Phillipe Chabasse, "The French Campaign," in Cameron, et al., op. cit., p. 63.

10. Ibid., p. 65. Cf., Ministere des Affaires Etrangeres, "Interdiction des mines anti-personnel—Communique du ministere des affaires etrangere," *La Politique etrangere de la France: texte et documents* (January-February, 1997), p. 51.

11. Brian W. Tomlin, "On a Fast Track to a Ban," in Cameron et al., op. cit., p. 201.

12. Chabasse, op. cit., p. 66.

13. Tomlin, op. cit., pp. 203–205; Norma Greenaway, "The Anatomy of a Landmines Agreement," *Ottawa Citizen*, November 29, 1997, p. B-1; Mark Gwozdecky and Jill Sinclair, "Landmines and Human Security," in Rob McRae and Don Hebert, eds., *Human Security and the New Diplomacy: Protecting People, Promoting Peace* (Montreal: McGill-Queens University Press, 2000), p. 31.

14. "Chairman's Agenda for Action on Antipersonnel Mines," Ottawa, October 5, 1996, http://pubx.dfait-maeci.gc.ca/00_Global/Pubs_Cat2.nsf/Welcome/welcome?opendocument.

15. Tomlin, op. cit., pp. 202, 205, 211–46.

16. Address by the Honorable Lloyd Axworthy, Minister of Foreign Affairs, at the Closing Session of the International Strategy Conference Towards a Global Ban on Antipersonnel Mines, Ottawa, October 5, 1996.

17. Interview with Robert Sherman, August 6, 2001.

18. Interview with White House official, August 6, 2001.

19. Mary Wareham, "Rhetoric and Policy Realities in the United States," in Cameron, et al., op. cit., p. 227.

20. Lawson, et al., op. cit., p. 162.

21. Ibid., p. 170.

22. Greenaway, op. cit.

23. Lawson, et al., op. cit., p. 169.

24. Ibid., pp. 163–164.

25. Interview with NSC official who drew on contemporaneous notes, March 18, 2003.

26. Text of Ambassador Stephen Ledogar's statement to the CD, January 20, 1997.

27. Rebecca Johnson, "Agenda But No Work at CD," Acronym Institute, March 17, 1997.

28. Interview with Eric Newsom, March 4, 2002.

29. Dana Priest, "56 in Senate to Press for Law Banning Use of Landmines by U.S.," *Washington Post*, June 12, 1997, p. A-12.

30. Jim Wurst, "Closing in on a Landmine Ban," *Arms Control Today*, 27, no. 4 (June/July 1997), p. 16.

31. By one account, Mexico's delegate to the CD misunderstood the US position and thought Washington was firmly committed to signing Ottawa in 2005. Robert Sherman says that he and Michael Matheson, the chief US negotiator, discovered

this "by chance" and convinced the Mexican to tell his government to reverse its position and ratify the CCW, but it was "already locked in" to Ottawa. Interview with Robert Sherman, August 6, 2001.

32. Johnson, op. cit.
33. Lawson, op. cit., p. 18.
34. Conversation with Austrian official, December 14, 2001.
35. Lawson, et al., op. cit., p. 168.
36. Thomas Hajnoczi, Thomas Desch, and Deborah Chatsis, "The Ban Treaty," in Cameron, et al., op. cit., p. 292.
37. Ibid., p. 293.
38. "Convention on the Prohibition of Antipersonnel Mines," Austrian Draft.
39. Hajnoczi, et al., op. cit., p. 293.
40. Ministry of Foreign Affairs, Austria, "Austria to Host Next Meeting on Antipersonnel Mines," in Department of Foreign Affairs and International Trade, *AP Mine Ban: Progress Report*, 1 (1997), p. 2.
41. Interview with White House official, August 6, 2001.
42. Interview with Eric Newsom, March 4, 2002.
43. Hajnoczi, et al., op. cit., pp. 293–294.
44. Ibid., p. 294.
45. Revised Austrian Draft, May 13, 1997.
46. Stuart Maslen, "The Role of the International Committee of the Red Cross," in Cameron, et al., op. cit., p. 91.
47. Interview with Stephen Goose, May 15, 2002.
48. Ibid.
49. E-mail from Caleb Rossiter to Robert Muller, Jody Williams, Tim Rieser, Tom O'Donnell, Stephen Goose, Sayed Aqa, Mary Wareham, Holly Burkhalter, Peter Herby, Penny MacKenzie, Tim Carstairs, and Rae McGrath, "Anti-Handling Exception," June 23, 1997.
50. Ibid.
51. Interview with Stephen Goose, May 15, 2002.
52. Interview with Robert Sherman, August 6, 2001.
53. Interview with Stephen Goose, May 15, 2002.
54. Office of the Assistant Secretary of Defense (Public Affairs), Background Briefing, "Antipersonnel Landmines," July 3, 1997.
55. George I. Seffers, "Pentagon May Resist Effort To Ban Antipersonnel Mines," *Defense News*, June 30/July 6, 1997, p. 11.
56. Interview with Tim Connolly, March 28, 2002.
57. Interview with Stephen Goose, May 15, 2002.
58. Interview with Tim Connolly, March 28, 2002.
59. Lawson, et al., op. cit., p. 171.
60. Hajnoczi, et al., op. cit., p. 301.
61. Maslen, op. cit., p. 92.
62. Wurst, op. cit., p. 15.
63. UPI, "Canada's Axworthy Meets with US Envoy," June 12, 1997; Lawson, et al., op. cit., p. 175.
64. Priest, op. cit.
65. Interview with Lee Feinstein, September 5, 2001.

66. Interview with Robert Sherman, August 6, 2001.
67. Bruce Wallace, "The Battle to Ban Landmines," *Maclean's*, July 1, 1997, p. 34.
68. Hajnoczi, et al., op. cit., p. 295.
69. Interview with Eric Newsom, March 4, 2002.
70. Jody Williams and Stephen Goose, "The International Campaign to Ban Landmines," in Cameron, et al., op. cit., p. 36.
71. Lawson, op. cit., p. 21.
72. "Declaration of the Brussels Conference on Antipersonnel Landmines."
73. Foreign Secretary Robin Cook, speech announcing the mission statement of the Foreign and Commonwealth Office, London, May 12, 1997.
74. Wurst, op. cit., p. 18.
75. Chabasse, op. cit., pp. 64, 66.
76. Interview with Robert Sherman, August 6, 2001.
77. Lawson, et al., op. cit., p. 175.
78. E-mail from Jody Williams to Robert Muller, Mike [?], May [?], Gail [?], Tim Rieser, July 1, 1997.
79. For example, ACDA Director John Holum, address to the CD, May 15, 1997.
80. E-mail from Jody Williams to Robert Muller, Mike [?], May [?], Gail [?], Tim Rieser, July 1, 1997.
81. Stephen Goose, draft paper, "Antipersonnel Landmines and the Conference on Disarmament," January 20, 1999.
82. Interview with Thomas McNamara, August 14, 2001.
83. Ibid.
84. Interview with White House official, August 6, 2001.
85. Interview with Eric Newsom, March 4, 2002.
86. Ibid.
87. Ibid.

CHAPTER 9

1. E.E. Schattschneider, *The Semi-Sovereign People* (Hinsdale, IL: Dryden Press, 1960), p. 71.
2. Robert J. Lawson, Mark Gwozdecky, Jill Sinclair, and Ralph Lysyshyn, "The Ottawa Process and the International Movement to Ban Antipersonnel Mines," in Maxwell Cameron, Robert Lawson, and Brian Tomlin, eds., *To Walk Without Fear: The Global Movement to Ban Landmines* (London: Oxford University Press, 1999), p. 167.
3. Jody Williams and Stephen Goose, "The International Campaign to Ban Landmines," in Cameron, et al., op. cit., p. 37.
4. Lawson, et al., op. cit., p. 173.
5. Ibid., p. 172.
6. Ibid., p. 172.
7. Margaret E. Keck and Kathryn Sikkink, *Activists beyond Borders: Advocacy Networks in International Politics* (New York: Cornell University Press, 1998), p. 12, describe a "boomerang pattern" in which NGOs "bypass their state" and engage in political action abroad to "bring pressure on their states from the outside." A more appropriate metaphor might be a carom shot.

8. "Chairman's Agenda for Action on Antipersonnel Mines," Ottawa, October 5, 1996, reprinted in Louis Maresca and Stuart Maslen, eds., *The Banning of Antipersonnel Landmines: The Legal Contribution of the International Committee of the Red Cross* (Cambridge: Cambridge University Press, 2000), pp. 483–484.

9. Williams and Goose, op. cit., p. 37.

10. Stuart Maslen, "The Role of the International Committee of the Red Cross," in Cameron, et al., op. cit., p. 90.

11. Resolution on the 1980 United Nations Convention on Certain Conventional Weapons and Problems Posed by the Proliferation of Antipersonnel Mines in Africa, 62nd Session of the OAU Council of Ministers, Addis Ababa, Ethiopia, June 22–23, 1995.

12. Williams and Goose, op. cit., p. 38.

13. Noel Stott, "The South African Campaign," in Cameron, et al., op. cit., p. 74.

14. Williams and Goose, op. cit., p. 37.

15. Alex Vines, *Still Killing: Landmines in Southern Africa* (London: Human Rights Watch, 1997).

16. Press statement by Defense Minister Joe Modise, South African Government Policy on Antipersonnel Landmines, February 20, 1997.

17. Final Declaration of the Fourth International NGO Conference on Landmines: Toward a Mine-Free Southern Africa, Maputo, Mozambique, February 25–28, 1997.

18. Final Declaration of the Regional Seminar for the States of the Southern African Regional Development Community, Harare, Zimbabwe, April 21–23, 1997.

19. E-mail from Jody Williams to Tim Rieser, Robert Muller, Mary Wareham, Robert Lawson, et al., May 30, 1997.

20. Ibid.

21. Lawson, et al., op. cit., p. 173.

22. Jerry White and Ken Rutherford, "The Role of the Landmine Survivors Network," in Cameron, et al., op. cit., pp. 99–100.

23. Interview with Jerry White, February 3, 2002.

24. White and Rutherford, op. cit., p. 100.

25. Interview with Jerry White, February 3, 2002.

26. White and Rutherford, op. cit., p. 100.

27. Interview with Jerry White, February 3, 2002.

28. White and Rutherford, op. cit., p. 100.

29. Interview with Jerry White, February 3, 2002.

30. White and Rutherford, op. cit., p. 100.

31. Ibid., p. 106.

32. Interview with Jerry White, February 3, 2002.

33. Interview with Stephen Goose, May 15, 2002.

34. White and Rutherford, op. cit., pp. 103–104.

35. Interview with Stephen Goose, May 15, 2002.

36. Interview with Jerry White, February 3, 2002.

37. Interview with Stephen Goose, May 15, 2002.

38. White and Rutherford, op. cit., p. 105.

39. Interview with Jerry White, February 3, 2002.

40. White and Rutherford, op. cit., p. 106.

41. Lawson, et al., op. cit., p. 165.
42. White and Rutherford, op. cit., p. 108.
43. Ibid., pp. 107–108.
44. Lydia Monin and Andrew Gallimore, *The Devil's Gardens: A History of Landmines* (London: Pimlico, 2002), pp. 13–14.
45. Interview with Jerry White, February 3, 2002.
46. Monin and Gallimore, op. cit., pp. 14-15.
47. Interview with Jerry White, February 3, 2002.
48. Ibid.
49. Ibid.
50. Letter from Diana, Princess of Wales, to Ken Rutherford, August 12, 1997.
51. White and Rutherford, op. cit., p. 112.
52. Interview with Jerry White, February 3, 2002.
53. Interview with Stephen Goose, May 15, 2002.
54. Interview with Jerry White, February 3, 2002.
55. White and Rutherford, op. cit., p. 111.
56. Interview with Jerry White, February 3, 2002.
57. White and Rutherford, op. cit., p. 112.
58. Maslen, op. cit., pp. 93–94.
59. Interview with Stephen Goose, May 15, 2002.
60. Ibid.
61. White and Rutherford, op. cit., p. 115.

CHAPTER 10

1. E.E. Schattschneider, *The Semi-Sovereign People* (Hinsdale, IL: Dryden Press, 1960), p. 16.
2. Robert J. Lawson, Mark Gwozdecky, Jill Sinclair, and Ralph Lysyshyn, "The Ottawa Process and the International Movement to Ban Antipersonnel Mines," in Maxwell Cameron, Robert Lawson, and Brian Tomlin, eds., *To Walk Without Fear: The Global Movement to Ban Landmines* (London: Oxford University Press, 1999), pp. 176–177.
3. Interview with Robert Sherman, August 6, 2001.
4. Dana Priest, "Shalikashvili Defends Use of 'Smart' Mines," *Washington Post*, August 29, 1997, p. A-33.
5. Interview with Eric Newsom, March 4, 2002.
6. Interview with Robert Sherman, August 6, 2001.
7. Interview with Eric Newsom, March 4, 2002.
8. Interview with Jerry White, February 3, 2002.
9. Interview with Eric Newsom, March 4, 2002.
10. Interview with Lee Feinstein, September 5, 2001.
11. Department of State, Daily Briefing, August 18, 1997.
12. Bradley Graham, "U.S. Dispatches Team to Discuss Mine Treaty," *Washington Post*, August 17, 1997, p. A-23.
13. Jody Williams and Stephen Goose, "The International Campaign to Ban Landmines," in Cameron, et al., op. cit., p. 43.

14. James Bennet, "U.S. Agrees to Join the Talks on Banning Some Land Mines; Change in Position Fails to Convince Critics," *New York Times*, August 19, 1997, p. A-6.
15. Michael Dolan and Chris Hunt, "Negotiating in the Ottawa Process: The New Multilateralism," in Cameron, et al., op. cit., p. 409.
16. Letter from the Joint Chiefs of Staff and the CINCs to Senator Strom Thurmond (R-SC), July 10, 1997.
17. "An Open Letter to President Clinton," July 21, 1977.
18. Interview with Eric Newsom, March 4, 2002. Christopher Kirkey, *Washington's Response to the Ottawa Landmines Process*, University of Maine Canadian-American Center, Occasional Paper No. 46 (August 2001), p. 12, has a somewhat different version that suggests the review was more foreordained.
19. Interview with Eric Newsom, March 4, 2002.
20. Interview with Lee Feinstein, September 5, 2001.
21. Interview with Jan Lodal, January 23, 2002.
22. Interview with Robert Sherman, August 6, 2001.
23. Interview with Eric Newsom, March 4, 2002.
24. Interview with Lee Feinstein, September 5, 2001.
25. Interview with Robert Sherman, August 6, 2001.
26. Ibid.
27. Interview with Lee Feinstein, September 5, 2001.
28. Interview with Eric Newsom, March 4, 2002.
29. Interview with Jan Lodal, January 23, 2002.
30. Interview with Eric Newsom, March 4, 2002.
31. Interview with Jan Lodal, January 23, 2002.
32. Ibid.
33. Ibid.
34. Ibid.
35. Interview with Stephen Goose, May 15, 2002.
36. Department of Defense press briefing, August 19, 1997.
37. Interview with Robert Sherman, August 6, 2001.
38. Department of State, Daily Briefing, August 18, 1997.
39. Department of State, Daily Briefing, August 21, 1997.
40. Interview with Lee Feinstein, September 5, 2001.
41. Ibid.
42. Graham, op. cit.
43. Interview with Eric Newsom, March 4, 2002.
44. Interview with White House official, August 6, 2001.
45. Interview with Jan Lodal, January 23, 2002.
46. Dolan and Hunt, op. cit., p. 409.
47. Thalif Deen, "U.S. Could Undermine Landmine Ban, Say NGOs," Inter Press Service, August 19, 1997.
48. E-mail from Jody Williams to Tim Rieser, Robert Muller, Mary Wareham, Robert Lawson, et al., May 30, 1997.
49. Williams and Goose, op. cit., p. 44.
50. Valerie Warmington and Celina Tuttle, "The Canadian Campaign," in Cameron et al., op. cit., p. 57.

51. Williams and Goose, op. cit., p. 43.

52. Interview with Mark Perry, May 3, 2001.

53. Maxwell A. Cameron, "Democratization of Foreign Policy: The Ottawa Process as a Model," in Cameron, et al., op. cit., p. 439.

54. Interview with Mark Perry, May 3, 2001.

55. Interview with Robert Muller, March 4, 2002.

56. Interview with Mark Perry, May 3, 2001.

57. Ibid.

58. Interview with Robert Muller, March 4, 2002.

59. Phillipe Chabasse, "The French Campaign," in Cameron, et al., op. cit., p. 67.

60. Interview with Mark Perry, May 3, 2001.

61. Thomas Hajnoczi, Thomas Desch, and Deborah Chatsis, "The Ban Treaty," in Cameron, et al., op. cit., p. 300.

62. Lawson, et al., op. cit., pp. 177–178.

63. Interview with US military officer, October 22, 2001.

64. Jacqueline S. Porth, "U.S. Is Negotiating to Reach a Global Landmine Ban in Oslo," US Information Agency, September 5, 1997.

65. Interview with Eric Newsom, March 4, 2002.

66. Interview with Robert Sherman, August 6, 2001.

67. Ibid.

68. Mary Wareham, "Rhetoric and Policy Realities in the United States," in Cameron, et al., op. cit., p. 235.

69. Department of Defense press briefing, August 19, 1997.

70. Jacqueline S. Porth, op. cit..

71. Interview with Jan Lodal, January 23, 2002.

72. Ibid.

73. Ibid.

74. Interview with Eric Newsom, March 4, 2002.

75. Ibid.

76. Interview with Jan Lodal, January 23, 2002.

77. Ibid.

78. Ibid.

79. Interview with Eric Newsom, March 4, 2002.

80. Interview with Jan Lodal, January 23, 2002.

81. Interview with Eric Newsom, March 4, 2002.

82. Ibid.

83. Ibid.

84. Norma Greenaway, "The Anatomy of Landmines Agreement," *Ottawa Citizen*, November 29, 1997, p. B-1.

85. Letter from Prime Minister Chretien to President Clinton, September 8, 1997, quoted in Dolan and Hunt, op. cit., p. 408.

86. Letter from Senator Jesse Helms to President Clinton, September 8, 1997, quoted in Dolan and Hunt, op. cit., p. 411.

87. Letter from General Henry H. Shelton to Senator James M. Inhofe, September 13, 1997.

88. Lawson, et al., op. cit., p. 179.

89. Spokesman James Foley, Department of State, Daily Briefing, September 15, 1997.
90. Interview with Tim Rieser, February 13, 2002.
91. White House, Office of the Press Secretary, Press Briefing by Robert Bell, Senior Director for Defense Policy and Arms Control, National Security Council, September 17, 1997.
92. Interview with Eric Newsom, March 4, 2002.
93. Dolan and Hunt, op. cit., p. 413.
94. International Committee of the Red Cross, "U.S. to Make Final Attempt to Maim Landmine Ban Treaty," September 15, 1997.
95. Dolan and Hunt, op. cit., pp. 413–414.
96. Interview with Eric Newsom, March 4, 2002.
97. Interview with Robert Sherman, August 6, 2001.
98. Interview with Lee Feinstein, September 5, 2001.
99. Interview with Michael Matheson, January 23, 2002.
100. Interview with Lee Feinstein, September 5, 2001.
101. Interview with Michael Matheson, January 23, 2002.
102. Interview with Tim Rieser, February 13, 2002.
103. Interview with Robert Sherman, August 6, 2001.
104. Interview with Eric Newsom, March 4, 2002.
105. Ibid.
106. Ibid.
107. Tim Burt, "US Threatens to Quit Anti-landmines Talks," *Financial Times*, September 11, 1997.
108. Ibid.
109. Interview with Lee Feinstein, September 5, 2001.
110. Interview with Eric Newsom, March 4, 2002.
111. Ibid.
112. Ibid.
113. Interview with Robert Sherman, August 6, 2001.
114. Wareham, op. cit., p. 235.
115. Interview with Jan Lodal, January 23, 2002.
116. Ibid.
117. Interview with Eric Newsom, March 4, 2002.
118. Ibid.
119. Ibid.
120. Ibid.
121. Interview with Rick Inderfurth, February 13, 2002.
122. Interview with Eric Newsom, March 4, 2002.
123. White House, Office of the Press Secretary, Remarks by the President on Landmines, September 17, 1997.
124. Interview with Robert Sherman, August 6, 2001.
125. Robert Bell, White House press briefing, September 17, 1997.
126. Dana Priest, "Clinton Directive on Mines: New Form, Old Function," *Washington Post*, September 24, 1997, p. A-23.
127. Lawson, et al., op. cit., p. 180; and Wareham, op. cit., p. 234.
128. Dolan and Hunt, op. cit., p. 415.

129. Australia, Parliament, *Bills Digest* No. 61 1998–99, Antipersonnel Mines Convention Bill 1998.
130. Interview with Rick Inderfurth, February 13, 2002.
131. Interview with Eric Newsom, March 4, 2002.
132. Bradley Graham, "U.S. Advocates $1 Billion Yearly to Remove World's Landmines," *Washington Post*, November 1, 1997, p. A-2. By the end of 2004, global funding for demining totaled $2.7 billion since 1997, $800 million of it from the United States. Wade Boese, "Clearing Mined Areas Now Treaty Aim," *Arms Control Today*, 35, no. 1 (January/February 2005): 39.
133. Memorandum in Patrick Leahy files, Certification Requirement on AP Landmines Moratorium in the FY 97 DOD Authorization Act, July 17, 1996, has a handwritten notation, "This certification did pass in 1998 in exchange for provisions in PDD-64."
134. Interview with Tim Rieser, February 13, 2002.
135. Memorandum in Patrick Leahy files, op. cit.
136. Letter from Samuel Berger to Patrick Leahy, May 15, 1998.
137. Interview with Tim Rieser, February 13, 2002.
138. Interview with Robert Sherman, August 6, 2001.
139. Interview with Eric Newsom, March 4, 2002.
140. Interview with White House official, August 6, 2001.
141. Interview with Lee Feinstein, September 5, 2001.
142. Interview with Robert Sherman, August 6, 2001.
143. Letter to the editor, *Los Angeles Times*, August 3, 2001; e-mail to the author.
144. Note for Secretary Cohen from Jan Lodal, Subject: Two Issues Raised by Sandy Berger, November 29, 1997.
145. Interview with Lee Feinstein, September 5, 2001.
146. Bureau of Politico-Military Affairs, US Department of State, "Landmines White Paper," February 27, 2004, and press briefing by Lincoln P. Bloomfield, assistant secretary of state for politico-military affairs, February 27, 2004.
147. Bradley Graham, "Bush Shifts US Stance on Use of Landmines," *Washington Post*, February 27, 2004, p. A-1.

CHAPTER 11

1. E.E. Schattschneider, *The Semi-Sovereign People* (Hinsdale, IL: Dryden Press, 1960), p. 2.
2. Stanley Hoffmann, "The United States and International Organizations," in Robert Lieber (ed.), *Eagle Rules* (Engelwood, NJ: Prentice-Hall, 2001), pp. 342–352.
3. Interview with Tim Rieser, February 13, 2002.
4. Interview with Jerry White, February 3, 2002.
5. Interview with Tim Connolly, March 28, 2002.
6. Jody Williams and Stephen Goose, "The International Campaign to Ban Landmines," in Maxwell Cameron, Robert Lawson, and Brian Tomlin, eds., *To Walk Without Fear: The Global Movement to Ban Landmines* (London: Oxford University Press, 1999), p. 24.

7. Robert Lawson, "Towards a New Multilateralism: Canada and the Landmines Ban," *Behind the Headlines*, 54, no. 4 (Summer 1997).

8. Ibid.

9. Jessica T. Mathews, "Power Shift," *Foreign Affairs*, 76, no. 1 (January/February 1997): 50.

10. Ibid., p. 51.

11. Ibid., pp. 53–54.

12. Peter J. Spiro, "New Global Communities: Nongovernmental Organizations in International Decision-Making Institutions," *Washington Quarterly*, 18, no. 1 (Winter 1995): 50.

13. Boutros Boutros-Ghali, "Foreword," in Thomas G. Weiss and Leon Gordenker, eds., *NGOs, the United Nations, and Global Governance* (Boulder, CO: Lynne Rienner, 1996), p. 7.

14. The evolution of the norm of humanitarian intervention, for instance, is traced in Martha Finnemore, "Constructing Norms of Humanitarian Intervention," in Peter J. Katzenstein, ed., *The Culture of National Security: Norms and Identity in World Politics* (New York: Columbia University Press, 1996), pp. 153–185.

15. An appropriate agenda for theorists is to study how states differ and how those differences affect their behavior toward other states and the operation of the international system, as well as to specify the conditions under which the state is a relatively autonomous actor or is a contingent actor—at once an independent and dependent variable—a plaything of deeper social forces or an arena for conflict and cooperation among social groups. The reconceptualizing of international relations along these lines is well under way, starting with disaggregation of the state by Graham T. Allison, *Essence of Decision* (Boston: Little, Brown, 1971); soon followed by the neoliberal emphasis on state vulnerability to international cooperation in Robert O. Keohane and Joseph S. Nye, *Power and Interdependence: World Politics in Transition* (Boston: Little, Brown, 1977); reemphasis on the centrality and autonomy of the state in Peter Evans, Dietrich Rueschemeyer, and Theda Skocpol, *Bringing the State Back In* (Cambridge: Cambridge University Press, 1985); the new institutionalism of Paul J. DiMaggio and Walter W. Powell, eds., *The New Institutionalism in Organizational Analysis* (Chicago: University of Chicago Press, 1991); the contesting of the very idea of the state by constructivists such as Alexander Wendt, "Anarchy Is What States Make of It: The Social Construction of Power Politics," *International Organization*, 46, no. 2 (1992): 391–425; focus on variations in state behavior in John G. Ruggie, "Continuity and Transformation in the World Polity: Toward a Neorealist Synthesis," in Robert O. Keohane, ed., *Neorealism and Its Critics* (New York: Columbia University Press, 1986), pp. 131–157; and by Thomas Risse-Kappen, ed., *Bringing Transnational Relations Back In* (Cambridge: Cambridge University Press, 1995); and reconception of the international system as an open one in Christopher K. Ansell and Steven Weber, "Organizing International Politics: Sovereignty and Open Systems," *International Political Science Review*, 20, no. 1 (January 1999): 73–94.

16. President Clinton, "Remarks Following a Meeting with Supporters of the Comprehensive Test Ban Treaty," October 6, 1999, *Weekly Compilation of*

Presidential Documents, 35, no. 40 (Washington, DC: US Government Printing Office, 1999), pp. 1936–1937.

17. US Army, Greenbook, Transformation Brief, 30 minutes, October 17, 2000.
18. Interview with Tim Rieser, February 13, 2002.
19. The White House, Office of the Press Secretary, Remarks by the President on Landmines, September 17, 1997.
20. Interview with Stephen Goose, May 15, 2002.
21. Interview with Robert Sherman, August 6, 2001.
22. Interview with Jan Lodal, January 23, 2002.
23. Interview with Eric Newsom, March 4, 2002.
24. Ibid.
25. Ibid.
26. Interview with Morton Halperin, December 6, 2001.
27. Michael Walzer, *Just and Unjust Wars: A Moral Argument with Historical Illusions* (New York: Basic Books, 1977), p. 133.
28. E.H. Carr, *The Twenty Years' Crisis*, 1919–1939 (New York: Harper and Row, 1964), p. 235.
29. Walzer, op. cit., p. 13.
30. Richard Price, *The Chemical Weapons Taboo* (Ithaca: Cornell University Press, 1997), pp. 30–35, 44–63, 70–99, 109–126.
31. Ibid., pp. 26–30, 35–36, 107–108.

Index